D1116258

# Political Leadership

# Political Leadership:

## Readings For an Emerging Field

EDITED BY GLENN D. PAIGE, UNIVERSITY OF HAWAII

Fp The Free Press   New York
Collier-Macmillan Limited   London

301. 5
P142 p
156893

Copyright © 1972 by The Free Press
A Division of The Macmillan Company

Printed in the United States of America
All rights reserved. No part of this book may be
reproduced or transmitted in any form or by any means,
electronic or mechanical, including photocopying, recording,
or by any information storage and retrieval system,
without permission in writing from the Publisher.

The Free Press
A Division of The Macmillan Company
866 Third Avenue, New York, New York 10022
Collier-Macmillan Canada Ltd., Toronto, Ontario
Library of Congress Catalog Card Number: 76–169237
printing number   1 2 3 4 5 6 7 8 9 10

# Preface

It is hoped that this book of readings plus an accompanying monograph and bibliography* will help to establish the study of political leadership as a special subject of inquiry in world colleges and universities or in other places where independent scientific thought is possible. Taken together, the readings, the monograph, and bibliography suggest the outlines of what such a field could be like and illustrate some of the foundations for it that are already available. They attempt to define the study of political leadership in a different sense than is usually implied by studies of charisma, political elites, political biography, and political leadership institutions. It is all of these—and more.

This attempt to focus attention upon a new field of inquiry, to combine old concerns into a distinctively new pattern, is intended as a continuing challenge, not as a final report. For the satisfactory future development of a special field of political leadership studies on a sound scientific basis will require a sustained process of world-wide cooperation among socio-behavioral scientists, humanists, political leaders themselves, and successive generations of inquisitive students. Hopefully, eventually we will achieve a global outlook that recognizes cultural pluralism yet rejects parochial cant and a knowledge structure so clear that its transmission and application to the solution of practical problems become relatively easy.

The present book of readings emerges out of a continuing process of self-education. In terms of intellectual interest many more items should have been included; practically, they could not. But since parsimony is a principle of science and poetry as well as of economics, the enforced constraint of this volume may have the virtue of encouraging both curiosity and imag-

---

* Glenn D. Paige, *The Study of Political Leadership* (New York: The Free Press, forthcoming).

ination. The challenge is to leap beyond the ideas collected here to envision what fuller knowledge of political leadership and better approaches to it might be like. There is a voluminous literature of potential relevance to explore (a literature that increases daily with the information explosion) and an even vaster resource in the concrete experiences of political leaders, past, present and future. This book will serve its purpose if readers approach both with a new sense of discovery.

The essays in this book are presented in five parts, each of which is intended to focus attention upon an important aspect of political leadership as a field of inquiry. Part One offers an overview and examines some attempts to conceptualize what is meant by "political leadership." Part Two suggests a simple conceptual framework consisting of six related variables: personality, role, organization, task, values, and setting. Part Three explores briefly some of the many strategies of inquiry that are available for political leadership research. Part Four raises questions about the education of political leaders. Finally, Part Five invites consideration of alternative modes of social orientation that students of political leadership may adopt toward their subject.

For unfailing assistance in preparing this book of readings I am especially indebted to Carolyn Kiyabu Ball of the Social Science Research Institute and the Graduate School of Library Studies, University of Hawaii. Mrs. Freda Hellinger and the staff of the Social Science Research Institute patiently assisted with typing and revision.

Enough has been said about the general goal of this volume and about the approach that has been taken. Each reader may now exercise his "logical," "critical," and "creative" imagination upon the results.*

Glenn D. Paige
Department of Political Science and
Social Science Research Institute
University of Hawaii

---

* I am indebted to Robert Jungk who elaborated these three modes of thought in his keynote address to the International Future Research Conference, Kyoto, Japan, April 10–16, 1970.

# Contents

# Part One

## Overview

INTRODUCTION

For one who approaches the study of political leadership here for the first time and who may be bewildered by what is being attempted, it may be comforting to recall that this is merely one of the latest efforts in more than 2000 years of attempts to focus attention upon a very important but very elusive subject. The objectives of Part One are to place the study of political leadership in past, present, and future perspective and to engage the imagination in efforts to create useful concepts of "political leadership" to guide inquiry.

Certainly one place to begin thinking about the study of political leadership—although not the only one—is to leap back in historical imagination to the beginnings of human life. Then, in a massive historical survey, emphasizing inevitably the most recent millenia, one might move gradually toward the present, scanning the remains of human experiences for evidence of individuals, institutions, and situations that seem to illustrate the emergence and operation of what might be called "political leadership." In relatively recent times, such a survey would call to mind such figures as Sargon and Hammurabi, Iknaton and Darius, Ch'in Shih Huang-ti and Caesar, Cleopatra and Catherine II, Alexander and Ashoka, Attila and Omar, Justinian and Constantine, Charlemagne and Genghis Khan, Yi Songgye and Tokugawa Iyeyasu, Napoleon and Lincoln, Bolivar and Bismarck, Horatio Seymour and Samuel J. Tilden, Lenin and Churchill, Lumumba and Mboya, Che Guevara and Luis Taruc, and so on. But however erudite, such a listing under present conditions is bound to be inadequate: evidence is irretrievably lost; dominant leaders are likely to be emphasized over sub-dominant ones; cultures with written records are likely to be stressed over those without them; leadership memories held in minor languages are

1

apt to be slighted in favor of major ones; and definitional indeterminancy is likely to confound identification. There is as yet no global data bank on historical political leaders to which might be addressed initial exploratory inquiries such as who they were, what they did, how they emerged, how they fell, and what influences they had, if any, upon human society. There should be one.[1]

Another place to begin the study of political leadership is to examine classics of world literature bearing on the subject. Most Western-educated persons immediately recall Plato's *Republic*[2] and Machiavelli's *The Prince*[3] in this connection. But world resources, although still neither adequately clarified nor appreciated, are more extensive than these. They include, for example, the model of moral suasion depicted in the *Analects* of Confucius,[4] the reward and punishment patterns prescribed in *The Book of Lord Shang*,[5] the crafty calculus of Kautilya's *Arthashastra*,[6] the earthly exercise of divine decree portrayed in Nizam-al-Mulk's *The Book of Government or Rules for Kings*,[7] and the portrait of the Aztec ruler-warrior contained in Bernadino de Sahagun's *Kings and Lords*.[8] Contemporary examples of this type of literature, not unworthy of their great tradition, are Stimson Bullitt's reflections on his experiences as a candidate for elected office in *To Be a Politician*[9] and W. Howard Wriggins' *The Ruler's Imperative: Strategies for Political Survival in Asia and Africa*.[10]

But even if supplemented by the discovery and assemblage of all recorded classics of model rulership (something that also needs to be done), we would still fall short of comprehensive global understanding. We would need also to comprehend the unwritten traditions of Africa and other parts of the world where man transmitted his political knowledge and experience by spoken word, song, and dance.[11] The recording and interpretation of the remnants of this tradition must also be accomplished.

A further approach would be to examine leaders in terms of their relationships to the great issues of an era. Outstanding twentieth-century issues, for example, include freedom versus dictatorship, poverty versus wealth, war versus peace, discrimination versus equality, and ecological survival versus eco-catastrophe. Many other salient issues are readily recognizable. Thus starting with a significant issue of interest we may trace its relationship to the behavior of local, provincial, national, and international political leaders. Important initial contributions to such an approach have been made by legislative voting studies[12] and community power studies,[13] but much remains to be done before a method specifically suited to illuminating the issue-connections of incumbent and aspiring political leaders of a total society can be usefully applied.

Still another, more immediate, approach to the study of political leadership would be to begin by inquiring into the concrete behaviors of political leaders in the contemporary environment. This means to begin here and now, with obvious, easily accessible outcroppings of political leadership behavior.[14] These are revealed, for example, in almost any daily newspaper. By way of illustration, *The New York Times* on a single day, October 5, 1970,[15] carried the following stories in which leaders figured prominently: President Nixon met privately with advisors on peace talks to end the Vietnam War; top Egyptian leaders discussed the idea of a collective ruling group to replace the late President Nasser; Bolivian President Orvando called upon army rebels to surrender to avoid bloodshed; Mayor Lindsay of New York agreed to hear prisoner complaints in a jail uprising after he had threatened an armed police invasion; former governor Scranton of Pennsylvania issued a presidential commission report on the killing of Kent State University students; Premier Golda Meir of Israel announced that she would attend the 25th anniversary celebration of the United Nations; Premier Bahdi Ladgham of Tunisia conferred as a peacemaker with opposing army and guerrilla leaders in Jordan to convince both sides to release prisoners; guerrilla chief Abu Bakr promised cooperation, saying he had been promised that the guerrillas will get what they want "if Allah is willing"; the speaker of the Egyptian National Assembly conferred to set the date for a special session of the 360-man group to deal with Nasser's succession; Israeli leaders planned West Bank elections for leaders to replace those formerly appointed by King Hussein; President Suharto of Indonesia moved to retire 86 generals; a Tanzanian village self-help leader explained, "The Government handles the technical side of things and we deal with ideology"; Senator William Fulbright charged that the Defense Department was using stories of a possible Soviet submarine base in Cuba to "alarm" the American people to support higher defense expenditures; Premier Papadopoulos of Greece pledged continuing support of the Western alliance; Edward Kardelj, Yugoslav politburo member, explained that a proposed six-man collective presidency to succeed President Tito would have a chairmanship that rotated annually among representatives of the six republics; Premier Pompidou of France prepared to leave for an eight-day visit to the Soviet Union to emphasize the "balanced position" of France versus the U.S.A. and the U.S.S.R.; Achutha Menon, a leader of the pro-Moscow Right Communist Party, was sworn in as head of the cabinet of India's Kerala State after an election victory; the wife of a former deputy speaker of the regional parliament in Sardinia was kidnapped and held for ransom; the homes of two Chilean right-wing political leaders were bombed; Mr. Tomic, who ran third in elections for the Chilean presidency, urged a Christian Democratic Party conference not to try to block the accession of victorious Marxist Dr. Salvador Allende in order to save Chilean democracy and to avoid civil war; a spokesman for Cleveland's mayor said he welcomed church efforts to get ethnic minority groups to identify with and cooperate with each other; state senators in Ohio received letters urging them not to confirm the appointment of a regent of a state university; the mayor of a small New Jersey town decided to sell his home and leave town because "taxes are too high"; Michigan's senators and governor were reported as being so "nice" that opposition candidates (including the wife of former Governor George Romney) found it difficult to attack them in the 1970 campaign; the grandson of President Eisenhower and the daughter of President Nixon, who are married, campaigned in Chicago for the brother of President Nixon's secretary; Hawaii's Governor John A. Burns was reported the Democratic primary election victor over his challenger Lieutenant Governor Thomas P. Gill; Vice-President Agnew, a Republican, made an election attack on Republican Senator Charles Goodell and received an editorial rebuke; Senator Goodell attacked Agnew for "inflaming the passions of the people"; an Indian chief of the Onondaga Nation refused to talk to a New York state legislative subcommittee on Indian reservation affairs because "a nation does not talk to a state"; political candidates in New York were reported making greater use of public opinion polls in plotting campaign strategy; Senator Edward Kennedy said he would not seek the Presidency in 1972 because "the uncertainties of higher office would place a great burden on our family"; and so forth. Although such reports are fragmentary and are not written systematically for facilitating research into political leadership, they suggest, like the top of an iceberg, the presence of underlying behavior that is of profound significance for individual societies, for regions, and for the world polity as a whole.

Thus, wherever one lives—in village, town, commune, city, state, province, territory, nation, or world (the one habitat shared by everyone) —a beginning can be made by looking sharply at the surrounding environment and asking such questions as, "Who are the political leaders? What difference do they make in social life? What alternative forms of political leadership are possible?" The first question will raise problems of identifying political leaders; the second will lead to analysis of leadership influences upon the political system and other aspects of society; the third will demand departure from the empirically given present to extrapolation, comparison, experimentation, and theoretical elaboration in search of action-relevant understanding.

In addition to these past and present-oriented modes of engagement in political leadership studies a futurist approach is also possible.[16] It may be asked what kinds of future societies are probable, possible, or desirable and then what forms of "political leadership" are likely, potentially achievable, or preferable. Another future-oriented approach would be to inquire into the implications for the future of present political leadership behavior and to examine the potential capacities of present leaders for creating desirable alternative futures. A future approach also raises naturally questions concerning the education of political leaders: what kinds of skills and knowledge do incumbent leaders have now for enabling them to shape desirable alternative futures; what kinds of continuing educational experiences might be useful for political leaders throughout their careers as they both create and respond to the future; and how should aspirants for political leadership —college students, for example—prepare themselves for leadership behavior in the onrushing twenty-first century and beyond? One not unthinkable approach to the study of political leadership from a future perspective is to hypothesize that neither past nor present forms of political leadership will permit human survival and advancement in the century ahead.

Initially it is not crucial just how the deliberate study of political leadership is begun—questions of interest to some may seem dull to others— but it is important that a beginning be made somewhere with a sense of alternatives. Where alternatives are appreciated, wiser decisions can be made. Thus the orientation may be toward the past, present, or future; toward the actual, possible, or preferable; toward the single case, comparison, aggregation, or experimentation; toward theory-building, teaching, research, administration, or action; or to varying combinations of these and other modes of behavior. What is important is that the study of political leadership begins to be perceived as a distinctive field worthy of further exploration.

This sounds obvious, but it is not. Take, for example, the publication record of the *American Political Science Review* from 1906–1963—a total of 2614 articles over a period of fifty-seven years.[17] Now if the subject of "political leadership" had been perceived as an important field for specialized study by the academic political science profession we could expect that this would be reflected in the titles given to the articles published during this period. Guess how many articles contained references to "leader" or "leadership"? Only seventeen (only one of them was really about the study of political leadership in a generic sense).[18] How about "politician"? Just one article.

Although these two figures dramatically symbolize the neglect, it would be inadequate to stop with them. Title references to other leadership roles of importance, at least in the American political system, should be sought. Variations on the word "president" (70 articles), "governor" (27 articles), "representative" (15 articles), and "senator" (5 articles)—but none on "mayor," are found. This means that only about 3% (85 of 2614) of the articles mentioned words directly related to the concept of leadership and leadership roles even within the American context.

But numbers require interpretation; and this is an inflated figure. Since all variants of the terms were examined, many articles of only marginal interest are included. More important, only a handful of them came close to an attempt to conceptualize the study of leadership in a general way. This means that on the basis of this literature it is virtually impossible to make political leadership role comparisons, even within the parochial American context. That is, it is not possible to compare the roles of president, governor, mayor, representative, senator, and other politicians. This cannot be done for functionally equivalent roles cross-culturally either. It must be concluded that, aside from specific pioneering insights, the study of political leadership, although intuitively recognized as important by probably all political scientists, has not yet been made a subject of specialized professional concern.

There is further evidence. Until recently few undergraduate courses or graduate seminars seem to have been offered in the general field of political leadership. It has usually not been defined as an area of graduate specialization in the same sense as fields such as political parties, legislatures, public administration, judicial behavior, and voting behavior. And consequently, few political scientists up to now identify themselves primarily as specialists in the study of political leadership. Yet as a bibliographical review suggests,[19] individual scholars have produced many important works that can serve as the foundation for a full-fledged field of political leadership studies.

How is this apparent neglect—or perhaps better, failure of conceptual focus—to be explained? Was it linked to the fact that the scientific study of politics, including the search for cross-level, cross-cultural, and cross-historical comparisons, is a relatively recent idea? Was it associated with anti-leadership biases in the American political culture or academic subculture? Or were taboos similar to those that once inhibited inquiry into sex and religion operative in blocking inquiry into the behavior of powerful political figures? Was there any significance in the fact that American political science first made its greatest scientific breakthrough in the study of voting behavior (the behavior of followers) rather than in the study of those who led, a field left largely to journalists? Was there a strain of determinism in American social science thought, reinforced by the surrounding political culture, that inhibited appreciation of the capacity of leaders to have independent impact upon political life? Was politics viewed as created by more basic economic and social forces? Were political leaders (politicians) viewed merely as the representatives or "tools" of these more basic interests? Or have they been viewed as trapped helplessly in the web of institutions? Was the neglect linked to the fact that although Americans established specialized schools for the education and advanced training of military and business leaders, they did not do the same for political leaders? And might not a chronic mutual disdain between politicians and professors have impeded nurturance of the cooperation necessary for the development of a full-fledged field of political leadership studies?

But if failure to focus was the story of the past, there is a perceptible emergence of concentrated attention in the present. Why? Did the crisis of World War II sensitize men to the importance of leadership as well as ab-

stract systems and forces in the behavior of Hitler, Mussolini, Stalin, Churchill, de Gaulle, Chiang, Roosevelt, and others? In the postwar period, was
not attention drawn to the important role of revolutionary leaders such as
Mao Tse-tung, Ho Chi Minh, and Fidel Castro? As scores of new nations
emerged to independence in the breakdown of the world colonial system, and
the names of men such as Sukarno, Nkrumah, Nasser, and Nehru flashed to
prominence, was there not a rediscovery of Montesquieu's dictum that "at
the birth of societies, it is the leaders of the commonwealth who create the
institutions; afterwards it is the institutions that shape the leaders"? [20] In
the divided nations particularly, were there not dramatic examples of the
importance for a people of common heritage of alternative political leadership: Ulbricht versus Adenauer in Germany; Mao against Chiang in China;
Ho Chi Minh versus Ngo Dinh Diem in Vietnam, and Kim Il Sung against
Syngman Rhee in Korea? And underneath the vast global changes of the
postwar period was there not felt the presence of departed leaders such as
Lincoln, Lenin, and Gandhi?

In American society itself, the assassinations of President John F.
Kennedy (November 22, 1963), Malcolm X (February 21, 1965), George
Lincoln Rockwell (August 25, 1967), Martin Luther King (April 4, 1968),
and Senator Robert F. Kennedy (June 6, 1968) constituted a shocking negative affirmation of the emotional and practical importance of leadership. And
the contemporary demands in American society for and against radical
change in willingness to wage war, race relations, income distribution, urban
life, industrial effects on the environment, property relations, abortion laws,
divorce laws, drug laws, the role of youth, and other matters constitute positive affirmation of needs for political leadership action.

But neither world nor contemporary local conditions are sufficient to
explain the current political science upsurge in political leadership studies;
there have been wars, revolutions, assassinations, and demands for radical
change before. What is perhaps new is the convergence of both behavioral
science and humanist concerns for individual human behavior combined with
increasing social science capacity for ever more sophisticated aggregative
analysis. Not only is political leadership behavior—incumbent, aspirant, or
revolutionary—perceived as a crucial element in efforts to define and solve
societal problems, but the behavioral science tools for observation, measurement, experimentation, and analysis plus the rationale for their employment
have gained wide acceptance in political science as a discipline. Methodo-
logically, political science is becoming increasingly more capable of studying
scientifically individual human behavior and of combining individuals through
aggregate analysis.

Although we have been speaking primarily of American political
science are there not similar trends in other societies that promise the eventual emergence of a world wide intellectual community devoted to the sci-

entific study of political leadership as a field of knowledge intrinsically interesting for its own sake as well as potentially contributive to man's capacity to solve his most pressing problems?

Thus far some alternative modes of engagement in the study of political leadership have been explored, some signs of intellectual failure to focus upon it have been indicated, and some possible reasons for its past neglect and present attraction have been suggested. It remains to take stock of some of the resources now available for making the study of political leadership a special field of inquiry and to question what needs to be done to move ahead.

Although neglected in a specialized sense, it would be a mistake to begin the study of political leadership with the idea that little of relevance previously has been accomplished. It would be equally erroneous to assume that existing studies constitute a coherent field of knowledge with organized potential for sustained advancement. There exists, indeed, an abundant literature that can serve as the foundation for such a field.[21] Among the intellectual resources that can be assembled for the development of a field of political leadership studies are the following:

1. *studies on charisma,* essays ranging from the seminal formulation of Max Weber[22] to the attempt to relate the concept to a variety of empirical examples by Ann Ruth Wilner.[23]

2. *didactic literature,* ranging from Machiavelli's *The Prince* and other works mentioned above through Lenin's *What Is to be Done*[24] to Cass' *How to Win Votes and Influence Elections.*[25]

3. *political biography and autobiography,* including the Georges' study of Woodrow Wilson;[26] Edinger's study of Kurt Schumacher;[27] Gottfried's study of Anton Cermak;[28] Wolfenstein's comparative analysis of Lenin, Trotsky, and Gandhi;[29] and innumerable primary sources such as de Gaulle's memoirs,[30] and Che Guevara's diary.[31]

4. *studies in political leadership values and ideas,* including original writings by political leaders themselves,[32] comparative ideological surveys,[33] and systematic comparative inquiries into relationships between values and other aspects of leadership behavior.[34]

5. *studies in leadership styles,* comprising both efforts to discover "operational codes" [35] and attempts to discover persisting patterns of personality influences upon political leadership behavior.[36]

6. *institutional role studies,* focusing upon individual or collective incumbents of formal positions of political leadership including studies of the American presidency,[37] senators,[38] congressmen,[39] governors,[40] state legislators,[41] mayors,[42] and local party leaders.[43]

7. *political elite studies,* aggregative studies ranging from the seminal contribution of Lasswell, Lerner, and Rothwell,[44] through

Frey's study of Turkish legislators,[45] to the recent incisive methodological critique by Searing.[46]

8. *community power studies* in which local political leaders are usually viewed aggregatively in relation to other community influentials, including such pioneering works as Hunter's discovery of a "power elite" complex in Atlanta,[47] Dahl's demonstration of a "pluralist" elite structure in New Haven,[48] and Agger, Goldrich, and Swanson's four-community comparative examination of the correlates of different political leadership groups, power structures, and regimes.[49]

9. *follower response studies,* inquiries that show how followers respond to the personalities, styles, organizational identifications, and issue positions of political leaders exemplified by the extensive research that has been done on the American voter.[50]

10. *area surveys,* combining various elements of the foregoing, studies that attempt to give an overview of the political leadership characteristics of a country or region; for example, studies of political leadership in Africa,[51] China,[52] Latin America,[53] Southeast Asia,[54] and the Soviet Union and Eastern Europe.[55]

11. *leadership studies in other socio-behavioral sciences, and applied fields,* including studies in psychology,[56] sociology,[57] anthropology,[58] economics,[59] and in public executive,[60] industrial,[61] labor,[62] military,[63] and religious[64] leadership.

The greatest resource, of course, lies in the living experience of political leaders themselves at every level and in every culture. In chains of learning stretching down from man's emergence as a human animal, there has been forged and transmitted variously changing knowledge about the nature of leadership in politics. This is the kind of knowledge that is passed on in schools of practical politics and in apprenticeship relationships. It is the gap between this kind of knowledge and what they perceive as academic knowledge that predisposes many leaders to treat political scientists with disdain. The appropriate response of the student of political leadership should be simply: "Teach me."

There is no doubt but that available intellectual resources are abundant both within the discipline of political science and without. So numerous are they in fact that one might be led to conclude either (1) that political leadership is so well treated by the discipline that no further specialized differentiation is necessary or (2) that a new field of political leadership studies would threaten to "take over" the entire discipline. Neither is true. In an academic discipline as in social life itself, it is expected that political leadership will be a subject of pervasive relevance; but it will not describe or explain all of human behavior. As an analytical cut across an entire discipline the study of political leadership may contribute a catalytic and linkage function for many political science concerns, but it will not have the eventual comprehensiveness and integrating power (both within and across disciplines) of more abstract formulations such as "decision making" and "the political system." [65] It will, however, contribute something to their further elaboration. As one aspect of political behavior both within and across polities, the study of political leadership will call attention to the actions of salient individuals from the largest to the smallest politically relevant unit—but it will not be all of politics nor all of political science.

What, then, needs to be done in order to establish the study of political leadership as a special field of inquiry? A set of minimum requirements would seem to be the following: (1) First of all, there is a need for general vision that such a special field of inquiry could exist. Just as a journey to the moon was envisioned before all the scientific, technological, and human capabilities for its attainment were created, so also the idea of a field of political leadership studies can serve as a general goal to guide subsequent efforts at attainment. (2) There is a related need for conceptual refinement: the creation and critical evaluation of alternative concepts of the nature of "political leadership." The more varied such concepts are, the less likely the neglect of important aspects of the subject by entrapment in influential or culture-bound formulations. On the other hand, the more the eventual conceptual convergence from different points of origin, the greater the sense of validity that analytical ideas are really focused upon vital aspects of political leadership behavior. (3) Methods need to be designed for enhancing our capacity to be surprised. Contentment with visions, concepts, and hypothesized or confirmed relationships will not lead to new knowledge. Thus we need to develop increasingly precise research methods that reveal not only what we think we know, but demonstrate dramatically what we do not. (4) There is needed what might be called nurturant interchange between the scholarly world of political leadership studies and the action world of political leadership itself. The one need not be "out there"; the other need not be "in here"; the one need not be "the establishment" or the "revolutionary enemy," the other its nemesis or puppet. Mutually beneficial relationships between the study and practice of political leadership from a wide range of positions need to be established. The reactive effects of involvement on both sides, while potentially distorting as well as enlightening, can themselves be made a subject of inquiry. The reciprocal influence processes of inquiry itself thus can become a part of what is studied, controlled for, and acted upon. (5) There is a need for developing means for the transmission of experience both about political leadership itself and about models of inquiry into it. No less than political leaders themselves, students of the subject have to devise ways of transmitting knowledge and of enhancing innovations in oncoming generations—or at least from inquiry to inquiry. (6) There is a need also for devising means to test the action usefulness of emerging knowledge in the study of political leadership. This can be done through experimental efforts in the laboratory or under natural field conditions.[66] (7) Finally, in developing the study of political leadership we need to encourage the critical monitoring of all its processes. These processes include conceptualization, research design and execution, transmission of experience, and the practical application of knowledge. The more diverse the critics, the more useful the expected criticisms. Thus the criticisms of scientists, humanists, political leaders, and other persons of varying background (including those of non-elite status) will be essential to engage in the monitoring process. Such criticisms may be technical, moral, or creatively imaginative: all can be helpful and become harmful only when accompanied by physical, psychological, or economic terror designed to injure or destroy the victim.

Not every student of political leadership will be able to do everything that will be required to advance this field of inquiry, but each can do something, and everything must be done by somebody.

The leading essay in this volume by Donald Searing (Selection 1) makes two contributions of special significance. First, in describing two models of social reality (the "organismic" and "mechanistic" models), the essay assists the conceptual clarification and sensitization to alternative formulations that is essential to the advancement of political leadership studies. Second, the essay demonstrates common problems and assumptions in the study of both individual political leaders and political elites as collectivities. Thus it contributes to appreciation of the idea that political leadership studies involve both studies of individuals and leadership groups that are empirically given (e.g., a legislature) or analytically defined (e.g., all state governors).

In attempting to link the concept of leadership with the concept of power, Kenneth F. Janda (Selection 2) makes a pioneering contribution to the conceptualization of political leadership. It may be questioned, however, whether a definition restricted to only one aspect (legitimate) of the five bases of social power identified by French and Raven[67] (reward, coercive, legitimate, referent, and expert) will be an adequate foundation for political leadership studies as a whole. It may also be asked whether making the perceptions of followers the crucial operational indicator of the presence of leadership may not contribute to the prolongation of customary "overemphasis" upon the question of why followers behave as they do, rather than opening up new inquiries into the description and explanation of the behavior of those persons who actually lead or aspire to leadership. Janda not only demonstrates the usefulness of continuing his efforts to relate political leadership to the concept of power but also suggests the potential utility of similar attempts to explore linkages with such concepts as "legitimacy" itself, "authority," "representation," "control," "conflict," "consensus," and "the political system."

These two essays naturally only begin to raise important problems of conceptualization. The reader is thus referred to the cited bibliography and to his own imagination as an approach to creative scientific conceptualization of political leadership as a subject for inquiry and action.

# Notes

to Part One: Overview

1. Progress toward a world data bank on political leadership will be facilitated by efforts to achieve a global overview of world history and by the elaboration of culture-specific monographs to undergird them. Outstanding overview efforts are represented by Arnold J. Toynbee, *A Study of History* (New York: Oxford University Press, 1954) and William H. McNeil, *The Rise of the West* (Chicago: University of Chicago Press, 1963).

The potentialities as well as shortcomings of attempts to list outstanding world leaders are illustrated by the 40,000 entries of *Webster's Biographical Dictionary* (Springfield, Mass.: G. & C. Merriam Co., 1964), and by the pioneering but crude and incomplete inventory contained in L. F. Wise and E. W. Egan, *Kings, Rulers and Statesmen* (New York: Sterling, 1967). The voluminous biographical literature in the English language alone is illustrated by the periodical reference work *Biography Index.*

2. Plato, *The Republic,* trans. by Francis Macdonald Cornford (New York: Oxford University Press, 1945).

3. Niccolo Machiavelli, *The Prince,* ed. by T. G. Gergin (New York: Appleton-Century-Crofts, 1964).

4. Confucius, *Analects,* trans. and annotated by Arthur Waley (London: G. Allen and Unwin, 1938).

5. J. J. L. Duyvendak, trans. (Chicago: University of Chicago Press, 1963).

6. R. Shamasastry, trans. (Mysore: Sri Raghuveer Printing House, 1956).

7. Hubert Darke, trans. (New Haven: Yale University Press, 1960).

8. Book 8 of *Florentine Codex,* trans. by Arthur J. O. Anderson and Charles E. Dibble (Sante Fe: The School of American Research, 1954).

9. Garden City: Doubleday, 1961.

10. New York: Columbia University Press, 1969.

11. An African example can be found in the Yoruba talking drum tradition "Oriki (Praise Names) for Lagunju of Ede," in Austin J. Sheldon (ed.), Chief Olunlade, trans., *The African Assertion* (New York: Odyssey Press, 1968), pp. 36–39.

12. E.g., Aage Clausen and Richard R. Cheney, "A Comparative Analysis of Senate-House Voting on Economics and Welfare Policy: 1953–1964," *American Political Science Review*, LXIV (March 1970), pp. 138–152.

13. E.g., Robert E. Agger, Daniel Goodrich, and Bert E. Swanson, *The Rulers and the Ruled* (New York: Wiley, 1964), especially chapter VI.

14. As Durkheim has advised, "We must approach the social realm where it offers the easiest access to scientific investigation. Only subsequently will it be possible to push research further and, by successive approximations, to encompass, little by little, this fleeting reality which the human mind will never, perhaps, be able to grasp completely." Emile Durkheim, *The Rules of Sociological Method* (New York: The Free Press, 1964), p. 46.

15. The importance of political leadership also can be seen readily or inferred by readers of Moscow's *Pravda* or Peking's *Jen-min Jih-pao,* although the variety and detail of the reported political leadership behavior is usually not as great as in some other leading world newspapers.

16. A useful contemporary introduction to future studies is John McHale, *The Future of the Future* (New York: George Braziller, 1969).

17. Kenneth Janda (ed.), *Cumulative Index to the American Political Science Review, Volumes 1–57: 1906–1963* (Evanston: Northwestern University Press, 1964).

18. Lester G. Seligman, "The Study of Political Leadership," *American Political Science Review*, XLIV (December 1950), pp. 904–915.

19. See the bibliography attached to Glenn D. Paige, *The Study of Political Leadership* (New York: The Free Press, forthcoming).

20. Quoted, for example, in Dankwart A. Rustow, *A World of Nations* (Washington: Brookings Institution, 1967), p. 135.

21. Consult, for example, George T. Force and Jack R. Van Der Slik, *Theory and Research in the Study of Political Leadership* (Carbondale: Southern Illinois University, Public Affairs Research Bureau, 1969); the bibliography appended to Lewis J. Edinger, *Political Leadership in Industrialized Societies* (New York: John Wiley, 1967); Carl Beck and J. T. McKechnie, *Political Elites: A Select Computerized Bibliography* (Cambridge: M.I.T. Press, 1967); and the 1155 items appended to Bernard M. Bass, *Leadership, Psychology and Organizational Behavior* (New York: Harper and Brothers, 1960).

22. See the essay on "Charismatic Authority" in Max Weber, *The Theory of Social and Economic Organization,* trans. by A. M. Henderson and Talcott Parsons (New York: The Free Press, 1957), pp. 358–364.

23. Ann Ruth Wilner, *Charismatic Political Leadership: A Theory* (Princeton: Princeton University, Center of International Studies, 1968).

24. V. I. Lenin, *What Is to be Done,* trans. by S. V. Utechin and Patricia Utechin (New York: Oxford University Press, 1963).

25. Don Pirie Cass, Chicago: Public Administration Service, 1962.

26. Alexander L. and Juliette L. George, *Woodrow Wilson and Colonel House* (New York: Dover, 1964).

27. Lewis J. Edinger, *Kurt Schumacher* (Stanford: Stanford University Press, 1965).

28. Alex Gottfried, *Boss Cermak of Chicago* (Seattle: University of Washington Press, 1962).

29. E. Victor Wolfenstein, *The Revolutionary Personality: Lenin, Trotsky, Gandhi* (Princeton: Princeton University Press, 1967).

30. Charles de Gaulle, *Mémoires d'espoir: le renouveau* (Paris: Plon, 1970.

31. Robert Scheer (ed.), *The Diary of Che Guevara* (New York: Bantam Books, 1968).

32. E.g., Mao Tse-tung, *Selected Works of Mao Tse-tung* (New York: International Publishers, 1954–1956), 4 vols., and Adolf Hitler, *Mein Kampf,* editorial sponsors John Chamberlain, *et al.* (New York: Reynal and Hitchcock, 1939).

33. Paul Sigmund, *Ideologies of the Developing Nations* (New York: Frederick A. Praeger, 1963).

34. Philip E. Jacob (ed.), *Values and the Active Community: A Cross-National Study of the Influence of Local Leadership* (New York: The Free Press, 1971).

35. Alexander L. George, *The "Operational Code": A Neglected Approach to the Study of Political Leaders and Decision Making* (Santa Monica: The Rand Corporation, 1967).

36. For example, Erwin C. Hargrove, *Presidential Leadership: Personality and Political Style* (New York: Macmillan, 1966) distinguishes between "presidents of action" ("dramatizing, moralizing, manipulative") and "presidents of restraint."

37. Richard E. Neustadt, *Presidential Power* (New York: John Wiley, 1960).

38. Donald R. Matthews, *U.S. Senators and Their World* (New York: Random House, 1960).

39. Charles L. Clapp, *The Congressman: His Work as He Sees It* (Washington: Brookings Institution, 1964).

40. Coleman B. Ransone, *The Office of the Governor in the United States* (Tuscaloosa, Ala.: University of Alabama Press, 1956).

41. James D. Barber, *The Lawmakers* (New Haven: Yale University Press, 1965).

42. Leonard I. Ruchelman, ed., *Big City Mayors: Crisis in Urban Politics* (Bloomington: Indiana University Press, 1969).

43. Samuel J. Eldersveld, *Political Parties: A Behavioral Analysis* (Chicago: Rand McNally, 1964).

44. Harold Lasswell, Daniel Lerner, and C. Easton Rothwell, *The Comparative Study of Elites: An Introduction and Bibliography* (Stanford: Stanford University Press, 1952).

45. Frederick W. Frey, *The Turkish Political Elite* (Cambridge: M.I.T. Press, 1965).

46. Donald D. Searing, "The Comparative Study of Elite Socialization," *Comparative Political Studies,* I (January 1969), pp. 471–500.

47. Floyd Hunter, *Community Power Structure: A Study of Decision Makers* (Chapel Hill, N.C.: University of North Carolina Press, 1953).

48. Robert A. Dahl, *Who Governs?* (New Haven: Yale University Press, 1961).

49. Robert E. Agger *et al., op. cit.* See also Charles M. Bonjean, Terry N. Clark, and Robert L. Lineberry (eds.), *Community Politics: A Behavioral Approach* (New York: The Free Press, 1971).

50. Angus Campbell *et al., The American Voter* (New York: John Wiley, 1965).

51. Norman K. Bennet, *Leadership in Eastern Africa; Six Political Biographies* (Boston: Boston University Press, 1968).

52. John Wilson Lewis (ed.), *Party Leadership and Revolutionary Power in China* (Cambridge: Cambridge University Press, 1970).

53. Robert J. Alexander, *Prophets of the Revolution: Profiles of Latin American Leaders* (New York: Macmillan, 1962).

54. Willard A. Hanna, *Eight Nation Makers: Southeast Asia's Charismatic Statesmen* (New York: St. Martin's Press, 1964).

55. R. Barry Farrell (ed.), *Political Leadership in Eastern Europe and the Soviet Union* (Chicago: Aldine, 1970).

56. Cecil A. Gibb, "Leadership: Psychological Aspects," in David Sills (ed.), *International Encyclopedia of the Social Sciences* (New York: The Free Press, 1968), IX, pp. 91–101.

57. Arnold S. Tannenbaum, "Leadership: Sociological Aspects," *ibid.,* pp. 101–107.

58. Marc J. Swartz, Victor W. Turner, and Arthur Tuden (eds.), *Political Anthropology* (Chicago: Aldine, 1966).

59. Harald Eidheim, "Entrepreneurship in Politics," in *The Role of the Entrepreneur in Social Change in Northern Norway,* ed. by Frederik Barth (Bergen, Norway: Universitet Bergen, Humanistisk Serie, 1967).

60. W. Lloyd Warner *et al., The American Federal Executive* (New Haven: Yale University Press, 1963).

61. William Henry, "The Business Executive: The Psychodynamics

of a Social Role," *American Journal of Sociology,* LIV (January 1949), pp. 289–291.

62. Lois MacDonald, *Leadership Dynamics and the Trade Union Leader* (New York: New York University Press, 1959).

63. Carl J. Lange, "Leadership in Small Military Units: Some Recent Research Findings," in *Defense Psychology,* ed. by Frank Geldard (New York: Pergamon Press, 1962), pp. 286–301.

64. D. Ray Lindley, "Types of Religious Leaders," *Encounter,* XXIII (1962), pp. 3–19.

65. E.g., Richard C. Snyder, "Decision Making as an Approach to the Study of Political Phenomena," in Roland Young (ed.), *Approaches to the Study of Politics* (Evanston: Northwestern University Press, 1958), pp. 3–38; David Easton, *A Systems Analysis of Political Life* (New York: John Wiley, 1965); and Gabriel A. Almond, "A Developmental Approach to Political Systems," *World Politics,* XVII, No. 2 (January 1965), pp. 183–214.

66. Suggestive introduction to the idea of experimental approaches to the acquisition of socially useful knowledge is contained in George W. Fairweather, *Methods for Experimental Social Innovation* (New York: John Wiley, 1968).

67. John R. P. French, Jr., and Bertram Raven, "The Bases of Social Power," in Dorwin Cartwright (ed.), *Studies in Social Power* (Ann Arbor: University of Michigan Press, 1959), pp. 150–167.

# 1

## Models and Images of Man and Society in Leadership Theory*

DONALD D. SEARING

Leadership theory construction has been confounded by two often dogmatic controversies. One is the great man-social forces dispute in individual leadership studies. The other is the pluralist-stratification debate in elite research.[1] The controversy has to some extent followed disciplinary lines, though it would be incorrect to characterize the disputants as neatly divided as all that, since disagreements continue within disciplines as well as among them.[2]

Donald D. Searing, "Models and Images of Man and Society in Leadership Theory." *The Journal of Politics,* XXXI, No. 1 (February 1969), pp. 3–31.

* I am grateful to Henry Shue, John Sprague, Lewis Edinger, and John Kautsky for their helpful comments on earlier drafts of this article.

[1] See: E. F. Borgatta *et al.,* "Some Findings Relevant to the Great Man Theory of Leadership," *American Sociological Review,* 19 (December 1954), pp. 755–759; Morris R. Cohen, "Great Men in History," in his *The Meaning of Human History* (LaSalle, Illinois: Open Court, 1947), pp. 214–224; Bernard M. Bass, *Leadership, Psychology and Organizational Behavior* (New York: Harper and Row, 1960); Sidney Hook, *The Hero in History* (New York: John Day, 1943); Lawrence Herson, "In the Footsteps of Community Power," *American Political Science Review,* 55 (December 1961), pp. 817–831; T. J. Anton, "Power, Pluralism, and Local Politics," *Administrative Science Quarterly,* 7 (March 1963), pp. 425–454; Nelson Polsby, *Community Power and Political Theory* (New Haven: Yale University Press, 1963); John Walton, "Substance and Artifact: The Current Status of Research on Community Power Structure," *American Journal of Sociology,* 71 (January 1966), pp. 430–439; and Richard M. Merelman, "On the Neo-Elitist Critique of Community Power," *American Political Science Review,* 62 (June 1968), pp. 451–460.

[2] Regardless of their methodological differences, historians often defend the great man in history thesis, while political scientists and sociologists typically maintain the social forces position. American political scientists frequently support the pluralist position in elite studies, with sociologists advancing the stratification argument. See John Walton, "Discipline, Method, and Community Power: A Note on the Sociology of Knowledge," *American Sociological Review,* 31 (October 1966), pp. 684–689.

This paper attempts to clarify discussion by explicating the following points. First, both controversies involve the same two alternative images of man and society, mechanistic and organismic. Secondly, current empirical research has frequently gone beyond these primitive images, thereby rendering unnecessary at least the dogmatic part of the controversies built upon them. Finally, when these mechanistic and organismic constructs are treated as heuristic or organizing models, they lose their mutually exclusive character and become complementary tools of scientific inquiry.[3]

In individual leadership analysis, great man in history studies usually construct the familiar mechanistic model of social action, whereas the social forces approach typically turns the organismic model to good account. In aggregate or elite studies we find the same two models again: pluralist analyses producing the mechanistic, and stratification studies the organismic in this case. I say *models* of social action, because few contemporary researchers explicitly argue that their model is applicable beyond a sub class of cases similar to the one from which it has been constructed. Confusion and controversy arise when these limited and tentative models are rigidified into images of man and society understood as isomorphic to *all* contexts of social experience. The manner in which mechanistic and organismic models cut across both individual leadership and elite controversies may be summarized as follows:

|                        | Individual Leadership Studies | Elite Studies |
|------------------------|-------------------------------|---------------|
| Mechanistic Models     | Great Man in History          | Pluralist     |
| Organismic Models      | Social Forces                 | Stratification|

Examination of the leadership literature then will demonstrate that mechanistic and organismic models have been repeatedly constructed to describe situational data in both individual leadership and elite studies. There

---

[3] There has recently been a growing awareness of the need for such a complementary approach. For example: Gerhard E. Lenski, *Power and Privilege* (New York: McGraw Hill, 1966); Fred I. Greenstein, "Personality and Politics: Problems of Evidence, Inference, Conceptualization," *American Behavioral Scientist,* 11 (November–December 1967), pp. 38–53; and Stanislaw Ossowski, *Class Structure in the Social Consciousness* (London: Routledge and Kegan Paul, 1963).

are two possible explanations of these apparently cumulative results. One is that relatively consistent patterns are repeatedly being discovered in comparative data and accurately described in research reports. The other is that researchers are bringing similar *a priori* images to their work and unwittingly structuring the data to fit these preconceptions. Social science is not yet sufficiently systematic that the second alternative can be dismissed as a remote possibility. In fact, such misinterpretation has frequently been the subject of exchanges in debates on leadership methodology. It should be emphasized, however, that mutual blanket rejections of the findings of one leadership school by another are frequently unsatisfactory, especially when supported only by *a priori* arguments. Logically demonstrating the limitations of these approaches does not always invalidate the results of all their applications. This is due to the rarity in contemporary social science of studies whose conclusions follow directly and unambiguously from deductive theories tested by rigorously applied methodologies. In short, at the present stage of behavioral research, distortion usually cannot be convincingly demonstrated without careful and intensive re-examination of the primary data for each specific research problem. Such a task is obviously well beyond the scope of this paper. Pending satisfactory replication of the studies to be discussed below, I shall therefore tentatively assume that the first explanation of their consistent results is correct—that each model adequately describes the data in question. We can then ask the following question. Given that these studies describe different situational contexts, and assuming that they have been satisfactorily executed, what can be concluded with regard to the debate in leadership analysis?

The conclusion, if a tautology may be drawn, is that situational contexts themselves differ, and that, *ipso facto,* different models do best apply to different situational contexts. This result is platitudinous and would seem pedantic were it not for some current controversy in leadership studies over attempts to generalize to all leadership contexts from either the mechanistic or the organismic model. What must be insisted on here is that in some situations great men are likely important, pluralism viable, and mechanistic models most appropriate. In other situations social forces prevail, stratification is more likely the rule, and organismic models are most reliable. In short, the controversy in leadership studies may be conditioned in part not by alternative models, but by monolithic images of man and society presented in the form of universal generalizations.

## IMAGES AND MODELS

It is indeed a commonplace of modern science that there seems to be no reason to believe in the existence of hard and fast "facts" which are subsequently discovered in the course of empirical inquiry. One need not be a cultural relativist to recognize that facts are abstractions, ordered and selected by observers who filter them out of experience by means of conceptual frameworks.[4] In behavioral research, these conceptual frameworks are usually structured by whatever the observer regards as valuable and as "real" in society. The important thing about such frameworks is whether they are introduced as unselfconscious *images* of society, or whether they are generated as tentative *models* for limited research purposes.

Images of man and society are familiar in the sociology of knowledge as closed systems of thought, supported by appropriate metaphors which at the same time furnish clues to the character of the image. For example, metaphors such as "balance" and "friction" are associated with a mechanistic image, while "stasis," "adaptation," and "health" are associated with an organismic image.[5] Their application is almost always unsatisfactory because they are regarded as literal truths about the way reality "really is." They blind us to alternative ways of looking at the same experience which might be more useful in inquiry.[6]

Models, in contrast, differ from such images by their greater precision and more limited scope. They can present tentative alternatives so that it becomes an empirical problem whether, for instance, a mechanistic or organismic model is more congruent with a given set of social institutions.[7] Models are partial isomorphs, aids to understanding based upon analogy. In this sense the term "model" is being defined quite loosely, following contemporary usage in political science which equates it at one level with constructed types such as *Gemeinschaft* and *Gesellschaft*. Here a model is distinguished from an image by its self-consciously explicit, limited and tentative character. It consists of statements identifying major characteristics

---

[4] See, *inter alia,* Carl L. Becker, "What are Historical Facts?" *Western Political Quarterly,* 8 (September 1955), pp. 327–340; and especially Kenneth E. Boulding, *The Image: Knowledge in Life and Society* (Ann Arbor: University of Michigan Press, 1956). *Cf.* Louis Kattsoff, "Facts, Phenomena and Frames of Reference in Psychology," *Psychological Review,* 60 (January 1953), pp. 40–44.

[5] Martin Landau, "On the Use of Metaphor in Political Analysis," *Social Research,* 28 (Autumn 1961), pp. 331–353. Landau links metaphors to these images of society and explores their historical impact upon the scope and method of American political science.

[6] See Abraham Kaplan, *The Conduct of Inquiry* (San Francisco: Chandler Publishing Company, 1964), p. 384; and Reinhard Bendix and Bennett Berger, "Images of Society and Problems of Concept Formation in Sociology," in Llewellyn Gross (ed.), *Symposium on Sociological Theory* (New York: Harper and Row, 1959), pp. 100 and 112.

[7] Eugene J. Meehan, *Contemporary Political Thought* (Homewood, Illinois: Dorsey, 1967), p. 30; and Carl G. Hempel, *Aspects of Scientific Explanation* (New York: The Free Press, 1965), p. 438.

and generalizations about their interrelationships.[8] Such models have been characterized as serving four functions: organizing, heuristic, predictive, and measuring.[9]

Models found in leadership studies usually serve the first two functions, belonging thereby to the context of discovery rather than validation. Nonetheless it is still necessary to decide which model is most appropriate for a given research context. This choice can be made on grounds of accuracy in correspondence to the empirical phenomena of relevance, or by economy as compared with other possible candidates.[10] By locating these mechanistic and organismic models at the ends of a continuum for leadership studies, it will be easier to discern where a particular social context tends. This can be done without losing sight of the fact that, from a slightly different problem perspective, the context may be located at a different place, and our model modified accordingly.[11] After briefly describing the two polar images as they have appeared in social thought, they will be examined in the context of leadership studies and treated as models therein.

---

[8] John C. McKinney's excellent discussion of constructed types is directly relevant to the organismic and mechanistic models as they have been used in leadership theory: *Constructive Typology and Social Theory* (New York: Appleton-Century-Crofts, 1966), pp. 100ff. See also Karl W. Deutsch, "Mechanism, Organism, and Society: Some Models in Natural and Social Science," *Philosophy of Science,* 18 (July 1951), p. 230; Marion Levy, "Some Problems for a Unified Theory of Human Nature," in Edward A. Tiryakin (ed.), *Sociological Theory, Values and Socio-Cultural Change* (New York: The Free Press, 1963); and Hempel, *op. cit.,* pp. 434–436. This obviously differs from more rigorously defined models which are discussed in Hubert M. Blalock Jr., *Causal Inferences in Nonexperimental Research* (Chapel Hill: University of North Carolina Press, 1961); and Herbert A. Simon, *Models of Man* (New York: John Wiley, 1957).

[9] Karl W. Deutsch, *The Nerves of the Government; Models of Political Communication and Control* (New York: The Free Press, 1963), pp. 8–11. Models are often used to mean many different things, ranging all the way from theory to any theoretical formulation other than theory. See Richard S. Rudner, *Philosophy of Social Science* Englewood Cliffs, N.J.: Prentice-Hall, 1966), p. 23. For a number of different meanings of models, see also Y. R. Chao, "Models in Linguistics and Models in General," in Ernest Nagel, *et al.* (eds.), *Logic, Methodology and Philosophy of Science* (Stanford: Stanford University Press, 1962).

[10] Deutsch, *The Nerves of Government, op. cit.,* pp. 11–16.

[11] This suggestion was made by Reinhard Bendix and Bennett Berger, "Images of Society and Problems of Concept Formation in Sociology," in Llewellyn Gross (ed.), *Symposium on Sociological Theory* (New York: Harper and Row, 1959), pp. 92–118. The proposal for pairing models in this fashion is analogous to the patriarchal-matriarchal pair applied by Radcliffe-Brown, who emphasized that no primitive society wholly corresponded to one or the other, but fell on a continuum somewhere between the two. A. R. Radcliffe-Brown, *Structure and Function in Primitive Society* (New York: The Free Press, 1965), p. 22. See also Ralf Dahrendorf, *Class and Class Conflict in Industrial Society* (Stanford: Stanford University Press, 1959), pp. 159ff.

## TWO IMAGES OF MAN AND SOCIETY

Mechanistic and organismic images of man and society are in evidence throughout the history of social thought. They have served as organizing principles for major figures in political philosophy,[12] and have alternated with one another as architectonic influences upon conceptualizations of contemporary social scientists.[13]

The mechanistic image begins with the notion that society and its human members are of a relatively constant and unchanging nature. Both are composed of discrete parts linked together in stable relationships of attraction, repulsion, and the like. Since the parts are not naturally integrated, they sometimes work against one another, as in conflict.[14] Analogies from Newtonian mechanics and Enlightenment clockwork are common frames of reference applied most conspicuously in the atomistic approaches of Hobbes, Locke, and Mill. Institutional aspects of social and political structure are often emphasized. Society, the whole, is an aggregate, equal to but no more than the sum of its parts. Priority falls to the part rather than the whole, to the institution or the individual person. Society is derived from these parts and can only be understood on the basis of this assumption.

The organismic image, on the contrary, emphasizes a perspective depicting society not as an aggregate of discrete parts, but rather as a system. It describes a closely woven pattern; an integrated whole greater than the sum of its component units. Its parts—institutions and individuals—are, in fact, derived from the whole and can only be understood and explained in terms of their relations to the complete social matrix. The parts cannot function in tasks beyond those assigned by the whole, for they are not integumented entities. Instead, the units are seen in terms of their adaptation to the interrelated whole of which they are a part.[15] Society is an open

---

[12] The two images are integral parts of the ancient natural right-modern natural right dialogue: Leo Strauss, *Natural Right and History* (Chicago: University of Chicago Press, 1953); and T. D. Weldon, *States and Morals* (London: John Murray, 1956).

[13] Raymond H. Wheeler has described the shift from a mechanistic to an organismic image with the growth of Gestalt psychology in the United States: "Gestalt Psychology," in Philip L. Harriman (ed.), *The Encyclopedia of Psychology* (New York: Philosophical Library, 1936). For description of a similar change from mechanistic to organismic images in American political science at this same time see Martin Landau, "On the Use of Metaphor in Political Analysis," *Social Research,* 28 (Autumn 1961), pp. 331–353.

[14] *Cf.* Karl W. Deutsch, "Mechanism, Organism and Society: Some Models in Natural and Social Science," pp. 230–252; Ralf Dahrendorf, *Class and Class Conflict in Industrial Society,* pp. 158ff.; and Landau, *op. cit.*

[15] Deutsch, "Mechanism, Organism and Society," Kenneth E. Boulding, *The Image: Knowledge in Life and Society,* p. 33. For discussion of the organismic image

system in relation to its environment: it grows and evolves while the institutions and individuals within it evolve in harmony with the larger organism.

Mechanistic and organismic images are involved in contemporary methodological controversies of the behavioral sciences. The need to articulate these vague formulations by replacing them with models is dramatized by a famous anthropologist's felicitous epigram, "Ordinarily we are unaware of the special lens through which we look at life. It would hardly be fish who first discovered the existence of water." [16] The use of these images and corresponding models in leadership studies is explored below. Note that the two models are ideal types. It is incorrect to assume that any of these studies utilizes a model which perfectly fits the polar types. Furthermore, the studies differ widely among themselves in the degree to which they approximate either polar model. They therefore should be thought of as dispersed along a continuum between the two extremes.

## INDIVIDUAL LEADERSHIP STUDIES: ORGANISMIC MODELS

Do leaders lead, or do they follow? That, paradoxically, is the question around which proponents of organismic and mechanistic images of man and society have argued for well over a century.[17] Would Germany have been united without Bismarck? Would the October Revolution have succeeded had Lenin not reached the Finland Station? By approaching such questions with images of man and society often embedded in philosophies of history, nineteenth century students of the problem inaugurated a confusing and

---

in sociology see Alvin W. Gouldner, "Reciprocity and Autonomy in Functional Theory," in Llewellyn Gross (ed.), *Symposium in Sociological Theory,* pp. 241ff.

[16] Clyde Kluckhohn, *Mirror for Man* (New York: McGraw Hill, 1949), p. 16. See also Dennis H. Wrong, "The Over Socialized Conception of Man in Modern Sociology," in Neil J. Smelser and William T. Smelser (eds.), *Personality and Social Systems* (New York: John Wiley, 1963), pp. 68–73; and Talcott Parsons, "Individual Autonomy and Social Pressure: An Answer to Dennis H. Wrong," *Psychoanalysis and the Psychoanalytic Review,* 49 (Summer 1962), pp. 70–79.

[17] The question has recently been examined in the small group context where methodological controls have reduced the propensity to philosophy of history found in the nineteenth century leadership studies at the total system level. On the whole, small group leaders have been described as followers of group norms, though this conclusion has recently been qualified. See Edwin P. Hollander, *Leaders, Groups and Influence* (New York: Oxford University Press, 1964); and Edgar F. Borgatta *et al.,* "Some Findings Relevant to the Great Man Theory of Leadership." To generalize directly from these early findings to all leadership at the total system level, however, would be to fall prey to the trap of creating a monolithic image of society. For valuable attempts to face the generalization problem see Sidney Verba, *Small Groups and Political Behavior* (Princeton: Princeton University Press, 1961), and Mancur Olson Jr., *The Logic of Collective Action* (Cambridge: Harvard University Press, 1965), pp. 57ff., and *passim.*

persistent controversy. The discussion continues today despite the fact that many contemporary scholars operate with tentative models which have undermined the monolithic images' claim to describe all social reality.[18]

Thomas Carlyle was the progenitor of an extreme version of the mechanistic image. The leader as hero, the creator of history, was accorded its most full blown expression in his grandiose and often mystical analysis. During the nineteenth century, Carlyle came under attack from historicists, who, in assaulting his extreme position, moved themselves to the other extreme: all leaders, from their point of view, became little more than ciphers in an inevitable historical progression. Although Hegel, Spencer, and Marx each identified different mainsprings within the historical process, they all agreed that individual leaders were unable to manipulate the controls. At most no leader was more than a catalyst for events; events which, from their deterministic perspectives, would have occurred with or without these heroic personalities.[19] The image generalizes to all social contexts. But, as we shall see below, when the problem is limited to particular contexts in case studies, the need to replace such monolithic formulations with tentative models becomes clear.

The most prominent characteristic of contexts to which organismic models best apply is their high degree of interdependence. An apt illustration is provided in a recent political leadership study of Kurt Schumacher.[20] Schumacher is described by his political biographer, Lewis Edinger, as confronting a post-war social context in Germany tightly integrated by two powerful forces: policies of the Allied occupation authorities, and the attitudes and behaviors of a defeated German people. This was the given social setting in which he would struggle for the leadership of post-totalitarian Germany. A more immediate and still more integrated setting existed within the party he intended to use as his vehicle to power, the S.P.D. It was tightly knit by the warp and woof of its traditions and organizational structure. Likewise, James McRandle's Adolf Hitler acts and reacts within the confines of a highly interrelated relevant milieu, although in this study the author draws attention to the social-psychological rather than organizational

---

[18] See Fred I. Greenstein, who reformulates this problem along lines similar to those suggested in this paper: "The Impact of Personality on Politics: An Attempt to Clear Away the Underbrush," *American Political Science Review*, 61 (September 1967), pp. 633–634.

[19] Sidney Hook, *The Hero in History* (New York: John Day, 1943), pp. 59–101, presents an excellent account of this intellectual thesis and antithesis.

[20] Lewis J. Edinger, *Kurt Schumacher: A Study in Personality and Political Behavior* (Stanford: Stanford University Press, 1965). See the formal presentation of the author's model, "Political Science and Political Biography I and II," *Journal of Politics*, 26 (May and August 1964), pp. 423–429, 648–677.

level in contrast to Schumacher's salient context.[21] German culture after 1918 embodied two dream stereotypes, worker and warrior (both creators and destroyers), which represented goals and values in the German national character.

While Edinger stresses the organizational cybernetics of Schumacher's immediate situation, and McRandle focuses on what might be regarded as part of the national character concept, Erik Erikson presents as Martin Luther's relevant context a *Zeitgeist* ranging across almost all of Europe.[22] His analysis of the impact of ideas on history during the Reformation depicts an almost equally integrated milieu focused at the level of Hegelian "ideologies." Each age has its guiding *Zeitgeist,* a total perspective, the ideology and internal processes of which are givens for a heroic leader. Luther faced the Renaissance ferment; his role was that of an "aqueduct" carrying its ideas into the Reformation era.[23] By contrast, James MacGregor Burns' study of Franklin D. Roosevelt finds a relevant context somewhat less thoroughly interwoven than those described by the other authors using an organismic model.[24] Perhaps owing to his proximity to Roosevelt's deeds, Burns' analysis moves still farther away from the polar type, encompassing immediately flexible policy situations within a loosely structured socio-political framework. Despite this difference, however, the framework is still found to impose constraints upon leadership behavior at this more general level.

Given the integrated nature of the relevant context, a second characteristic associated with organismic models relates the interdependent parts by processes of evolutionary social change. The total ideological climate of Luther's age is described as evolving by its own impetus until ripe for transformation into another stage. The Reformation represented this next historical phase into which history was moving. Young man Luther thus stood at the edge of a stepwise change in the Western historical process. Hitler's action context was also one of structured, on-going social forces: Germany between the wars was an unstable society experiencing rapid,

---

[21] James H. McRandle, *The Track of the Wolf* (Evanston: Northwestern University Press, 1965).

[22] Erik Erikson, *Young Man Luther: A Study in Psychoanalysis and History* (New York: W. W. Norton and Company, 1962).

[23] *Ibid.,* pp. 194–195. Gaetano Mosca has similarly treated the ideological climate of an age: *The Ruling Class,* trans. and ed. Arthur Livingston (New York: McGraw Hill, 1939), pp. 173ff. A somewhat different interpretation of Erikson's model has been developed by Lucian Pye, "Personal Identity and Political Ideology," in Dwaine Marvik (ed.), *Political Decision Makers* (New York: The Free Press, 1961), pp. 290–314.

[24] James MacGregor Burns, *Roosevelt: The Lion and the Fox* (New York: Harcourt, Brace, Jovanovich, 1956).

but evolutionary, institutional change. Hitler, unlike the ultimately unsuccessful Schumacher, was well equipped to mesh with the evolving leadership needs set by his time and place. F.D.R.'s context again is further removed from the organismic pole, but his leadership is nevertheless analyzable as enmeshed within an evolving political environment beyond the reach of his manipulative skills.

This points to a third feature of organismic models as applied in leadership studies. Human action is analyzed from the perspective of the whole or the contextual situation. The whole system is causally dominant over the parts (leaders in this case) because these parts are well integrated with, and structured by the whole. They can best be understood in their contextual matrix. This context shapes *recruitment* parameters, and molds the *roles* the leader can play. Edinger's Schumacher is analyzed with a model employing three key variables: personality, role, and political setting. The leadership role was given by the situation. In order to be successfully recruited to the role, the leader had to perceive correctly its expectations, and have a personality structure suitable to fulfilling them. If his personality precluded playing the required role, he would fail, as did Schumacher. Schumacher's personality needs are persuasively shown to have restricted his role choice in such fashion that he compulsively acted to satisfy his inner demands, rather than those presented by the setting's leadership role. He acted dysfunctionally in terms of his manifest power goals and failed in his bid for national leadership.[25]

Social forces then, are the selective processes which make great men. The latter, in these models, are the "mediums" or responding mechanisms through which social forces operate.[26] Adolf Hitler, for example, was successfully recruited to politics because his personality needs, in contrast to Schumacher's, permitted him to respond to the needs of his situation—in his case, latent cultural tendencies in Weimar Germany. The context did not structure as highly defined a role as Edinger found in Schumacher's situation. But a role was defined nonetheless, embodying and verbalizing the cultural themes of worker and warrior, creator and destroyer. Hitler's personality development paralleled these themes of creation and destruction. He was aptly suited to a role which could evoke responsive chords in many

---

[25] The causes of leaders' successes and failures, wrote Machiavelli when reflecting on republics, depend upon their ability to act in accordance with the needs of their contexts. *Discourses,* Third Book, Chapter IX. Roosevelt too is described as operating in a political context calling forth a particular leadership role: broker-leadership, for which his personality was well suited. When the role definition changed however, he was unable to fill its requirements adequately, and lost some power as a result.

[26] Though he takes the model for an image, William F. Ogburn's well known article offers valuable comments on this theme: "The Great Man Versus Social Forces," *Social Forces,* 5 (December 1926), pp. 225–231.

German personalities. The National Socialist movement itself was achieving snowballing successes because of its archetypal verbalization of these themes. Hitler rode its crest through successful recruitment.

Like Hitler, Erikson's Luther played out a role cast by an ideological context. In such situations the organismic models approach leaders not as discrete parts that can be studied in isolation, but rather as behavior, as interactions in contexts. The formula for successful Reformation leadership in Luther's case was a function of congruence between personality growth (particularly Erikson's concept of *identity crisis*) and historical change. Class, ideology, culture, and historical period all converged on the outcome of the crisis in Luther's personality development. In the course of his crisis he found a new meaning for his life, a new identity which, at the same time, adumbrated the "social identity crisis" of his age.[27] Luther was a successful political leader because the role he was prepared to assume by virtue of his identity crisis was congruent with ideological changes of his era. His struggle formed a bridge between individual crisis and historical change. Fear drove him to act as a medium for social change, moving society to its next historical stage which could offer greater harmony with his individual personality needs.[28]

## INDIVIDUAL LEADERSHIP STUDIES: MECHANISTIC MODELS

Perhaps the most striking aspect of studies employing relatively mechanistic leadership models is that social change is characterized as less integrated

---

[27] Compare Erikson's analysis of Luther's situation with that of Mohammed as treated in Tor Andrae's classic, *Mohammed: The Man and His Faith* (New York: Harper Torchbooks, 1955). There are striking psychoanalytic parallels between Luther's identity crisis and Mohammed's call. Moreover, in both cases, the religious leaders discovered new meaning for their lives in doctrines whose congruence with the needs of their social contexts evoked mass responses carrying them both to power. See also James D. Barber's discussion of political recruitment: *The Lawmakers* (New Haven: Yale University Press, 1965), pp. 237ff.

[28] Daniel Lerner calls Luther's role that of "The Spokesman," who "defines new identities for changing persons, reshapes old expectations, formulates new demands to fit the new lifeways." *The Passing of Traditional Society* (New York: The Free Press, 1958), p. 407. He believes that this is the role of the leader of every revolutionary movement in the twentieth century. Political change in institutional transfer contexts structures the role of charismatic leaders, writes David Apter, *Ghana in Transition* (New York: Atheneum, 1963), pp. 273ff. I take this role to be similar to Lerner's "Spokesman" and Erikson's "medium for social change." Seymour Martin Lipset develops this notion in the comparative context of legitimacy crises in founding new nations, *The First New Nation* (New York: Basic Books, 1963), pp. 16–23. It is just these sorts of crises and founding situations moreover, with which Machiavelli deals. He describes ancient practices and reformulates them in terms of generalizations about functionally successful behavior in such situations. See his *Prince* and *Discourses*.

than in situations to which the organismic model best applies. The integration of organismic models can be thought of as "system dominance," while mechanistic models are, by contrast, "sub-system dominant." The dominant sub-system can be any role-set or even the personality system of an individual such as Stalin during Russia's industrialization. For instance, Robert C. Tucker has explained the terror programs of Nazi and Soviet totalitarianism as an *ad hoc* technique, applied by psychotically motivated leaders during militant phases of two movement-regimes.[29] He calls attention to the leader's personality as a possible source of explanation for phenomena which may not necessarily be recurrent evolutionary phases in totalitarian political systems. Such situations are often more atomized than highly integrated. Erwin C. Hargrove found in his study of six Presidential leadership styles that, "In a sense, the Presidential office is shapeless, and each President fills it out to suit himself." [30] Indeed, Hargrove's studies have as one of their common themes, the shaping of the Presidential office by Presidents themselves. Social events are sufficiently open-textured to permit semi-autonomous individual actions, just as in the Chicago political context where Boss Cermak was able to realize ubiquitous outlets for his power needs.[31]

Mechanistic models which lack natural interdependence rely upon mechanisms such as attractions, repulsions, and the like for holding together their parts. One such mechanism evident in leadership studies is the emphasis on conflict, both within the leader's personality and between the leader and his environment. An illustration of this feature may be found in studies applying Harold Lasswell's famous approach to individual political leadership.[32] The pleasure principle serves as nexus: man is conceived as an animal driven to a pursuit of pleasure through gratifying his needs and desires. Political men to whom the approach applies, seek power to mitigate suspicions of their own inadequacy. They experience uncertainty and conflict within their personalities. Abraham Lincoln grew up in an ambivalent home atmosphere which engendered deep uncertainties that he was loved.[33] James Forrestal experienced acute insecurity as a child owing to a dearth of family

---

[29] Robert C. Tucker, "The Dictator and Totalitarianism," *World Politics,* 17 (July 1965), pp. 555–584. See also the same author's, "The Theory of Charismatic Leadership," *Daedalus,* 97 (Summer 1968), pp. 731–756.

[30] Erwin C. Hargrove, *Presidential Leadership: Personality and Political Style* (New York: Macmillan, 1966).

[31] Alex Gottfried, *Boss Cermak of Chicago: A Study of Political Leadership* (Seattle: University of Washington Press, 1962).

[32] Source materials for the approach are Harold Lasswell, *Psychopathology and Politics* (New York: Viking Press, 1960) and his *Power and Personality* (New York: Viking Press, 1962).

[33] Harold Lasswell, "Personality," chapter in his *Politics: Who Gets What, When, How* (New York: Meridan Books, 1960), pp. 131–147.

love within a matriarchal family structure.[34] Boss Cermak struggled with a similar diffidence related to his parent's immigrant status. And Woodrow Wilson came to harbor fears that he was "ugly, worthless, and unlovable," exacerbated by his suppressed rage at an authoritarian father.[35] The inner personality conflict felt by each of these men was then transferred in their adult lives to social contexts (displaced upon public objects in Lasswell's formulation). They all were driven to compensatory power-seeking through conflict in the public arena. Wilson, for example, bore the scars of the lost battle against his father. He would never again submit his will to another man's, and was driven to engage Princeton's Dean West and Senator Henry Cabot Lodge in aggressive conflict situations. The world was perceived by these men in terms of a struggle between forces of good and evil. Forrestal became inflexible on policy issues as his displacement of private motives led to a militant posture toward his sons and toward the Soviet Union.

In mechanistic models the leader is treated as dominant over the whole, the situation. Action is considered from the leader's perspective because the situation is not well integrated. Hargrove's study of six American Presidents, for instance, divides them into Presidents of action and Presidents of restraint according to their leadership styles in office. Personality is the chief variable structuring the role played by each incumbent. Their role choice is described as a function of their personality which is broadly understood to encompass needs or drives, skills or mental traits, and values. Emphasis is accorded individual actions, their psychoanalytic genesis, and the style in which they are executed. In the same vein, a situational variable is used in the study of Boss Cermak, but the relevant situation is not the context structuring a role for the mature leader. Rather it is the immediate situation of his *childhood* relevant to socialization processes in his early personality development.[36]

---

[34] Arnold Rogow, *James Forrestal: A Study of Personality, Politics, and Policy* (New York: Macmillan, 1963).

[35] Alexander L. and Juliette L. George, *Woodrow Wilson and Colonel House: A Personality Study* (New York: Dover Publications, 1964). *Cf.* Victor E. Wolfenstein's similar findings for Lenin, Trotsky and Gandhi, *The Revolutionary Personality* (Princeton: Princeton University Press, 1967).

[36] Traditional narrative political biography is also exemplary of this point. Alan Bullock's study of Hitler, for example, in contrast to McRandle's treatment of the Führer's recruitment, focuses on his actions in power as having a decisive impact on political and social events in Germany. Alan Bullock, *Hitler: A Study in Tyranny* (New York: Harper and Row, 1962). Note that whereas Lasswell's mechanistic approach places the usual Freudian benchmark on the *childhood phase* of personality development (which is later carried largely as is into adult life), Erikson's more organismic model allows for personality development through identity crises which occur throughout life. Environment crucially structures personality *before* recruitment to leadership in the first instance, whereas with Erikson there is also emphasis

Since the part is relatively dominant over the whole in mechanistic models, the leader's actions are explained more by the internal psychological sources of his behavior, than by the influence of the systemic leadership context. Stress is often placed therefore on the psychoanalytic *genesis* of personality traits, because these factors do importantly affect the way the leader plays his role. In the Lasswellian studies, individual action and psychoanalytic motivation hold center stage. If leaders whose cases fit this model had behaved in patterned roles completely determined by situational contexts, then study of their personality would be irrelevant to explaining their behavior.[37] For example, the Georges' explanation of Wilson's leadership behavior begins with his early family life. Here the youth's most significant relationship was with his authoritarian father who demanded inordinate erudition and precision of expression from his son. The boy responded with feelings of diffidence and inadequacy, the rigid Calvinism of the father supplying ready reinforcement for these doubts. He was deeply resentful, but terrified of his father and completely submitted to his will. These experiences fostered an overwhelming need to dominate and seek power, which was later displaced upon public objects in ways structured by residues of the emotive sets acquired during his earlier father-son relationship.

Finally, mechanistic models, lacking strong integration, often include parts that may be considered discrete since they do not modify one another's essential natures. The *trait* approach to leadership is a particularly apposite illustration. Instead of analyzing leadership behavior as an interaction phenomenon, it is attributed to the leader's possession of leadership traits. Alan Bullock's study of Hitler found that his behavior was best approached from his characteristic will to power and leadership traits of elocution and manipulative skills. The Lasswellian studies also include in their models discrete parts which are usually innate properties. A prominent example is the need for pleasure, which is related to similar needs for tension reduction and power. Emphasis remains upon an integumented personality structure which is less subject to alterations through others' expectations than are personality structures found in mechanistic interaction models.

In the foregoing discussion of individual leadership models, I have tried to stress that neither all the studies discussed as organismic, nor all those treated as mechanistic, perfectly fit either polar type. Nor do all the studies in one group or the other use exactly the same model. That is

---

on socialization processes *after* recruitment—the environment more immediately structures leadership behavior from this perspective.

[37] An exception, of course, is that personality might still be relevant to their recruitment—to whether or not they were able to play the given role. But then this mechanistic model of their incumbent behavior would still not apply to their subsequent leadership behavior.

precisely the point. Many different leadership models are found spread out along a continuum between the organismic and mechanistic poles, just as will be found in analyzing similar models in elite studies. The important thing about these results is the finding that organismic and mechanistic models are constructed in the leadership literature, and that different models have been found to fit best different leadership situations.

The model characteristics can now be drawn together in summary form to facilitate following them through the elite literature below. It should be emphasized that these models were constructed from empirical research, and are not necessarily logically interrelated in a way that would make it impossible to interchange their characteristics.

| Organismic Models | Mechanistic Models |
|---|---|
| 1. Interdependent parts | 1. Atomistic parts |
| 2. Evolutionary change | 2. Conflict relationships |
| 3. System dominant | 3. Sub-system dominant |

## ELITE STUDIES: ORGANISMIC MODELS

Turning our attention to elite studies, the stratification-pluralist controversy will be seen to straddle the same two images of man and society found in individual leadership studies: organismic and mechanistic.

The organismic image of society goes back at least to Plato whose carefully described Republic was a highly integrated system. In this ideal society, just as in the properly ordered human psyche, each unit would perform its natural function as part of a unified, organic whole. Since integration facilitates communication and control, the Republic's elite-mass relationships could easily be controlled by a cohesive group of philosopher kings. Here we find many characteristics of the organismic image writ large in a monument to social unity. It was just this extreme unity, however, which Plato's student Aristotle criticized as impossible to attain. Aristotle's alternative conceptualization of mixed regimes and polity corresponded more to what has been identified as the mechanistic image of society, with less integration and greater competition among groups.

Although Plato and Aristotle were describing normative ideals rather than images in our sense, their constructs had many features in common with what soon became images of man and society. In this regard, it has been often suggested that value positions are somehow built into such images and affect analyses beginning with such frameworks. Normative judgments of this type can be found in the history of social thought where organismic images tend to be found associated with conservative values, and mechanistic images with anti-conservative values. From this point of view, when constructing tentative models for empirical analysis one must be careful to avoid being led to certain value premises without being aware of them. The Philosophical Radicals, for example, fell into this confusion with their mechanistic construct which attempted to deny the social wood for the individual trees. They moved back and forth between an analytic model for social inquiry and an image of society from which they drew normative conclusions. It is unnecessary to trace the intellectual history of these constructs any further than mentioning Pareto's and Mosca's counter-reaction against the Philosophical Radical's fragmented mechanistic image.

Pareto understood society as an integrated system of interdependent parts: atop hierarchical social organizations stand both ruling elites and potential elites. Natural processes within the evolving social organism precipitate circulation between speculator and rentier elite types as part of the mechanisms of social change. Gaetano Mosca also saw a social world organized in integrated systemic configurations, subclassifiable by historical periods. He argued that recruitment to a ruling class follows selective standards set by a society's esteemed values and attributes in any given period. Much of the appeal of Pareto and Mosca grew from the elegant simplicity of their formulations. They tended to describe images of *all* social reality, as opposed to tentative models of limited application. As valuable as their work has been—and remains—to contemporary elite analysis, they have set the tone of an unnecessary debate in leadership studies by aiming their theoretical efforts too high at too early a stage in research. Their attempts at general theories often shade off into monolithic philosophies of history. In summarizing the more restricted models of contemporary elite research below, the rationale for a paired-model research strategy will again be the underlying theme.

The stress on interdependence in organismic models is associated with descriptions of relations among components in terms of evolutionary change. For example, one observer attempting a synthesis of Marx and Pareto seeks to locate elites in a total system context through comparative study of social stratification and political hierarchy. The social system is then understood as interrelated and evolving through a developmental process.[38] In Suzanne Keller's similar model of Western industrial society, achievement-recruited, functionally organized elite groups alternate in holding power according to the sorts of problems that the developing social

---

[38] Raymond Aron, "Social Structure and the Ruling Class," *British Journal of Sociology*, 1, 1 and 2 (March 1950), pp. 1–16, 126–143. *Cf.* Peter Bachrach, *The Theory of Democratic Elitism* (Boston: Little Brown, 1967), p. 34; and Donald MacRae, "Darwinism and the Concept of Social Evolution," *British Journal of Sociology*, 10 (June 1959), pp. 105–113.

organism requires for solution at a given time.[39] The trends that Lasswell, Lerner, and Rothwell proposed to map in the original RADIR project are developmental.[40] The enterprise is set in the framework of Lasswell's configurative method which emphasizes integrated social systems evolving as on-going processes through phases of development and equilibrium. This is only slightly modified by the fact that the process is understood as open to a modicum of manipulation by leaders.

Highly interrelated components characteristic of organismic models have been found useful in studies stressing the integration of social contexts. Interrelatedness in elite research is often treated on two distinct levels. One is the elite-elite focus which describes internal characteristics of governing groups. The other is the elite-mass focus which describes relations of these rulers to the ruled. On the elite-elite level, several scholars have constructed typological categories for "closed" or "unified" elites.[41] Similarly, C. Wright Mills has underscored this component in developing the model with reference to the United States.[42] By using the positional method of elite identification associated with organismic models, he finds that corporation executives, military leaders, and weaker political leaders constitute an American power troika exercising control over the society's "big decisions." More importantly, these three spheres are integrated so that their roles become increasingly interchangeable as incumbents' educations, living styles, values, and friendships merge in a continuing trend. Keller's model of an integrated elite is interesting in its similarities and differences with Mills' work. In contradistinction to Mills' analysis, she finds that interchangeability among American elite groups is becoming increasingly difficult. She describes integration, but it is integration of functions rather than people. Strategic elites are functionally specific and highly interdependent. They are each so specialized that they vitally need the support of the others.

---

[39] Suzanne Keller, *Beyond the Ruling Class: Strategic Elites in Modern Society* (New York: Random House, 1963). Compare John Porter's similar findings of institutional-independent, but functionally interdependent elite groups in Canada. He describes the situation as a "confraternity of power," *The Vertical Mosaic* (Toronto: University of Toronto Press, 1965), p. 522.

[40] Harold D. Lasswell *et al., The Comparative Study of Elites: An Introduction and a Bibliography* (Stanford: Stanford University Press, 1952). A revised version of parts of this monograph has been republished along with several of the empirical elite studies in the RADIR series: Harold D. Lasswell and Daniel Lerner (eds.), *World Revolutionary Elites* (Cambridge: M.I.T. Press, 1965).

[41] Raymond Aron, "Social Structure and the Ruling Class," *op. cit.;* and Carl Beck and James J. Malloy, "Political Elites: A Mode of Analysis," unpublished paper presented at the Sixth World Congress of the International Political Science Association, Geneva, Switzerland, 1964.

[42] C. Wright Mills, *The Power Elite* (New York: Oxford University Press, 1956).

Turning to elite-mass relationships William Kornhauser finds that although from the perspective of the individual citizen mass society may appear atomized, when viewed as a whole its major characteristics are homogeneity and integration.[43] On the local community level, Floyd Hunter and Vidich and Bensman likewise found highly homogeneous social contexts in the communities they studied.[44] Moreover, in his research Hunter introduced the reputational method of elite identification, which is often employed in association with organismic models, in contrast to the decisional method used with the mechanistic models to be considered below.

A third characteristic of organismic models is that owing to the system dominant character of the social context, socio-economic factors are often accorded primacy in determining relations among the parts. C. Wright Mills found that in American society property is identified so closely with power that economic elites have the most weight in decisions at the pinnacles of leadership. Similarly, Arthur Vidich and Joseph Bensman describe Springdale as a community where businessmen's values ultimately prevail because they are the chief values in the community culture. And Robert Presthus found in cohesive Edgewood that economic leaders were more like prime movers than like firsts among equals.[45] In the same vein, system dominance includes sufficient interdependence that experiences are very similar in structurally equivalent socialization agencies such as families and schools. These similar experiences generate similar attitudes. Elite groups with structurally similar life experiences are therefore believed likely to hold similar attitudes. This is true of Keller's functionally specific strategic elites, of Mills' makers of big decisions, and of the leaders studied in Vidich and Bensman's Springdale as well. To a limited extent, the widely used social background approach to elite studies is also germane. Social background categories receive heavy emphasis under the assumption that in highly integrated environments contexts of socialization experiences can function as reliable indices of elite attitudes and behaviors.[46]

---

[43] William Kornhauser, *The Politics of Mass Society* (New York: The Free Press, 1959).

[44] Floyd Hunter, *Community Power Structure* (Chapel Hill: University of North Carolina Press, 1953). Arthur J. Vidich and Joseph Bensman, *Small Town in Mass Society* (Garden City, New York: Doubleday, 1960).

[45] Robert Presthus, *Men at the Top: A Study in Community Power* (New York: Oxford University Press, 1964).

[46] This assumption has been examined by: Donald D. Searing, "Elite Socialization in Comparative Perspective," *Comparative Political Studies*, 1 (January 1969), pp. 471–500; Lewis J. Edinger and Donald D. Searing, "Social Background Variables in Elite Analysis," *American Political Science Review*, 60 (June 1967), pp. 428–445; Donald R. Matthews, *The Social Background of Political Decision Makers* (Garden City, New York: Doubleday, 1954); and Morris Janowitz, "The Systematic Analysis of Political Biography," *World Politics*, 6 (April 1954), pp. 405–412.

Finally, in organismic models the system is dominant over its parts. These components are not discrete entities, but are treated analytically in terms of their functions in wholes. Hunter, Presthus, and Vidich and Bensman all found necessary a comparatively holistic analysis of the communities they studied. The reputational method used by the first two authors was directed toward this goal. They were interested in a method which would examine the whole configuration of community power, including potential and behind the scenes power which may not be overtly exercised. Vidich and Bensman concluded that business elites prevailed in Springdale because their values were the most salient ones in the total community context.[47] Keller's strategic elites can only be understood in terms of their specific societal functions, while Mills and Kornhauser treat the elites they study as products of specific socio-economic configurations in total societal types.

## ELITE STUDIES: MECHANISTIC MODELS

Mechanistic models in elite studies present less interdependence among their parts than is found in organismic models. The parts are not highly integrated, existing as they do in a somewhat more atomized environment. Here, as in the previous set of studies, elite-elite and elite-mass levels of analysis can be distinguished. At the elite-elite level, T. B. Bottomore finds that the most salient fact about elite groups in several industrial societies is that they are not part of a homogeneous whole. Instead they are best understood as competing and jostling for power among themselves.[48] In studying British rulership, another analyst concludes that British elites are characterized by similar habits, customs and values, and may also to some extent mix socially with one another. But he argues that they do not constitute an integrated power elite. He finds that Mills' organismic model with its homogeneous elite composition would not fit the British political context.[49] In New Haven,

---

[47] In such social contexts power becomes a function of community social structure—and this is why Nelson Polsby has labeled analyses based on the organismic model, stratification studies. *Community Power and Political Theory* (New Haven: Yale University Press, 1963). *Cf.* Reinhard Bendix and Seymour Martin Lipset, "Social Stratification and Political Power," in Reinhard Bendix and Seymour Martin Lipset (eds.), *Class, Status and Power* (New York: The Free Press, 1953), pp. 596–609.

[48] T. B. Bottomore, *Elites and Society* (New York: Basic Books, 1964). A similar finding for the United States in particular has been reported by Arnold Rose who goes on to construct a mechanistic model: *The Power Structure* (New York: Oxford University Press, 1967). In the same vein, Wendell Bell describes a decrease in Jamaican inter-elite links during the transition to independence: *Jamaican Leaders* (Berkeley: University of California Press, 1964).

[49] W. L. Guttsman, *The British Political Elite* (New York: Basic Books, 1963). On the limitations of the organismic model for study of British rulership, see also

Robert Dahl found different sorts of leaders making decisions in different issue areas, and in Riverview, Presthus described similar patterns of elite composition.[50] With regard to elite-mass relationships, the question turns on the degree of mass participation in decision-making and/or the permeability of the elite group. It seems correct to interpret these as empirical questions in both instances. And whether or not one wants to call the results pluralism would appear to be a matter of definition and perhaps of values.[51] In any case, many scholars believe in the viability of such access in industrial societies. In New Haven, for example, Dahl found that "from time to time elections clearly have a decisive effect on public policies." [52] One of Dahl's students has argued further that mass participation of this nature is related to the existence of a fragmented and relatively uncoordinated social context.[53]

Lacking strong interdependence, the parts of mechanistic models have been related by checks and balances. Elite groups engage in conflict and struggle for political power rather than naturally acquire the commodity as a result of systemic changes as in Keller's more organismic model. Since power relations are not usually found completely grounded in socio-economic positions, there is more room for group conflict over value preferences. For example, a process involving the balancing of economic interests was found in New Haven by Dahl, who describes the city's mayor as acting to avoid and resolve the group conflict. In such cases power is not held by economic elites alone. It is instead often the political leaders such as New Haven's Mayor Lee who hold the scepter of authority, even though this may only mean being more equal than others, and then only in limited contexts. Bottomore also locates British political elites at the center of the decision-making stage. And Presthus too finds political elites holding more power than economic leaders in his relatively fragmented Riverview. Presthus' comparative study of two communities (Edgewood, the more homogeneous of the two, was discussed as illustrative of the construction of organismic models) em-

---

Jean Blondel, *Voters, Parties and Leaders: the Social Fabric of British Politics* (Baltimore: Penguin Books, 1963), p. 248.

[50] Robert A. Dahl, *Who Governs?* (New Haven: Yale University Press, 1961). Robert Presthus, *Men at the Top, op. cit.*

[51] On this problem see the following exchange: Jack L. Walker, "A Critique of the Elitist Theory of Democracy," *American Political Science Review,* 60 (June 1966), pp. 285–295; and Robert A. Dahl, "Further Reflections on 'The Elitist Theory of Democracy,'" *American Political Science Review,* 60 (June 1966), pp. 296–305. See also Peter Bachrach, *The Theory of Democratic Elitism* (Boston: Little Brown, 1967).

[52] Dahl, *Who Governs?*, p. 220.

[53] Nelson Polsby, *Community Power and Political Theory, op. cit.* For a similar analysis of Oberlin, Ohio: Aaron Wildavsky, *Leadership in a Small Town* (Totowa, N.J.: Bedminister Press, 1964).

ployed both the reputational and decisional or issue methods of elite identification. He concluded that the reputational method best identifies the repositories of potential power. Therefore it is perhaps best suited to the study of relatively homogeneous contexts where power is more subtly located in socio-economic structures. The decisional method, on the other hand, focused on those who exercise overt power. It is therefore best suited to relatively fragmented contexts where the power of political sub-systems may be more important. Since it seems unlikely that social reality is ever accurately represented by models at the organismic or mechanistic poles, his results point to the value of a paired-model approach in leadership research.

Lastly, mechanistic models treat the part as more important than the whole. Because elite groups are not as functionally integrated with their contexts as they are in situations better fitting more organismic models, more attention is paid to the elite itself than to its situational context. In particular, the analysis often emphasizes the impact of the elite upon its context rather than the other way around. Because elite groups—especially political ones such as have been described in Great Britain—are relatively discrete parts, they can engage in conflict and are not best analyzed as determined in their action patterns by the configurations of an evolving milieu. In some instances they may be said to represent a given number of variables in a closed, not an open systemic context.

Once again it should be emphasized that I am not claiming that models discussed in either the organismic or mechanistic groupings are all the same, or that they fit either polar type. Quite the contrary. In most cases only a few model characteristics have been described in order to make two points. The first is that they are strung out along a continuum between organismic and mechanistic poles. The second is that, on the basis of the extensive case study research already done in elite analysis, we may conclude that different models have been found most appropriate for different leadership situations.[54]

## CONCLUDING REMARKS: "A COMBINATION OF OPPOSITES"

We began with the suggestion that theoretical work in both individual and elite leadership studies was impeded by similar controversies, and that this was somewhat unnecessary because of the confused character of the disagreements. In developing these thoughts this article has attempted to interrelate and clarify some of the literature in the leadership field, while ex-

---

[54] On variation in situational circumstances in light of their impact upon leadership see Fred I. Greenstein, "Personality and Politics: Problems of Evidence, Inference, Conceptualization," *American Behavioral Scientist,* 11 (November–December 1967), pp. 44–45.

amining a source of the controversy in two images of man and society. They are images of man *and* society because the two levels of analysis are necessarily associated. The organismic image of an interdependent, system-dominant social whole leaves little room for autonomous individual or group control over events already structured by evolutionary historical processes. The whole system seems clearly dominant over its sub-systems, while almost the reverse is true looking through the lense of a mechanistic image. Social forces and social stratification are the keys to history in the first instance; great men and group conflict in the second.

Perhaps it was the philosophies of history from the nineteenth and early twentieth centuries which, in inaugurating the contemporary study of leadership, created a debate over images as either-or alternatives which continues today on a less grandiose scale. Whatever the intellectual origins of the dispute, a review of recent case studies on the subject has found it based in part upon unsatisfactory methodological interpretations. When the images are concretized in relatively precise and tentative models constructed from empirical research we not unexpectedly find a differentiated world. Some leadership contexts are more integrated than others, while different models along an organismic-mechanistic continuum do best correspond to these different leadership situations.

Although this conclusion may seem *prima facie* plausible from several perspectives, it should be emphasized that it has been drawn here under the assumption that most of the studies examined do not represent serious distortions of their subject matter. This seems a reasonable assumption—at least for purposes of the present argument—in the absence of evidence to the contrary. Of course, replication might yet discover that in some cases a scholar has structured his data to fit a preconceived image of man and society.[55] If the majority of these studies are satisfactory, however, then the conclusion follows and a paired model approach would seem appropriate for the early stages of leadership inquiry.

---

[55] For example, Carl J. Friedrich argues that Pareto and Mosca frequently overlooked contextual differentiation: *Man and His Government* (New York: McGraw Hill, 1963), pp. 319ff. The point that some contexts are more integrated than others has often been made in criticizing the interdependence postulate of functional analysis. See Alvin W. Gouldner and Richard A. Peterson, *Notes on Technology and the Moral Order* (New York: Bobbs Merrill, 1962), pp. 2ff.; 65. Paralleling our analysis above, Terry N. Clark *et al.*, have suggested with regard to community studies, that, "Following this interpretation, the variable explaining differences in findings reported by different researchers would not be political ideology, or discipline, or research method, but the actual differences in power structures between communities." "Discipline, Method, Community Structure, and Decision-Making: The Role and Limitations of the Sociology of Knowledge," *The American Sociologist,* 3 (August 1968), p. 215.

The great man—social forces, and pluralist—stratification exchanges may therefore be unnecessarily confusing as a result of relatively unsystematic model construction and concept formation in the above case studies. But this is only a footnote on sources of the controversy and is currently being ameliorated. Furthermore, rigorous precision may be lacking in some cases for understandable, if not ultimately desirable circumstances: these are typically organizing and heuristic models in the context of discovery rather than validation. Terminological disputes have to some extent also compounded the confusion, particularly in national and community elite studies in relatively modernized societies. Scholars are often in greater factual agreement over the amount of possible mass influence on decision making processes in these contexts, for instance, than the labels "elitist" and "pluralist" would seem to imply.[56] A related procedural problem concerns the use of positional, reputational, and issue techniques of elite identification.[57] These techniques have been found more or less associated with particular model types, but there is no theoretical reason preventing the use of several techniques in the same research context. Finally, some additional difficulties may stem from problems of collecting and organizing the enormous store of empirical evidence on the total system level. This point has been made by a reviewer in commenting upon the selectivity of C. Wright Mills' evidence in *The Power Elite*.[58] The scope of research and diffuseness of evidence may indeed make it easy to misinterpret what one sees in light of preconceived notions. These considerations represent still another reason to utilize a paired-model approach which stresses the tentative nature of the constructs.

Having said this much, what more can be added by way of research suggestions? One of the most salient questions raised here relates to the

---

[56] Another example is the confusion surrounding the concept "Establishment" in Great Britain, particularly over whether it refers to a potential and/or overt elite, and over the actual composition of either. Hugh Thomas (ed.), *The Establishment* (London: Clarkson N. Potter Inc., 1959). In addition, Presthus observes, "To some extent, where the sociologists found monopoly and called it elitism, the political scientists found oligopoly but defined it in more honorific terms as pluralism," *op. cit.,* p. 430.

[57] Robert A. Dahl, "A Critique of the Ruling Elite Model," *American Political Science Review,* 52 (June 1958), pp. 463–469; John Walton, "Discipline, Method and Community Power: A Note on the Sociology of Knowledge," *American Sociological Review,* 31 (October 1966), pp. 684–689; Raymond E. Wolfinger, "Reputation and Reality in the Study of 'Community Power,'" in Nelson W. Polsby *et al.,* (eds.), *Politics and Social Life* (Boston: Houghton Mifflin, 1963), pp. 703–711; and Richard M. Merelman, "On the Neo-Elitist Critique of Community Power," *op. cit.*

[58] Talcott Parsons, "The Distribution of Power in American Society," *World Politics,* 10 (October 1957), pp. 123–144.

nature of the different research contexts themselves. In the first place, the relevant situational context(s) should be clearly identified. Is it interpersonal, institutional, socio-economic, or cultural? All four have been used in the case studies above. Is a holistic analysis necessary, or will one of more limited scope likely prove adequate? These questions obviously depend very much on the specific research problem, and are answerable only after achieving some familiarity with the data. However this may be, some guidelines can be helpful in identifying the relevant context and making rough preliminary characterizations of its structure.

One of the most valuable research suggestions comes from Ralf Dahrendorf's approach of "paired models," also elaborated by Reinhard Bendix and Bennett Berger as "dual tendencies," and by Robert Redfield as a "combination of opposites." [59] The approach has been in use for some time and includes such famous social sciences pairs as Societas and Civitas, Culture and Civilization, and *Gemeinschaft* and *Gesellschaft*. This article has emphasized the need for its *explicit* use in leadership studies, employing the organismic-mechanistic pair which is already applied in much empirical research. The idea is simply that by approaching a research problem in leadership studies with these paired models in mind, the scholar is likely to modify one of them carefully in the course of research for use in his particular problem context. This would preclude his unwittingly bringing one member of the pair to the research as an *a priori* image of all social reality.[60]

Several considerations are involved here. On the one hand, we have seen that different modifications of these polar models will likely best apply in different leadership contexts. But it is also clear that the problem studied may involve *several* relevant contexts (*e.g.,* institutional and socio-economic). Secondly, even within the same broad context, we might want to use different models to study different problems. Dahrendorf has stressed

[59] Ralf Dahrendorf, *Class and Class Conflict in Industrial Society, op. cit.,* pp. 159ff.; Reinhard Bendix and Bennett Berger, "Images of Society and Problems of Concept Formation in Sociology," in Llewellyn Gross (ed.), *Symposium on Sociological Theory* (New York: Harper and Row, 1959), pp. 92–118; Robert Redfield, *The Little Community and Peasant Society and Culture* (especially chapter 9) (Chicago: University of Chicago Press, 1956), and the literature cited therein.

[60] This approach seems to be useful for many of the leadership studies with which I am familiar. However, I obviously would not claim that it would be equally valuable for all possible leadership studies, or that all social reality could be organized along such an organismic-mechanistic continuum. What I wish to emphasize is that, for scientific discovery, the two models become complementary rather than mutually exclusive. See Reinhard Bendix and Seymour M. Lipset, "The Field of Political Sociology," in Lewis A. Coser (ed.), *Political Sociology* (New York: Harper and Row, 1967), p. 29.

choosing between the complementary models only for studying specific problems. He consciously did this himself in his own monograph.[61] In the individual leadership studies reviewed above, McRandle, who was primarily interested in the problem of Hitler's *recruitment* constructed an organismic model, while Bullock in focusing on Hitler's *policy actions,* especially when in power, employed a mechanistic model. Likewise, Burns found an organismic model useful in *relating F.D.R. to his context,* while Hargrove turned a more mechanistic model to good account in studying the problem of the *impact of his personality and style upon the institution.*

Perhaps the best illustration of this point is provided by Robert Redfield in his sensitive and subtle work, *The Little Community.*[62] Redfield studied a large Mexican village, Tepoztlán, and found it well integrated and harmonious. A number of years later, Oscar Lewis studied the same village and found violence, corruption, and disease. In reflecting upon the differences in their analyses, Redfield concludes, "that Lewis is especially interested in the *problems* of economic need and personal disharmony and unhappiness, topics which I did not investigate." [63] In short, Redfield investigated harmonious relationships and Lewis problems of conflict and disharmony. Let us suppose, however, that they had both investigated the same problem: whether social interaction in Tepoztlán was characterized overall by harmony or disharmony, for example. It seems correct in this case to assume that an overall characterization is possible and that one model will be more satisfactory than another. When studying exactly the same problem in precisely the same context, one model will usually prove more useful than its alternatives. Usefulness here may be judged on the basis of economy and accuracy of correspondence of "fit" with the relevant empirical phenomena.[64]

In any event, simply to consider model construction is to transform the dogmatic controversies of competing images into questions for empirical

---

[61] Dahrendorf, *op. cit.* Inasmuch as his problem was authority and conflict relations he used what he calls a "coercion" model. See pp. 157–165.

[62] Redfield, *op. cit.* His entire chapter 9 is the best discussion of this problem I have found.

[63] *Ibid.,* p. 136. Redfield also generously discusses the possibilities that a particular image of society may have influenced his work. To avoid such problems in the future, he proposes the use of the "combination of opposites" or paired model approach.

[64] In the local community context, Dahl offers his decisional or issue method as something of a test of a model's "fit." "A Critique of the Ruling Elite Model," *op. cit.* Giovanni Sartori has objected, however, that a conclusive test is extremely difficult even in the relatively small community: *Democratic Theory* (New York: Frederick A. Praeger, 1965), pp. 114–115. One limitation here is that the specific problem interest needs to be made explicit first. If Sartori is correct, then this is a still stronger reason for proceeding cautiously with tentative paired models.

research. It is hoped that this paper will contribute to the further development of this end, and that eventually even these heuristic and organizing models will be replaced by more rigorous models within the context of validation.

# 2

## Towards the Explication of the Concept of Leadership in Terms of the Concept of Power[1]

KENNETH F. JANDA

The task of this paper is to present a conception of leadership as a particular type of power relationship. By way of an introduction to this presentation, some remarks will first be made concerning concept construction and social research. Two approaches to the study of leadership will then be examined, setting the stage for a discussion about the development of the concept of leadership. After examining some of the conceptual difficulties which have plagued the study of leadership, this paper will comment briefly on the re-lationship between the study of leadership and the study of power. Finally, attention will be directed to the main task of considering leadership as a power phenomenon.

## CONCEPT CONSTRUCTION AND SOCIAL RESEARCH

The development of a cumulative body of knowledge depends, in part, upon the development of a precise vocabulary which can provide exact descrip-tions for the specific phenomena under study. Prefatory to developing their own technical vocabulary for identifying the things they study, scientists

Kenneth F. Janda, "Towards the Explication of the Concept of Leadership in Terms of the Concept of Power." *Human Relations,* XIII, No. 4 (1960), pp. 345–363.

[1] This paper was produced during my research training period as a pre-doc-toral Fellow of the Social Science Research Council. I wish to thank the Council for its support during this period. I am especially grateful to Dorwin Cartwright of the Research Center for Group Dynamics for his encouragement and helpful criti-cism regarding this paper. Also due for thanks are George Psathas and Henry Teune, both of Indiana University, whose cautious skepticism led to some valuable re-formu-lation of my arguments.

generally utilize the common vocabulary of the language in which they communicate. Of course, as used in everyday language, a word will frequently have several quite different denotations, more than one of which might be related to the subject of study. Moreover, conventional words sometimes acquire additional connotations which add to their richness but subtract from their precision.

Notwithstanding these semantic barriers to precise understanding, scholars are often led, for a variety of reasons, to adopt a familiar word, associated with related but diverse meanings, and use it in a more restricted, technical sense from that in which it is normally used in ordinary conversation. When employed in a specialized sense as a nominal definition for an independently defined phenomenon, our conventional word becomes a label for a scientific concept and eventually comes to stand for that concept itself. These word-labels then become candidates for inclusion within the technical vocabulary associated with the field of study. "Leadership" and "power" (i.e., the concept of leadership and the concept of power) are examples of conventional words which have been incorporated into the technical vocabulary of those attempting to construct a systematic body of knowledge about social behavior.

Although obvious benefits accompany the practice of identifying a scientific concept with a word which possesses some related meaning in normal use, there are at least two difficulties attending the use of familiar words in this manner. The first will be called the *delusion of sufficiency,* pertaining to a premature satisfaction with the analytical utility of the concept being proposed. The delusion of sufficiency sometimes results in concepts which are not independently defined but which incorporate the wealth of denotations and connotations associated with the normal use of the word. At other times, the delusion of sufficiency might lead to the hasty adoption of a fairly explicit common meaning without consideration of the problems involved in utilizing that meaning to support rigorous analysis. However it arises, the delusion of sufficiency produces concepts which are not analytically tight and are therefore inadequate for exacting study.

The second difficulty, called *confusion by similarity,* relates to the entanglement of a carefully formulated concept with one or more other analytically distinct concepts that share the same label. A clear concept might be confused with one prepared under the delusion of sufficiency, or perhaps the confusion would result when alternative analytically tight concepts were similarly named. Both the delusion of sufficiency and confusion by similarity present obstacles to the development of a cumulative body of knowledge, and —in view of social scientists' disinclination to abandon common words for neologisms—both are particularly troublesome for the systematic study of social behavior.

Despite their special susceptibility to these two kinds of difficulty, the social sciences have only recently begun to grapple in earnest with the problems that these difficulties present. A great deal of fresh effort is now being directed to concept clarification in these disciplines. On the nature and function of concept clarification, Robert K. Merton (1957) has this to say:

> It is, then, one function of conceptual clarification to make explicit the character of data subsumed under a concept. . . .
>
> In a similar fashion, conceptual analysis may often resolve apparent antimonies in empirical findings by indicating that such contradictions are more apparent than real. This familiar phrase refers, in part, to the fact that initially crudely defined concepts have tacitly included significantly different elements so that data organized in terms of these concepts differ materially and thus exhibit apparently contradictory tendencies. The function of conceptual analysis in this instance is to maximize the likelihood of the comparability, in significant respects, of data which are to be included in research (pp. 90–1).

Unfortunately, the recent emphasis on conceptual clarification has lagged badly behind the development and application of methodological techniques used in operationizing concepts. As a result, our literature has become cluttered with a wealth of disparate findings on poorly defined, similarly named concepts. Both the study of leadership and the study of power offer prime examples of this conceptual-operational imbalance. However, the task of this paper will only be to inquire at length into the conceptual status of one of these, the study of leadership. A thorough treatment of the concept of power—the subject of another work—is precluded at this time. Nevertheless, the final portion of this paper will draw from the literature on power in an attempt to explicate a concept of leadership in terms of power. But, first, the study of leadership must be investigated in some detail.

## APPROACHES TO THE STUDY OF LEADERSHIP

Anyone at all familiar with the literature of sociology and social psychology will readily grant that the topic of leadership has commanded considerable attention from students in these fields. However, it is not unfair to say that these disciplines have distinguished themselves more by accumulating *studies* on leadership than by cumulating *knowledge* on leadership.

The heroic efforts of some students to synthesize disparate findings by editing and categorizing these studies usually fail to satisfy anyone—including the persons who undertake the task. In a recent attempt to impose some order upon this literature, Browne and Cohn (1958) corroborate this general viewpoint of the study of leadership. They introduce their work with these comments:

> Through all of the subsequent history of man's attempts to record human experiences, leadership has been recognized to an increasingly greater extent as one of the significant aspects of human activity. As a result, there is now a great mass of "leadership literature" which, if it were to be assembled in one place, would fill many libraries. The great part of this mass, however, would have little organization; it would evidence little in the way of common assumptions and hypotheses; it would vary widely in theoretical and methodological approaches. To a great extent, therefore, leadership literature is a mass of content without any coagulating substances to bring it together or to produce coordination and point out interrelationships (Introduction, first page).

The history of the study of leadership is somewhat less chaotic than the study itself. Most students have identified two main approaches used in studying leadership. The earlier is commonly known as the "trait" approach, and the other is usually called the "situational-interactional" approach.

The old trait approach originally considered the "leader" as a personality type that tends to assume a position of dominance in almost every social situation, and its early followers tried to discover the particular personality factors common to all such persons. With the acknowledgement that the same pepole do not always "lead" in every social situation, the focus of the trait approach was shifted to discover the different personality traits demanded of a leader by each situation, but students following this approach were still concerned with identifying and examining the personalities of individuals considered to be leaders.

The obvious limitations of this method of study caused some students to divert their attention from cataloguing personality traits and led them to study leadership in terms of "situational-interactional" factors. By focusing upon the interaction among individuals in their activities as group members, this approach removed personality traits of the leader from their determinant status and relegated them to the position of a contributing factor to be examined in conjunction with three other factors: (1) the social and physical nature of the environment within which the group must operate, (2) the nature of the group task, and (3) the personality characteristics of the other group members.

Whereas the student of the trait approach sought to account for the leadership phenomenon solely by studying the personality factors of the leader himself, situational-interactionalists argued that there were other relevant variables that had to be taken into account. The existence of these other variables could be advanced to account for the disturbing fact that individuals who possessed leadership "traits" frequently were not designated as leaders. The explanatory superiority of the situational-interactional approach demonstrated itself to the extent that current research on leadership is conducted almost exclusively in this framework.

## THE CONCEPT OF LEADERSHIP, THE DELUSION OF SUFFICIENCY, AND CONFUSION BY SIMILARITY

The preceding section, while discussing two approaches to the study of leadership, used "approach" to refer to the evaluative framework within which variables are judged for importance and are selected for examination. However, the *concepts* employed in these approaches have not yet been examined for their adequacy in defining the leadership phenomenon in terms of general characteristics which can be used to identify the specific phenomena to be studied by these approaches.

It is usually much easier to discover what specific phenomena people have been studying than to find out what conceptions have guided the selection of these phenomena, for in many cases the conceptions are implicit whereas the items under examination are nearly always explicit. What basic conception underlies the entire body of leadership literature when this literature is viewed in the aggregate; i.e., what concept provides the lowest common denominator that can be used to accommodate the findings on leadership? First, it appears that all students would agree that leadership is some type of group phenomenon, for virtually no one writes on leadership apart from group behavior. Moreover, the leadership phenomenon would appear to be concerned with the activities of "salient" group members—those who could be positively differentiated from the other group members on the basis of behavior, perceptions, group structure, or personal factors. However, our common denominator cannot be reduced beyond this point and still be used to accommodate the entire body of literature on leadership; the collective conceptual and operational definitions advanced in the name of leadership are too disparate to be combined under a denomination more precise than that referring to some form of saliency attributable to individual members within a group.

In a general manner, the development of the concept of leadership can be traced through the trait approach and the situational-interactional approach in terms of the delusion of sufficiency and confusion by similarity. On the whole, it can be said that the concept used to guide inquiry into leadership under the trait approach was prepared almost completely under the delusion of sufficiency, as most inventories of leadership traits were conducted with only simple, commonsense notions of leadership. This point was brought out very clearly in Stogdill's review (1948), which noted that, in many cases, the notion of leadership was never independently defined. Instead, "leaders" were designated by some manner—Stogdill listed five primary methods—and then leader*ship* was assumed to be operative because of the existence of an individual named as a leader. However, it was seldom made clear whether leadership then referred to (1) the behavior of this individual in interaction with other group members, (2) the behavior of this individual as a group member—perhaps with differentiated role functions to perform, (3) the behavior of other group members in interaction with the member designated as leader, (4) the social relationship which existed between the leader and other group members, (5) all of the above, or (6) none of the above.

Although many students following the situational-interactional approach also operated with dictionary definitions of leadership, some penetrated through the delusion of sufficiency to formulate more precise concepts of leadership. For example, R. B. Cattell (1952) has presented a conception of leadership which involves a group member's effect upon group syntality, and Stogdill (1953, p. 41) defined leadership as "the process (act) of influencing the activities of an organized group in its efforts toward goal setting and goal achievement." Each of these conceptions has a fairly explicit meaning, but they both bear different implications for research and theory. However, as they carry the same label, these conceptions are susceptible to confusion by similarity. The possibility of this confusion would not be bothersome if these were the only conceptions in competition, but of course there are many more. As a matter of fact, Stogdill (1957, p. 7) superseded his definition given above with another quite different one which views leadership as "the behavior of an individual when he is directing the activities of a group toward a shared goal." Furthermore, there are still many scholars writing on this topic who have yet to dispel the delusion of sufficiency and establish exactly what it is that they are studying. Their highly ambiguous ideas of leadership complicate the general concept even further.

Of course, these difficulties are not confined to the study of leadership; no doubt all disciplines are plagued by these problems. However, the case being made here is that the concept of leadership has been characterized by the delusion of sufficiency and confusion by similarity to such an extent. as to render the accumulated literature on leadership almost valueless in the aggregate. Both difficulties have surrounded the concept of leadership with an ambiguity that it clearly reflected in the study of leadership. Regarding the chaotic state of this literature, Thibaut and Kelley (1959, p. 289) have this to say:

> Not much smaller than the bibliography on leadership is the diversity of views on the topic. Many of the studies essentially ask: what do people mean when they speak of a leader? Other studies begin with a conceptual or empirical definition of leadership and then proceed to determine the

correlates or consequences of leadership so defined. Even a cursory review of these investigations shows that leadership means many different things to different people.

In witness that leadership means "different things to different people," Shartle (1951) and Morris and Seeman (1950) offer similar listings of five criteria frequently used to identify leaders. According to Shartle's list, a leader has been identified as:

    1. An individual who exercises positive influence acts upon others.
    2. An individual who exercises more important positive influence acts than any other member of the group or organization he is in.
    3. An individual who exercises most influence in goal-setting or goal-achievement of the group or organization.
    4. An individual elected by the group as leader.
    5. An individual in a given office or position of apparently high influence potential (Shartle, 1951, pp. 121–122).

Gibb's listing (1954) of leadership criteria includes all these under fewer headings and also adds two others:

    6. The leader as a focus for the group.
    7. The leader as one who engages in leadership behavior.

As to what is involved in "leadership behavior," Morris and Seeman would include:

    A. Behavior involved in the execution of a given position.
    B. All the behavior of an individual selected as leader.
    C. Any positive influence act.
    D. Behavior of any individual that makes a difference in the behavior or characteristics of the group.
    E. Behavior of an individual when he is directing the activities of a group (p. 51).

The literature on leadership has, at one time or another, utilized all these criteria to identify "leaders." Although students of the subject are often troubled by the obvious differences in the phenomena selected for study by these various criteria, they reluctantly do what Festinger (1955, p. 208) did and include studies under a heading of leadership "only because those reporting such studies call it leadership."

## CONCEPTUAL DIFFICULTIES AND THE STUDY OF LEADERSHIP

The question might be raised, "Why *not* include all studies which purport to examine leadership under a general heading of 'leadership'?" Of course, the answer to this question involves considerations of a concept's utility for guiding research which can contribute to a cumulative body of knowledge about the phenomenon being studied. Simply put, research findings about different phenomena do not become additive merely by labelling these phenomena as if they were identical. Furthermore, this practice of indiscriminate labelling is a step *away* from concept clarification rather than a step toward it, and the study of leadership reflects enough muddy analysis because of conceptual difficulties without the need for further obfuscation.

In order to support this general indictment of the literature on leadership, four specific charges against this literature will be set forth along with their substantiating statements.

*1. Little comparability exists among leadership studies in the aggregate, for these studies, being guided by widely differing notions of the phenomenon called leadership, have not concerned themselves with common phenomena.*

Numerous reports (see Borgatta *et al.,* 1955; Cattell & Stice, 1954; Chowdhry & Newcomb, 1955; Gibb, 1954; Stogdill & Coons, 1957) have documented the easily understood fact that two or more operational definitions of a leader, applied to the same group, generally identify *different* individuals as the leaders of the group. As Cattell and Stice (1954) have shown with regard to personality factors, the specific criterion used to designate a leader conditions the findings about personality variables associated with the phenomenon of leadership. Nevertheless, findings on leadership are seldom categorized according to the operational definitions used to identify leaders but, instead, these incomparable findings have assumed a false compatibility under the general label of leadership.

As long as findings can be identified with specific criteria used to identify leaders, *some* measure of comparability is still maintained. However, even this thin thread, tying the operational measure to some common conceptual basis, is sometimes snipped off. Chowdhry and Newcomb (1955) were guilty of this act when they added together the scores from sociometric questions based on four criteria of leadership: those individuals most capable of acting as president of the group, those who most influence the decisions of others, those most worthy of acting as group representatives to a convention, and those most liked as friends—and then called the individuals receiving the highest one-fifth of the total choices the "leaders." This highly arbitrary procedure was also followed by Borgatta, Couch, and Bales (1955) but with different criteria and a different cut-off point. Both these studies became successful candidates for the literature on leadership simply by virtue of their titles.

2. *Much of the research on leadership has been influenced by a conception which, upon inspection, blurs into another more fundamental concept employed in the study of group processes.*

It has been suggested that the one thing which various leadership criteria have in common is their insistence upon some kind of saliency within the group. Clearly, a member cannot be salient unless he can be differentiated from other group members on one or more criteria, and, of course, almost every group member can be differentiated from other group members on the basis of one or more of these criteria. From this realization, it is just a short step to conclude that every group member can be, and often *is,* a leader. Moreover, this step has been taken by many students. For example, Bass (1960, p. 89) has claimed, "Any member of the group can exhibit some amount of leadership. Members will vary in the extent they do so." Again, Haythorn (1955) produced findings in express support of Cattell's hypothesis that every man in a group is to some extent a leader in so far as every man has some effect upon group syntality. Haythorn's conclusion was, "At least in small groups of this nature it seems probable that each individual member makes some contribution to the characteristics of the total group" (1955, p. 339). Finally, Cartwright and Zander (1953, p. 538) state that *if* "Leadership is viewed as the performance of those acts which help the group achieve its objectives," *then* "In principle, leadership may be performed by one or many members of the group."

Thus, we are confronted with a conception of leadership based on *quantitative* instead of *qualitative* considerations. Under this conception, the group is no longer studied to discover *who* leads, for *everybody* leads. The important thing to find out is how *much* they lead. In fact, this is the logical conclusion to an approach which equates leadership with contributions to group performance. Question: Whatever became of the concept of group *membership?* Is there no residual of group activity left anywhere to attach to this concept? Apparently, "membership" now only identifies the particular group to which each leader belongs, although there was a time when group members were expected to contribute to group performance.

Of course, the point being made here is that the current use of "leadership behavior" is essentially the same as that of "membership behavior" in that both seem to refer to behavior which contributes to group performance. Although some articles on leadership are still bold enough to hold that "A group may or may not have leaders" (Stogdill, 1953, p. 41), the general conception of leadership has become sufficiently blurred into the concept of membership to produce a number of statements which contend that "Every group member is thus in some degree a leader" (Cattell, 1952, p. 182).

*3. The study of leadership has suffered under a dubious distinction between "leadership" and "headship" which has adversely conditioned much of the conceptualizing about leadership.*

The literature on leadership reflects a tendency to dissociate the concept from considerations of group structure. Stogdill (1953) is one of the few who have presented a conception of leadership as a function of group organization, and Stogdill's conception was attacked by Gibb (1954, p. 880) who contended that it "represents an unnecessary restriction on the concept of leadership and has no operational advantage in research." Alone, these words conceal the frame of reference Gibb undoubtedly used in formulating this remark, for Gibb has held that leadership disappears and headship results when group activity is conducted under structure and organization. Gibb's criteria (1955a) for distinguishing between the concepts of headship and leadership are these:

1. The position of headship is maintained through an organized system and not by the spontaneous recognition of the individual contribution to the group goal.

2. In headship, the group goal is not internally determined.

3. Headship does not really involve *a group* at all, since there is no sense of shared feeling or joint action.

4. A situation of headship involves a wide social gap between the group members and the head, who works to maintain this distance.

Why does Gibb bother with four criteria when his third one alone would suffice? If "groupness" is requisite for leadership and "non-groupness" is requisite for headship—where is the problem? Rarely can social scientists deal with concepts which dovetail so well. However, these other criteria of differentiation are erected to bolster a doubtful distinction. *Each* criterion dissolves upon close examination and serious reflection. Is leadership, however defined, predicated on "the spontaneous recognition of the individual contribution to the group goal"? In leadership, is the group goal always "internally determined"? Does leadership never involve the maintenance of a "wide social gap"? A quick recollection of the literature reporting on research in leadership will produce a "no" to all three of the above questions.

This is not the time or place to conduct an inquiry into this tangential concept. Simply stated, the issue at hand is that the leadership-headship dichotomy is not quite as sharp as frequently claimed. Perhaps the criteria *can* be supplemented and adjusted to produce a conceptual distinction between the terms which accords to an intuitional basis for that distinction.

The fact is, this still remains to be done, and studies of leadership in even the most *formalized* social structures cannot be excluded purely on cries of "headship."

No doubt some readers will interpret the debunking of headship as an unnecessary parry of a fanciful thrust, but the thrust has a real basis in the literature. Writings on leadership radiate a genuine feeling that studies of leadership based on positional status in an organized group are somehow "missing" the *real* leaders of a group. Apparently, the presumption is that such studies become so preoccupied with the investigation of relationships as they *should* be that they frequently overlook relationships as they *are*. This has probably been done in the past and may be done in the future, but the fact that some research has been conducted poorly should not preclude efforts to pursue similar research properly. The tendency to explicitly dissociate the concept of leadership from group status is hardly fanciful; it is a real force.[2]

*4. The study of leadership has emerged as a separate field in the study of group processes and has been conducted as if leadership were a totally unique phenomenon, although virtually all of the existing conceptions of leadership can be explicated in terms of more basic concepts of social psychology.*

Normal usage of the word "leadership" has cloaked the term with a false concreteness which students have tried to capture in constructing conceptions of leadership. However, the intuitive notion of leadership is too ambiguous to elicit agreement upon any single conception; alternative conceptions appear equally satisfying to our commonsense ideas. Moreover, the conceptions of leadership which have been formulated can frequently be interpreted as special cases of phenomena associated with more basic concepts of social psychology. This assessment of the literature finds support in the comments of Thibaut and Kelley (1959, p. 289) who say that "among the complex aspects of leadership, there do not seem to be any properties unique to the phenomena. In virtually all cases leadership seems to be analyzable in terms of other, simpler concepts."

In order to substantiate this contention, let us review the previous listing of leadership criteria (p. 51). Criteria 1, 2, and 3 all employ the concept of influence in identifying leaders; criterion 4 is based on perception processes; and number 5 involves considerations of group structure and influence processes. Criterion 6—at least as proposed by Redl (1955)—is dependent upon concepts of group psychoanalysis. Within the set of criteria

---

[2] See Gouldner (1950, p. 16) for the position of another student of leadership who is concerned over the implications for research and theory produced by the perpetuation of the "headship"-"leadership" distinction.

included under No. 7, leadership behavior, A and E are both concerned with concepts of role differentiation; B includes practically every notion used in the study of human behavior; D involves concepts which attend the study of groups in general; and C once more employs the concept of influence.

Among the different concepts utilized in formulating criteria to identify leaders, the most prominent one appears to be the concept of influence. Indeed, this concept is utilized to such an extent that the study of influence itself might be expected to command considerable attention from those studying leadership. However, the actual relationship between these areas of study does not match this expectation.

## THE RELATIONSHIP BETWEEN THE STUDY OF LEADERSHIP AND THE STUDY OF POWER (INFLUENCE) [3]

The first thing to be noted in a comparative review of the literature on leadership and that on power is that *there is almost no overlap between the two.* Studies of leadership and studies of power have been conducted almost independently of each other. By this, it is meant that, in the main, those who write on leadership do not write on power and *vice versa.* Moreover, the number of cross-references between the two bodies of literature is amazingly small. Footnotes appearing in the literature on leadership *seldom* cite studies of power, and the reverse again holds true. Of course, verbal references to the other will be found in the literature on either concept, but these references are clearly of a superficial nature.

As an indication of the separation between the studies, consider the practice followed to 1959 in each volume of the *Annual Review of Psychology.* In each of these volumes, there is a chapter dealing with the literature on "Social Psychology and Group Processes." With the exception of the first volume of the *Review,* in which Jerome Bruner (1950) passed only very lightly over some general literature on "group dynamics," every subsequent chapter has, with minor modifications, devoted *separate* sections to the literature on "leadership" and that on "influence processes." Moreover, the literature cited in one section usually does not receive acknowledgement in the other. This practice was followed by Katz (1951), Smith (1952), Newcomb (1953), Crutchfield (1954), Festinger (1955), French (1956), Cartwright (1957), Heyns (1958) and Gilchrist (1959) from 1951 through

---

[3] Although both labels, "power" and "influence," have been employed by different students investigating the same type of social relationships, "power" has probably been used more frequently in the literature on the subject. However, an excellent case, based on the delusion of sufficiency and confusion by similarity, can be made for employing "influence" as a label for this concept while excluding all references to "power." Notwithstanding this fact, *for the purpose of this paper,* power and influence will be used synonymously.

1959. Of these authors, only French explicitly refers the reader on leadership to the other section on influence processes.[4]

Furthermore, it may be said that, whenever the two concepts *are* considered together in the same work, one of the two clearly becomes the real subject for analysis, and the treatment accorded to the subordinated concept is usually quite sophomoric, ignoring relevant literature on the topic. In short, we have two separate, practically self-contained bodies of literature—one on leadership, the other on power. The remainder of this paper will attempt to relate these literatures by presenting a concept of leadership in terms of power.

## LEADERSHIP AS A POWER PHENOMENON

The conceptual complexities surrounding the power phenomenon are too involved to be discussed in detail at this time, and reference will only be made to what recent writers (Cartwright, 1959; Dahl, 1957; March, 1955; Simon, 1953) might agree on as a conceptual definition of power. These writers would view the power phenomenon as a particular type of social relationship in which one person adjusts his behavior to conform with a pattern of behavior communicated to him by another person. This concept supports these specific definitions:

> *power,* used as an adjective modifying "relationship"—a particular type of social relationship which demonstrates the features involved in the conceptual definition
>
> *power,* noun—the ability to cause other persons to adjust their behavior in conformance with communicated behavior patterns
>
> *power-wielder*—the individual who prescribes patterns of behavior which are followed by other individuals
>
> *power-recipient*—the person who adjusts his behavior to conform with the prescribed pattern of behavior.

Regarding leadership and power, it should be immediately noted that this conceptual formulation of power is already close to some students' formulation of leadership. For example, Warriner (1955, p. 367) conceives leadership "as a form of relationship between persons [which] requires that

---

[4] Riecken's recent chapter on "Social Psychology" in the 1960 volume of the *Annual Review* is the first to consider the literature under a heading of "Leadership and Power." However, Riecken reported mainly on research which examined the power variable in leadership behavior, and he did not review any works which attempted to relate the concepts.

one or several persons act in conformance with the request of another."
According to this formulation, the concepts of leadership and power can
hardly be differentiated from each other.

However, it is contended that a theoretically significant and operationally useful conception of leadership can be provided by considering
leadership phenomena as a particular subset within the larger set of power
phenomena. Thus, all leader-follower relationships are power-wielder–power-
recipient relationships, but not all power relationships involve leadership.
Leadership phenomena can be distinguished from other power phenomena
when power relationships occur among members of the same group and
when these relationships are based on the group members' perceptions that
another group member may, with reference to their group activities, legiti-
mately prescribe behavior patterns for them to follow. Thus, in a situation
of leadership, the power-recipients do not object to the power-wielder's demands upon their behavior as group members. Essentially this same concept
of leadership was advanced by Gouldner in 1950, but his presentation has not
seemed to have much influence on the literature. In his words, "a leader
would be an individual in a group who, in *some* situations, has the *right* to
issue *certain* kinds of stimuli which tend to be accepted by others in the
group as obligations" (Gouldner, 1950, p. 19).

In order to examine this idea of legitimacy further, we must first
answer some basic questions about power relationships in general. Why does
anyone "accept" influence? That is, why do power relationships exist at all?
For now, the answer can be given that power relationships exist because some
individuals can motivate other individuals to perform specific acts of behavior. Cartwright links motivation to power in this manner:

> . . . "motive base" refers to the sorts of phenomena variously referred to
> as "need," "motive," "drive," "tension system," or "instinct." The im-
> portant feature of motive base as it relates to the conception of power is
> that an act of an agent must "tap" a motive base for it to activate a
> force (Cartwright, 1959, pp. 204–5).

> . . . In our formulation, O can activate a force on P only if some act of
> O can tap a motive base of P. In this sense, P's motive base may be
> thought of as a basis of O's power (ibid., p. 206).

According to the conception proposed in this paper, the base of a
power relationship provides the identifying element for distinguishing leadership phenomena from power phenomena in general. Writing in the same
volume of studies as Cartwright, French and Raven (1959, pp. 155–6) ex-
pand upon this notion of the bases of power:

By the basis of power we mean the relationship between O and P which is the source of that power. . . . Although there are undoubtedly many possible bases of power which may be distinguished, we shall here define five which seem especially common and important. These five bases of O's power are: (1) reward power, based on P's perception that O has the ability to mediate rewards for him; (2) coercive power, based on P's perception that O has the ability to mediate punishments for him; (3) legitimate power, based on the perception by P that O has a legitimate right to prescribe behavior for him; (4) referent power, based on P's identification with O; (5) expert power, based on the perception that O has some knowledge or expertness.

Now some students of leadership would probably call all intra-group power relationships "leadership," regardless of the power base used to support that relationship. Apparently, Warriner (1955) would subscribe to this position along with Bass (1960, p. 94), who contends that "leadership may be viewed as influence occurring among members of the same group." However, the conception of leadership offered in this paper obviously excludes reward, coercive, referent, and expert power from being considered as a basis of leadership. According to this paper's conception, leadership does not occur unless the power-wielder secures the desired behavior from the power-recipient on the basis of *legitimate* power—that is, when the influence attempt comes from a group member who is perceived as having the "right" to prescribe behavior for other group members to follow.

## LEGITIMACY AS A POWER BASE AND THE STUDY OF LEADERSHIP

At this point it must be emphasized that legitimate power *per se* is not sufficient to support this conception of leadership. Simple equation of leadership with legitimate power is essentially the conception proposed by Gouldner. However, this paper identifies leadership with a particular *type* of legitimate power. That is, the power-wielder must be perceived as having a particular right *with reference to the activities of power-recipients as group members* to prescribe behavior patterns for them to follow.

It is necessary to emphasize the association of leadership with a particular type of legitimate power, for legitimacy itself stems from different sources. French and Raven (1959, p. 160) disclose three important sub-bases for legitimate power:

> Cultural values constitute one common basis for the legitimate power of one individual over another. O has characteristics which are specified by the culture as giving him the right to prescribe behavior for P, who may not have these characteristics. . . .

Acceptance of the social structure is another basis for legitimate power. If P accepts as right the social structure of his group, organization, or society, especially the social structure involving a hierarchy of authority, P will accept the legitimate authority of O who occupies a superior office in the hierarchy. . . .

Designation by a legitimizing agent is a third basis for legitimate power. An influencer O may be seen as legitimate in prescribing behavior for P because he has been granted such power by a legitimizing agent whom P accepts. . . . An election is perhaps the most common example of a group's serving to legitimize the authority of one individual or office for other individuals in the group.

The inclusion of cultural values as a base of legitimacy reveals the necessity of adding a restriction to Gouldner's equation of leadership with legitimate power. Legitimate power based on cultural values includes power relationships that we would want to exclude from our conception of leadership, which would encompass only those power relationships produced by the power-recipient's perception that the power-wielder has the right to prescribe behavior for him as a member of a particular group.

We have not yet discussed the way in which group members develop perceptions of leaders. Acceptance of the social structure and designation by a legitimizing agent are obviously only operative in on-going groups of long duration. However, the leadership phenomenon can also be found in newly formed traditionless groups. In such groups, an individual may emerge as a leader because of his personality, abilities, resources, special knowledge, etc. In short, the group members identify his behavior requests with the group goal and, in the process of conforming to these requests, develop perceptions that this individual has the right to prescribe behavior patterns for them with reference to their activities as group members.

However, in on-going groups of long duration—which probably include the groups of most interest to social scientists—the last two bases of legitimate power, acceptance of the social structure and designation by a legitimizing agent, assume great importance for students of leadership. A group member occupying a position in an accepted social structure or given formal status by a legitimizing agent may thereby acquire legitimate power and only need exercise that power base to demonstrate leadership. Of course, these two factors and leadership do not necessarily coincide. The extent to which these factors do coincide is, in fact, a subject for empirical examination. However, the literature dealing with leadership as a *concept*—apart from the literature reporting on *research*—distinctly subordinates the importance of these factors as determinants of leadership. Perhaps this failure can be attributed to the over-concern with promoting a distinction between "headship" and "leadership." In any case, the literature on power has not ignored investigating these factors, and some of these findings may be reviewed with profit for leadership.

French and Snyder (1959) have produced findings which, in general, support their contention that formal group status in itself is a source of power. Raven and French (1958b, p. 83), conducting research specifically designed to examine several aspects of legitimate power, claim to "have experimentally demonstrated that a member whose group has elected him to a position of authority will thereby achieve legitimate power over remaining members." Furthermore, in another article experimenting with differences in the degree of influence demonstrated by elected and non-elected supervisors, Raven and French (1958a) clearly establish the superior influence of the elected supervisor but discover an unexpected finding in the amount of influence demonstrated by the non-elected supervisor. They explained this observation by stating, "It thus seems likely that the very occupation of a key position in a structure lends legitimacy to the occupant" (*ibid.*, p. 409).

In strong contrast to the literature conceptualizing about leadership, research studies provide an important place for formal group status, employing it as an indicator of the leadership phenomenon. The examinations of political leadership conducted by Seligman (1955) and Moos and Koslin (1951, 1952) are certainly studies of individuals possessing formal group status. Similarly, Seeman (1953) investigates role conflict among leaders by concentrating on the individuals who hold top positions in social institutions. Kahn and Katz (1953) are two more students of leadership concerned with persons who possess formal group status. Morris and Seeman (1950, p. 152), reporting on early progress in the Ohio State Leadership Studies Program, also state that "the method used to date in the various studies made by the staff has been the selection of individuals in high office as persons to examine for leadership. . . ."

The articles by Lewin and Lippitt (1955) and White and Lippitt (1953) utilize formal group status as a technique for inducing leadership, the type of which was then varied among "authoritarian," "democratic," and "laissez-faire" roles. Preston and Heintz (1953) and Hare (1955) also equated leadership with formal group status while varying the leader's role between "supervisory" and "participatory" leadership. Torrance's study (1955) differed in that his formal leadership was altered between "directive" and "non-directive" roles. Gibb (1955b) and Maier and Solem (1953), explicitly considering groups without formal leaders as "leaderless," examine the effect of leadership on group performance by comparing these groups with ones which elected leaders. Finally, the legitimization of the formal status of the conference chairman was specifically acknowledged by Berkowitz (1955).

As mentioned before, many studies identify "leadership" on the basis of criteria other than formal group status. It is suggested that the variations discovered in the behavior of formally designated leaders from that shown by other types of leaders might be due to the different bases of power upon which each can draw in establishing power relationships. The findings of Carter, Haythorn, Shriver, and Lanzetta (1953) on "emergent" versus "appointed" leaders would tend to indicate different bases of power were attached to each type. Maier and Solem also suggest a shift in the bases of power available to group members who still possess formal group status but who have suffered a loss in legitimate power. They hold, "The great limitation to autocratic leadership is that such a leader has difficulty in having his decisions accepted so that appropriate action will follow" (1953, p. 561).

## SUMMARY AND CONCLUSION

This paper has presented a conception of leadership as a particular type of power relationship characterized by a group member's perception that another group member has the right to prescribe behavior patterns for the former regarding his activity as a member of a particular group. This conception carries certain implications which were not discussed in the text. Some of these implications are immediately obvious: different group members can perceive different individuals as leaders; the same member can perceive more than one individual as his leader; leadership may or may not exist in a given group; etc. It would seem that these implications, when expanded upon and drawn more sharply, can account for much of the diversity existing within the literature on leadership. The task of strengthening this concept through further delineations of its implications for research and theory is the subject of a future effort; this brief sketch of leadership in terms of power must suffice for now.[5]

For those students who *already* view leadership as involving power relationships, this paper can be interpreted as a recommendation for them to raise the concept of power from its subordinated position and conduct

---

[5] Other "forms" of leadership cannot always be easily related to this conception based on legitimate power. For example, "leadership by coercion" contains a possibility of contradiction within the context of this conception, for this phrase appears to describe a power relationship based on coercive power *as well as* on legitimate power. Although it is generally thought that the operation of one base of power precludes the operation of another, this is, of course, an empirical question which must await a more precise formulation of the variables involved as well as further research on the nature of the bases of power, including the conditions under which they operate. However, the familiar concept of "charismatic leadership" can be accommodated within this conception with little difficulty by considering charismatic leadership as a particular type of leadership which can be characterized either by the strength of the power base available to the power-wielder or by his personal qualities which invoke the intense feelings of voluntary obedience within the group members.

their study with a greater attention to power relationships in general. This would involve drawing distinctions as to the type of power relationship being studied under the heading of leadership and utilizing findings on power relevant to power relationships among group members. It seems inconceivable that students of leadership who define their conceptions in terms of power can afford to ignore the large and growing body of literature on this subject and fail to incorporate its findings in their study. One of the results of this redirection of emphasis would involve paying greater attention to the behavior of the follower than is normally given, for, as Katz (1951, p. 140) says, "Leadership is a relation involving two terms and it is impossible to study the influencing agent without also studying the people being influenced."

For those students of leadership who are not satisfied with a conception of leadership explicated in terms of power, this paper urges that they re-examine precisely what it is that they are studying. Admittedly, there is no monopoly granted for the exclusive use of labels, and if one person chooses to call something else "leadership," he is privileged to do so. Undoubtedly, we will always be subject to some degree of confusion by similarity as long as we are committed to the use of common words as labels for scientific concepts. However, this might be a small price to pay for retaining the benefits which accompany easy translation into common language.

As for the merits of other conceptions of leadership, the standard of utility must be the final arbiter, and the proof of utility must be borne by the advocates of these conceptions. As Cartwright (1959, p. 187) says, "One must rely in the long run upon a sort of inverse 'Gresham's law' which holds that good conceptual systems drive out bad." Indeed, the conception proposed in this paper must also win its way, if it is to be won, through such competition. Furthermore, it is not thought that this conception is in anywhere near a perfected stage; it can probably be improved now and most certainly will be improved in the future, as new findings on power are brought to light and as new thinking is conducted on the concept of legitimacy.

Nevertheless, it is thought that this specific conception of leadership has advantages which will yield rewards for its users. It seems apparent that this conception—as well as any—closely approximates an "intuitive" notion of leadership. As Seeman (1950, p. 41) said, "Though specific definitions of leadership may vary considerably, the core of the concept—regardless of whether we define leadership as 'acts which make a difference in group effectiveness'—is the idea of a stratification in terms of power or influence." If the association of leadership and legitimate power is adopted, the study of power can hardly be avoided in the study of leadership, which has been isolated, to a large extent, from other aspects of social psychology. In Seeman's words:

The extent to which status attributes and leadership ideology are correlated has an important bearing on the extent to which we may profitably
conceive of "leadership" as a distinct research "area" separable from the
more general problems of power, influence, or social status. Myrdal has
pointed out that the concern with "leadership" is a distinctly American
phenomenon, and it may well be that our research *per se* simply reflects
this "American bias," and that from a social scientific point of view our
work might be more profitable if we adopted such a more general framework. . . . (*ibid.,* pp. 47–8).

The general attitude of this paper is mirrored by the concluding comments of Thibaut and Kelley in their recent book, *The Social Psychology of
Groups* (1959, p. 290):

> It is our opinion that leadership research will be most fruitful when
> it adopts an indirect and analytical approach to its task. Rather than going
> directly into the complex phenomena and surplus-meaning-laden termi-
> nology encompassed by the term leadership, research must first be directed
> toward clarifying problems of power structures, norms and goals, task
> requirements, functional roles, etc., each of which is complex and chal-
> lenging enough in its own right. In short, an understanding of leadership
> must rest on a more basic understanding of the structure and functioning
> of groups.

And this paper urges an approach to leadership which draws upon a
basic understanding of power.

## REFERENCES

Back, Kurt W. (1951), "Influence Through Social Communication," *Journal of
Abnormal Social Psychology,* 46, January, pp. 9–23.
Bass, Bernard M. (1960), *Leadership, Psychology, and Organizational Behavior*
(New York: Harper and Row).
Berkowitz, Leonard (1955), "Sharing Leadership in Small, Decision-making
Groups," in A. Paul Hare, Edgar F. Borgatta, & Robert F. Bales (eds.),
*Small Groups: Studies in Social Interaction* (New York: Alfred A.
Knopf), pp. 543–555.
Borgatta, Edgar F., Couch, Arthur S., & Bales, Robert F. (1955), "Some Find-
ings Relevant to the Great Man Theory of Leadership," in A. Paul Hare,
Edgar F. Borgatta, & Robert F. Bales (eds.), *Small Groups: Studies in
Social Interaction* (New York: Alfred A. Knopf), pp. 568–574.
Browne, C. G., & Cohn, Thomas S. (eds.) (1958), *The Study of Leadership*
(Danville, Illinois: The Interstate Printers and Publishers).
Bruner, Jerome S. (1950), "Social Psychology and Group Processes," in Calvin
P. Stone (ed.), *Annual Review of Psychology* (Stanford: Annual Re-
views), pp. 119–150.

Carter, Launor, Haythorn, William, Shriver, Beatrice, & Lanzetta, John (1953), "The Behavior of Leaders and Other Group Members," in Dorwin Cartwright & Alvin Zander, *Group Dynamics* (Evanston: Row, Peterson), pp. 551–560.

Cartwright, Dorwin (1957), "Social Psychology and Group Processes," in Paul R. Farnsworth (ed.), *Annual Review of Psychology* (Stanford: Annual Reviews), pp. 211–236.

Cartwright, Dorwin (1959), "A Field Theoretical Conception of Power," in Dorwin Cartwright (ed.), *Studies in Social Power* (Ann Arbor: Research Center for Group Dynamics, Institute for Social Research, University of Michigan), pp. 183–219.

Cartwright, Dorwin, & Zander, Alvin (1953), "Leadership: Introduction," in Dorwin Cartwright & Alvin Zander, *Group Dynamics* (Evanston: Row, Peterson), pp. 535–550.

Cattell, Raymond B. (1952), "New Concepts for Measuring Leadership, in Terms of Group Syntality," *Human Relations,* 4, 161–184.

Cattell, Raymond B., & Stice, Glen F. (1954), "Four Formulae for Selecting Leaders on the Basis of Personality," *Human Relations,* 7, pp. 493–507.

Chowdhry, Kamla, & Newcomb, Theodore M. (1955), "The Relative Ability of Leaders and Non-leaders to Estimate Opinions of Their Own Groups," in A. Paul Hare, Edgar F. Borgatta, & Robert F. Bales (eds.), *Small Groups: Studies in Social Interaction* (New York: Alfred A. Knopf), pp. 235–245.

Crutchfield, Richard S. (1954), "Social Psychology and Group Processes," in Calvin P. Stone (ed.), *Annual Review of Psychology* (Stanford: Annual Reviews), pp. 171–202.

Dahl, Robert A. (1957), "The Concept of Power," *Behavioral Science,* 2, July, pp. 201–215.

Festinger, Leon (1955), "Social Psychology and Group Processes," in Calvin P. Stone (ed.), *Annual Review of Psychology* (Stanford: Annual Reviews), pp. 187–216.

French, John R. P., Jr., & Raven, Bertram (1959), "The Bases of Social Power," in Dorwin Cartwright (ed.), *Studies in Social Power* (Ann Arbor: Research Center for Group Dynamics, Institute for Social Research, University of Michigan), pp. 150–167.

French, John R. P., Jr., & Snyder, Richard (1959), "Leadership and Interpersonal Power," in Dorwin Cartwright (ed.), *Studies in Social Power* (Ann Arbor: Research Center for Group Dynamics, Institute for Social Research, University of Michigan), pp. 118–149.

French, Robert L. (1956), "Social Psychology and Group Processes," in Paul R. Farnsworth (ed.), *Annual Review of Psychology* (Stanford: Annual Reviews), pp. 63–94.

Gibb, Cecil A. (1954), chapter 24: "Leadership," in Gardner Lindzey (ed.), *Handbook of Social Psychology,* Vol. II (Cambridge: Addison–Wesley), pp. 877–920.

Gibb, Cecil A. (1955a), "The Principles and Traits of Leadership," in A. Paul Hare, Edgar F. Borgatta, & Robert F. Bales (eds.), *Small Groups: Studies in Social Interaction* (New York: Alfred A. Knopf), pp. 87–95.

Gibb, Cecil A. (1955b), "The Sociometry of Leadership in Temporary Groups," in A. Paul Hare, Edgar F. Borgatta, & Robert F. Bales (eds.), *Small Groups: Studies in Social Interaction* (New York: Alfred A. Knopf), pp. 526–542.

Gilchrist, J. C. (1959), "Social Psychology and Group Processes," in Paul R. Farnsworth (ed.), *Annual Review of Psychology* (Stanford: Annual Reviews), pp. 233–264.

Gouldner, A. W. (ed.) (1950), *Studies in Leadership* (New York: Harper and Brothers).

Hare, A. Paul (1955), "Small Group Discussion With Participatory and Supervisory Leadership," in A. Paul Hare, Edgar F. Borgatta, & Robert F. Bales (eds.), *Small Groups: Studies in Social Interaction* (New York: Alfred A. Knopf), pp. 556–560.

Haythorn, William (1955), "The influence of individual members on the characteristics of small groups," in A. Paul Hare, Edgar F. Borgatta, & Robert F. Bales (eds.), *Small Groups: Studies in Social Interaction* (New York: Alfred A. Knopf), pp. 330–341.

Heyns, Roger W. (1958), "Social Psychology and Group Processes," in Paul R. Farnsworth (ed.), *Annual Review of Psychology* (Stanford: Annual Reviews), pp. 419–452.

Kahn, Robert L., & Katz, Daniel (1953), "Leadership Practices in Relation to Productivity and Morale," in Dorwin Cartwright & Alvin Zander, *Group Dynamics* (Evanston: Row, Peterson), pp. 612–628.

Katz, Daniel (1951), "Social Psychology and Group Processes," in Calvin P. Stone (ed.), *Annual Review of Psychology* (Stanford: Annual Reviews), pp. 137–172.

Lewin, Kurt, & Lippitt, Ronald (1955), "An Experimental Approach to the Study of Autocracy and Democracy: a Preliminary Note," in A. Paul Hare, Edgar F. Borgatta, & Robert F. Bales (eds.), *Small Groups: Studies in Social Interaction* (New York: Alfred A. Knopf), pp. 516–523.

Maier, Norman R. F., & Solem, Allen R. (1953), "The Contribution of a Discussion Leader to the Quality of Group Thinking: the Effective Use of Minority Opinions," in Dorwin Cartwright & Alvin Zander, *Group Dynamics* (Evanston: Row, Peterson), pp. 561–572.

March, James G. (1955), "An Introduction to the Theory and Measurement of Influence," *American Political Science Review,* 49, June, 431–451, reprinted in Heinz Eulau, Samuel J. Eldersveld, & Morris Janowitz (eds.), *Political Behavior* (New York: The Free Press, 1956), pp. 385–397.

Merton, Robert K. (1957), *Social Theory and Social Structure* (New York: The Free Press).

Moos, Malcolm, & Koslin, Bertram (1951), "Political Leadership Re-examined: an Experimental Approach," *Public Opinion Quarterly,* 15, Fall, pp. 563–574.

Moos, Malcolm, & Koslin, Bertram (1952), "Prestige Suggestion and Political Leadership," *Public Opinion Quarterly,* 16, Spring, pp. 77–93.

Morris, Richard T., & Seeman, Melvin (1950), "The Problem of Leadership: an

Interdisciplinary Approach," *American Journal of Sociology*, 56, September, pp. 149–155.

Newcomb, Theodore M. (1953), "Social Psychology and Group Processes," in Calvin P. Stone (ed.), *Annual Review of Psychology* (Stanford: Annual Reviews), pp. 183–214.

Preston, Malcolm G., & Heintz, Roy K. (1953), "Effects of Participatory vs. Supervisory Leadership on Group Judgment," in Dorwin Cartwright & Alvin Zander, *Group Dynamics* (Evanston: Row, Peterson), pp. 573–584.

Raven, Bertram H., & French, John R. P., Jr. (1958a), "Group Support, Legitimate Power, and Social Influence," *Journal of Personality*, 26, September, pp. 400–409.

Raven, Bertram H., & French, John R. P., Jr. (1958b), "Legitimate Power, Coercive Power, and Observability in Social Influence," *Sociometry*, 21, June, pp. 83–97.

Redl, Fritz (1955), "Group Emotion and Leadership," in A. Paul Hare, Edgar F. Borgatta, & Robert F. Bales (eds.), *Small Groups: Studies in Social Interaction* (New York: Alfred A. Knopf), pp. 71–86.

Riecken, Henry W. (1960), "Social Psychology," in Paul R. Farnsworth (ed.), *Annual Review of Psychology* (Stanford: Annual Reviews), pp. 479–510.

Seeman, Melvin (1950), "Some Status Correlates of Leadership," in Alonzo G. Grace (ed.), *Leadership in American Education* (Proceedings of the Co-Operative Conference for Administrative Officers of Public and Private Schools. Chicago: The University of Chicago Press), pp. 40–50.

Seeman, Melvin (1953), "Role Conflict and Ambivalence in Leadership," *American Sociological Review*, 18, August, pp. 373–380.

Seligman, Lester G. (1955), "Development in the Presidency and the Conception of Political Leadership," *American Sociological Review*, 20, December, pp. 706–712.

Shartle, Caroll L. (1951), "Studies in Naval Leadership," in Harold Guetzkow (ed.), *Groups, Leadership and Men* (Pittsburgh: Carnegie Press), pp. 119–133.

Simon, Herbert A. (1957), "Notes on the Observation and Measurement of Political Power," *Journal of Politics*, 15, November, pp. 500–516, reprinted in Herbert Simon, *Models of Man, Social and Rational* (New York: John Wiley), pp. 62–78.

Smith, M. Brewster (1952), "Social Psychology and Group Processes," in Calvin P. Stone (ed.), *Annual Review of Psychology* (Stanford, Annual Reviews), pp. 175–204.

Stogdill, Ralph M. (1948), "Personal Factors Associated With Leadership: a Survey of the Literature," *Journal of Psychology*, 25, pp. 35–71.

Stogdill, Ralph M. (1953), "Leadership, Membership, and Organization," in Dorwin Cartwright & Alvin Zander, *Group Dynamics* (Evanston: Row, Peterson), pp. 39–51.

Stogdill, Ralph M., & Coons, Alvin E. (1957), *Leader Behavior: Its Description and Measurement* (Columbus: Research Monograph Number 88, Bureau of Business, The Ohio State University).

Thibaut, John W., & Kelley, Harold H. (1959), *The Social Psychology of Groups* (New York: John Wiley).

Torrance, E. Paul (1955), "Methods of Conducting Critiques of Group Problem-solving Performance," in A. Paul Hare, Edgar F. Borgatta, & Robert F. Bales (eds.), *Small Groups: Studies in Social Interaction* (New York: Alfred A. Knopf), pp. 560–567.

Warriner, Charles K. (1955), "Leadership in the Small Group," *American Journal of Sociology,* 60, January, pp. 361–369.

White, Ralph, & Lippitt, Ronald (1953), "Leader Behavior and Member Reaction in Three 'Social Climates,' " in Dorwin Cartwright & Alvin Zander, *Group Dynamics* (Evanston: Row, Peterson), pp. 585–611.

# Part Two

## A Conceptual Framework

### INTRODUCTION

A conceptual framework consists of a set of concepts hypothesized to call attention to important aspects of behavior that are related in ways still to be verified. A conceptual framework states: Here are some important aspects of the subject; they may be related in such and such ways; if we understood these relationships more clearly, then we would probably be able to explain better the behavior in which we are interested. Behavioral science, like life itself, is based upon a certain amount of faith.

A conceptual framework may be embodied in or derived from a definition. The definition of political leadership that underlies the structure of this collection of essays and the accompanying monograph and bibliography is as follows:

> Political leadership consists in the interaction of personality, role, organization, task, values, and setting as expressed in the behavior of salient individuals who contribute to variance in a political system (however defined) and in four dimensions of human behavior (power, affect, instrumentality, and association).[1]

In this definition attention is focused upon individual persons who are studied either singly or aggregatively according to purpose. Six concepts are suggested as sources of explanation of that behavior: *personality,* taken first as the sum total of the characteristics that identify an individual human being and second as characteristics that may be shared with others; *role,* a set of socially defined expectations of behavior independent of personality; *organization,* the interpersonal interaction system, both direct and mediated, by which the individual is related to human society; *task,* objective requirements for decisions to be made, problems to be solved, or things to be done; *values,* ideas about desirable states of affairs and desired means for attaining them; and *setting,* the physical, technological, economic, social, and cultural features of the environment of behavior.

In this definition, the "political system" is taken as a dependent variable—it can also be taken, of course, as an independent or intervening variable—something to be explained of which leadership behavior is taken to contribute at least a partial explanation. There is as yet no consensus among world political scientists about the nature of a "political system" in a generic sense. It is variously described in terms of power relations, authoritative distribution of values, the making of societal decisions, the relations between structures and functions, and so on. Thus, the definition accepts the concept of political system as a variable term, the content of which remains to be specified in any particular investigation. What the definition attempts to convey is that the study of political leadership and the common effort to gain scientific understanding of a political system as a whole are potentially mutually instructive. Advances in one may illuminate the other. Thus we may ask: For any given conception of a political system, what are the implications for political leadership behavior? And conversely: For any given finding in the study of political leadership behavior, what is its significance for emerging ideas about a political system?

Finally, mention is made of four major dimensions, or aspects, that seem to characterize all human behavior: power, affect, instrumentality, and association. By *power* is meant actual or attempted control of one part by another. By *affect* is meant feelings and emotions. *Instrumentality* refers to task or problem-solving requirements. *Association* means the structure by which the various parts of a behavioral aggregate are related one to the other.

Such a sweeping assertion requires further explanation. The first three dimensions are supported by what seems to be a striking contemporary convergence among certain fields of psychology, social psychology, and sociology. Three approaches are now dominant in personality psychology: theories of reinforcement (power), emotions (affect), and cognition (instrumentality). Social psychological studies of small groups, as analyzed by Robert F. Bales,[2] have repeatedly identified three "dimensions of social evaluation" that are related to leadership needs. These might be termed "powerability" (power), "likability" (affect), and "taskability" (instrumentality). In sociological studies, Amitai Etzioni[3] has identified three types of social institutions: "coercive" (power), "expressive" (affect), and "utilitarian" (instrumentality). Thus these three dimensions seem to characterize the behavior of individuals, groups, and large-scale social institutions.

The fourth dimension, "association," is not usually included. Perhaps this is because the psychologist assumes the human body as given, the social psychologist assumes that the group is formed, and the sociologist assumes the society as pre-existing. The political scientist, however, is perhaps less apt to take a pattern of political institutions as given. He sees political institutions, parties, legislatures, judiciaries, and administrations as subject either to peaceful change by constitutional engineering or to violent transformation by revolution. Whether a society has a single party or a competitive multi-party system, for example, is not accepted as "given" in the same sense as the human body, the small group, or a human society as a whole. Thus the concept of association is intended to convey the idea of the emergent structure of the body, the very creation of the group, and the very process by which men become aggregated in various institutions, as well as the associative combination of men in political life.

The conceptual framework may be summarized as in Figure 1.

**Figure 1.** A Conceptual Framework for the Study of Political Leadership

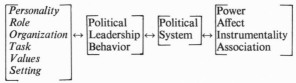

The readings that follow in this section are devoted to exploring each of the six suggested independent variables of the conceptual framework.

## PERSONALITY

Since political leaders are persons, the study of personality correlates of their behavior is inescapable. The guiding question for political leadership studies is not whether leaders have personalities different from followers but rather the effects of whatever personalities they do have. Adequate understanding of the contribution of personality factors in political leadership will require the cooperation of many kinds of specialists: among them, personality psychologists, psychiatrists, political scientists, research methodologists, and, of course, political leaders themselves.

Barber (Selection 3) presents a study of personality correlates of presidential leadership and discovers three styles ("rhetoric," "business," and "personal relations") that emerged, he asserts, in initial political successes of college student days. This approach to personality is reminiscent of the "earliest recollection technique" as proposed by Alfred Adler, who argued that a person's subsequent life style would be revealed in memories of his earliest experience in childhood.[4] In any case, the whole life cycle, from birth and childhood through old age and death, should be of potential interest in political leadership studies.

## ROLE

Historically, political leaders often have occupied very conspicuous formal offices such as "king," "president," "governor," "mayor," "chief," and so forth.[5] Also they have been recognized in informal positions of great actual power such as "revolutionary." Thus it would seem important to attempt to develop a useful concept of role in political leadership studies that can be used to describe the nature of leadership positions aside from the personalities of the men who occupy them. This is no easy task, since the concept of "role" is at least as elusive as that of personality, with which it is commonly confounded. But upon reflection it will be appreciated that attention to the concept of role is of practical as well as of academic importance. The structure of expectations imposed socially upon men who rise to lead may be a critical element in societal survival and may well merit the engineering application of at least as much intellect as goes into the building of a bridge.

The selection from the study of state legislators by Wahlke and others (Selection 4) represents the most influential recent study of leadership roles by political scientists. Their studies suggest, as do other studies in the same vein, that for any given role (e.g., "state legislator"), a small number of different incumbent "orientations" can be identified. Difficult questions concerning the possible confounding of role and personality by basing research on incumbent responses, and the possible usefulness of an effort to define role independently of incumbent definitions, are usually not raised. Another way to clarify this problem is to ask, "What was it (the role of the legislator, party worker, etc.) that originally allowed divergent styles of performance by incumbent personalities?" or, "What was it that placed patterns of permissible behavior of incumbent personalities in such narrow constraints that only limited variations in style were possible?"

If role is to become a precise tool of analysis in political leadership studies, then appropriate research instruments will have to be created and applied. We will have to advance beyond initial exploratory questions such as, "What is the most important thing you do?" or "How do you describe your job as _____?" Role analysis presents a great challenge to students of political leadership. Much remains to be done to perfect it as a conceptual and operational research tool.

## ORGANIZATION

Surprisingly, the great activity in the study of organizational behavior over the past twenty years, primarily industrial and military in nature, has not been linked to the study of political leadership. The task, then, is to place political leaders within an organizational context ranging from the dyad, through small groups and formal organizations, to macro-societal and sub-societal segmental relationships. It is not so much a question of whether leadership behavior as manifested in small groups can be extrapolated to apply to an entire political system (although this is a useful question),[6] but more narrowly whether small group theory helps to explain political leader behavior *in a small group context* itself. The same question would arise about the applicability of formal organizational theory for political leadership in relation to large-scale organizations. This is important, for example, when a political leader seeks to control (or must respond to) an army, an industrial organization, or a public bureaucracy. Beyond this, the leader can be seen as related to various interest groups, classes, occupational groups, ethnic groups, and potentially to all persons in his area of activity.

By now it should be apparent that the term "organization" is being used in a peculiar way as a suggested variable for political leadership studies. What is meant are all direct or indirect interpersonal interactions in which the leader is a participant.[7] We want to know what influences a political leader has upon persons related to him in various ways and what influences they, in turn, have upon him. For example, Pigors has analyzed four types of "followers" that may be found in any organization; these he terms "constructive," "routine," "impulsive," and "subversive." [8] What are the implications for political leadership behavior of having various combinations of persons like these (and others that may be identified) in leader-related organizations? [9]

Political scientists already have accomplished much through the study of political parties, legislatures, public administration, and voting behavior. What needs to be done now is to focus more precisely upon "political leadership" as an independent source of variation in these behaviors and to place the whole within general theories and sub-theories of organizational behavior (ranging from dyads, through group and formal organizations, to total societies as organizational units). Admittedly this is a gigantic intellectual task; it is no wonder that it has scarcely begun. But at least three starting points are clear: to view organizations from the standpoint of political leaders, to view political leadership behavior from the perspective of related organizations, and to examine the relevance of both for emerging theories of organized human behavior.

Relationships need to be examined between political leaders and small groups (family, staff, cabinet, faction, council), large formal organizations (party, legislature, bureaucracy, police, army), ad hoc aggregates (mobs, assemblies, coalitions), societal segments (voters, interest groups, social strata, ethnic groups, elites, counter-elites, non-elites), and total societies as organizational units, as well as various combinations of the foregoing. Every leader can be viewed as being located within a matrix of organizational relationships of this sort. Analysis by case studies and comparison may then determine the most salient relations of mutual influence for any given problem. Not all organizational relationships will be crucial determinants of leader behavior all the time. We need to know which, when, and how.

A pioneering effort to link political leadership with theories of formal organization is presented by Eric Josephson (Selection 5). Reversing a commonly held image of top leadership as the prisoner of "rational" formal organization, Josephson argues the possibility that "irrational" leadership may have far-reaching dysfunctional effects upon large bureaucratic organizations. He cites Hitler as his principal political leadership example and might have considered Stalin as well. The study of political leadership will have to extend this type of investigation to explore more precisely the interacting effects of formal organizational properties and leadership behavior. We need to know much more about the qualities of organizations that amplify or diminish political leader influence.

## TASK

Much discussion and evaluation of political leadership implies that task is an important independent variable. It is asserted, for example, that crisis tasks call forth leaders of unusual abilities, or break those of less competence; that the tasks associated with one leadership role (e.g., the presidency) may be critically different from those of another (e.g., senator); that some types of tasks are more difficult than others within a given leadership role (e.g., foreign relations versus domestic tasks); that undramatic leaders may be cast aside when confronted with tasks requiring dramatic action; that fast moving tasks overwhelm slow-witted leaders; that leaders should be selected on the basis of anticipated task requirements; and so on.

The concept of task makes possible the direct linkage of political leadership studies with the most pressing problems of any age: for example, war and peace, poverty, population, health, housing, transportation, industrialization, pollution, agriculture, crime, the quality of personal or communal life, education, the vitality of the arts, science, and any other aspect of society where problem-solving needs, demands, or opportunities exist.

Nevertheless, the concept of "task" has not been precisely articulated in the socio-behavioral sciences, although such concepts as "stimulus," "problem," and "occasion for decision" are closely related. In leadership studies the idea of a task often is embedded in the catch-all concept of "situation"; sometimes "task" is mentioned but without analytical clarification. Thus the study of political leadership faces the challenge of justifying attention to the concept of task, articulating its nature, and showing its theoretical or practical usefulness. A rough analog from the world of practical politics is the idea of an "issue," something "wrong" in community life that requires corrective leadership action. As a point of departure, task may be regarded broadly as a stimulus providing an opportunity for response, a problem to be solved, an occasion for decision, or an issue to be settled.

It may be found useful to distinguish between two types of tasks: metatasks (tasks about tasks, their identification and interrelation) and substantive tasks (tasks about specific empirical concerns). Also it may be helpful to view substantive tasks in relation to each of four dimensions that have been suggested as important correlates of leadership behavior: power tasks, affective tasks, instrumental tasks, and associative tasks. Power tasks include gaining, maintaining, using, augmenting, diminishing, and transferring power. Affective tasks include such things as emotional control of the self, emotional empathy for others, and management of emotional aspects of social conflict and consensus. Instrumental tasks include the creation and application of problem-solving knowledge, the utilization of productive resources, the management of change, the resolution of conflict, response to crisis, and planning for the future. Associative tasks include such things as organizing, communicating, mediating, developing alliances and coalitions, and managing external relations.

Another approach to the identification and categorization of political leadership tasks will be to combine insights into operational task requirements from the point of view of leaders and leadership task requirements inferred from emerging conceptions of the nature of a political system. For example, W. Howard Wriggins has analyzed eight "strategies for aggregating power" employed by political leaders in Asia and Africa: "projecting the personality, building an organization, promoting an ideology, rewarding the faithful and susceptible, intimidating the opponent and wavering ally, developing the economy, expanding (or contracting) political participation, and using foreign policy." [10] Such formulations can be viewed in relation to the functional categories proposed for a political system by Gabriel A. Almond: ". . . generating inputs (demands and supports); processing inputs (articulation, aggregation, rule conversion, rule application, political communication); generating outputs (extraction, regulation, allocation, symbolic production); and the exercise of performance capabilities (extractive, regulative, distributive, symbolic, and responsive)." [11] Consider also the implications for political leadership at various levels of the five crises of political development that have been suggested by the SSRC Committee on Comparative Politics: legitimacy, participation, distribution, integration, and regulation.

It will be important for political leadership studies to envision both the necessity for leaders to respond to objective tasks thrust upon them as well as the opportunity for leaders to define their own task objectives. Tannenbaum and Schmidt,[12] for example, have suggested how a leader can choose among seven different leadership styles based on his assessment of three variables: himself, his associates, and the situation. This implies that task characteristics are an important element. An illustration of a leader's opportunity for task innovation is given by Herbert Simon:[13]

> The main task of the leader is innovation—which involves creative problem-solving activity for him and for his organization. He accomplishes this task by managing his own allocation of attention and effort, and by paying particular attention to the organization's scanning and program development functions. He contributes to creative innovation throughout the organization by seeing that it has a constantly-revised, clear, simple picture of the world in which it is operating and its goals in that world. Through these processes, he is able to contribute to the organization not merely his energy, but also the means to release in creative ways the energies of others.

The essay by David C. Korten (Selection 6) suggests how task might function as an independent variable to bring about changes in other aspects of political leadership behavior. Although the analysis is not specifically focused upon the concept of task—but more generally upon "stress"—the essay presents a paradigm for experimental inquiry involving task as an independent variable. Korten suggests that increasing stress is associated with changes toward high "goal structure" and from democratic to authoritarian leadership. In terms of the present conceptual framework, this suggests that changes in task are associated with changes in values and organizational behavior. Further elaboration of Korten's paradigm to encompass different kinds of tasks and different dependent variables seems definitely promising, including the addition of the influence of past learning and future expectations as elements of the conditions antecedent to task-coping leadership behaviors.

Neither the tasks of political leaders nor the problems associated with scholarly analysis of them can be expected to be simple. They offer another important challenge to political leadership studies.

## VALUES

Concepts of values will be vital for advancing the study of political leadership even though, as in many of life's most important things, gaining a precise understanding of their operational influence may be difficult. As Soejatmoko, a leading Indonesian intellectual, has explained, "A large part of the really important problems in the development process are not to be empirically tested. They are of a normative nature, and if . . . research in the social sciences wants to be more relevant, I think it cannot escape somehow to relate to these problems that are of a normative nature." [14]

The world of political action seems to provide abundant indications of the importance of values. Men deem it important whether or not their leaders espouse and pursue "liberal," "conservative," "socialist," "communist," or "fascist" means toward their associated ends. Even the disavowal of an ideological label itself implies a value system; usually it consists of an eclectic assemblage of values drawn from historically given ideological systems. Although many observers of political leaders are sceptical of their public value utterances, and although leaders of different ideological persuasions may share certain common values both within and across cultures, the contemporary world provides dramatic evidence that political leadership values do make a difference in the direction of societal development. This is strikingly illustrated by comparing political, social, economic, and cultural differences that have been brought about in divided China, Germany, Korea, and Vietnam by different dominant political leadership groups. Other examples of the potential significance of strong leadership values are Gandhi's devotion to non-violence and Hitler's hatred of Jews, the former inspiring peaceful resistance, the latter inciting to genocide.

Assigning a position of clearly differentiated importance to values in the study of political leadership will permit the establishment of linkages with areas of deep human concern that are not usually given prominence in political science analysis. These are law, religion, economics, and the arts. The latter may be an especially promising area of investigation. Political leaders may serve as patrons, destroyers, or creators of artistic values. What are the implications for leadership behavior and its impact upon society of Hitler as an architect, Mao as a poet, Churchill as a painter, Sihanouk as a composer, and Disraeli as a novelist? It may be that a concern for exploring linkages between political leadership and artistic values will lead to asking the question, "Is it beautiful?" of a political system as well as, "Does it work?" or "Is it just?"

Four principal tasks confront value analysis in the study of political leadership. The first is the identification of operative values as they relate to political leadership behavior both within and across cultures. Important beginnings have been made by Harold Lasswell's eightfold value classification ("power, enlightenment, wealth, well-being, skill, affection, respect, and rectitude"),[15] by Ralph K. White's categories[16] for value content analysis of war propaganda as extended by William Eckhardt for the study of conflict mindedness ("denunciation, strength, justified aggression, 'war/peace' values, and lack of concern for the welfare of others"),[17] by the effort of Alexander L. George[18] to extend the study of the "operational codes" of political leaders as pioneered by Nathan Leites,[19] and by the comparative studies of Philip E. Jacob and his international colleagues of local political leadership values and community activism in India, Poland, Yugoslavia, and the United States ("concern for economic development, conflict resolution-avoidance, participation, selflessness, localism, action propensity, honesty, equality, and political responsibility").[20]

In further pursuit of the first task, values associated with accession to power, normal role performance, crisis management, and disengagement from positions of political leadership will be of special interest. The nature, relationships, and effects of values associated with the person, family, friend-ship dyad, faction, organization, community, class, sub-societal group, so-ciety, nation, region, international organization, and world society (or global village) will deserve exploration. So also will values associated with problems such as poverty, violence, and injustice. Attention will need to be given not only to how values operate independently to influence the be-havior of leaders but how the values publicly espoused or privately acted upon by leaders influence the value life of a society. And attention should not be limited to inquiry into the bright, "polite," positive values; the dark, "dirty," negative ones need to be examined as well.

A second task for value analysis in the study of political leadership will be to inquire into origins, combinations, and patterns of change and extinction of leadership-related values. This means to go beyond description and correlation of values at a given time into the structure of reinforcing conditions and future expectations that permit the emergence, maintenance, adaptation, change, and abandonment of values. This kind of analysis will assist students of leadership to pursue a third task: the exploration of the introduction of new values into the realm of political leadership behavior through laboratory and field experiments.

A fourth task, to be conducted both independently and in cooperation with political leaders, will be to contribute to the description and creation of evaluative criteria for judging political leadership performance under vary-ing conditions. A starting point will be to examine the professional criteria by which political leaders judge each other both within and across levels and systems as well as to inquire into follower evaluations. This may be supple-mented by objective knowledge about actual patterns of political leadership behavior that emerges from scientific inquiry and by exploring creative potentials in normative criticism by any member of society.[21] Since one view of political leadership is that it has the social function of transforming actual conditions through the possible toward the ideal, the description of existing normative feedback systems and the engineering of more adequate ones for the future are appropriate subjects of concern.

The overview essay by Milton Rokeach (Selection 7) in this section discusses the concept of values with unusual clarity. After defining value, instrumental value, terminal value, value system, and attitude, he presents a model of value-attitude change. This model is based on assumed functional relationships among many attitudes, relatively fewer instrumental values, and a very small number of terminal values. Of special interest for political leadership studies are his findings that sometimes single values are good predictors of behavior (e.g., "salvation" as a terminal value tended to be a good predictor of church attendance); and that relative emphasis upon a pair of values, "freedom" and "equality," tended to differentiate fascist, communist, socialist, and conservative political leaders.

Rokeach's formulations suggest that it will be fruitful to study carefully the terminal and instrumental values of political leaders, and to experiment with predicting attitudes and other behaviors based on this knowledge. Appreciation of the independent importance of values undoubtedly will be aided by clarifying and correlating other variables of the conceptual framework such as task. The model for value change proposed by Rokeach merits further investigation by observation of political leader behavior in a natural setting and by laboratory experimentation. Finally, continued comparative research on value sets needs to be pursued across cultures, political systems, and roles.

## SETTING

The final variable of the suggested conceptual framework may be called the "setting." At the present time, no single definition of setting seems entirely satisfactory. Alternative formulations will have to be posited and tested as the study of political leadership progresses. The main idea of the concept of setting is that political leadership behavior takes place in an environment that includes human, man-made, and natural elements. For example, a political leader may act in a context characterized by linguistic diversity, a low level of technology primarily devoted to agriculture, and a large-scale territory. It is hypothesized that political leadership behavior is affected by and in turn affects this environment, either directly or indirectly. It will be the task of political leadership studies to discover what kinds of things in what ways enter into this relationship of mutual influence.[22]

Two principal approaches to the concept of setting seem promising. The first is wholistic; the second is segmental. Among the wholistic approaches can be included the concepts of culture, historical era, and stages of development. The anthropological concept of culture conveys the idea of a patterned tapestry of life woven by men, artifacts, and nature; e.g., agricultural, nomadic, and urban industrial cultures. The historical idea of an age, epoch, or era, marked by a complex configuration of characteristic elements, also conveys a wholistic conception of setting; e.g., ages of peace, war, expansion, consolidation, contentment, invention, and revolution. A wholistic approach to the idea of setting is illustrated also by various interpretations of stages in human development; e.g., Marxist-Leninist portrayals of human progress from primitive communism, through feudalism, capitalism, and socialism to communism; Organski's outline of four stages of political development as primitive unification, industrialization, national welfare, and abundance;[23] and the frequent tripartite division of human experience into traditional, transitional, and modernizing or developing periods.

Wholistically viewed, human society, or any given subunit of it, is seen to be characterized by a distinctive pattern of associated features, growing out of the past, conditioning the present, and providing both opportunities for and limitations upon the future. Analytically viewing political leadership in such a context—holding identifiable personality, role, organizational, and value variables constant—research must clarify the influence of the whole upon it. A wholistic approach to setting analysis will be benefited by extension of the efforts of Samuel Klausner and others to develop the scientific study of total societies.[24]

Another approach to setting is segmental. This means to concentrate upon certain aspects of the environment rather than attempting to characterize the effects of the setting as a whole. Naturally there is a relationship between the whole and a part, but one may be emphasized over the other. Examples of segmental emphases with wholistic aspirations that differ in relative strength are contained in such academic disciplines as psychology, economics, political science, geography, and various fields of the humanities. Sub-specialties in more wholistic disciplines such as history, sociology, and anthropology also illustrate segmental accentuation. From a segmental point of view political leadership studies will wish to explore the relationships of such variables as the following to leader behavior: systems of economic production and ownership; population characteristics; spatial location of persons and artifacts; technological capabilities, especially for transportation and communication; social structure; and cultural institutions.

The essay by Tateisi, Yamamoto, and Kon (Selection 8) challenges students of political leadership to envision a progression from past to future settings for leadership behavior, to imagine types of political leadership most suitable for such settings, and to examine the role played by political leadership in shifts from one setting to another. Again explicit linkages to political leadership have not been provided by the authors but must be supplied by specialists on political leadership who can appreciate their relevance. This essay can remind students of political leadership that their analysis of setting variables can be accomplished on a futuristic as well as a historical or contemporary basis.

The relationships among components of a conceptual framework may be hypothesized to be something like those among the fingers of a hand: they are related, some closer than others, and in different circumstances they assume positions of varying relative importance. The objectives of research and theory-building efforts with respect to any given conceptual framework in the study of political leadership will be to describe and explain the nature of the concepts and the linkages among them. Gradually out of these efforts increasingly more adequate bodies of theory should emerge; and if the emerging theories are valid, then anticipations and actions based upon them should be increasingly more accurate and effective.

# Notes

to Part Two: A Conceptual Framework

1. This definition may be compared to that proposed by Edinger (Selection 9): "Political leadership is thus a position—or in the language of the cognitive approach to role analysis—the location of an actor or actors in a group, characterized by the ability of the incumbent to guide the collective behavior of this group in the direction of a desired authoritative distribution of values in a political community. The political leader, in this sense, is a *central actor* occupying a *focal position* which relates to various *counter-positions* in a particular *role-set*. As the incumbent of such a position, the central actor is perceptually related to the occupants of these counter-positions in terms of reciprocal expectations and evaluations associated with these positions. He perceives himself, and may be perceived by other relevant actors, as playing one or more roles oriented toward the exercise of decision-making authority in a political community by himself and/or other members of his particular group."

2. Robert F. Bales, "Interaction Process Analysis" in David I. Sills (ed.), *International Encyclopedia of the Social Sciences* (New York: Macmillan, 1968), VII, pp. 465–471.

3. Amiati Etzioni, *A Comparative Analysis of Complex Organizations* (New York: The Free Press, 1961).

4. Harold M. Mosak, "Early Recollections as a Projective Technique," *Journal of Projective Techniques,* XXII (1958), pp. 302–311.

5. Some societies, such as the Eskimo, however, are known not to have formal leadership roles associated with individuals.

6. An important political leadership study on this question that may be overlooked because "political leadership" is not mentioned in its title is Sidney Verba, *Small Groups and Political Behavior* (Princeton: Princeton University Press, 1961).

7. This does not apply only to "polite" relationships; relations with

gangsters and strongarm men, where applicable, should be examined as well.

8. Paul Pigors, "Types of Followers," *Journal of Social Psychology,* V, No. 3 (August 1934), pp. 378–383.

9. The relationship between Colonel House and Woodrow Wilson, for example, shows how an initially "constructive" follower comes to be perceived as "subversive" by the leader. Alexander L. and Juliette L. George, *Woodrow Wilson and Colonel House* (New York: Dover, 1964), also give a classic description of how an intimate adviser can manipulate a leader. See especially chapter III, "Formula for Success," pp. 113–132.

10. W. Howard Wriggins, *The Ruler's Imperative: Strategies for Political Survival in Asia and Africa* (New York: Columbia University Press, 1969).

11. Gabriel A. Almond, "A Developmental Approach to Political Systems," *World Politics,* XVII (January 1965), pp. 183–214.

12. Robert Tannenbaum and Warren H. Schmidt, "How to Choose a Leadership Pattern," in Robert Tannenbaum *et al.* (ed.), *Leadership and Organization* (New York: McGraw-Hill, 1961), pp. 67–79.

13. Herbert Simon, "The Decision Maker as Innovator," in Sidney Mailick (ed.), *Concepts and Issues in Administrative Behavior* (Englewood Cliffs, N.J.: Prentice-Hall, 1962).

14. Soejatmoko, remarks at a conference on "American Research on Southeast Asian Development: Asian and American Views," sponsored by the Asia Society and the East-West Center, Honolulu, January 28–30, 1968.

15. A recent statement is contained in Harold D. Lasswell, "A Note on 'Types' of Personality: Nuclear, Co-Relational, Developmental," *Journal of Social Issues,* XXIV (1968), p. 83.

16. Ralph K. White, "Hitler, Roosevelt and the Nature of War Propaganda," *Journal of Abnormal and Social Psychology,* XLIX (1949), pp. 157–174; and Ralph K. White, *Value Analysis: Nature and Use of the Method* (Ann Arbor: Society for the Psychological Study of Social Issues, 1951).

17. William Eckhardt, "The Values of Fascism," *Journal of Social Issues,* XXIV (1968), pp. 89–104.

18. *The 'Operational Code' A Neglected Approach to the Understanding of Political Leadership* (Santa Monica: The Rand Corporation, 1967).

19. *The Operational Code of the Politburo* (New York: McGraw-Hill, 1951).

20. Philip E. Jacob *et al., Values and the Active Community: A Cross-National Study of the Influence of Local Leadership* (New York: The Free Press, 1971).

21. This implies, of course, cross-professional evaluation of political leadership behavior. The same could be said to be desirable for evaluation of scholarly contributions to the theory and practice of political leadership.

That is, the criticism by leaders and followers of scholarly contributions to knowledge of this subject should be elicited as well.

22. In their study of the historical evolution of the American presidency Rienow and Rienow mention several examples of the effect of technological influences upon political leadership behavior: e.g., the invention of the telephone freed presidential candidates from reliance on a small number of local bosses for information about voter attitudes (p. 134); and the emergence of television has meant that candidates must possess "the mystical ability to 'project' on a television screen" (p. 204). Other influences mentioned include printing, the train, radio, the airplane, jet plane, and helicopter. Robert Rienow and Leona Train Rienow, *The Lonely Quest: The Evolution of Presidential Leadership* (Chicago: Follett, 1966).

23. A. F. K. Organski, *The Stages of Political Development* (New York: Alfred A. Knopf, 1965).

24. Samuel Klausner, ed., *The Study of Total Societies* (New York: Frederick A. Praeger, 1967). Perhaps "societal syntality" and "global syntality" will be developed as concepts reminiscent of Cattell's formulation of "group syntality."

# 3 Personality

Classifying and Predicting Presidential Styles:
Two "Weak" Presidents

JAMES D. BARBER

In the United States, no one can be president but the President. If he withholds his energies or fritters them away ineffectively, we endure or enjoy a period of national stalemate. So we need to know as much about why some presidents fail to lead as about why others succeed. Indeed, it can be argued that our periods of political drift have been as fateful for the nation as our eras of New Freedom, New Deal and New Frontier.

But the dull presidents are a trial for the political analyst, particularly for the student of personality and political leadership. It is not just that they sap one's intellectual verve, but that their personality configurations are, on the surface, indistinct. They thus provide "hard-case" tests for the supposition that personality helps shape a president's politics. If a personality approach can work with Coolidge and Hoover, it can work with any chief executive. I mean to show here how these two men illustrate some recurrent dynamics of presidential style and how these dynamics can be caught in a theory with predictive possibilities.

The following pages take up these themes in order. First I shall set forth a scheme for classifying presidents according to the major dimensions of their political styles and demonstrate the applicability of the classification scheme to Coolidge and Hoover. The purpose of this section is to define and apply concepts potentially useful for classifying political leaders in terms of patterned regularities in political styles, not simply to describe each president as a unique case. The data I shall use are biographical; their presentation in small space requires radical summarization.

The second section poses a theory, focusing primarily on the president's first independent political success, of the development of a political

---

James D. Barber, "Classifying and Predicting Presidential Styles: Two Weak Presidents." *Journal of Social Issues,* XXIV, No. 3 (July 1968), pp. 51–80.

style. In brief, I argue that a president's style is a reflection of the ways of performing which brought him success at the time, usually in late adolescence or early adulthood, when he emerged as a personality distinctive from his family heritage, in a role involving relatively intensive participation in a socially organized setting. It is at this point that argument moves from classification to prediction, from an emphasis on naming to an emphasis on explaining. Biographical materials are then treated in a more dynamic fashion, in an effort to reveal the psychological functioning which sustains an integrated pattern of behavior, that is, a distinctive and consistent political style.

## "STYLE"

"Style" in this context means a collection of habitual action patterns in meeting role demands. Viewed from outside, a man's style is the observed quality and character of his performance. Viewed from inside, it is his bundle of strategies for adapting, for protecting and enhancing selfesteem. The main outlines of a political style can be usefully delineated, I have argued, by the interaction of two main dimensions.[1] The first is *activity-passivity* in performing the role. Presidents have often been typed in this way. The question here is not one of effectiveness but of effort. Political roles, including the presidency, allow for wide variation in the amount of energy the person invests in his work. Such investment has a large voluntary component and typically reflects to a high degree the man's personal habits as these interact with the demands of the situation. The second dimension is *positive-negative affect* toward his activity. Action *per se* tells us nothing of affect. The way one feels about his work—specifically, whether he goes about his tasks reasonably happily or with an air of discouragement and sadness—tells much about the fit between his needs and his duties. His affect toward his work represents the self's way of registering that fit. Like activity-passivity, the affect dimension links personality with political leadership.

Put together, these two crude and simple variables delineate four political types. Briefly, the active-positive shows a style oriented primarily toward productiveness; the active-negative toward personal ambition; the passive-positive toward affection; and the passive-negative toward (minimal) performance of duty. Within these general nuclear types, a series of per-

---

[1] See James David Barber, *The Lawmakers: Recruitment and Adaptation to Legislative Life* (1965); and "Leadership Strategies for Legislative Party Cohesion." David Shapiro's *Neurotic Styles* (1965) is helpful in understanding styles in general and several specific style patterns.

sonality dynamics relate the self-system, reactions to political experience, strategies of adaptation to political roles, types of vulnerability to political persuasion and effectiveness in performing political tasks. In psychological terms, activity and affect interact to give, respectively, generally adjusted, compulsive, compliant and withdrawn types. There is no one "political man," no universal pattern of leadership performance.

For the analysis of political behavior in collegial bodies such as legislatures, this classificatory scheme may capture the main comparisons. For the Presidency, an office of immense individual power, we need more precise characterizations. I propose here to deepen the analysis within each category by elaborating three subcategories. These subcategories emerge when we ask (extending the major dimensions of activity and affect) to what extent and with what adjustive purpose the president takes advantage of the main opportunities the role affords him. Specifically, how does he integrate his personal style with the role's opportunities for:

> *Rhetoric:* A leader may accentuate certain kinds of expressiveness to audiences, ranging from the world audience to his companions at dinner.
> *Business:* He may or may not concentrate on managing the endless flow of details that flood onto his desk, the studying and budget calculations, the reviewing of memoranda, the personnel problems, etc.
> *Personal Relations:* A president may concentrate in various ways on bargaining with, dominating, combatting and depending on the political elite close around him.

Obviously all presidents do all of these things. But equally obviously they vary in their devotion to each and in their style of performance in each. The first task in analyzing a presidential style, then, is to characterize, within the general framework of activity and affect, the way the man habitually meets the role's demands that he speak, that he manage ordinary business, and that he operate with others at close range. The examples presented— and they are only that—show how these style elements can be distinctive and habitual for the man and politically significant for the nation.

Once the styles are understood, we move to an even more difficult question: how might they have been predicted? How might we have supposed, on the basis of the man's known history, what he would do with the office?

## THE COOLIDGE STYLE

Calvin Coolidge as president fits the passive-negative, or withdrawn type. Of the three main dimensions of style he emphasized rhetoric. His rhetorical style was sharply compartmentalized according to the audience: witty banter with reporters, highminded addresses to the nation, silence at social occasions. He avoided detailed work on presidential business. His personal relations were coolly detached. These patterns are evident as the main themes of the Coolidge presidency.[2]

## RHETORIC

Coolidge complained that "One of the most appalling trials which confront a President is the perpetual clamor for public utterances." But this "foster-child of silence" was anything but quiet in public. In office 67 months, he held 520 press conferences, an average of 7.8 per month, compared with Franklin Roosevelt's 6.9. He gave radio addresses about once a month. He got off to an excellent start with reporters, cracking jokes at this first conference; their "hearty applause" on that occasion made it "one of my most pleasant memories." They were "the boys" who came along on his vacations. Clearly he enjoyed their enjoyment, particularly when he could surprise or titillate them with Yankee humor. He carefully stage-managed his "I do not choose to run for President in nineteen twenty-eight" statement, releasing the news at noon on the fourth anniversary of taking office, grinning broadly. His wife was as surprised as the reporters were. He let himself be photographed in full Indian headdress, cowboy chaps and hat, overalls and any number of other outfits; there is a picture of him presenting a sap bucket to Henry Ford. When a friend protested that his antics made people laugh, Coolidge said, "Well, it's good for people to laugh."

His formal addresses had a completely different tone. They were sermons from the church of New England idealism. "When the President speaks," he wrote, "it ought to be an event," by which he meant a serious and dignified and uplifting event. He spoke on "Education: the Cornerstone of Self-Government," "The High Place of Labor," "Ordered Liberty and World Peace," "Authority and Religious Liberty," "Religion and the Republic," "The Genius of America," "Destiny is in you," "Do the day's work," "The things of the spirit come first," and "The chief ideal of the American people is idealism"—this was Coolidge in the presidential pulpit. And he was quite serious. When Will Rogers imitated his nasal twang and penchant for clichés, he was much offended and refused Rogers' apology.

---

[2] On Coolidge, I have found most useful the biographies by Fuess and White, and Coolidge's *Autobiography*. McCoy's new biography, which appeared as I finished this piece, seems to confirm its interpretation. The short quotations, too numerous to attribute individually here, are from the above three books and from Cornwell's, on which I have relied for much material on presidential rhetoric. Lowry (1921) is also helpful.

## BUSINESS

Coolidge sincerely believed in hard work. He felt busy, even rushed, but his constant routine included a daily nap and often eleven hours of sleep in twenty-four. Often tired and bored, he gradually abandoned all physical exercise except for brief walks and spent much time in silent contemplation, gazing out his office window. His strength was not effort but patience. "Let well enough alone," was his motto. He was the "provincial who refuses to become excited over events for which he has no direct responsibility." He kept Harding's cabinet, let Daugherty hang on for a long time, tried to delay his friends' efforts to boost him in 1924. Asked how he kept fit he said, "By avoiding the big problems." Most of the time Coolidge simply did not want to be bothered.

Underneath these tactics, supporting and justifying them, was a strain of mystical resignation. "I am only in the clutch of forces that are greater than I am," he wrote, despite being "the most powerful man in the world." He bore his young son's death with Roman stoicism: "The ways of Providence are beyond our understanding." The dedicated man, he wrote in his newspaper column, "finds that in the time of need some power outside himself directs his course." Coolidge could wait, storing up his meager energies with a feeling of rightness in entrusting himself to fate. "Government is growth," he said, and added: "—slow growth." He and Providence presided while the rate slowed down.

## PERSONAL RELATIONS

Coolidge got rid of much work by giving it to others, and he believed in doing just that. "One rule of action more important than all others consists in never doing anything that some one else can do for you." He appointed or retained "men of sufficient ability so that they can solve all the problems that arise under their jurisdiction." He rarely interfered and he resented others interfering with him. His loyal helper Frank Stearns got repeated rebuffs for his trouble. Coolidge seldom discussed political matters with his wife. He complained of Hoover as Secretary of Commerce (Coolidge called him "the wonder boy" or "the miracle worker"): "That man has offered me unsolicited advice for six years, all of it bad!"

Yet he was always surrounded by people. He and Grace entertained more than any previous family in the White House. Alone, he said, he got "a sort of naked feeling." His poker face, his long impenetrable silences at social affairs were known to all Washington and gave rise to scores of anecdotes as matron after matron tried to pry a few words from him. Occasionally he could be induced to talk about Vermont. More often, he simply sat. This was "a form of defense," his biographer says. "Can't hang you for what you don't say," said Coolidge. "In order to function at all," he warned his successors, the President "has to be surrounded by many safeguards. If these were removed for only a short time, he would be overwhelmed by the people who would surge in upon him." He learned not to smile, as smiling encouraged longer office visits. He had very little interest in women and was, his biographer says, "embarrassed when left for even a short period in the company of the other sex." Undoubtably much of Coolidge's acerbity at dinner parties was a reaction to intensified shyness at having to cope with the matron to his left and right. When he did speak, it was some tart, pithy puckishness, mildly aggressive, disconcerting, with a quality of surprise in a conventional conversational setting. In a rare and revealing confession, he once told Frank Stearns why:

> Do you know, I've never really grown up? It's a hard thing for me to play this game. In politics, one must meet people, and that's not easy for me . . . When I was a little fellow, as long ago as I can remember, I would go into a panic if I heard strange voices in the kitchen. I felt I just couldn't meet the people and shake hands with them. Most of the visitors would sit with Father and Mother in the kitchen, and the hardest thing in the world was to have to go through the kitchen door and give them a greeting. I was almost ten before I realized I couldn't go on that way. And by fighting hard I used to manage to get through that door. I'm all right with old friends, but every time I meet a stranger, I've got to go through the old kitchen door, back home, and its not easy (Fuess, 1965, 25).

Coolidge "tried deliberately to suppress 'aggressive wittiness,' " but "it broke out repeatedly in quaint comments."

Even this brief account shows the main features of the Coolidge style. Clearly he belongs in the withdrawn type. Aside from his banter with reporters, he did not particularly enjoy being President, given all the demands that made on him, and he conserved his energies stingily. Many of his characteristics—his rural Yankee background; his persistent turning back to his past, his father, his homeplace; his avoidance of controversy and patient faith in Providence; his penchant for reverie and retreat; his sense of strangeness in a cosmopolitan environment ("Puritan in Babylon")—concord with empirical findings on this type in a very different environment. His style within that type is also clear. Words for Coolidge were shaped heavily by his relations to different audiences. The "serious" audience was the nation, to which he addressed sermons on common virtue, purveying the illusion of specificity through epigram. In fact, his abstract pseudo-

Hegelian fatalism had little clear connection with the political issues of the day. His humor at news conferences was badinage with the boys, a show with much audience participation, full of little surprises. There, as in his dinner table silences and mild insults, the focus was on Coolidge as a clown, one who could touch the heart but leave the political brain and brawn of the nation relaxed.

His philosophy helped him rationalize his leisurely pace. His method was to concentrate on matters only the President had to decide, and to define that category as narrowly as possible. Most everything could wait. And Coolidge himself could wait, with utter, unflappable calm for longer than the last of his advisors. He also managed to rationalize his independence of others; clearly his style in close interpersonal relations cut him off effectively from much of the Washington conversational froth—but also from any effective political bargaining with administrative or legislative or party leaders. He was a loner who endured in order to serve, while the nation drifted.

## THE HOOVER STYLE

Hoover belongs in the active-negative category, the compulsive type. He emphasized hard work on detail and endless conferences behind the scenes. He avoided and detested the rhetorical demands of the office. In personal relations, his was a stance of highly restrained aggression. Again, some illustrative evidence is necessary to make this pattern clear.[3]

## RHETORIC

The rise of Herbert Hoover coincided with an immense expansion in the mass media, particularly newspapers and radio. Hoover was a genuine hero; his remarkable effectiveness in European relief activities cannot be seriously questioned. He was the subject, not the instigator, of a vast public relations build-up largely due to increased media demands for news and to the drama and success of his works. But Hoover in the presidency "transmuted all adventure into business," as Arthur Schlesinger (1957) complains. He detested the office's demands for dramatization. "The presidency is more than an executive responsibility," he wrote; "it is an inspiring symbol of all that is highest in American purpose and ideals." Yet he could not bring himself to practice the pretense such inspiration requires. "This is not a showman's

---

[3] On Hoover, the most useful sources are Irwin, Lyons, and Hoover's *Memoirs*. Here again Cornwell's chapters have supplied much material. The short quotations are too numerous to attribute individually. They are taken from the above and from Liggett, 1932; Myers, 1934; Warren, 1967; Wolf, 1956; Wood, 1932; and Hinshaw, 1950.

job," he said, "I will not step out of character," and "You can't make a Teddy Roosevelt out of me." He felt uncomfortable when forced to perform in public: "I have never liked the clamor of crowds. I intensely dislike superficial social contacts. I made no pretensions to oratory and I was terrorized at the opening of every speech." The "miracle worker" disdained "the crowd" which "only feels: it has no mind of its own which can plan. The crowd is credulous, it destroys, it hates and it dreams—but it never builds."

Extremely sensitive to criticism, Hoover reacted to personal abuse with "hurt contempt." He was rarely aggressive, normally suffering in silence with only an occasional private complaint. He got off to a good start with the press, setting more liberal rules for the conference, but even before the stock market crash he began to restrict the reporters, became more secretive and admonished them for the error of their ways. Often he withdrew to his forest camp in Virginia without notice to the press; there he set up guards to keep the newsmen away. He began to play favorites among them and to go over their heads to editors and publishers. He cancelled conferences on short notice, ignored questions and took to reading prepared statements. Eventually, most of the White House reporters turned against him. He met them less and less frequently and virtually eliminated conferences near the end of his term.

Hoover's public addresses rarely discussed specific policies in detail. His twenty-one radio addresses were mainly "greetings" to specific groups, full of vague moral precepts. Speech-writing was as hard for him as speechmaking. He drafted each one in longhand, went through a dozen or more drafts and heavily edited proofs to produce a labored and ordinary address. But perhaps the most peculiar feature of the tone of Hoover's presidential statements was their public optimism in the midst of social disaster. As the Depression deepened, again and again he found business fundamentally sound, the worst of the crisis over, employment gradually increasing, government efforts remarkably successful, no one actually starving—or so he said, giving rise to a "credibility gap" of modern proportions. His pollyanna reassurances stand in stark relief against both the condition of the country and the character of the man. His secretary put it more kindly: "Figuratively, he was the father protecting his family against the troubles impending, shouldering their burdens for them, keeping the 'bad news' to himself, outwardly trying to be as smiling and cheerful as possible."

## BUSINESS

Meanwhile, he slaved and suffered in silence. Long before the Depression Hoover was frequently discouraged. At the Paris Peace Conference in 1919, Colonel House found him "simply reveling in gloom"; Ike Hoover remembered that in the White House he "never laughed aloud" and "always had a frown on his face," and his secretary recalls that "he worried as have few Presidents in our history, with discouragement at his lot most of the time." He was glad when it was all over: "All the money in the world could not induce me to live over the last nine months. The conditions we have experienced make this office a compound hell." He worked as hard as he worried. Even before the crash his routine was a rigorous one, beginning with an energetic medicine ball game first thing in the morning. After his inauguration he immediately set about a series of programs for change and reform. Then when the panic hit, "he began that grinding, brutal, self-lacerating labor, often eighteen or twenty hours a day or clear around the clock, which would continue unbroken until the blessed hour of release more than three years later. No galley slave of old was more firmly riveted to his drudgery, for he was chained by his surpassing sense of duty." "So tired that every bone in my body aches," Hoover trudged on. Near the close of his tenure he allowed himself one bitter outburst in public, significantly in reply to charges that he had "done nothing." In "the one harsh word that I have uttered in public office," he called such charges "deliberate, intolerable falsehoods."

And so they were. He had done plenty, but to little effect. Hoover was immersed in detail. As Bernard Baruch put it, "To Hoover's brain facts are as water to a sponge. They are absorbed into every tiny interstice." He had a "card index" mind which could grasp and retain details and figures without notes. He commissioned endless policy studies to produce the facts on which to base programs. His whole orientation, in other words, was away from the vagaries of opinion and toward the hard precision of fact.

Much of his energy went into an endless round of conferences. Hoover appeared to believe that if only he could bring the right people together and give them the right proposal, they would agree and march off to execute his plan. John Kenneth Galbraith called these "no-business meetings," designed to accomplish nothing, but there is little doubt Hoover had high hopes for this technique of "coordination." In almost all such encounters he had more pertinent information and had worried through a more thoroughly organized proposal than any other participant. And he was President of the United States. The others he expected to behave as had his subordinates in business, in the European relief organization, and in the Department of Commerce: as willing endorsers and enforcers. When cabinet members and congressmen failed to respond in this way, Hoover's gloom deepened. His personal discouragement proved contagious; to Henry L. Stimson, his Secretary of State, a private conversation with Hoover was "like sitting in a bath of ink."

## PERSONAL RELATIONS

Hoover kept his aggressive feelings tightly controlled in close relations as in public ones. At a time when, as he complained, "My men are dropping around me," when H. G. Wells found him a "sickly, overworked and overwhelmed man," Hoover was often tempted to lash out. Deep inside he may have been, as his apologist Lyons believed, "a sensitive, soft-hearted person who craves affection, enjoys congenial company, and suffers under the slings of malice," but he could also feel intense anger. "I'll rattle his bones" was his typical expression when thwarted by some obstructionist. In 1932 he meant to "carry the fight right to Roosevelt . . . We have got to crack him every time he opens his mouth." But he would quickly rein in these feelings:

> He was almost always the master of his emotions, however provoked he might be. If something went wrong, if some individual really aroused him he would, in common parlance, "blow off steam." But it was only for a moment. The next minute he would be pressing his buzzer. When the stenographer was seated beside his desk, instead of telling Mr. Blank cryptically what he thought, he dictated a most diplomatic communication. There was never a barb in it. Rather, it represented earnest and skillful effort to induce that individual to see eye to eye with him (Joslin, 1934, 19).

With his immediate staff "there were no cross words if a subordinate made an error." Nor would he "let himself be baited into a controversy if he could possibly avoid it." Many a time it was tried out on him. His usual comment, made with supreme contempt, was: "A man should not become embroiled with his inferior." His expression was one of "pained disbelief" when other political and congressional leaders failed to keep their commitments.

Of course his demeanor affected his political relations. His inability to enter into genuinely cooperative relations with others, relations involving compromise, an appreciation for the irrational in politics, a sense for the other man's position, meant that his endeavors to induce an enthusiastic response were doomed to failure. He could lead an organization of committed subordinates, but he could not create that commitment among leaders with their own bases of power and their own overriding purposes.

Hoover did accept renomination in 1932, but reluctantly. He "had no overpowering desire to run again," expressed his indifference to the subject, anticipated defeat, and found the campaign a "miserable experience." But he "felt that he must follow through to the end of the struggle. Be that as it may, he had a desperate desire for vindication of himself and his policies."

The purpose was defensive, not any positive achievement. The expected defeat brought relief, not despair.

No brief account can do justice to a complex character, but it seems clear that Hoover belongs in the compulsive type of political leader, outlined by much activity and much unhappiness in the role. Many themes fit this pattern: his struggles with the "exposure" element of the public figure role, resulting in the adoption of a propagandistic orientation; his history as a rapidly upward mobile young man whose links to politics developed out of his nonpolitical occupation; his feelings of frustration and powerlessness in the face of an unresponsive or hostile environment; his anxious, unremitting labor; his suffering and struggle to restrain his aggression. Deeper analysis, one would predict, would reveal a self dominated by the conflict between conscience and ambition, alternating between feelings of guilt and feelings of impotence.

The main distinctive elements in Hoover's style can also be readily summarized. Words were difficult for him; he resisted expression and fell back on a rhetoric of exaggeration when forced into the limelight. Work was his main strategy for success, intensely compulsive work on detail. And in his relations with others he stressed restraint of aggression, an anticipation that his plan would win and succeed in execution. These strategies failed. That Hoover sustained them in the face of repeated negative messages from the environment attests to their rootedness in his personality. The office no more made the man than it made his successor.

## TOWARD A PREDICTIVE THEORY

Where did these styles come from? Our problem is not to discover why Coolidge and Hoover became presidents while others with similar background took different paths, but to find out why, being presidents, they acted as they did. Furthermore, we want an *economical* method for answering that question, a method amenable to *generalization* to other cases, and a method which produces *predictive* statements. That requires a theory. Let me set mine out as starkly as I can.

## FIRST INDEPENDENT POLITICAL SUCCESS

In the lives of most political leaders there is a clearly discernible period, usually in late adolescence or early adulthood, in which a style is adopted. Typically that period can be identified (a) by marked infusions of confidence from relative success, (b) by a relatively new and special relationship to group life, and (c) by a relatively sudden emergence from obscurity to wider attention. The way in which the man finds words to relate himself to an expanded audience, the role of work in bringing him new success, and the mode of his more intimate links with others around him presage his style in the presidency. If we can discover how future presidents met and resolved these fundamental problems in their own critical periods, we should be able to predict how they are likely to attempt (not necessarily successfully) to solve similar problems as chief executives.[4]

## MOTIVES

How can one understand this formative period? First one must view it against the background of compensatory needs inherited from childhood. It is important to highlight the significance of change in the person's life situation. We want the meanings his new development had for him, and that requires knowledge of what he was before. A style's staying power, its persistence and resurgence, depends on its rootedness in strong motives. Viewed retrospectively, a style offers important compensations; viewed prospectively, it promises the continuation and extension of rewards. There is a turning away from an unsatisfactory prior condition to a possibly more satisfactory condition for the future. These satisfactions, and the anticipation of them, are the motive forces which energize the new system.

## RESOURCES

Second, the formative period can only be discerned in the light of the resources a man brings to it. The condition of one's body is a simple example of personal resource. The condition of one's mind is a subtler case, depending as it does on learning and on the collection of relevant experiences and perceptions a person brings to the formative period. These constitute a repertoire of potential style elements upon which he can draw when his time comes. His learning until then can be considered as a rehearsal, though rarely in any conscious sense, for a decisive commitment to a particular style. His experiments in self definition, real and vicarious, set out boundaries and pathways for his map of the future.

## OPPORTUNITIES

And last, a style is not formed in a vacuum but in a context of opportunities. Just as we do not expect a person who has always had all the affection he

---

[4] On the significance of compensation in political leadership, see Lasswell, 1930 and 1945. On the expansion of a potential leader's "field of power," see Alexander L. George, "Power as a Compensatory Value for Political Leaders," *Journal of Social Issues,* XXIV, No. 3 (July 1968), pp. 29–49.

has wanted to seek an unending succession of affection in adulthood, and just as we do not expect an illiterate to adopt an identity as a writer, so not every environment available at the time offers the same chances for personal development. These constraints and stimuli in the immediate culture may have a great deal to do with the kinds of strategies one translates into part of his personal identity.[5]

As a beginning test, then, the following pages examine Coolidge and Hoover at the time of their first independent political success, introduced in each case by a radically summarized account of the needs and resources brought from childhood. A final section draws together these themes with the conclusions derived from the material on their presidential styles.

## COOLIDGE: NEEDS FROM CHILDHOOD

John Calvin Coolidge, Jr., was born in Plymouth, Vermont, on the Fourth of July, 1872, the first child, after four years of marriage, of John Calvin Coolidge and Victoria Josephine Coolidge, nephew of Julius Caesar Coolidge, grandson of Calvin Galusha Coolidge, descendant of five generations of his family in a Vermont village. His mother was a quiet, delicately beautiful person, a chronic invalid since shortly after her marriage. Coolidge remembered "a touch of mysticism and poetry in her nature." His father was a big, stern-visaged man, a storekeeper and pillar of the community who had held many town offices and went to the state legislature. His son admired him for "qualities that were greater than any I possess," and accepted much paternal admonition without complaint.

Calvin's early hero was his grandfather "Galoosh," tall, spare and handsome, an expert horseman and practical joker, said to have a trace of Indian blood, who raised colts and puppies and peacocks and taught the boy to ride standing up behind him. His grandmother ("The Puritan severity of her convictions was tempered by the sweetness of womanly charity") read the Bible to him and when he misbehaved shut up in the dark, windowless attic, "dusty with cobwebs."

Calvin's younger sister Abbie, his constant playmate, was "a lively affectionate girl, with flaming red hair, who was full of energy and impressed everybody by her personality"—almost the exact opposite of her shy brother. Calvin himself was small and frail, with his mother's features, punctual and methodical, only occasionally joining in the schoolyard teasing.

So much for the cast of characters. Life began its hammer blows at this shy boy when he was six. His hero Galusha died as Calvin read him the

---

[5] On the interactions of motivations, resources and opportunities in accounting for political action, see Barber (1965, 10–15, 217–240).

Bible. Six years later his invalid mother, "who used what strength she had to lavish care upon me and my sister," died as a result of an accident with a runaway horse. Her passing left an indelible mark on him:

> In an hour she was gone. It was her thirty-ninth birthday. I was twelve years old. We laid her away in the blustering snows of March. The greatest grief that can come to a boy came to me. Life was never to seem the same again (Coolidge, 1929, 13).

Calvin was despondent too long. His family became concerned; but he kept up his school work "with no tardy marks and good deportment."

Later at the nearby Black River Academy, where his parents and grandmother had gone to school, he was unhappy and homesick, though his father brought him home nearly every weekend. In his third year Abbie joined him there; Calvin had written he hoped she could come. A year and a half later, at age fifteen, she was dead of appendicitis. Calvin came home to be with her in her last hours.

There was another unsettled time for Calvin, like that following his mother's death. He failed the entrance examinations for Amherst College. He had caught cold and stayed home "for a considerable time." In late winter he went back to Black River Academy to get "certified" for Amherst. There he worked hard, "made almost no acquaintances," and in two months was approved for Amherst. In September his father married a Plymouth neighbor, a spinster Calvin had known all his life. "For thirty years," Coolidge wrote much later, "she watched over and loved me." They corresponded regularly until her death in 1920.

Amherst was an all-male place where three-quarters or more of the students belonged to fraternities, "the most unique feature of Amherst life . . . strongly recommended by the members of the faculty," as the *Students' Handbook* said. Calvin needed no urging. He had written his father from school that he and a friend should visit the college "to see about getting me into a society there." But the scheme did not work. Calvin moved into a boardinghouse. The others there were quickly pledged. He remained an "Ouden," an outsider in a small community of clans. "I don't seem to get acquainted very fast," he wrote home in October. After Christmas he wrote that "Every time I get home I hate to go away worse than before and I don't feel so well here now as the first day I came here last fall but suppose I will be all right in a day or two." Two days later: "I feel quite reconciled to being here tonight but felt awful mean yesterday and the day before. I don't know why, I never was homesick any before." In his first two years at Amherst Coolidge was "to say the least, an inconspicuous member of the class." He faithfully attended class meetings, but did not join in the myriad activities, formal and informal, scholarly and athletic, religious and amorous, going on around him. He took long walks in the woods.

Nor was his social isolation balanced with scholarly achievement; his first term marks averaged 2 on a scale of 5. "The marks seem pretty low, don't they"? he wrote his father. He remembered much later that "It needed some encouragement from my father for me to continue." He had begun with the hope that he could do well in his courses with plenty of time to spare.

156893

Thus at twenty-one Calvin Coolidge was an indistinct personality, inarticulate, ineffective, alone. Particularly in affection and achievement he stood on the threshold of adulthood much deprived.

## COOLIDGE: RESOURCES FROM CHILDHOOD

In his mind he had been gathering impressions and registering experiences which would later be useful. He had known his father and grandfather as political leaders in the community. He saw how his father made decisions— "painstaking, precise, and very accurate"—and came to understand government as "restraints which the people had imposed upon themselves in order to promote the common welfare." In the summer before he entered Amherst his father took him to a gathering in Bennington to hear President Benjamin Harrison; there he heard much high oratory about the "high consecration to liberty."

As a boy he had taken a minor part in speaking "pieces," acting in amateur plays, and was even an "end man" once in a local minstrel show. Cicero's orations stuck with him from Latin classes. At graduation from Black River Academy, in a class of five boys and four girls, he delivered an address on "Oratory in History," the newspaper called it "masterly" and his teacher said his speech was "the best one he had seen." After his freshman year at Amherst, at the Independence Day celebration in Plymouth— "Of course, the Fourth of July meant a good deal to me, because it was my birthday"—he delivered a speech on "Freedom," "burning with fervor, replete with denunciation of Proud Albion, and rich with the glorification of our Revolutionary heroes." Perhaps inspired by his freshman rhetoric teacher, this was his last experiment in the florid style of oratory.

Had Coolidge's life taken a different turn, other events, other impressions would have lasted into his autobiographical years. As it was, he had in his mind a number of important images: of small scale Yankee democracy, of his mother reading the romantic poets, of his father succeeding by being careful, of the familial legitimacy of politics, and of himself surviving before audiences. So far he had made nothing of these resources. But they were waiting.

## COOLIDGE: FIRST INDEPENDENT POLITICAL SUCCESS

Of the events in his first two years at Amherst, Coolidge wrote:

> In the development of every boy who is going to amount to anything there comes a time when he emerges from his immature ways and by the greater precision of his thought and action realizes that he has begun to find himself. Such a transition finally came to me. It was not accidental but the result of hard work. If I had permitted my failure, or what seemed to me at the time a lack of success to discourage me, I cannot see any way in which I would ever have made progress. If we keep our faith in ourselves, and what is even more important, keep our faith in regular and persistent application to hard work, we need not worry about the outcome (Coolidge, 1929, 60).

As a matter of fact, what he calls his "transition" was triggered by events nearly "accidental"; his success did not result primarily from "hard work"; and he was, as we have seen, "discouraged" by his earlier lack of success. (Perhaps every autobiography is a mixture of real memories and new meanings, a last attempt to join together life and belief.) In any case, Coolidge did begin his junior year an isolated boy with no real achievements and left Amherst as a young man with a distinctive style of action. In between the whole intensity of his experience, its pace and significance were revolutionalized.

Amherst upperclassmen could wear high derbies and carry canes. Each fall the members of the junior class raced from one end of the athletic field to the other, clad in "topper" and stick. The last seven across the line had to provide dinner and entertainment for the rest. Coolidge was not last, but was one of the losers. His assignment was a speech on "Why I Got Stuck." He began in silence by turning his pockets inside out to show that he had lost all his money on the race. Then: "You wouldn't expect a plow horse to make time on the race track or a follower of the plow to be a Mercury," he said. Pitching hay didn't fit one as a sprinter. And other such comments. Then, in conclusion: "Remember, boys, the Good Book says that the first shall be last and the last shall be first." The speech was a success—the whole class laughed and gave him an ovation. It was his first such appearance and it brought him more attention and notoriety than anything he had done at Amherst so far. He began to emerge as a character, although the incident is not mentioned in his *Autobiography*.

That same year he began to attract attention as a debater. Public speaking and debating were compulsory parts of the curriculum. One of his classmates wrote: "It was in his junior year that we discovered Coolidge. In that year we began debating, and in the debates we found that he could talk. It was as if a new and gifted man had joined the class." Coolidge now became more and more adept at brief and direct statement. He won frequently in debating, perhaps every time in the junior debates. In November of that year he wrote his father proudly: "In view of the fact that yesterday I put up a debate said to be the best heard on the floor of the chapel this term . . . can you send me $25"? In January he wrote home another glowing report of a successful debate. At the end of his junior year the students in the public speaking class voted to split the prize between Coolidge and another speaker. He continued debating in his senior year. In September he was elected to present the "Grove Oration" at the graduation exercises the following June. This was meant to be a humorous speech following the ponderousness of more formal addresses. In June, after a long series of in-door sermons and addresses, the students went to the College Grove, lit up their corncob pipes and settled back on the grass. Coolidge began this way: "The mantle of truth falls upon the Grove Orator on condition he wear it wrong side out," and went on through a series of in-house jokes, continually interrupted by hecklers and shouts of laughter. "The oration was packed with what today would be called 'wisecracks,' " his biographer says, "many of them sarcastic observations on members of the faculty—remarks which, although good-natured in tone and intention, had nevertheless something of a bite." The speech was a smashing success.

In parallel with these oratorical victories, Coolidge achieved social ones. He was elected a member of Phi Gamma Delta on January 15th of his senior year. This began a life-long, active tie, his only fraternal connection. From the start he entered into the group's affairs; a classmate recalls that

> He took a deep interest in the chapter, was most faithful in attending "goat" and committee meetings, and while he did not live at the house, he passed considerable time there. We soon began to rely upon his counsel and judgment, and he was a distinct help to us in many serious problems we had to meet at that time (Fuess, 1965, 54).

He wrote his father that "being in a society" would cost a little more money. From that time on, Coolidge was a faithful "Fiji," raising money, acting as the chapter's lawyer, returning to inspect the house carefully from cellar to garret, organizing (while he was President) the "Fiji Sires and Sons." His role in his brief membership as a student was that of the faithful attender and business helper; he skipped the dances and card games and "wild parties." At long last he had found a band of brothers. He was not a central figure in this group, but it is obvious that his membership meant a great deal to him after years of being left out. The moral he draws from this in the *Autobiography* is touching: "It has been my observation in life that, if one will only exercise the patience to wait, his wants are likely to be filled."

## GARMAN'S INFLUENCE

He had found a voice and developed a relationship to his audience; he had a club of friends. At the same time, Coolidge found a model, an idol with whom to identify and a set of philosophical beliefs to guide him. This was Charles E. Garman, professor of philosophy, whose course, as Coolidge took it, ran from the spring term of junior year through senior year, moving from psychology to philosophy to ethics. "It always seemed to me that all our other studies were in the nature of a preparation for the course in philosophy," Coolidge remembered. Garman, a tall, cadaverous man with piercing black eyes, was a dramatic character, "a middle-aged Hamlet," extremely popular among the students.

Garman was in reality "a devout and rather orthodox New England Congregationalist" with a strong neo-Hegelian bent. Our interest is less in what he taught than in what Coolidge carried away from him and retained for thirty-five years. Garman did not carry his question-raising method to the point of not providing answers. Coolidge recalled his emphasis on rational judgment in ethical matters, the existence of a personal God and of "the complete dependence of all the universe on Him," man as set "off in a separate kingdom from all other creatures," the "spiritual appeal" of art as Divine revelation, the essential quality of men, the dignity of work and industry's right to work's rewards, "that might does not make right, that the end does not justify the means, and that expediency as a working principle is bound to fail." All of this Coolidge lays out in an unusually lengthy passage of his memoirs. Garman posted aphorisms on the walls of his classroom— "Carry all questions back to fundamental principles," "Weigh the evidence," "The question *how* answers the question *what*," "Process not product," and so forth. But perhaps the key lesson Coolidge retained is found later in the *Autobiography* in the context of his early steps in politics, when he was elected Mayor of Northampton, Massachusetts:

> Ever since I was in Amherst College I have remembered how Garman told his class in philosophy that if they would go along with events and hold to the main stream, without being washed ashore by the immaterial cross currents, they would some day be men of power (Coolidge, 1929, 99–100).

Already the echoes of Coolidge as President are apparent.

Coolidge remembered that "We looked upon Garman as a man who walked with God," and that he was "one of the most remarkable men with whom I ever came in contact," a man who "was given a power which took his class up into a high mountain of spiritual life and left them alone with God," who had "no pride of opinion, no atom of selfishness," "a follower of the truth, a disciple of the Cross, who bore the infirmities of us all." Coolidge did not try to defend Garman's position theoretically. But

> I knew that in experience it has worked. In time of crisis my belief that people can know the truth, that when it is presented to them they must accept it, has saved me from many of the counsels of expediency (Coolidge, 1929, 67).

He had found a rule of life, and the words to express it with.

## THE BREAK WITH HIS PAST

Coolidge had written a romantic story for the Amherst *Literary Monthly* in the summer between his junior and senior years. In his senior year, he tried his hand at a very different literary task, undertaken in secret: an essay for a national contest on "The Principles Fought for in the War of the American Revolution." The Amherst History Department awarded his piece a silver medal; the following December when he was working in a law office in Northampton, Coolidge learned he was also the national winner. One of the partners asked him, "Have you told your father"? To which he replied, "No, do you think I'd better"? In his *Autobiography* Coolidge recalled that

> I had a little vanity in wishing my father to learn about it first from the press, which he did. He had questioned some whether I was really making anything of my education, in pretense I now think, not because he doubted it but because he wished to impress me with the desirability of demonstrating it (Coolidge, 1929, 74).

Coolidge had moved from an emotional psychology, a sentimental dramatism in his story ("Margaret's Mist") to the logic of principles, the metier of ethical philosophy which he would continue to emphasize all his life. But his "No, do you think I'd better"? also represented a change. Right after graduation he returned to the farm for a summer's work and then went to Northampton to learn law. As late as January of his senior year he had not yet decided whether the law or storekeeping would be his profession. He wrote his father then, "You will have to decide." He did know that he wanted "to live where I can be of some use to the world and not simply where I should get a few dollars together." By graduation he had decided that the law was "the highest of the professions." On his own, Coolidge sought a place and in September 1895 he went to work in a law office in Northampton. When he joined the law office Coolidge made a break with his past. The boy whose name had been recorded in various forms now discarded the "John" and became plain Calvin Coolidge. And "during these first years he worked so hard that for three years he did not find time to go back to Plymouth." The distance was about a hundred miles.

"That I was now engaged in a serious enterprise of life I so fully realized that I went to the barber shop and divested myself of the college fashion of long hair." He who had so often written home of his successes kept the largest one a secret. He found a job without his father's help. None of the Coolidges had been lawyers. Calvin had formed his style and begun his own life. He had found a way to be; he was not entirely certain where he was going.

As we have seen, Coolidge himself attributed to his experience in the last two years at Amherst a shaping influence on his mind and heart. His biographers agree. Fuess is convinced that "he was, during his first two years at Amherst, acutely conscious of his slow progress. His ambitions had been thwarted; he had failed to make a fraternity, he was unnoticed by those around him, his marks were only mediocre, and he had no compensating successes." Then "perhaps his entire political philosophy" was shaped by his junior and senior teachers as he combined a spurt of learning with social success. William Allen White goes farther: his "spirit awoke in Amherst," Garman "unlocked for him the philosophic mysteries of life," he was "baptized for life," "this reborn spirit whom Garman begot," and "Body and mind and spirit were cast into the iron mold of a fate which guided him through life."

Clearly Coolidge had found at Amherst the major features of the style that served him as President. The similarity in his rhetoric, business management, and personal relations habits in these widely separate periods of his life are striking.

## HOOVER: NEEDS FROM CHILDHOOD

Five generations of Coolidges lived in the confining culture of a small New England town; five generations of Hoovers lived in the confining culture of Quakerism, moving about from time to time but retaining their religion and its peculiar community practices. Gentle and free in ideology, Quakerism was often harsh and repressive in practice. Quaker meetings left Hoover with a sense of "the intense repression upon a ten-year-old who might not even count his toes."

Herbert Clark Hoover was born on August 10, 1874 in West Branch, Iowa, two and a half years after his brother Theodore and two years before his sister May, to Jesse Clark Hoover, a blacksmith and farm implement salesman of 27 and Huldah Minthorn Hoover, a seminary-educated lady of 26. An aunt present at his birth wrote that "Jesse and Huldah always made much of thee because thee represented the little girl they hoped soon to have." Hoover remembered his mother vaguely as "a sweet-faced woman."

She was very religious, spoke often in meeting, an efficient and serious-minded person. His father had a teasing humor, but was capable of punishing Herbert severely.

A plump baby, Herbert nearly died of croup in his second winter and suffered many other illnesses and accidents. But as he grew stronger and older he became a healthy, outdoor-loving boy.

His father died suddenly in the summer of Herbert's sixth year. His mother became "less and less a creature of this world after her husband died," leaving the children for long periods while she travelled about preaching. Herbert was passed around from uncle to uncle, each of whom worked him hard but also let him play in the woods and fields. In the winter after his eighth birthday, his mother died of pneumonia. "Bereavement put a sudden end to his little-boyhood, as it had to his babyhood," Will Irwin writes.

Separated from his brother and sister and sent to an uncle's farm, Herbert "took it hard—but with his mouth shut and grief showing only in his eyes." At age ten, he was again uprooted and sent to Oregon to live with his mother's brother, Henry John Minthorn, whose only son had just died. "Thee is going to Oregon," he was told, and "his lips closed very tight." Minthorn put him to school and chores, for a time of "sober routine." His uncle was a severe taskmaster; once Herbert "stalked out in anger and boarded with other relatives." At fifteen he was taken with his uncle to open a "Quaker land-settlement business" in Salem. A visitor told him of opportunities for engineering education at the newly opening Stanford University. Over the family's objection—and this is the first report of Herbert arguing—he took the Stanford entrance examinations, failed them, but was admitted for special tutoring in the summer.

Hoover thus left home and childhood with understandable enthusiasm. The major deprivations are clear: he lost both his parents, suddenly and unexpectedly, by the age of eight, a severe loss of affection and stability, and he had been shuffled about, against his will, from one stern relative to another, separated from his brother and sister, powerless to shape any segment of his own life. He needed others, and he needed to get his own place in the world and hold it. All his work so far had brought him nothing but more work. Words were not yet part of his equipment; he had kept a tight-lipped sense of humiliation as person after person he relied on had agreed to abandon him to others.

## HOOVER: RESOURCES FROM CHILDHOOD

Neither the political nor the rhetorical emphasis in Coolidge's upbringing were there for Hoover. His uncle Laban was an Indian agent and his Uncle Henry Minthorn had been one; Hoover vaguely remembered the Garfield campaign of 1880 and the lone (and drunken) Democrat in West Branch. That appears to have been the extent of his political exposure. Nor is there any record of early appearances before an audience. He did not like school: years later, asked to name his favorite study, he replied "None. They were something to race through—so I could get out of doors." He remembered some of his teachers with affection, but their lessons appear to have made no substantive impression on him. At home there were no novels, "save those with Total Abstinence as hero and Rum as villain." He and his brother read —surreptitiously—"Youth's Companion," a mild thriller of the day, and, with their cousin George acted out the parts. At first "Bertie" acted as look-out in case someone should discover this sinful behavior; then he was pro-moted to "super parts":

> When Tad commanded the Colonial army, Bertie was that army; he was also the white maiden bound to the stake, while George as the Indian Chief tortured her and Tad as the *Deerslayer* came to the rescue (Irwin, 1928, 15).

Not even at play, then, did he take the lead.

But these indoor intellectual forays never compared in Hoover's ex-perience or memory with the outdoors and the physical. The early pages of his *Memoirs* read like a nature book, full of owls and rabbits and fish. He and his cousins played with machinery and put an old thresher back to-gether; in Oregon he and another office boy tried to repair sewing machines for sale. The heritage was much stronger from the males of his line—the farmers and blacksmith—than from his mother's religiousness. In the office he was efficient in detail, learned to run a typewriter, and spent as much time as he could in the hills. The focus was on things, not words. He recalls a kind teacher who got him started on *Ivanhoe,* an "opening of the door to a great imaginative world" which "led me promptly through much of Scott and Dickens, often at the cost of sleep," but "Oregon lives in my mind for its gleaming wheat fields, its abundant fruit, its luxuriant forest vegetation, and the fish in the mountain streams." On Sunday evening he was allowed to read "an improving book," but one wonders how much of that there was after the Sabbath routine:

> On Sunday mornings, when work of necessity was done, came Sabbath school; then the long meeting; then dinner; then a period of sluggish rest followed by a Band of Hope meeting, where the lecturer or teacher dis-played colored prints of the drunkard's dreadful interior on each stage of his downward path, with corresponding illustrations of his demeanor and conduct (Irwin, 1928, 30).

Unlike most men who have become President, Hoover had in his background virtually nothing of legitimating family example, identification with political figures, or practice in expressing ideas to audiences.

## HOOVER: FIRST INDEPENDENT POLITICAL SUCCESS

The same September that Coolidge entered Amherst, Hoover entered Stanford. At seventeen he was the youngest and, reportedly, the youngest-looking student in the first class at that new university. Will Irwin describes the effect the next four years had on Herbert Hoover:

> He had lived, so far as he was aware, a happy childhood. But after all, that sympathetic brooding which makes childhood supremely happy had been lacking to his life since he was nine (sic) years old; for the greater part of another seven years a repressed atmosphere, wherein his extraordinary intelligence had no proper soil for growth; and hard work at menial or mechanical tasks. The atmosphere of freedom, of high animal spirits, the intellectual stimulus of those original young professors who went adventuring to Stanford—these struck in. Here he knew his first joy of the intellect, here he felt the initial stirring of his higher powers, here he found his wife. Stanford became a kind of complex with Herbert Hoover. Within fifteen years his interests and his wanderings were to embrace the globe; but those golden hills above Palo Alto were always the pole to his compass (Irwin, 1928, 33–34).

Hoover came to Stanford early in the summer of 1891 to be tutored. Still one subject short of the number required at the end of the summer, he studied a couple of physiology textbooks for two straight nights and passed an examination. He was admitted "conditioned in English"—the language came hard for him, "then and for many years he was impatient with words." He took English examinations twice a year for the next several years without success. In his senior year he failed German. The English "condition" was finally removed to allow him to graduate, when two of his engineering professors argued that his technical reports showed sufficient literary skill. In class and out of class he "said little and listened a lot; there was a wordless eagerness about him," as Lyons puts it. As a sophomore he was "shy to the point of timidity—rarely spoke unless spoken to," his classmate Lester Hinsdale recalled from their lunches together. Irwin remembers Hoover visiting him in the infirmary when Hoover was a senior.

> He did not say a word of sympathy for me—in pain and forever out of football—but I felt it nevertheless. Then, at the door he turned for an instant and jerked out: "I'm sorry." Just that; but it was as though another man had burst into maudlin tears (Irwin, 1928, 60).

When he met his future wife in geological laboratory—he was a senior, she a freshman—he was tongue-tied and red-faced. No other girls were among his close friends at Stanford, nor were there any "frivolous flirtations." It is important to note, then, that verbal expressiveness had no part in Hoover's success at Stanford. He never found there a way to attract attention or to achieve his goals through speechmaking or even facile conversation. That mouth so tightly shut at critical moments in his childhood symbolized his verbal restraint at Stanford and as President (though not as Secretary of Commerce). Typically Hoover talked haltingly, rarely looking the other in the eye, with one foot thrust forward as he jingled the keys in his pocket.

## SUCCESS CAME FROM SYSTEMATIC AND ORDERED WORK

Hoover's success at Stanford came from work, not words, and from a way of relating to others. He began his extracurricular working career at college by hiring on as a clerk in the registration of the new class. The skill exercised was meticulous attention to detail. Later in his freshman year Professor Branner employed him to do typing, again a matter of careful mechanical work. Then he branched out; he and two partners established a newspaper route and a laundry service for the students. These were soon sublet to other students, providing a small but regular income for Hoover. His entrepreneurial talents were beginning to emerge. Later he sold out the laundry for $40 and he and a new friend started a cooperative residence for students in Palo Alto, a project he dropped soon because it kept him away from the campus.

In the summer after Hoover's freshman year, Professor Branner got him a job with the Geological Survey of Arkansas, of which Branner had been State Geologist, at $60 a month and expenses. In his two subsequent Stanford summers he worked for the United States Geological Survey in California and in Nevada. That first summer "I did my job on foot, mostly alone, stopping at nights at the nearest cabin" in the Ozarks, making systematic notes, gathering and filing away facts, observations. The mountaineers were suspicious of travelling inquirers: "I finally gave up trying to explain." In the subsequent summers Hoover was "far happier," he writes. He worked as a "cub assistant" to Dr. Waldemar Lindgren, riding a horse all day and camping out with the survey team at night. Hoover very much wanted this job. At the first of the post-sophomore summer he was not yet employed, so he and a friend canvassed San Francisco for contacts for putting up billboard advertising. They signed up "a few hundred dollars" worth of contracts and went to work. Then Hoover heard of the geological survey and that there was a place for him with it. He walked 80 miles in three days to take it on.

Hoover's exact role in these two latter summers needs specification. He was, "as the youngest member of the Geological party," the disbursing officer: "I had to buy supplies and keep the accounts according to an elaborate book of regulations which provided wondrous safeguards for the public treasury." Carefulness by the book again, combined with outdoor energy and listening to the experts around the campfire.

Hoover returned to Stanford and extended his business enterprises. For a brief time he was a shortstop on the baseball team but soon became manager, "arranging games, collecting the gate money and otherwise finding cash for equipment and uniforms." He did so well at that that he was advanced to manager of the football team. One game produced $30,018. Hoover was acquiring a reputation for management. Operating in a new and developing environment without precedents he was under demand as the man who could—and would—take care of a wide variety of chores and enterprises for his fellows. Branner knew him for his efficiency; when other students complained that Hoover seemed to have too much pull with the famous geologist, he replied "But I can tell Hoover to do a thing and never think of it again." These talents also gave him his start in campus politics.

## HIS START IN CAMPUS POLITICS

Like Coolidge, Hoover was a "Barbarian" at Stanford. Fraternities developed quickly among the richer students interested in social prominence. He was not one of those. Sam Collins, one of the oldest members of Hoover's class, had proposed the cooperative rooming house at the beginning of their sophomore year. Collins was impressed with Hoover's system and order in straightening out the finances. Under Collins' tutelage Hoover first got involved in college politics when he was brought in with a group of "Barbarians" that organized to overthrow fraternity control of the student offices and activities. A zealot named "Sosh" (for "socialist") Zion declared his candidacy for student body president; "Collins swung in behind him in this campaign, and Hoover followed." He was assigned to canvass the "camp," the students who lived in rough shacks left over by the workers constructing the new college. Still he was "rather inarticulate—this repressed boy of eighteen" but he did what he could and the Barbs won, in a close vote.

The next summer Hoover worked for Dr. Lindgren, but he also thought about ways of organizing the many student activities at Stanford some of which had been very sloppily run and one of which had had a scandal. Hoover returned in the fall with a draft of a new constitution in which student activities would be brought together under the control of the student body. In addition to a president and a football manager, a treasurer, bonded and double-audited, would handle the finances. Hoover's plan was modified in some detail in bull sessions with Collins and others; they decided to put off a move for it until electing, under the existing rules, a student government sympathetic to the plan the following spring.

In the spring term, this group gathered again and developed a ticket, with Lester Hinsdale as candidate for president, Herbert Hicks for football manager, and Herbert Hoover for treasurer. Hoover was reluctant. He thought the treasurer, who would collect a salary, should be a graduate student.

> "But there's the salary," they said: "you can drop your work for Doc Branner and your laundry agency. The job will support you."
> "No, sir"! responded Hoover, emphatically. "If I accept this nomination and get elected, there's one thing sure. I take no salary. Otherwise, they'll say I'm backing the new constitution just to get a paid job" (Irwin, 1928, 54)!

The "3-H" ticket won. Sosh Zion opposed the salary. Hoover refused to take it, though he worked like a demon for the remaining two years at Stanford as treasurer. The new student government got the student body to pass the new constitution.

Hoover spent the following summer working again for Dr. Lindgren, who put Hoover's name with his own on the various maps and reports. "Years later, Hoover confessed to a friend that no subsequent honor had puffed him up so much as this."

The next autumn, Hoover's junior year, he was busy running a lecture series, keeping the records and accounts for athletic events, and generally making himself useful. As Will Irwin recalled.

> In the conferences over this or that problem of our bijou party in a toy state he seemed hesitant of advancing an opinion. Then, when everyone else had expressed himself, he would come in with the final wise word . . . After all, ours was the world in miniature. I lived to see him in councils whose decisions meant life or death for millions; yet it was always the same mind and the same method (Irwin, 1928, 62).

Hoover, in other words, was one of the boys, but at the edges of the group in most of their activities. He was the reliable treasurer, the arranger of meetings, the hard-working but shy and restrained person. He was valued for his virtues, particularly his energy and carefulness, his thoroughgoing honesty. He was never a charismatic leader at Stanford. In nearly all of his activities, someone else—usually someone older like Professor Branner or Professor Lindgren or Sam Collins or Lester Hinsdale took the lead, and Hoover followed and served. Things got solved at Stanford in the caucus and Hoover took his part there. But there is not, in all of this student political and business activity, any record of his ever having spoken to a large gathering of his classmates. He was the man behind the scenes. He made friends, but many were the sort of friends whose respect is stronger than their affection.

In words, then, Hoover was restrained and not very expressive. In work he devoted all his energies to concentrated effort. In his personal relations he was a quiet, behind-the-scenes coordinator, not a leader. And so he was as President of the United States.

## A SUMMARY OF MAIN THEMES

The links between each style at the time of first independent political success and in the presidency are clear in these two cases. Briefly put:

For Coolidge, *rhetoric* in the presidency consisted of (a) serious, abstract, epigrammatic addresses, full of themes from Garman, delivered much like his serious debates and speeches at Amherst and (b) witty banter with reporters, much like his funny speeches to his fellow undergraduates. As president he avoided as much of the *business* of the office as he could; work on detail had played little or no part in his Amherst success. As president he avoided close personal relationships, keeping others at a distance with mildly aggressive wit; at Amherst intimate friendship or close cooperation had never been his style.

For Hoover, *rhetoric* was impossibly hard, and he failed at it, as words had so often failed him at Stanford. Forced to speak, he fell back on his mother's Quaker mysticism and his uncle's phony advertising. His whole soul was poured into the *business* of the office, meticulous attention to detail, and careful designs for the arrangement of things. At Stanford very similar efforts had brought him money, independence, respect and acceptance. In *personal relations,* President Hoover tried desperately, in conference after conference, to repeat his success at Stanford in gaining cooperation by mastering details and presenting his plan.

The similarities are evident. Analyzed retrospectively here, they seem amenable to discernment in their earlier forms by an analyst attuned to the role demands of the presidency.

## PRESIDENTIAL STYLE AND FIRST INDEPENDENT POLITICAL SUCCESS

There are fundamentally three steps in this argument. One is that there is such a thing as presidential style, in the sense of habitual patterns of performance in response to recurrent role demands. I have tried to illustrate how the flow of energy and affect in three channels captures, within a broader typological framework, the major dimensions of such styles. Presidents tend to solve their rhetorical problems, their problems of managing business, and their problems of adapting in close personal relations in characteristic, patterned ways, not randomly or simply as flexible, rational responses to historical events.

Second, there is an identifiable formative period, that of first independent political success, in which the major elements of presidential style are exhibited. Personality formation is a long, developmental process, subject to change before and after this period. But the *main, adaptively strategic, politically-relevant action patterns* are evidenced most clearly when a young man, drawing together themes from his past, present and anticipated future, answers for himself the question, "What works for me?" The fit between presidential style and the style of the formative period is not vague or mysterious, but direct: in rhetoric, business management, and personal relations presidents tend to behave as they did when they first found a way to succeed with these tools.

The third step in the argument is less clear. Why does this congruence occur? The answers are speculative. Most probably, the strength of the adaptive pattern derives from the confluence, in its original formation, of (a) satisfaction of strong needs for compensation for earlier deprivations, (b) at least some resources from the past applicable to present achievement, and (c) a favorable set of opportunities. At a deeper level of analysis, this pattern's staying power derives from a solution to the Eriksonian identity crisis; it may represent the behavioral manifestations of intensely emotional late-adolescent trial and victory. The outward signs of the formative period are a new surge of success on one's own, a new way of linking oneself to others and a new fame. To the psychoanalyst, these may be signs only, referents to much deeper developments in the meanings of work and luck, love and hate, thought and word. Psychoanalytical data would reveal, one suspects, such factors contributing strongly to habit formation in this critical period.

At an even more speculative level, the analogy between being president and emerging as a successful young adult with an individual style can be posed. Both are in some sense culminations of preparatory stages, modes in the curve of life, high points of achievement beyond which one may never go. Both are unique experiences, in the double sense that neither ever happens twice in the same life and that no two persons work them out in the same ways. Both highlight the lone individual discovering what he can make of a situation in which a great deal depends on his personal choices. A new president, scanning (though seldom consciously) his life's repertoire of successful strategies, might well turn to those which had worked so well for him as he became a man.

A few cases plus speculation do not make a theory. Yet as these ideas are refined they may find application in stylistic analysis not only of past presidents but also of men yet to be presidents. At that point we may be able to move beyond some of the many uncertainties of prediction, to guess better than we have, and before the fact, what the most powerful politician in the world will do with that power.

## REFERENCES

Barber, James David, *The Lawmakers: Recruitment and Adaptation to Legislative Life* (New Haven: Yale University Press, 1965). *Journal of Politics,* 28, 1966.

Barber, James David, "Leadership Strategies for Legislative Party Cohesion,"

Coolidge, Calvin, *The Autobiography of Calvin Coolidge* (New York: Cosmopolitan, 1929).

Cornwell, Elmer E. Jr., *Presidential Leadership of Public Opinion* (Bloomington: Indiana University Press, 1965).

Fuess, Claude M., *Calvin Coolidge: the Man from Vermont* (Hamden, Conn.: Archon Books, 1965).

Hinshaw, David, *Herbert Hoover: American Quaker* (New York: Farrar, Straus, 1950).

Hoover, Herbert, *The Memoirs of Herbert Hoover: 1874–1920, Years of Adventure* (New York: Macmillan, 1951).

Hoover, Herbert, *The Memoirs of Herbert Hoover: 1920–1933, The Cabinet and the Presidency* (New York: Macmillan, 1952).

Irwin, Will, *Herbert Hoover: a Reminiscent Biography* (New York: Century, 1928).

Joslin, Theodore G., *Hoover: Off the Record* (Garden City, N.Y.: Doubleday, Doran, 1934).

Lasswell, Harold D., *Psychopathology and Politics* (New York: Viking Press, 1960).

Lasswell, Harold D., *Power and Personality* (New York: Viking Press, 1962).

Liggett, Walter N., *The Rise of Herbert Hoover* (New York: H. K. Fly, 1932).

Lowry, Edward G., *Washington Close-ups: Intimate Views of Some Public Figures* (Boston: Houghton Mifflin, 1921).

Lyons, Eugene, *Our Unknown Ex-President: a Portrait of Herbert Hoover* (Garden City, N.Y.: Doubleday, 1948).

McCoy, Donald R., *Calvin Coolidge: the Quiet President* (New York: Macmillan, 1967).

Meyers, William Starr (ed.), *The State Papers and Other Public Writings of Herbert Hoover.* Vol. 2 (Oct. 1, 1931 to March 4, 1933) (New York: Doubleday, Doran, 1934).

Schlesinger, Arthur M. Jr., *The Age of Roosevelt: the Crisis of the Old Order, 1919–1933* (Boston: Houghton Mifflin, 1957).

Shapiro, David, *Neurotic Styles* (New York: Basic Books, 1965).

Warren, Harris Gaylord, *Herbert Hoover and the Great Depression* (New York: W. W. Norton, 1967).

Wolfe, Harold, *Herbert Hoover: Public Servant and Leader of the Loyal Opposition* (New York: Exposition Press, 1965).

Wood, Clement, *Herbert Clark Hoover: An American Tragedy* (New York: Michael Swain, 1932).

# 4 Role

## The Roles of Legislators in the Legislative Process

JOHN C. WAHLKE, HEINZ EULAU, WILLIAM BUCHANAN,
AND LEROY C. FERGUSON

### THE LEGISLATOR AS A DECISION MAKER: PURPOSIVE ROLES

Since "lawmaking" is accepted as the central function of American state legislatures, participation in the making of decisions is not only expected of the legislator but is authorized and legitimized by his occupancy of the official position. But "participation in lawmaking or decision making" is hardly a satisfactory characterization of the role of legislator. Rather it is role orientations which are the specifications of the legislative role, without which the central concept of "legislator" does not, and probably cannot, have much analytical meaning.

His role orientations are probably not unrelated to the legislator's perception of the power pattern of a political system and the kinds of functions which the legislature is called on to perform. For instance, in a party-disciplined legislature the individual legislator is unlikely to find much room for independence or inventiveness; the purely routine aspects of his job probably loom large in his legislative role orientations. In a legislature particularly exposed to the pulls and pressures of interest groups, role orientations are likely to derive from the need to arbitrate, compromise, and integrate group conflicts. In the legislature subservient to the whims and wishes of the electorate, the spokesman function is likely to be accentuated in legislative role orientations. In a legislature which enjoys relatively great independence from

John C. Wahlke, Heinz Eulau, William Buchanan, and LeRoy C. Ferguson, "The Roles of Legislators in the Legislative Process." *Role Theory: Concepts and Research*. Edited by Bruce J. Biddle and Edwin J. Thomas. New York: John Wiley & Sons, Inc., 1966, 243–254. Copyright © 1966 by John Wiley & Sons, Inc. Abridged from pages 245–422 of a book by the same authors entitled *The Legislative System: Explorations in Legislative Behavior*. New York: John Wiley, 1962. Copyright © 1962 by John Wiley & Sons, Inc. Reprinted by permission of the authors and Wiley. This study was supported in part by a grant from the Committee on Political Behavior.

the executive, legislative role orientations may stress the creative, policy-making aspects of the job. Moreover, legislative role orientations need not occur in pristine singularity. Two and three, or even more, orientations may be held by a legislator.

The complexity of institutionally derived legislative role orientations becomes even more apparent if we place them in a historical perspective. They may be, and probably are, patterned by past as well as current configurations in the power structure of the political system. For as institutions, legislatures are phenomena in time, with memories of their own going beyond the limitations of time. These memories are transmitted by legislators themselves from generation to generation, consciously or unconsciously shaping the perceptions of the present. The past may thus continue to serve as a model for contemporary role orientations.

A legislature is the product of a long and slow growth over centuries, with a veritable maze of rules, procedures, privileges, duties, etiquettes, rituals, informal understandings and arrangements. Every phase of the lawmaking process—from the introduction of bills through their deliberation in committee and debate on the floor to the final vote—has gradually become circumscribed by appropriate strategies and tactics. The legislator was always expected to master the rules of parliamentary procedure and be familiar with available strategies. Hence the legislator could traditionally orient himself to the job of lawmaking in terms of the parliamentary rules and routines, rather than in terms of legislative functions as they may be shaped by the power situation in the political system. Parliamentary ritual rather than parliamentary goals would absorb his attention. One may call this orientation to the legislative role that of the *Ritualist.*

A second orientation is particularly deeply rooted in American political history. It was probably generated by the conflict between the British Crown, acting through the agency of the appointed governor, and the colonial legislatures. In the course of this conflict the legislature came to be viewed as the instrument through which colonial interests could be defended against what were perceived as royal encroachments on colonial rights. It does not matter, in this connection, that the colonists differed among themselves with regard to the proper object of legislative activity—whether the defense of property rights or the natural rights of man were the goals of colonial claims. The crucial point is that the legislature and legislators were expected to be advocates or defenders of popular demands. Wilfred E. Binkley has aptly described the role orientation of the colonial legislator—what we shall call the role orientation of *Tribune:* "The assemblyman, chosen by popular election as a representative of his neighbourhood . . . set forth to the provincial capital, commissioned, as he believed, to fight the people's battle against the governor" (Binkley, 1947, p. 4).

A third major orientation seems to have originated at a later stage of colonial-executive relations, the stage when the legislature asserted itself as an institution capable of performing independent, policy-making functions. As Alfred De Grazia has summarized this later development, "The Colonial legislatures already conceived of themselves as possessed of a positive legislative capacity removed from the ancient English idea of Parliament as an agency for wresting concessions from the Crown. They had learned well the lessons of the seventeenth century revolutions as well as those to be obtained from the Bill of Rights. Legislatures, they had come to realize, could govern" (De Grazia, 1951, p. 70). Once the colonial legislature was expected to be an instrument of governance, rather than an instrument of obstruction, a role orientation more appropriate to the legislature's new functions was likely to emerge. We shall call this the orientation of *Inventor*. The legislator was now expected to be sensitive to public issues, discover potential solutions and explore alternatives, both with regard to means as well as ends. The problems of government were deemed soluble by way of rational deliberation and cogent argument in debate, partly because the issues were relatively simple, not requiring technical, expert knowledge; partly because the range of governmental activity was seen as very limited.

Just as the role orientation of inventor derived from the conception of the legislature as a creative, policy-making institution, a fourth orientation— we shall call it that of *Broker*—developed in response to the rise of interest groups and the increasing number of demands made on legislatures by pressure groups. The legislature became, in the course of the nineteenth century, a major integrating force in the pluralism of American political, social, and economic life. This development had been foreshadowed by the struggle of interests in the Constitutional Convention, in early Congresses and state legislatures, and had suggested to the authors of *The Federalist* the balancing function of legislative bodies. The role orientation of broker was probably implicit in Hamilton's notion of the disinterested representative (*The Federalist,* 35), and though everyday politics seemed to confirm this conception of the legislator's role as a working principle, it was not articulated in political theory until fairly recently.

This review of legislative role orientations, whether theoretically derived from the legislature's place in the power structure of the political system or historically reconstructed, has suggested four major types—ritualist, tribune, inventor, and broker. There may be others. For example, journalistic accounts suggest many legislators have an orientation which might be called *opportunist*—the legislator who holds the office without really "taking" the associated role, who accepts the bare minimum of expectations, such as voting on roll calls and attending committee meetings or sessions as a passive participant, but who mainly uses the legislative office, or "plays *at*" the legislative role while concealing that he is really playing other, essentially nonlegislative roles.

## THE LEGISLATOR AS REPRESENTATIVE: REPRESENTATIONAL ROLES

The problem of representation is central to all discussions of the functions of legislatures or the behavior of legislators. For it is through the process of representation, presumably, that legislatures are empowered to act for the whole body politic and legitimized. And because, by virtue of representation, they participate in legislation, the represented accept legislative decisions as authoritative. It would seem, therefore, that legislation and representation are closely related. And if they are related, the functional relevance of representation to legislative behavior needs to be articulated.

But agreement about the meaning of the term "representation" hardly goes beyond a general consensus regarding the context within which it is appropriately used. In the following we shall describe [three] orientational types as they were defined by legislators themselves.

### Trustee

The role orientation of trustee finds expression in two major conceptions of how decisions ought to be made. These conceptions may occur severally and jointly. There is, first, a moralistic interpretation. The trustee sees himself as a free agent in that, as a premise of his decision-making behavior, he claims to follow what he considers right or just, his convictions and principles, the dictates of his conscience. There is also a judgmental conception of the role of trustee. The trustee is not bound by a mandate because his decisions are his own considered judgments based on an assessment of the facts in each decision, his understanding of all the problems and angles involved, his thoughtful appraisal of the sides at issue.

A great variety of conceptions of representation are involved in the role orientation of the trustee. In particular, it seems that this orientation derives not only from a normative definition of the role of the representative, but that it is also often grounded in interpersonal situations which make it functionally inevitable. The condition that the represented do not have the information necessary to give intelligent instructions, that the representative is unable to discover what his clientele may want, that preferences remain unexpressed, that there is no need for instructions because of an alleged harmony of interests between representative and represented—all of the circumstances may be acknowledged as sources of the role orientation of trustee, at times even forced on the representative against his own predilection for a mandate if that were possible.

## Delegate

Just as the trustee role orientation involves a variety of conceptions of representation, so does the orientation of delegate. All delegates are agreed, of course, that they should not use their independent judgment or principled convictions as decision-making premises. But this does not mean that they feel equally committed to follow instructions, from whatever clientele. Some merely say that they try to inform themselves before making decisions by consulting their constituents or others; however, they seem to imply that such consultation has a mandatory effect on their behavior: "I do ask them (i.e., constituents) quite often, especially where there's doubt in my mind." Others frankly acknowledge instructions as necessary or desirable premises in decision making: "I do what they want me to do. Being re-elected is the best test"; or, "A majority of the people always gets their way with me." Finally, there is the representative in the delegate role who not only feels that he should follow instructions, but who also believes that he should do so even if these instructions are explicitly counter to his own judgment or principles: "Some things I'm not particularly sold on but if the people want it, they should have it"; or, "Reflect the thinking of my district even if it is not my own private thinking."

What strikes one in the comments [of delegates], in contrast to those made by trustees, is the failure to elaborate in greater detail the problem of why the representative should follow instructions in his decision-making behavior. Delegates, it seems, have a simpler, more mechanical conception of the political process and of the function of representation in legislative behavior. Perhaps most noticeable, in contrast to the trustee orientation, is the omission of delegates to raise the question of political responsibility under conditions of strict instructions. Apparently, the problem is ignored by the delegate precisely because he rejects the possibility of discretion in his decision making. It is a matter of speculation whether the role orientation of delegate is based on a conscious majoritarian bias which he could elaborate and defend if necessary, or whether it simply reflects lack of political articulation and sophistication. On the other hand, the fact that the delegate seems to have so little doubt about this role suggests that, whatever his reasons and regardless of whether his decisions are really in accord with the views of different groups among his clientele, he is likely to be characterized by a fairly high sense of personal effectiveness in his approach to law-making.

## Politico

As suggested earlier, the classical dichotomization of the concept of representation in terms of independent judgment and mandate was unlikely to
exhaust the empirical possibilities of representational behavior. In particular,
it would seem to be possible for a representative to act in line with both
criteria. For roles and role orientations need not be mutually exclusive.
Depending on circumstances, a representative may hold the role orientation
of trustee at one time, and the role orientation of delegate at another time.
Or he might even seek to reconcile both orientations in terms of a third.
In other words, the representational-role set comprises the extreme orientations of trustee and delegate and a third orientation, the politico, resulting
from overlap of these two. Within the orientational range called politico, the
trustee and delegate roles may be taken simultaneously, possibly making for
role conflict, or they may be taken seriatim, one after another as legislative
situations dictate.

Because our data do not permit us to discriminate too sharply between these two possibilities, we shall speak of legislators who express both
orientations, either simultaneously or serially, as politicos.

In general the politico as a representational-role taker differs from
both the trustee and the delegate in that he seems to be more sensitive to
conflicting alternatives, more flexible in the ways in which he tries to resolve
the conflict among alternatives, and less dogmatic in his orientation towards
legislative behavior as it is related to his representational role.

## THE LEGISLATOR AND HIS DISTRICT: AREAL ROLES

Representation of geographical areas introduces a certain amount of ambiguity into the relationship between representative and represented. Part
of this ambiguity involves the widely held expectation, contested by Ed-
mund Burke but shared by many citizens and politicians alike, that the
legislator is a spokesman of the presumed "interests" of his district. Implicit
in this expectation is the assumption that a geographical unit has interests
which are distinct and different from those of other units. This assumption
has been challenged on a variety of grounds: that the geographical area as
such, as an electoral unit, is artificial; that it cannot and does not generate
interests shared by its residents; that it has no unique interests; and so on.
Schemes of proportional or vocational representation have been advanced to
make possible the representation of allegedly more "natural" interest groupings, such as minority, skill, or economic groups.

Yet, the assumption that geographical districts have unique interests
which are, or ought to be, taken into consideration when legislative decisions

are made, continues to be shared not only by voters, politicians, and others involved in policy making, but also by scientific students of the political process. It underlies many studies which seek to relate legislative roll-call votes to socio-economic characteristics of electoral districts, as well as those studies which analyze the socio-economic composition of legislatures.

Such an interpretation is most tenuous under modern conditions. Electorial districts tend to be so heterogeneous in population attributes, so pluralistic in the character of their group life, so diverse in the kinds of values and beliefs held, that whatever measures of central tendency are used to classify a district are more likely to conceal than to reveal its real character. The notion that elections are held as a method to discover persons whose attributes and attitudes will somehow mirror those most widely shared by people in their district appears to be of dubious validity. The function of representation in modern political systems is not to make the legislature a mathematically exact copy of the electorate.

But the difficulty of finding an identity between representative and represented does not mean that a legislator's point of reference in making decisions cannot be his district. It may or may not be, and whether it is or not is a matter of empirical determination. We may doubt that what orients a legislator towards his district rather than some other focus of attention is the similarity between his district's characteristics and his own. Or we may assume that a legislator incorporates in himself the characteristics of his district—which, for argument's sake, may be admitted when he comes from a relatively homogeneous area. But it is still an empirical question whether or not the legislator is subjectively concerned with his district and seeks to discover its "interests."

In spite of the considerations just mentioned, state legislators perceive representation of the interests of some geographical area as a proper function of their legislative activities. On the basis of their responses, we classified legislators into "district oriented," "state oriented," and "district-state oriented."

### District Oriented

District-oriented legislators indicated two types of response patterns: some simply mentioned their district or county as an important focus of their areal role orientation; others explicitly placed district above state in defining this orientation.

A second major group of district-oriented legislators specifically pointed to the importance of placing the interests of their district above those of the state. Their concern with the state's interests usually appeared as an afterthought. But, as one respondent put it, "you cannot actually disassociate one from the other."

### State Oriented

State-oriented legislators either mentioned the state alone as the salient focus of their areal orientation, or they also mentioned the district, but clearly tending to place the state above district in importance. Some of them emphasized the need for state policy or state program as an overriding consideration. A second group of state-oriented legislators pointed to both the state and the district as relevant foci of their role orientation, but tended to give the benefit of doubt to the state. Finally, some of the state-oriented legislators explicitly stressed the desirability of overcoming parochial considerations in favor of the state.

### District-State Oriented

A third group of legislators who spontaneously concerned themselves with the areal focus of their legislative role mentioned both district and state as equally relevant to their legislative or service activities. Apparently, they did not envisage the possibility of conflict arising out of these orientations and thought that they could attend to the interests of both state and district without undue complications.

## LEGISLATORS' ROLE ORIENTATIONS TOWARD PRESSURE GROUPS

Further insight into the character and function of pressure politics requires examination of individual legislators' postures toward pressure groups and their reasons for them—both "reasons" they adduce and correlations between legislators' postures and analytic variables established by analysts. We are concerned here, it should be emphasized, with the functioning of the legislative *institution* and not with unique historical events or outcomes. Similarly, we are concerned with legislators' orientation toward pressure groups as a *generic* class of "significant others," not with their particular individual group affiliations and identifications.

With respect to the bearing of pressure politics on the function of representation, the basic question is, how, and how much, are demands of interest groups considered by a legislature in the course of its decision making? In general some members will accommodate the demands of organized interest groups in the legislative process. Others will resist consideration or accommodation of these demands. Still others, presumably attuned to other persons or factors, will play a neutral or varying and indeterminate role toward such group demands.

It seems obvious that a legislator's reaction to the activities of pressure groups and lobbyists will depend in part upon his general evaluation of pressure politics as a mode of political activity in the world he lives in. It likewise seems obvious that legislators' reactions to pressure groups or lobbyists will vary with their different degrees of knowledge or awareness of group activities. The legislator who knows what the Municipal League is, what it wants, who speaks for it and when, will react differently to cues from the League than one who never heard of it and doesn't identify anyone as its spokesman.

Assuming, then, that any given legislator's behavior with respect to pressure groups will depend largely upon his general affective orientation toward pressure politics and his awareness of such activity when it occurs around him, one can construct the following very simple typology of legislators' role orientations toward pressure groups:

> Facilitators: Have a friendly attitude toward group activity *and* relatively much knowledge about it.
>
> Resistors: Have a hostile attitude toward group activity *and* relatively much knowledge about it.
>
> Neutrals: Have no strong attitude of favor or disfavor with respect to group activity (regardless of their knowledge of it), or, have very little knowledge about it (regardless of their friendliness or hostility toward it).

## THE NETWORK OF ROLES: AN IDEAL-TYPE CONSTRUCT

The analytical distinction between clientele, representational, and purposive roles is helpful in dissecting the legislator's total role. Actual behavior, however, is not a function of discrete roles, but of a system of roles. It is the network of interpenetrating roles which gives structure and coherence to the legislative process. Comparative analysis of the eight chambers of four states included in this study supports the notion that roles are meaningfully related to each other. Moreover, the patterning of observed relations and differences is such that it is possible to develop an ideal-type construct of the total network. Such an ideal-type construct is, of course, an exaggeration of empirical reality, but it can serve two valuable purposes: first, it can demonstrate the logic of the postulated network; and, second, it can serve as an independent criterion for comparing the concrete, empirical role systems.

Figure 1 presents a diagram of the ideal-type network of legislators' roles suggested by the clustering of role orientations empirically found in the four states and by the theoretical considerations. The diagram reflects the observed tendency of certain orientations in one sector to be associated with particular orientations in others. Thus, the upper half of the diagram idealizes the following pairs of role orientations: majority-state-oriented,

Figure 1. Ideal-type Network of Roles.

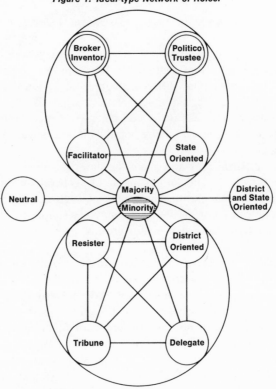

majority-facilitator, state-oriented-facilitator, facilitator-politico, majority-politico, majority-broker, state-oriented-trustee, state-oriented-inventor/broker, facilitator-broker, broker-trustee/politico, and inventor-trustee. The lower half idealizes these pairs: minority-district-oriented, minority-resister, district-oriented-resister, resister-delegate, minority-delegate, minority-inventor/tribune, district-oriented-delegate, district-oriented-tribune, resister-tribune, and tribune-delegate. The diagram thus suggests two essentially reciprocal sets of relationships or dimensions, one represented in the upper, the other in the lower half of the diagram. The neutral and district-state orientations do not associate readily in theory with either of these, but, as the diagram shows, stand more or less outside and between them.

Any individual legislator is likely to be located more in one than another dimension of this network of available roles. Moreover, it is the network as such, rather than simple adoption of one orientation instead of another, which is crucial to the individual's behavior. That is to say, the difference between one role and another in a given subsystem—such as, for instance, the difference between facilitator and resister, or between trustee and delegate—is a function of the total network of roles. In such a network, each role is somehow related to every other role, and the character and extent of these relations gives any one empirical legislative role system its peculiar character.

We have not attempted to characterize the different patterns or clusterings of role orientation which might be manifested by the individual legislator, in terms of the ideal-type network illustrated in Figure 1. We have, instead, sought to characterize the system differences resulting from the various constellations of role orientation found to prevail in the four legislatures. In other words, although the diagram represents the coincidence of particular role orientations for the individual legislator, we are interested in it as a representation of the aggregates of role orientations and role relationships constituting a system of role relationships among legislators in particular legislatures. We wish to use the ideal-type construct of the network of roles to characterize differences among legislative systems. It is to this that we turn in the next section.

## LEGISLATIVE ROLE STRUCTURES

Ideally, it would be desirable to identify and specify the entire matrix of all role combinations in a given legislative system. Unfortunately, even the largest chamber in this study includes too few cases to isolate empirically the theoretically possible matrix of roles in combination. However, we can construct a partial framework by dealing with the most frequent individual pairs of roles that are taken in a legislative chamber. Each of these "dominant pairs" may or may not be linked because any one role in one pair may also be linked with a third role in another pair.

Table 1 presents the dominant (i.e., the most frequent) pairs of roles in the two chambers of each state legislature. The base of the proportions is the total number of legislators whose individual roles appeared in the dominant pairs. For instance, of the California House members for whom data were available, 30 per cent are district-oriented minority members, 26 per cent are majority-neutrals, 27 per cent are district-oriented facilitators, and so on.

### House Role Structures

The distributions in Table 1 yield some interesting results, but they are difficult to inspect and appraise. There are two ways in which we can simplify the emerging structures—one numerical, the other graphical. First, we can single out the number of times a given role appears in a dominant pair. Table 2 presents this alternative. The patterns for each role set are clear. They sensitize us to the significance of particular distributions in the more complex array of Table 1. In the first place, in the New Jersey and Ohio Houses, where "party government" has genuine meaning, the role of majority member appears among the dominant pairs, but the role of minority member does not. In California, where "party control" has little meaning,

**Table 1.** Proportions of Dominant Role Pairs in the Four Legislatures

| Lower Chambers | | | | | | | | | | | |
|---|---|---|---|---|---|---|---|---|---|---|---|
| Ohio | N | % | N.J. | N | % | Calif. | N | % | Tenn. | N | % |
| Ma/Di-St | 94 | 31 | Ma/Di-St | 38 | 34 | Mi/Di | 50 | 30 | Ma/Di | 38 | 42 |
| Ma/Fa | 125 | 32 | Ma/Fa | 57 | 28 | Ma/Ne | 68 | 26 | Ma/Re | 87 | 31 |
| Di-St/Ne | 89 | 19 | Di-St/Fa | 37 | 19 | Di/Fa | 44 | 27 | Di/Re | 38 | 23 |
| Ma/Tr | 94 | 35 | Ma/Tr | 39 | 41 | Ma/Tr | 37 | 30 | Ma/Tr | 61 | 59 |
| St/Tr | 75 | 20 | Di-St/Tr | 26 | 23 | Di/De | 23 | 30 | Di/Tr | 31 | 29 |
|  |  |  | St/Tr | 26 | 23 |  |  |  |  |  |  |
| Fa/Tr | 92 | 24 | Fa/Tr | 39 | 26 | Ne/Tr | 32 | 31 | Ne/Tr | 59 | 36 |
| Ma/Br | 130 | 36 | Ma/Tri | 58 | 47 | Mi/Tri | 78 | 28 | Ma/Tri | 89 | 48 |
| Di-St/Br | 95 | 27 | Di-St/Tri | 37 | 32 | Di/Tri | 49 | 47 | Di/Tri | 37 | 49 |
| Fa/Br | 125 | 24 | Fa/Tri | 57 | 23 | Ne/Tri | 68 | 22 | Ne/Tri | 87 | 28 |
| Br/Tr | 120 | 23 | In/Tr | 55 | 31 | In/Tr | 47 | 19 | Tri/Tr | 66 | 41 |
| Senates | | | | | | | | | | | |
| Ma/Di-St | 18 | 22 | Ma/Di | 16 | 25 | Ma/Di | 28 | 25 | Ma/Di | 8 | 50 |
| Ma/Di | 18 | 22 | Mi/Di | 16 | 25 |  |  |  |  |  |  |
| Mi/Di | 18 | 22 |  |  |  |  |  |  |  |  |  |
| Ma/Fa | 32 | 28 | Ma/Fa | 21 | 29 | Mi/Fa | 29 | 28 | Ma/Re | 29 | 38 |
| Di/Fa | 19 | 27 | Di-St/Fa | 16 | 31 | Di/Ne | 24 | 21 | Di/Re | 8 | 38 |
| Ma/Tr | 20 | 50 | Ma/Tr | 15 | 33 | Ma/Tr | 12 | 33 | Ma/Tr | 17 | 76 |
| Di/Tr | 13 | 23 | Di/De | 13 | 31 | Di-St/Tr | 12 | 34 | Di/Tr | 5 | 80 |
| St/Tr | 13 | 23 |  |  |  |  |  |  |  |  |  |
| Ne/Tr | 20 | 30 | Fa/Po | 15 | 27 | Fa/Tri | 12 | 50 | Re/Tr | 17 | 41 |
| Ma/Br | 32 | 28 | Ma/In | 21 | 38 | Ma/Tri | 35 | 34 | Ma/Tri | 31 | 42 |
| Di/Tri | 17 | 41 | Di/Tri | 16 | 44 | Di/Tri | 28 | 29 | Di/Tri | 8 | 63 |
|  |  |  |  |  |  | St/Tri | 28 | 29 |  |  |  |
| Fa/Br | 32 | 22 | Fa/Tri | 23 | 38 | Ne/Tri | 29 | 28 | Re/Tri | 29 | 28 |
| In/Tr | 24 | 25 | In/Po | 21 | 19 | Br/Tr | 17 | 24 | Tri/Tr | 18 | 50 |
| Br/Tr | 24 | 25 | Tri/De | 21 | 19 | Tri/Po | 17 | 24 |  |  |  |

*Key:*
Ma = majority   De = delegate   In = inventor   Re = resister
Mi = minority   Di = district   Ne = neutral   Tri = tribune
Br = broker   Di-St = district-state   Po = politico   Tr = trustee
   Fa = facilitator

both the roles of majority and minority member are encountered in the dominant pairs. Tennessee represents a special case: although formally the role of "majority member" alone occurs in the dominant pairs, we know that the "majority" is factionalized and not a majority in the same sense as in the competitive party states. The Tennessee House is actually composed of competing "minorities," and though the role of majority member seems present in the dominant pairs, it cannot be taken in a literal sense.

Second, in the representational-role set, the role of trustee occurs in the dominant pairs almost exclusively, with the single exception of California, where the delegate role appears in one dominant pair. This role of trustee is, as we noted earlier, so universal that it is necessarily linked to any cluster in the total network of dominant pairs. In other words, it does not serve as a discriminating factor in a topology of role structures.

**Table 2.** Number of Times a Role Appears in Combination with Another in a Dominant Pair, Lower Chambers

| Role | Ohio | N.J. | Calif. | Tenn. |
|---|---|---|---|---|
| Party | | | | |
| Majority member | 4 | 4 | 2 | 4 |
| Minority member | 0 | 0 | 2 | 0 |
| Representational | | | | |
| Trustee | 4 | 5 | 3 | 4 |
| Politico | 0 | 0 | 0 | 0 |
| Delegate | 0 | 0 | 1 | 0 |
| Purposive | | | | |
| Inventor | 0 | 1 | 1 | 0 |
| Broker | 4 | 0 | 0 | 0 |
| Tribune | 0 | 3 | 3 | 4 |
| Areal | | | | |
| State oriented | 1 | 1 | 0 | 0 |
| District-State oriented | 3 | 4 | 0 | 0 |
| District oriented | 0 | 0 | 4 | 4 |
| Pressure group | | | | |
| Facilitator | 3 | 4 | 1 | 0 |
| Neutral | 1 | 0 | 3 | 2 |
| Resister | 0 | 0 | 0 | 2 |

Third, in the purposive-role set, the Ohio House role structure differs from the other three lower chamber structures in the pervasiveness of the broker role in dominant pairs, while elsewhere the tribune role is more prominent, suggesting a more "populist" milieu than prevailed in 1957 in the Republican-dominated Ohio House.

Fourth, of the areal-role set, the district role is present in dominant pairs in California and Tennessee, but not in Ohio and New Jersey. In the latter two states, the district-state role occurs in the dominant pairs, as does the state role in one pair, but neither of these two roles is present in the dominant California and Tennessee pairs. The pattern suggests that the areal-role orientations held by legislators may serve as critical discriminating devices in the characterization of legislative role structures.

Finally, the pressure-group-role set seems to perform a similar function. The facilitator role is prominent in Ohio's and New Jersey's dominant pairs, and the neutral role in California. Only in Tennessee does the resister role appear in dominant pairs, and it does so twice, while the facilitator role is altogether absent from dominant pairs.

The frequency of a role's appearance in dominant pairs, and the pattern of occurrences from state to state, give a first view of what one might expect when the linkages between those roles which constitute the dominant pairs are constructed graphically. The diagrams of the House structures presented in Figure 2 can be readily compared with the ideal-type construct [Figure 1]. This comparison makes it possible to develop an empirical typology of legislative role structures.

The Ohio diagram of Figure 2 shows a relatively highly integrated role cluster of what we may call the "majoritarian type." Almost all the ideal-type linkages are present, and where they are not they are replaced by "intermediate" roles in the dominant pairs (such as the district-state instead of the "pure" state role, or the neutral role instead of the facilitator role). But the linkages in no way penetrate into the reciprocal "minoritarian" cluster of the ideal-type model. Minority members are totally eclipsed as role takers in the dominant structure, as are such minority-linked roles of the ideal-type model as tribunes, resisters, delegates, and district oriented.

In the New Jersey House structure, also, the role of minority member and its ideally associated roles of delegate, resister, and district oriented are missing from the dominant majority-centered cluster. But, in contrast to Ohio, the tribune role of the minority cluster is linked three times to majority-anchored roles, and the reciprocal roles of the purposive-role set, ideally located in the majoritarian cluster, are not among the dominant pairs. With this one exception, then, the New Jersey House role structure is very similar to Ohio's. We can characterize the Ohio House structure as "broker-majoritarian" and the New Jersey House structure as "tribune-majoritarian."

By way of contrast, the California House role structure reveals a bipartisan pattern. The structure is not solely, as in the Ohio case, centered in the majority role (though the "majority" had organized the lower cham-

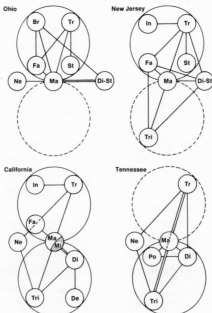

Figure 2. Role Structures of Four Lower Houses.

ber), nor is it predominantly so centered as in the case of New Jersey. The California structure includes elements of both the ideal-type majoritarian and minoritarian clusters. And not only do both majority and minority member roles appear in the dominant pairs, but the linkages cut across the boundaries of the reciprocal sets of the ideal-type model. The "populist" component is outstanding: the tribune and district-oriented roles are linked across cluster boundaries, but the majority-related roles of inventor and facilitator each appear in dominant pairs. The California House role structure reflects the strongly "atomistic" orientation of California legislators, and it is indicative of the low salience of party roles as premises for legislative behavior. We may term the California House role structure "populist-bipartisan."

Finally, the Tennessee House role structure is altogether different from the previous types. Though formally "majoritarian," it is in fact minority geared: the tribune and district roles are most pervasive, and, alone among the four chambers, the role of resister appears in at least one dominant pair. At the same time, such majority-anchored roles as inventor or broker in the purposive-role set, facilitator, and state oriented are missing altogether in the Tennessee House structure. Only the trustee, ideally located in the majority cluster, is present. Apparently, it is a role which cannot be shed

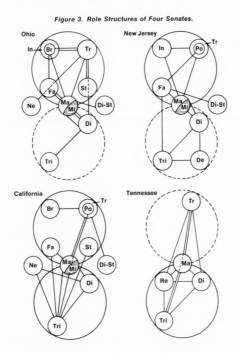

Figure 3. Role Structures of Four Senates.

in contemporary empirical reality, even in a system which is so clearly minority geared. These results, we already suggested, are easy to explain, and they confirm that the "majority" in Tennessee is only a pro forma majority. In fact, the "majority" Democrats are divided into competing fractions, none of which can permanently control the legislature, and which behave more like minority parties in a multi-party system. We can characterize this structure as "populist-minoritarian."

### Senate Role Structures

Tables 1 and 3 show that in the four Senates more pairs are tied for dominance, making the over-all picture somewhat more complex. But a glance at Figure 3 will indicate that, in spite of the greater complexity, the general patterns observed in the role structures of the lower houses are maintained from state to state, but a number of differences may be noted.

In the first place, in the Ohio and New Jersey Senate the role of minority member seems to be somewhat more integrated into the dominant majority pattern than is the case in the respective Houses. This is quite plausible. In the smaller chambers, the minority is more likely to be in closer contact with the majority, it is more likely to be given attention, and it is more likely to play an active role in the legislative process. As a result, ideally minority-centered roles are likely to be more frequently linked to majority-anchored roles. In New Jersey, for instance, we may note that the

**Table 3.** Number of Times a Role Appears in Combination with Another in a Dominant Pair, Senates

| Role | Ohio | N.J. | Calif. | Tenn. |
|------|------|------|--------|-------|
| Party | | | | |
| Majority member | 5 | 4 | 3 | 4 |
| Minority member | 1 | 1 | 1 | 0 |
| Representational | | | | |
| Trustee | 6 | 1 | 4 | 4 |
| Politico | 0 | 2 | 1 | 0 |
| Delegate | 0 | 2 | 0 | 0 |
| Purposive | | | | |
| Inventor | 1 | 2 | 0 | 0 |
| Broker | 3 | 0 | 1 | 0 |
| Tribune | 1 | 3 | 5 | 4 |
| Areal | | | | |
| State oriented | 1 | 0 | 1 | 0 |
| District-State oriented | 1 | 1 | 1 | 0 |
| District oriented | 5 | 4 | 3 | 4 |
| Pressure group | | | | |
| Facilitator | 3 | 4 | 2 | 0 |
| Neutral | 1 | 0 | 2 | 0 |
| Resister | 0 | 0 | 0 | 4 |

facilitator-tribune combination among the dominant pairs, or in Ohio the facilitator-district pair.

Secondly, we note that in the Ohio and New Jersey Senates the district-oriented role appears in dominant pairs, while this is not the case in the respective Houses. Also, in New Jersey the delegate role and in Ohio the tribune role are paired with some other roles, while this pairing does not occur (with the exception of the tribune in New Jersey) in the lower chambers. These three roles—tribune, delegate, and district-oriented—seem to loom as latent premises of their behavior in Senators' self-conceptions of their legislative role in general. Senates have been historically looked on as performing more distinctly "ambassadorial functions" in the representative system. And though now popularly elected just as the members of the "popular" lower houses, the notion that Senates are, in part at least, conclaves of ambassadors from geographically-based constituencies may linger on in Senators' self-definitions. This, of course, we cannot prove, but as a hypothesis it is congruent with the fact that in the lower houses these "populist" roles are minority centered. Minority members are likely to perceive themselves as "ambassadors"—spokesmen of the "outs"—vis-à-vis the controlling majority with its predominant state orientation.

The "constructions" of legislative chambers as role structures suggest that through the use of non-conventional analytical categories, in our case derived from a role analysis of legislators, we can describe the structure of a legislative chamber, not as it is embodied in rules and bylaws (which are important parameters for behavior), but as it represents a system of action.

## REFERENCES

Binkley, W. E., *President and Congress* (New York: Alfred A. Knopf, 1947).
De Grazia, A., *Public and Republic, Political Representation in America* (New York: Alfred A. Knopf, 1951).
*The Federalist*, No. 35.

# 5 Organization

## Irrational Leadership in Formal Organizations

ERIC JOSEPHSON

It is now recognized that so-called "rational" institutions may be sources and victims of "irrational" behavior within the units and also exerting pressure from outside. Numerous studies have drawn our attention to the stresses and strains operating within the structure of a formal organization, or to the interplay between rational and irrational behavior. In this paper, attention will be focussed on the role played by leadership in contributing to irrational behavior, reflected by an institution's inner life and policy.

Formal organization, represented at its highest stage by bureaucracy, requires certain structural conditions that have been described systematically by sociologists, following Weber, and need not be catalogued here. Bureaucracy, which, Weber claimed, enjoys the advantage of a machine over non-mechanical modes of production, attempts to maximize possibilities of rational action by employing the most effective means to reach designated ends. Chief among its methods, as Merton notes, is "the complete elimination of personalized relationships and of nonrational considerations (hostility, anxiety, affectual involvements, etc.)." [1]

Simon likewise observes that by integrating the behavior of its members, formal organization permits self-coordination,[2] or what Mannheim called "self-rationalization." That is, the organization substitutes group alternatives for individual choice. While it is difficult for an isolated individual to reach a high degree of rationality, the "environment of choice" itself can be selected and deliberately modified and the "stimuli surrounding decisions"

---

Eric Josephson, "Irrational Leadership in Formal Organizations," *Social Forces,* XXXI, No. 2 (December 1952), pp. 109–117.
[1] Robert Merton, "Bureaucratic Structure and Personality," *Social Forces,* 18 (May 1940), pp. 560–568.
[2] Herbert Simon, *Administrative Behavior* (New York, 1948), chaps. 2, 4–5, 10–11.

controlled by the organization, thereby making it possible for the participant to approach the goal of objective rationality.

What determines the level of efficiency achieved by an administrative organization is, in this view, a series of "limits" to rationality: limits to a participant's ability in performing his tasks and limits to his capacity for making "correct" decisions. To the extent that these limits are removed, administrative organization nears its aim: high efficiency. Administrative theory, Simon claims, must deal with such limits to rationality and the way an organization affects these limits for the person making a decision.

There is, however, an "area of acceptance" within which the individual will behave "organizationally." If institutional demands fall outside this area, personal motives will reassert themselves. When a participant behaves impersonally, an organizational scale of values is substituted for his personal scale as the criterion of "correctness" in his decisions. If it is questioned whether one can so easily draw a line between "personal" and "organizational" behavior, evidence for change of character, according to Simon, is to be found in organizational "identification." When identification is imperfect, the resulting discrepancies between personal and institutional values or goals may result in a decline of efficiency. On the other hand, when the organization's structure is well conceived, the process of identification permits institutional arrangements to govern decisions of participants and enables human rationality to transcend the limits otherwise imposed upon it. Ideally, an organization must be so constructed that a decision which is subjectively rational from the standpoint of the responsible individual will remain rational when reassessed from the standpoint of the group.

Recognition of limits to rationality in organizational behavior serves to correct the earlier "pure" theory of bureaucracy and maximum rationalization.[3] However, as Merton observes, Weber, at least, was not interested in the weaknesses of bureaucratic structure.[4] In addition, such writers as Roethlisberger and Dickson, Barnard, and Whitehead have placed considerable stress on the structural and functional position of "informal" leadership and groups within formal organizations. According to this view, although

---

[3] Routinization is implicit, but as Neumann observes, the decisions of bureaucrats are not necessarily routine; they may be creative, unprecedented, deviate from rules, and be highly discretionary. Franz Neumann, "Approaches to the Study of Political Power," *Political Science Quarterly,* LXV (June 1950), 161–180.

[4] "Weber played down the non-rational overtones which breathe authority into any office held. The managerial executive of a large industry certainly has more authority than that which his office defines. He can, for example, draw on the legendary image which his type has in the American social structure, tapping non-rational sources which lie outside bureaucratic definition." Jeremiah Wolpert, "Toward a Sociology of Authority," in *Studies in Leadership,* ed. by Alvin Gouldner (New York, 1950), pp. 689–90.

informal behavior in such circumstances can be disruptive, it can also be regarded as a defense of the individual personality against the disintegrative effects of formal organizations, and plays an essential role in producing stability. However, while there has been great interest in activities of informal groups (which may or may not be rational in terms of institutional objectives) little attention has been paid to the effect of irrational, or possibly delinquent *leadership within the organization*.[5] It is perhaps significant that, until recently, the bulk of literature in the field of industrial sociology has dealt with irrationality at subordinate levels.

As Merton observes, although bureaucratic structure attains a high degree of reliability, based on discipline (which can become an end in itself), conflict may arise when "personalized relationships are substituted for the structurally required impersonal ones." This conflict is the "intrusion of primary group attitudes when secondary group attitudes are institutionally demanded." [6]

In this connection, it has been recognized that a major factor responsible for irrationality in formal organizations is what Lasswell calls "continual interplay between office and personality." [7] This feature has been noted by many observers. After referring to the "trained incapacities," "occupational psychoses," and "professional deformation" that may result from rigidity and formalism in bureaucratic structure, Merton raises a number of pertinent questions: To what extent are particular personality types selected and modified by bureaucracies? Do bureaucracies select personalities of particularly submissive or ascendant tendencies? [8]

Bureaucrats themselves have been described by Lasswell as "compulsive" personalities, insofar as the compulsive manner of dealing with men is to develop a set of rigid molds into which they are supposed to fit.[9] A more fundamental, although paradoxical, characteristic of the bureaucrat, according to Lasswell, is the avoidance of responsibility. At first, the bureaucrat appears to submit readily to authority and to exaggerate his own importance by identifying himself with authorized power. But this view overlooks the most important feature of the personality. A bureaucrat who says he will not "stick his neck out" is incapable of assuming an authoritative role. Actually, his tension and hostility are such that apparent devotion to

---

[5] Certain students of leadership "emphasize the role of a leader in *satisfying* the needs of his group, almost to the complete exclusion of the leader's role in *frustrating* the needs of his group." Alvin Gouldner, *op. cit.,* Introduction, p. 48.

[6] Robert Merton, "Bureaucratic Structure and Personality," *loc. cit.*

[7] For illustration of this concept see Harold Lasswell, *The Analysis of Political Behavior* (London, 1948), Part III, chap. 1, "The Participant-Observer: A Study of Administrative Rules in Action," pp. 261–278.

[8] Robert Merton, "Bureaucratic Structure and Personality," *loc. cit.*

[9] Harold Lasswell, *Power and Personality* (New York, 1948), pp. 89–91.

established ways of doing things is counteracted by unrecognized forces within him; unconscious demands on the personality aim to destroy authority. In addition to delay and uncertainty about rules, there is "passing the buck up higher." This state of affairs can upset administrative stability and frustrate authority which is supposedly being so carefully served. Administration is "knifed by the undisclosed hosility of frustration. . . . Hostility toward authority is . . . clearly expressed in the bureaucratic tensions that rise in the process of interpreting authority," concludes Lasswell, with public service in mind.

Mutual impact of personality and office has long been a matter of intense interest to novelists and historians, as well as sociologists. It is striking that many writers remain convinced that bureaucracy simultaneously selects and produces mediocrity in its *subordinate* personnel.[10]

Broadening our inquiry, we wish to investigate some effects which certain types of personality in the position of *authority* have upon formal organizations within which they are found. As we have seen, there has been considerable interest in "bureaucratic personality" and the influence which institutional experience has upon individuals who are exposed to it; we are concerned here with the effect of varying conditions of leadership upon bureaucratic structure and operations. If, as Moore notes, "managerial functions and activities *will always include elements not planned in the organizational scheme,*"[11] personality of the executive must count far more heavily than that of subordinates, who are bound more by bureaucratic rigidity and controls, while to a considerable extent the executive is freer from such restraint.

At this stage of our knowledge about leadership, any conclusions drawn from studying the impact of personality upon formal organizations

---

[10] Balzac, convinced that there is an "administrative type," in a novel about French government bureaucracy, questioned whether bureaucrats "became idiots in their calling, or whether they are somewhat idiotic at birth. Perhaps nature and the government play an equal part in this process. . . . But in the case of the employee, offices constitute nature. . . . Employees . . . form a sort of class where there are exercises to be done, where the chiefs take the place of school-masters, where rewards are given to *protégés,* like prizes for good conduct, and where there exists nevertheless a kind of intimacy. . . . The office is the world in miniature, with its peculiarities, friendships, hatreds, its envy and its cupidity, its fluctuations . . . frivolous discourse . . . and . . . ceaseless spying." *Les Employes* (Paris, 1862), pp. 228–229. Later, Warnotte also referred to the bureau as a little community, with an atmosphere of secrecy and anxiety. In his study of "professional deformation" he has described "tragedies" of the "internal life" of bureaucracy. Daniel Warnotte, "Bureaucratie et Fonctionnarisme," *Revue de l'Institut de Sociologie,* No. 2 (April-June 1937), pp. 219–260.

[11] Wilbert Moore, *Industrial Relations and the Social Order* (New York, 1946), p. 122.

must be guarded. It has been found difficult to distinguish between "personal" and "organizational" behavior. In any situation of leadership a great number of external, as well as internal factors will mitigate the influence of the leader's character upon the organization and its subordinates. Nevertheless, without attempting to "over-psychologize," it has been recognized in certain instances, particularly where the presence of a personality disorder may be detected, that the impact of character upon the structure and operations of an organization can be decisive. At the same time, it cannot be denied that the personality of a leader in an organization may very well undergo change, as in cases of "professional deformation," at levels of leadership, as well as among subordinates. However, if it can be demonstrated that the character of an administrator, or executive, can influence the "atmosphere" and operations of an organization, we will have extended our picture of the limits to rational behavior.

Leadership[12] can be understood as a role that makes demands upon character and, under particular circumstances, selects distinctive personality types.[13] In hierarchies of formal organizations, leadership and power require marked traits. By their very nature, such organizations find considerable, if not exclusive, use for autocrats and the picture of the "authoritarian personality" produced by psychologists has considerable bearing on this problem. Significantly, Gardner Murphy has observed that for an authoritarian, rules may become ends in themselves and hence be a central implement of the power drive. An extreme position on this issue is taken by Comfort, who proposes that centralized, coercive government attracts to its positions of power delinquent and psychopathic personalities; here, institutional power and those who seek it are identified with criminological traits.[14] Does the theory of authoritarian personality have a place in the analysis of leadership in formal organizations? What evidence do we have?

---

[12] With Gouldner, we recognize that a leader is anyone who influences group behavior, in organizations that may be democratic or authoritarian, formal or informal. Gouldner, *op. cit.*, Introduction.

[13] See S. De Coster, "l'Exercise de l'Autorite, probleme de psychologie sociale," *Revue de l'Institut de Sociologie* (1951), No. 1, pp. 35–65; and William Henry, "The Business Executive: "The Psychodynamics of a Social Role," *American Journal of Sociology*, LIV (January 1949), 286–291.

[14] Alex Comfort, *Authority and Delinquency in the Modern State: A Criminological Approach to the Problem of Power* (London, 1950), p. x. Oliver Garceau has criticized this approach. "Most anal, compulsive neurotics do not become effective political leaders, nor do leaders appear consistently to have disturbed personalities of definable categories. Less compulsive and more flexible typologies have still to be applied systematically to political leadership." The personal pathology of certain totalitarian leaders does not necessarily clarify democratic leadership. "Research in the Political Process," *The American Political Science Review*, XLV, No. 1 (March 1951), 77.

Psychological aspects of leadership in industrial organizations have been described by McGregor, who discusses the manner in which superiors affect subordinates striving to satisfy their needs.[15] The outstanding characteristic of this relationship is the dependence by the subordinate upon superiors for gratification of his needs. Industrial organizations are generally authoritarian in structure, writes McGregor, and psychologically, this relationship between subordinate and superior is important "because of its emotional similarity to the dependence characteristic of another earlier relationship: that between . . . child and . . . parents."

Subordinates face real or imagined threats to the satisfaction of their work-situation needs and actions of superiors may be perceived as the source of these threats. In their dependence upon superiors, subordinates desire a sense of security, which is produced chiefly by an atmosphere of approval, created only by the superior in his underlying attitude toward his subordinates. "Many superiors are themselves so insecure that they . . . are unconsciously afraid to have capable and developing subordinates," notes McGregor. It is not surprising, therefore, that in cases in which they are denied consistent discipline, a sense of participation, and a share in responsibility, subordinates may display sharp feelings of insecurity.

A second statement of the relationships between the personalities of leaders and the responses of subordinates is offered by McMurray, who proposes that an organization tends to reflect, in its behavior and policies, the character of its top executives.[16] "There is no reason to assume that executives are less subject to emotional maladjustment than are their subordinates." In other words, the doctrine that an "employer is the natural leader of his men" offers no guarantee that positions of leadership will be occupied by those best qualified to conduct affairs in a rational manner. One type of leader may try to compensate for strong feelings of insecurity or inadequacy by authoritarian behavior: power drives become a form of defense mechanism, as Fromm and others have suggested. The morale of an organization subject to an autocratic personality, of course, may suffer. Another type of leader found in executive positions may be emotionally immature and seek desperately, if in vain, the good will of his subordinates. Finally, there may be the admittedly selfish leader who regards employees merely as a means to personal profit, prestige and power. Cases of naked exploitation, or terrorization of subordinates are familiar examples. Consequently, distrusted superiors and policies may be responsible for resistance on the part of

---

[15] Douglas McGregor, "Conditions of Effective Leadership in the Industrial Organization," in *Readings in Social Psychology,* ed. by T. N. Newcomb and E. L. Hartley (New York, 1947), pp. 427–435.

[16] Robert McMurray, "Management Mentalities and Worker Reactions," in *Human Factors in Management,* ed. by Schuyler Hoslett (New York, 1946).

subordinates, voluntary limitation of output, or what has been called "bureaucratic sabotage." [17]

"A little recognized but potent source of employee dissatisfaction," writes McMurray, "is the fact that the structure of management is military or totalitarian. Business organizations are usually dictatorships. . . . The flow of power is almost exclusively downward." (This view, of course, contrasts sharply with Barnard's image of "co-operative organizations" where the "determination of authority lies with the subordinate individual.") Although McMurray believes in the "superior efficiency" of authoritarian institutions, he recognizes that authority gives ample opportunity for aggressiveness, usually directed toward subordinates.

So far, we have tried to modify the classical theory of bureaucracy by observing certain limits to rational action on the part of formal organizations, with particular stress on interplay between personality and leadership. Accepting the hypothesis that formal organization tends to be authoritarian by nature, a number of theoretical approaches to the problem have been examined. Executive power, it would appear, can select or indulge personality types whose behavior may have serious consequences for the operation and stability of the organizations concerned. What is the evidence for this proposition? In order to suggest possible clues, five case studies of leadership in action are described briefly.

1. The experiments of Lewin and his group on leadership among groups of adolescents, although not concerned with formal organizations, are pertinent, and familiar enough so that few details need be presented here. Lippitt, in the first study, demonstrated that "authoritarian" and "democratic" group "atmospheres" can be measured by reference to the character of the leadership in the respective groups.[18] An authoritarian leader, dominating his subordinates, imposed his goals upon them and produced submissive behavior on the part of group members. While conflict was observed among members of the authoritarian group, cooperation and unity marked the democratic group. While strong individual goals arose in the authoritarian group, related to a need for status, but conflicting with group objectives and the leader's power, group goals were much more potent and creative in the democratic group and constructive activity was achieved.

In a later study, Lippitt and White elaborated the original experiment

---

[17] For a case study of resistance to change of leadership and "bureaucratic sabotage" see Alvin Gouldner, "The Problem of Succession and Bureaucracy," in Gouldner, *op. cit.*, pp. 644–659.

[18] Ronald Lippitt, "An Experimental Study of the Effects of Democratic and Authoritarian Group Atmospheres," in *Studies in Topological and Vector Psychology,* I, University of Iowa Studies in Child Welfare, XVI, No. 3 (1940).

on leadership.[19] Here, a "laissez-faire" group was added to the original authoritarian and democratic units. On this occasion, it was noted that there could be both passive and aggressive responses to authoritarian leadership, although in both cases, subordinates were more dependent upon leadership than in the democratic or laissez-faire groups.

In short, striking differences in efficiency, *esprit de corps,* aggressiveness, and level of frustration were found by comparing the behavior of group "climates" produced by the three basic patterns of leadership. Variations in the structure of group behavior were attributed directly to differences between "induced social climates," rather than to constant characteristics of club personnel. The adult-leader role was found to be a strong determinant of patterns of social interaction and emotional development in the groups. Although such material is illuminating with regard to leadership-effect, it has not been extended, unfortunately, to adult behavior in less artificial, formal organizations.[20]

2. On the other hand, the studies of mental breakdown in the Army Air Forces by Grinker and Spiegel offer valuable insight into problems of leadership and morale in tightly-knit groups facing critical situations.[21] Describing air combat groups, the authors indicate that fliers felt toward each other as "brothers" and toward the leader as a "father" who could expose them to danger or extricate them from the most difficult combat situations. (It must be noted that there was a high degree of cohesion in the groups, perhaps unique in military forces. Furthermore, the air combat situation is unusually sharp and dramatic.) Due to his psychological position as "father" of his men, the character of a commander had profound effect upon the combat group to which he was attached.[22]

Identification with group by a flier was related to his need for a sense of belonging. Faith in leadership was one of the most important factors contributing to high morale. Men appeared to be "fighting more *for* someone than *against* somebody." It was the personality of a leader upon which

---

[19] Ronald Lippitt and Ralph White, "An Experimental Study of Leadership and Group Life," in Newcomb and Hartley, *op. cit.,* pp. 315–330.

[20] It is regrettable that what must have been golden opportunities for experiment in leadership-effect were missed by Stouffer and his associates, by their own admission, in the massive studies of adjustment to army life and combat.

[21] Roy Grinker and John Spiegel, *Men Under Stress* (Philadelphia, 1945).

[22] Significantly, in air combat groups, leaders usually had had little training in large-scale administration and its problems. Conversely, as Robert Nisbet notes, while the factory manager or executive is primarily an administrative technician, often he is not a leader. "Leadership and Social Crisis," in Alvin Gouldner, *op. cit.,* pp. 702–720. This view is supported by T. N. Whitehead, in *Leadership in a Free Society* (London, 1937).

depended his capacity to influence morale. In exchange for loyalty and sacrifice, men expected attention in return. A successful air combat leader had to be technically competent, strong in character and courageous: such a leader communicated his own strength. Commanders could neither demand too much, nor too little; fliers went to incredible lengths of sacrifice and effort for a leader who had their confidence and affection. To keep the men's good will, the commander had to be a just and impartial "father" and had to give every possible consideration to his men's needs. Incompetent leadership, on the other hand, compelled fliers to become self-centered and lose interest in their group.

Grinker and Spiegel analyzed many pathological cases and a number of them bear directly on the problem of leadership and morale. In two instances, where airmen became casualties, failure of leadership had been directly responsible; the subordinates reacted subsequently by expressing hostility toward authority in general, specifically related to their own leaders and generalized to cover the whole army. Justifiable contempt for their commanders and loss of confidence in leadership was extended to all authoritative "father-figures."

What is particularly interesting in the material presented by Grinker and Spiegel is the emphasis on emergence of familiar emotional attachments within a formal organization (to which attention has been drawn by many writers on industrial psychology). Most striking, however, is the suggestion of direct connection between breakdown of leadership and personality disorders among subordinates, at least in highly cohesive groups.

3. An experiment in training subordinates to become more democratic and self-reliant, after experience in an authoritarian organization, is reported by Meltzer.[23] Here, the problem was whether six key functionaries could be developed into leaders themselves, having been conditioned, as followers, to look toward a general manager for direction in a small company. Originally, all power led to one individual, the general manager. When he resigned, the organization had to learn to carry on democratically without him. Nevertheless, for a period after the departure of the dominant official, the six men did well on their own; however, it soon appeared there had been no real change: they soon reverted to submissive patterns of behavior. Only when the "clinical approach" was employed by consultants, involving intensive interviews and group discussion, did adjustment to freedom begin to take place. Particularly notable in this study is the fact that the personality of the authoritarian general manager is not described directly.

---

[23] H. Meltzer, "Humanizing Relations of Key Personnel," in Schuyler Hoslett, op. cit.

The emphasis is entirely on the influence that his *absence* had upon the organization.[24]

4. Goldsen and Low conducted an intensive study of a crisis in labor-management relations.[25] Two top executives in a branch office of a national company were faced suddenly with unionization of their nine salesmen. According to the observers, the executives were in a state of "shock" upon learning of this development. One of them was literally unable to command himself, and then cope with the problem calmly and objectively. Such was his self-preoccupation that he "personalized" the entire crisis. Unionization was felt to be a personal attack upon *him*. Guilt-feelings, however, made him assert his innocence and blame others for the turn of events. Self-centeredness and a distorted view of reality prevented this executive from understanding his subordinates' problems. In his view, unionization represented betrayal and rejection of the paternal role he wished to play, since the men had proceeded secretly in their plans, without consulting him. Hence, the "shock." The traumatic nature of his response showed how a wounded ego may try to fortify itself. The rejected "father" now turned against his "sons." Ultimately, this executive's rationalizations placed him in a vindicative position from which there could be little retreat. Possibility of settlement in the dispute was reduced by the presence of "immature" leadership.

5. As a final, and perhaps extreme, case illustrating interplay between personality and institutional behavior, we refer to the effect of Hitler's leadership upon operations of the German Army during World War II.[26] There is considerable evidence that the Fuehrer was responsible for major strategic

---

[24] This test of leadership-effect has been employed elsewhere. In the Lippitt and White experiment, described in "An Experimental Study of Leadership and Group Life," *loc. cit.*, leaders of the three groups arrived late for meetings deliberately. During the interval, club behavior was observed. In the authoritarian clubs, no initiative was shown by members when alone; in the democratic club, participants were active and productive; while in the laissez-faire group, members were active, but not productive. Such data give striking evidence of the extent to which work motivation was leader-induced in the two authoritarian situations. In the democratic group, absence or presence of the leader had practically no effect.

[25] Joseph Goldsen and Lillian Low, "Manager Meets Union: A Case Study of Personal Immaturity," in Hoslett, *op. cit.*

[26] This account is based on Oron Hale, "Adolf Hitler as Feldherr," *Virginia Quarterly Review*, 24 (Spring 1948), pp. 198–213, from which all quotations are taken. See also: F. H. Hinsley, *Hitler's Strategy* (Cambridge, 1951), and Felix Gilbert, ed., *Hitler Directs His War* (New York, 1950). The serious limits of rationality in military operations are, of course, well recognized. In *Thoughts on War* (London, 1944), Liddell Hart writes that "the conduct of war must be controlled by reason if its object is to be fulfilled" (p. 177) but also that armies "for tactical success . . . need to cultivate *irregularity*." (p. 158)

decisions made by Germany and can be credited both with early victories and subsequent defeats. In 1938, the turning point, uncooperative, independent army leaders were removed and the command structure of the armed forces reorganized to permit co-ordination and direction of total war under Hitler himself, and to ensure the submission of the army to his will. However, as long as military operations were directed through established agencies,

> the machinery of the German High Command functioned efficiently, from 1939 to 1941, when it began to break down and disintegrate. That it did not improve with use and experience is largely attributable to the inadequacies of the men who used it, and of these Hitler was . . . most important.

Never reconciled to assumption of supreme power by Hitler, "the highly trained military scientists of the . . . General Staff regarded" the Fuehrer's headquarters with suspicion.

> The opposition between Hitler's Armed Forces High Command and the Army General Staff . . . represented a conflict of principles: Hitler's unorthodox military ideas and his intuitive art of command were incompatible with the General Staff concept of scientific planning and adherence to established military doctrines.

When Hitler assumed direct personal command of the armies in 1941, breakdown of the structure and operations of the High Command followed, as well as a turning point in German conduct of the war. The Fuehrer himself, neglecting other leadership functions, was unqualified for such enormous tasks, lacking the professional training necessary for an Army commander-in-chief.

> Hitler's overvaluation of willpower, morale and ideological indoctrination as factors in military operations amounted to illusionism. "Fanatical determination" was one of his favorite and oft-repeated phrases. Enemy superiority in manpower and material could be overcome, in his opinion, by sheer willpower and determination. Sober calculation and objective estimates of enemy capabilities, in which the General Staff officer was trained, led, in his opinion, to loss of spirit, lack of daring, weakening of willpower, even to defeatism. . . . Hitler apparently never doubted his asserted infallibility. His experience with the . . . General Staff between 1938 and 1941 [when his intuition was often right and General Staff thinking wrong] confirmed his opinion of the essential superiority of his own judgment in military affairs. Thereafter he paid slight attention to "expert advice," dismissing . . . experienced military authorities as "professional obstructionists."

On the other hand, it is significant that Hitler consistently refused to assume responsibility for disasters suffered by the German army under his leadership, and at the same time, would not delegate authority to subordinates. Moreover, the rapid turnover in army command positions, engineered by Hitler, scarcely produced bureaucratic stability, and it was precisely commanders "highly trained, experienced, and steeped in the tradition and doctrines of the German Army" who aroused his suspicions and became victims of his wrath.

After 1943, when Germany had lost the initiative and faced defeat, Hitler became completely opportunistic in his strategy. As the situation worsened, he "immersed himself more and more in the tactical situation at the fronts until he lost all perspective for larger strategic problems." Hitler's reaction to the plot of the generals in 1944, of course, was to make a farce of the German army's operational structure. "Henceforth, distrusting every one, he issued all operational orders and made all decisions personally." Shortly before the end of the war, he threatened

> "draconic punishment" for disobedience, [and] ordered all Commanders from Army Group to Division . . . to report to him every operational decision they proposed to execute in sufficient time to permit his personal intervention and the issuance of a counter-order if the proposed action did not meet with his approval. During these last months, he spent his time ordering counter-attacks by units already overrun, demanding last-ditch defense of strong-points that had already fallen, and planning troop movements for which there were neither troops nor transport.

It is striking that the great German military machine, professional and traditional in its outlook, could be wrecked by a psychopath.[27] Before the

---

[27] "Hitler's Russian campaigns will be studied and described minutely by students of military history. But there are elements of the story that will always escape the historian—the elements that relate to human personality, the elements outside the domain of human reason. . . . The strategic blunders, the reckless disregard of professional advice, the illusion that 'the Russian is dead,' cannot be explained by reference to any fundamental laws in world history; they are manifestations of the mystery of human personality. . . . The orders were those of a madman." Oron Hale, "The Fuehrer and the Field Marshal," *Virginia Quarterly Review,* Vol. 26, No. 4 (Autumn 1950), pp. 492–511. Perhaps a supreme example of the effect of Hitler's personality upon German military operations is to be found in the case of General Paulus, who, ordered needlessly by the Fuehrer to sacrifice his army at Stalingrad, found himself incapable of acting logically and rationally, i.e., by ordering a break-out attempt on his own account. Such was the submission of the military machine to the pathological Hitler that, while it is revealing that Hitler himself never ordered the break-out, the subordinate commander, paralyzed, was incapable of assuming the responsibility. In this classical case of "trained incapacity," the problem could not be solved.

war, the General Staff, "limited and practical in its aims, cold and rational in its methods," was not opposed to Hitler since he was expected to produce the results which it desired by following a practical policy: gradual and limited expansion of the army, maintenance of professional standards, avoidance of impractical plans of unlimited conquest.[28] However, by a clever process of infiltrating Nazis into key positions, Hitler was able to capture and "politicize" the military bureaucracy and eventually master the generals, who had joined forces with him in the hope that they could ultimately assume direction of state policy themselves. Perhaps a more rational military leadership would have been able to delay the final outcome of the war, but it has been shown that the quality of army leadership deteriorated by a selective process as Hitler assumed direct command. This conflict between charismatic leader and bureaucratic organization would be fatal to both forces.

Reviewing briefly a number of theoretical contributions to the study of institutional life and case studies of leadership in action, we have tried to enlarge our picture of irrational behavior in formal groups. Certainly, it is not personality alone that may "sabotage" the operations of an organization. Nevertheless, both the classical description of "ideal" bureaucracy and field studies of institutional behavior neglect irrational leadership, in the first instance, due to exaggeration of logical behavior, and in the second, by stressing irrational activity on the part of subordinates. However, as we have seen, there are occasions when executives, or leaders, may themselves behave in a manner "dysfunctional" from the standpoint of organizations they serve, as when provoking hostility and resistance on the part of subordinates, leading in turn to inefficiency and low morale.

Ideally, bureaucracy assumes that in the process of "self-rationalization" a participant will identify himself sufficiently with logical goals of an organization to permit maximum rationalization of behavior. In practice, however, the process of identification may be reversed: the *executive* may identify the organization with *his* goals and needs. By virtue of his superior power he may frustrate institutional operations far more easily than subordinates. The danger is increased when bureaucracy indulges autocratic leadership, and discrepancy occurs between group goals and the leader's behavior, if, in extending his authority and consolidating his position, he disregards group values and institutional needs.

Weber's view of history conceived a cyclical rotation between bureau-

---

[28] Today, in their apologies, German generals claim that they opposed Hitler from the start, remembering that before his time, they regarded the army as a non-political corporation concerned only with efficiency and the welfare of its members [perfect bureaucratization]. See H. Trever-Roper, "Hitler's Generals Create a Dangerous Myth," *New York Times Magazine,* February 19, 1950; and *Nazi Conspiracy and Aggression,* Vol. 2 (Washington, 1946).

cratic power and charismatic leadership, the latter, in its hostility to routine and formalized organization, disrupting the process of rationalization. Mannheim, following Weber in a theory of balance between rational and irrational forces in society, observed that the modern world creates highly rational forms of action that depend on a series of repressions and renunciations of impulsive satisfactions. In this delicate state of affairs, "the slightest irrational disturbance can have the most far-reaching effects." May this historical generalization be transposed and applied to the "inner life" of formal organizations? Executive positions, where power and responsibility for decision remain, would appear to hold greater dangers to the smooth operation of organizations than "informal groups" among subordinates, even in an age of interlocking control over leadership itself in industry, labor, government and war.

It is obvious that further historical and experimental research is required in this field. The synthesis presented here is intended to show various approaches that may guide investigations into the impact of personality upon formal organizations. Ideally, the closest collaboration would be necessary between the psychology of personality and leadership and the study of formal social structure. It appears likely that such an endeavor would be rewarding for both. A clue for the sociological detective engaged in this research may very well appear in Weber's claim "that irrational behavior [is] more predictable in its course than rational."

# 6 Task

## Situational Determinants of Leadership Structure

DAVID C. KORTEN

Leadership has long been a topic of considerable interest in the social sciences. Nearly every aspect of leadership has been the subject of some degree of study. The present paper is concerned with some of the situational factors which determine the form of leadership which will arise and be accepted in a group. Two basic questions will be considered:

1. Under what conditions will there be pressure toward centralized authoritarian leadership?
2. Under what conditions is a more participative democratic form of leadership likely to arise?

While this is certainly not a new topic, this paper attempts to develop a somewhat more systematic approach than has ordinarily been undertaken toward this subject. I feel that the "model" developed in this paper provides a framework or structure for further experimentation and theoretical development that has perhaps previously been lacking.

My initial interest in making such a study was stimulated by observations made last summer in Indonesia and Burma of a strong desire, particularly among certain high government officials, for centralized control. I observed this same trend beginning to develop in Malaya. Recent releases from Ghana suggest that this situation is not confined to Asia.

Particularly in Indonesia, which is the situation most familiar to me, there was an original attempt at developing a free society and a free enterprise economy. In each of the countries mentioned there was no revolu-

David C. Korten, "Situational Determinants of Leadership Structure." *Journal of Conflict Resolution,* VI, No. 3 (September 1962), pp. 222–235. Copyright © 1962 by The University of Michigan. Reprinted by permission.

tion in depth establishing the centralized control over more democratic institutions, nor has there been any other single totally disrupting occurrence which might account for the shift toward centralization. Though stress is certainly present, the overt crisis situation which is usually used to account for the rise of dictatorship is not entirely relevant. A more refined approach is needed.

Although each of these countries is unique in its own way, they all seem to have certain common elements in their situations which may be very important in exerting pressure for these centralizing trends. Mention of these seems helpful as a starting point for discussion.

1. Each of them is in a sense in a high drive state. There is great desire, at least among major elements of the population, for improvement and development.

2. In addition to the drive for development, there is a related but separate drive for national status to compensate for feelings of inferior status developed through years of colonial suppression.

3. A sense of crisis exists which is closely related to the high drive state and results in part from the self-imposed adverse results of many of the programs which have been attempted.

4. A reasonably definite goal structure is established which may be spelled out in great and specific detail as evidenced in the five-year plans, eight-year plans, etc., which establish production goals and welfare measures to be attained at specific points in time.

5. All possess a low level of technical skill and an ill-developed understanding of the economic forces with which they must deal. The path to their goal is unclear and they are attempting to force clarity through control, although they lack the real understanding in many cases which is needed to accomplish effective control.

## DEVELOPMENT OF A CONCEPTUAL MODEL

The first problem is one of developing a framework within which the important variables causing pressure for structural shifts can be studied and interrelated. From this framework, or model, it may then be possible to trace the forces leading a group or society from democratic to authoritarian forms of leadership and to compare these with the forces which lead the group in the opposite direction from an authoritarian to a democratic form.

This paper offers a very simplified proposal in order to facilitate initial study, even though simplification to the extent currently proposed may not be entirely realistic and certainly does not cover all possible cases. For example, no attempt has been made at this point to deal with laissez-faire forms of leadership.

We will, for the present, think in terms of a two-dimensional space represented by a four-cell matrix. The purpose is to represent discrete dimensions of authoritarian and democratic leadership against discrete dimensions of high goal structure and low goal structure. This is illustrated in Figure 1. The reasons for including the high and low goal structure dimensions should become clear later in the discussion.

In the following discussion the attempt is made to characterize each of these dimensions. While it is realized that these dimensions in fact exist as continua, they are treated here as discrete for purposes of simplicity.

### Goal Structure

Although I am not really satisfied with the terms *high* and *low goal structure* as being clearly descriptive of the concepts which I have in mind, I have not yet found a term which is substantially better in this respect. For this reason I suggest that preconceptions as to what the terms represent be avoided and their meaning instead be developed from the following discussion.

The consideration of goals came into the study at the very beginning in a comparative discussion of Russian communism with its presently au-

### Figure 1

|  | High Goal Structure | Low Goal Structure |
|---|---|---|
| **Democratic** |  |  |
| **Authoritarian** |  |  |

thoritarian leadership, and American democracy. In the United States approach we stress more how we want progress, rather than *where,* thus placing somewhat more emphasis on the method than on the outcome. Our goal is actually a continuing one and although we look for continual material and spiritual progress, we set no specific terminal goals and establish no time schedule. Our goals are to a large extent *non-operational.*[1]

---

[1] March and Simon developed the concept of *operational* and non-operational goals. "When a means of testing actions is perceived to relate a particular goal or

On the other hand, the Russians seek to build a way of life not yet attained. Their stated orientation is toward future attainment and involves emphasis on change rather than on preservation. Their goals are fairly concrete or *operational* in such things as surpassing free world industrial output and communizing the world. Such terminal goals as these assume great importance, and lead to the establishing of a definite time-table of accomplishment.

I feel these goal differences may have a great importance in helping to explain the differences in the forms of government adopted. It was consideration of these factors which led to adopting the terms high and low goal structure which referred to the clarity of impression or structuring of future goals which the group was seeking to attain. As the model developed further, this description broke down to some extent as it was found that the cognitive clarity was not so essential as the terminal quality. Still no alternative has been suggested which seems to be a real improvement. The original concept still fits very nicely into the final model, but the present model is not so limiting as the original concept.

### High Goal Structure

In this situation we are concerned with groups which have rather specific goals which are of importance in the consensus of group opinion. The group is looked upon as a means of carrying out tasks or operations which will lead to these goals. It is not generally characterized by the desire to maintain the status quo, but rather by the desire to work toward a new situation or to attain something which the group has not presently attained. Group goals assume considerably more importance than individual goals. Individuals see the attainment of the group goal as prerequisite to the attainment of their own goals.

In some situations there may be a specific threat to the status quo which is introduced from a source external to the group. In this case the "new situation" would be the status quo with the threat removed. If a crisis has already occurred, the goal might be *reattainment* of the *old* status quo, but it would *not* be *maintainance* of the *present* status quo.

### Low Goal Structure

The group in the low goal structure situation will have fewer or much less important shared *achievement* goals. Such goals as exist will more likely relate to maintaining routine functions necessary to maintaining the status

---

criterion with possible courses of action, the criterion will be called operational. Otherwise the criterion will be non-operational" (March and Simon, 1958, p. 155).

quo or making slight readjustments in it. There will be less commonality of individual goals, and attraction to the group might be considered more social in nature. Emphasis will tend to be on individual rather than on group goals. To the extent that the person does identify with the group, the identification is likely to be based on personal attractiveness or on the means which the group offers for the facilitation of personal efforts to attain individual goals.

### Descriptive Examples

A study carried out by Back is very useful in describing or characterizing the interactions expected in the high and low goal structure situations (Back, 1958). This study provides a discussion of differences in social interactions under different orientations toward group membership.

Two of the situations studied were cohesiveness based on the performance of a task and cohesiveness based on personal attraction.

It may be expected that interaction in the high goal structure group will be most closely characterized by that found in Back's task-oriented group where "group members wanted to complete the activity quickly and efficiently; they spent just the time necessary for the performance of the task, and they tried to use this time for the performance of the task only" (Back, 1958, p. 196). There was an absolute minimum of social as opposed to task-oriented interaction.

The low goal structure situation would probably be more closely characterized by the group where cohesiveness was based on personal attraction and there was little emphasis on the group task. This group was essentially interested in enjoying the status quo. The activity of these groups tended toward "longish, pleasant conversation" (Back, 1958, p. 196).

Sussman's study of the "Calorie Collectors," an organization of women supposedly drawn together to participate in weight losing activities, also provides a smilar characterization of the two goal structure situations (Sussman, 1956).

The members of this club could be divided into one of two classes. The first were those who were primarily interested in looking for social support and sympathy for their problem. These would be in the low goal structure situation. The other group was described as the serious dieters who were really interested in undertaking activities leading to the loss of weight. These would be in the high goal structure situation.[2]

---

[2] It might be pointed out that a group can be in both of the goal structure situations at the same time as suggested by the Sussman observations. This is probably always true to some extent, but it also seems from the study that there were

A reasonably clear example could be described at the level of the local community. In the usual case, the function and orientation of this unit of organization will be toward providing the services upon which individuals are dependent for maintenance of their personal pursuits. Emphasis would be on such relatively routine functions as maintenance of the streets, law enforcement, fire protection, garbage collection, provision of utilities, and other common services. This would be an example of a low goal structure situation.

This same community might be considered in the high structure situation if the citizens were strongly intent upon making certain changes in their community. These might take the form of a massive community beautification campaign or an all-out effort to attract new industries, etc. Individual goals of having personal prosperity would be aroused and their attainment would be seen as dependent upon accomplishment of these group goals.

## LEADERSHIP

In the discussion of democratic and authoritarian leadership, I have relied on the operational definitions developed by White and Lippitt (1960, pp. 26–7). Further elaboration will be made at a later stage concerning additional characteristics. For the present these operational definitions seem appropriate for either large or small groups. Since these are both well-known concepts, little further elaboration at this point seems necessary.

### Authoritarian Leadership

1. "All determination of policy by the leader.

2. "Techniques and activity steps dictated by the authority, one at a time, so that future steps are always uncertain to a large degree.

3. "The leader usually dictates the particular work task and work companion of each member.

4. "The leader tends to be 'personal' in his praise and criticism of the work of each member, but remains aloof from active group participation except when demonstrating."

---

essentially two distinct groups within the "Calorie Collectors." When such a situation exists, the two subgroups may tend to work at cross purposes and the total effect may be very disruptive of group performance as was the case in this situation. This may account for the ineffective performance of many small informal organizations. While this would make a very interesting area for further study, it does not appear directly relevant to the present discussion.

### Democratic Leadership

1. "All policies a matter of group discussion and decision, encouraged and assisted by the leader.

2. "Activity perspective gained during discussion period. General steps to group goal sketched, and where technical advice is needed the leader suggests two or more alternative procedures from which the choice can be made.

3. "The members are free to work with whomever they choose, and the division of tasks is left up to the group.

4. "The leader is 'objective' or 'fact-minded' in his praise and criticism, and tries to be a regular group member in its spirit without doing too much of the work."

## THE DYNAMIC CHARACTERISTICS OF THE MODEL

So far we have been concerned only with the development of static definitional concepts. The real interest, however, is in the dynamic characteristics of the model—the forces causing shifts from one to another of the cells of the matrix.

### The Influence of Stress

The term stress is used here to include actual stress, motivation, desire, etc., regardless of the source from which it might arise. The stress may have one of two origins. First would be from natural disaster or from some other form of externally imposed threat. The second would be motivation arising from increased level of expectation, changes in values, etc. In other words stress arising in the first case is essentially a threat to the status quo as in the cases of the crisis studies where a present equilibrium is threatened. In the second case stress results rather from an increase in the level of equilibrium along some dimension of desire.

The outcome seems much the same regardless of the source of the stress, but the two situations may appear somewhat different when they are experienced, and may have later implications for refinements in the model. Probably the first will tend to be more severe in its effects.

Our attention will be directed first to movements along the goal structure continuum, or rather shifts between high and low goal structure cells while the leadership pattern remains constant. At this point the assertion will be tested that an increase in situational stress will cause an increase in goal structuring, while reduction in stress will lead to a reduction in goal structuring. This is diagramed in Figure 2.

### Figure 2

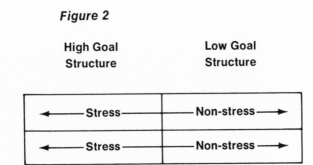

Stress and Tolerance for Ambiguity

There have been a number of studies attempting to relate stress and tolerance of ambiguity. Wispe and Lloyd did a study of 43 life insurance representatives in which they related sales productivity, preference for permissive or structured group organization, and amount of threat perceived in the organizational environment (Wispe and Lloyd, 1955). Using a $\chi^2$ test they find a significant tendency for persons who perceived little threat in their environment to prefer permissiveness in the group organization. Those with a higher threat orientation preferred the more highly structured group situation.

Smock found that groups placed under stress showed a greater tendency to make an early attempt to recognize structure in an ambiguous situation (Smock, 1955). Furthermore, they tended to adhere more strongly to their prerecognition hypothesis in spite of increasing incongruity between their hypothesis and the stimuli.

Cohen reports, from a study using an interview situation, that a highly significant relationship exists between lack of situational structure and the perception of threat in the power exercised by others (Cohen, 1959). This experiment seems to suggest that a perception of threat and the anxiety or stress caused by such a perception can be reduced by seeking to increase situational structure.

Stress and Goal Clarity

Though specific empirical evidence has not been found, it might be suggested that in the absence of stress a group will tend to maintain less structured goals or objectives. This is only to say that we tend to seek to maintain the status quo when our drives are satisfied and we feel secure. The development of specific goals which might be difficult to attain develops the possibility of failure and creates anxiety or the pressure for attaining these goals. A less structured goal situation is safer and less threatening.

When stress is introduced, the status quo is no longer satisfactory and change is sought to reduce the anxiety. The highly non-operational goal of anxiety reduction is introduced. If the cause of the stress is ambiguous, this in itself will further serve to increase the anxiety. It can be expected that the first efforts will be made to reduce the ambiguity by attempting to identify or give structure to the source of the anxiety.

Another source of ambiguity will be present when, even though the source of the stress is clear, it is not exactly clear what actions can be taken to remove the source of the stress.

Anxiety seems to serve as a motivation for three actions, which must logically be made in sequence. The completion of any one of these will serve to reduce a part of the anxiety.

1. Identify the source of the anxiety.
2. Identify the steps which must be taken to remove the anxiety.
3. Carry out the steps identified in 2.

The first two parts of the sequence are concerned primarily with reduction of ambiguity, but are nearly essential to successful purposeful (as opposed to random) actions to reduce the anxiety. The ambiguity is a frustrating experience because it stands as a barrier to successful action. As Lewin points out, "An unstructured region has the same effect as an impassable obstacle. Being in unstructured surroundings leads to uncertainty of behavior because it is not clear whether a certain action will lead to or away from a goal" (Lewin, 1959, p. 255).

Torrance, who studied a group of 200 Air Force personnel downed over enemy territory during World War II or Korea, relates the results of situations where the ambiguity is not reduced (Torrance, 1954). He found that in this very stressful survival situation two types of structural unclarity were likely to be evident: (1) Unclear field structure, or the "degree to which certain patterns of interdependencies or linkages have been stabilized." He found that these were likely to lead to either random, trial-and-error behavior, or to development of a feeling of hopelessness which usually led to surrender to the enemy.

Studies have found that in stressful situations where goal and path clarity is not established, there will be a tendency to avoid the situation or to leave the group.

Gerard reported that low-status subjects whose group goals were unclear tended to withdraw from their group, become dissatisfied with their roles, and to devaluate their own effectiveness (Gerard, 1960, p. 397).

Weitz conducted a study of 474 life insurance salesmen who tend, as the nature of their occupation, to be under considerable competitive stress. A detailed book describing the work to be done was given to 226 of them. The other 248 were not given the book. There was a considerably higher rate of termination among those for whom the situation was not clearly defined (Weitz, 1956).

It should be quite clear that once a goal is attained, it is no longer a goal. If the goal has been attained and the anxiety reduced, the group has almost automatically relocated itself in the low goal structure situation. Of course this is looking to a sort of "pure" case. Particularly in a larger organization it would be highly unlikely that all goals would be attained and all anxieties removed at any particular point in time. It seems at least conceptually possible, however, to think in terms of an over-all index of anxiety and degree of goal structuring in order to place the group along the goal structure continuum.

## CHANGES IN LEADERSHIP

The shifts from one goal structure cell to another are merely incidental to a unified hypothesis regarding the development of pressures for shifts between democratic and authoritarian leadership.

### The "Natural" Shifts in Leadership Patterns

While it is possible for these shifts between democratic and authoritarian leadership to take place at either the high or low goal structure levels, the hypothesis to be tested suggests that *unless outside pressure or force is exerted,* the direction of the shifts in the high goal structure situation will be only from democratic to authoritarian and in the low goal structure situation it will be only from authoritarian to democratic. This is represented very simply in Figure 3.

*Figure 3*

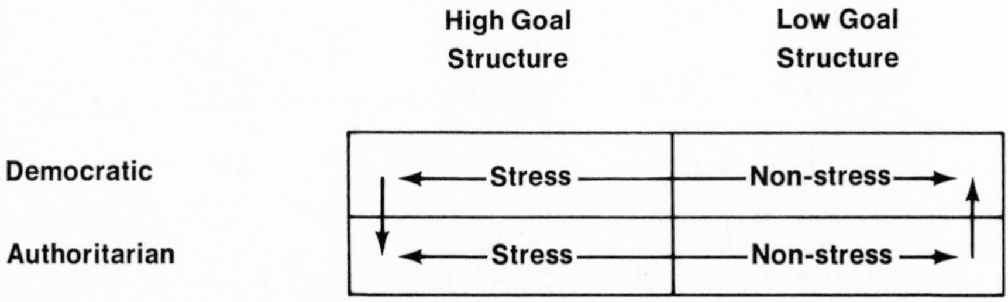

|  | High Goal Structure | Low Goal Structure |
| --- | --- | --- |
| Democratic | ←——Stress—— | ——Non-stress——→ |
| Authoritarian | ←——Stress—— | ——Non-stress——→ |

## High Stress Shift from Democratic to Authoritarian Leadership

We have already established that under stressful conditions there will be strong pressures exerted for the development of clear goals and clearly defined methods of attaining them. In going one step further, we may also expect that the more compelling and/or the more clearly structured the goal, the greater will be the desire to take a direct approach to the attainment of the goal. Pleasant socializing is replaced with more intense emphasis on achievement. This would suggest attempting to attain complete control over any ambiguities in the environment, especially those ambiguities which take the form of deviant individuals or subgroups. The greater the immediacy or urgency, the greater the demand that all available resources be channeled directly toward the attainment of this goal. This is sometimes difficult to do while still attempting to maintain truly democratic institutions.

Deviants loom as frustration-creating barriers to the goal attainment. The most direct way to remove the barrier is to control it and move it at will. There are two basic forms which this control may take. Of course, here again we must realize that we are in reality dealing with a continuum. The first is the control common to democratic institutions where certain limits are set on action, and control is carried out by the policing of exceptions. Actual attainment of goals is more likely to depend on conformity attained through perceived commonality of interest or through group social pressures. The second form of control is the authoritarian form which seeks to maintain absolute control over every action taking place within the organization. The greater the pressures for collective action and the greater the tendency for deviation within the group, the more likely it is that this form of control will have the greater appeal.

The assertion is explicit in the model that a democratic organization can maintain itself with a well-defined goal structure. It now remains to establish the conditions under which this is likely to be the case, as well as stating those conditions under which the appeal of authoritarianism will be more overpowering.

When is democracy retained?

We can see from the nature of the control methods available under democracy that the success of democracy in the face of crisis depends to large degree on the cohesiveness of the group and its ability to apply sanctions through social pressure. This is most assured if the goal is clear, the path to the goal is clear, and individuals identify their own objective with group objectives and agree on the methods of attaining these. This means essentially a minimum of unresolved ambiguity. The statement is to some extent redundant in that when the goal and path are clear it is almost a definitional matter that all who agree on the goal or identify with the group will also agree on the path. To the extent that there is disagreement, we might consider the goal or the path to contain elements of ambiguity.[3]

When is there a shift to authoritarianism?

Stress reduction in itself does not provide a unifying group goal due to its rather extreme non-operational, ambiguous character. Cohesiveness under stress is dependent, on some agreement as to the source of the stress, or on the goal, the attainment of which will reduce the stress. Further cohesiveness can be developed through agreement on the path to the attainment of the goal. Since the cohesiveness of the group becomes more and more task-oriented as the stress increases, the group will be evaluated in terms of its potential for providing a means of completing the task-stress reduction. Thus the less the agreement within the group with regard to how the objective may be attained, the less the individual who disagrees with the group view will be attracted to the group and the more he will attempt to take independent action, form opposition groups, etc.

This situation may be expected to lead to more overt action on the part of leaders to control these deviants in order to reduce the ambiguity which they face in their decision-making. Control over the deviants gives them greater control over their environment and removes impediments to what they consider to be effective action. The greater the stress, and the less the clarity and general agreement on goals and path, the greater the compulsion among the group members to give power to a central person who in essense promises to remove the ambiguity and reduce the stress. Hook points out that, ". . . insofar as alternatives of action are open, or even conceived to be open—a need will be felt for a hero to initiate, organize, and lead" (Hook, 1943, p. 13).

That there is a tendency toward reliance on a power figure in ambiguous situations may be demonstrated at even very low levels on the continuum as is demonstrated in a study by Waring, Dwyer, and Junkin (1951, p. 255). They found that during meals on the first day of nursery

---

[3] Although this seems the situation most conducive to maintaining democratic leadership in time of stress or even crisis, it may be seen that there is also a danger in complete agreement, because in this case there may be too little concern with maintaining restrictions on the power of leaders. If those in power are opportunists, this provides their opportunity to establish authoritarian control. Thus even when the real crisis is passed, the people may find that now they are unable to regain the power which they originally passed to the central authority. "Where a democracy is wise, it will wholeheartedly cooperate with its leaders and at the same time be suspicious of the powers delegated to them—a difficult task but one which must be solved if democracy is not to become, as often in the past, a school for tyrants" (Hook, 1943, p. 14).

school, children were more ready to acquiesce to the advice of the adult than later on when they felt themselves to be on better known ground for resisting. In other words, during the period of initial ambiguity, they tended to submit to an authoritarian leader on whom they relied to help structure the situation.

Hamblin found in laboratory groups subjected to apparent crisis in a problem-solving experience a tendency to replace the old leader with a new leader if the old leader did not have an obvious solution to the crisis problem (Hamblin, 1960). Hertzler did an analysis of 35 historical dictatorships. Although his method was not as systematic and objective as might be desired, his conclusion is consistent with the one reached here.

> A befuddled and fearsome mass in time of crisis is nearly always ready, nay anxious, to give over control to anyone who gives evidence of ability to wield it efficiently. This situation, in turn, both demands and provides the opportunity for a leader or a cohesive minority group which offers a ready made formula of social procedure and which promises a dynamic attack upon the problems [Hertzler, 1940, p. 160].

Other experiments have demonstrated increased suggestibility in situations of ambiguity which point up the increased possibility for an authoritarian leader to introduce distorting suggestions when ambiguity is present. Luchins and Luchins presented subjects with a picture identification task (Luchins, 1955). Subjects were influenced by an overheard judgment and by the experimenter's evaluation of the communication as right or wrong. Although there was more agreement with the true than with the false communications, the conformity with false communications, and failures to respond were higher for the ambiguous than for the clear-cut pictures.

Coffin conducted a series of studies which are relevant to the present problem. In one case he used the Rorschach ink-blot tests as the ambiguous stimulus (Coffin, 1941). Subjects were given a fictitious journal article stating that business and professional men would see the blot in one way while laborers would see them in another way. Using college students as subjects, the conclusion was reached that "subjects may be influenced by suggestion not only to accept or assent to a suggested statement, but actively to construct the imaginative situation in accordance with the suggestion given" (p. 64). From this not-very-surprising conclusion we see a laboratory demonstration of an often used political technique to force judgments in unfavorable situations. "A good American will recognize that . . . etc."

Another experiment by Coffin revealed low but consistent correlation between suggestibility and difficulty of a set of math problems (1941). The degree of suggestibility declined with years of mathematical training. This may have particular relevance in the underdeveloped countries where the tasks are indeed difficult, yet the level of training is very low. It is in these countries where there seems to be the greatest susceptibility to authoritarian leadership.[4]

Still another experiment conducted by Coffin, used sound stimuli and again found that suggestibility increased as the ambiguity of the assigned task increased (Coffin, 1941).

### Shifts from Authoritarian to Democratic Leadership Under Low Stress

In the low stress situation, it would seem difficult for authoritarian leadership to maintain itself. We can expect that the power held by the authoritarian figure will be reduced as was found in a study by Hamblin (1960). He found that the person with highest influence in a group had the greatest influence (relative to other members of the group) during periods of crisis. This influence decreased as the goal was attained and the crisis was thereby reduced or removed.

Once major group goals have been attained, the cohesiveness of the group will once again come to depend more upon the socializing process. Greater importance will be placed on the attempt to satisfy individual needs which may have been either sacrificed or frustrated by the authoritarian leadership.

As in the case of the White and Lippitt study there will be decreased satisfaction with the authoritarian structure and the opportunity for greater individual participation and self-determination will be desired. In many cases the surface expressions of this discontent exhibited in the presence of the authoritarian leader are such as to probably go unnoticed, but at least in the White and Lippitt study these showed up clearly in careful analysis.

The following expressions of the discontent were noted (White and Lippitt, 1960, pp. 74–6).

1. Four boys dropped out of the clubs during the experimental situation and all did so during periods of autocratic leadership.

---

[4] When Hook points out that, "A successful democracy, . . . , may honor its statesmen: but it must honor its teachers more . . ." (1943, p. 238), he is in a way suggesting that a democracy must be able to decrease situational ambiguity through increased knowledge of the situations likely to be encountered rather than relying upon a hero leader to provide this structure.

2. Nineteen of twenty boys who made direct comparisons between the autocratic and democratic leaders stated preferences for the democratic leader.

3. The boys made significantly more discontented remarks to each other under autocratic than under democratic rule.

4. There were more expressions of discontent directed at the leader.

5. There was more ignoring of the leader's approaches.

Over a longer period of time as these resentments built up under the confining authority, we might expect that more overt signs of discontent would develop.

### "Unnatural!" Shifts in Leadership Patterns

One can hardly imagine shifts between democratic and authoritarian leadership taking place in directions opposite to those just discussed *if* indeed the important variables are as they have been described. Cases can easily be found, however, of shifts counter to the direction indicated. It might be established that *these* shifts do not usually take place as a matter of group acceptance or from other internal pressures, but rather are forced upon the group through superior strength. A military dictator may arise in a time of indifference and establish military control; a department or office of a larger firm may be suddenly assigned a new administrator who introduces a more centralized control, etc. These shifts do take place, but they are of a somewhat artificial nature compared with the processes which we have been discussing.

A shift from authoritarian to democratic leadership in a situation of high stress would also seem to be very unlikely unless an outside force dedicated to democratic leadership overthrew or replaced the former leaders and then significantly reduced the source of the stress that had kept the authoritarian leader in power. Other special cases might be presented where an authoritarian leader apparently gave up his power voluntarily in time of high stress, but such occurrence is rare and such cases would have to be examined individually to determine their relationship to the present model.

### THE EQUILIBRIUM CELLS

It should be clear that there are resistances to shifts in leadership patterns taking place. These are created by tradition and vested interest. There are thus important restraining factors involved to prevent the shifts previously indicated. The hypothesis we have developed establishes only the direction of the pressures which exist for change, but does not promise that the change will actually take place.

The direction of the pressures suggests that in the highly structured goal situation the equilibrium cell is one in which authoritarian leadership is exercised, while in the low goal structure situation, it is democratic leadership which exists in the equilibrium situation. In the low goal structure group, the emphasis will be on individual subgoals rather than super organization goals. In a sense this might be considered the characteristic nature of the democracy with its emphasis on the individual rather than the group. In this situation the group leadership will be sought which will serve the advancement of the individual. The autocrat will be hard put to maintain his position.

When a more all consuming group goal is developed, the individual's role becomes subservient to the group and his only importance comes in his contribution to the group. This is the situation in the high goal structure condition and it is here that the autocracy will be in equilibrium. The democratic government will be in constant danger of running into new ambiguities and losing its consensus support.

### Maintaining Authoritarian Equilibrium

It seems that authoritarian leaders have a particular appreciation of the equilibrium acting to maintain their power in the high stress, highly structured goal situation. Thus it can be seen that one of the most important activities of a dictatorship is that of stressing the threats created by both external and internal enemies in order to maintain the stress and produce the super goals which can be used to unite the populace. These must be constantly internalized by the people.

In Indonesia this is represented by the "struggle for West Irian" which is reiterated in nearly every public utterance by every public official. For the Communist countries, the "foe" is the menace of capitalism, represented by the United States in particular. The most extreme emphasis is placed on this in Communist China, where the internal problems are much more severe than in Russia for example. Considerable dependence is placed on these central goals in directing the people's attention away from the frustration experienced in satisfying their true personal goals.[5]

---

[5] It will be noted that China is an especially complex case, as the "manufactured" crisis is used to structure the stress created by a real internal crisis. The attempt is to develop a structure more consistent with retaining the present government in power than would be the case if the structure were allowed to develop around the true source of the stress.

In Sussman's study we find a case where a group leader was attempting to maintain an essentially authoritarian leadership position; however, this leader made little pretense of establishing or working toward group goals. "Leadership as it existed in Calorie Collectors was one of attainment of personal influence and power by Mrs. Lott rather than achievement of group goals. The result was ultimate factionalism and disorganization" (Sussman, 1956, p. 354). The group disintegrated and later reformed around another woman who was oriented more toward group objectives of planning programs to encourage weight reduction. This gives one example of loss of control by an authoritarian leader in a situation where the leader did not identify with group goals.

It is interesting to note a further technique used by the authoritarian to maintain his leadership. This is mentioned in the operational definition by White and Lippitt. "Techniques and activity steps dictated by the authority, one at a time, so that future steps are always uncertain to a large degree" (White and Lippitt, 1960, p. 26).

This serves several functions. It provides reduction of immediate anxiety, but retains dependence on the authoritarian leader for further reduction of the ambiguity when the present step is completed. It also makes it difficult for failure to be evaluated, as it is not possible to determine the actual importance of any particular step that is taken. It is further not possible to certainly establish whether or not the current step is truly leading toward the *stated* goal. Considerable faith must be placed on the authoritarian. If his work is not accepted, the situation again becomes intolerably ambiguous.

## IMPLICATIONS

It is difficult at this point to discuss specific applications of detailed knowledge of the influence of these situational pressures on leadership. However, it is possible to suggest where applications might be sought.

This study was undertaken from the point of view of an advocate of democratic, or participative leadership. In order to insure the preservation of the democratic structure, it seems essential to understand the forces which cause pressure for a shift from democratic structure to more highly authoritarian structure.

Through greater understanding, possibly either the situations leading to the pressures may be avoided, or effective countermeasures can be established to resist the pressures expected under certain circumstances. Not only does this have implication at the national and international political level and in particular in dealings with newly independent nations, but it might also prove of value in the implementation of the relatively new group-centered theories of management and organization. Systematic study and organization of the forces which resist the successful introduction and application of participative management are the first steps in finding suitable implementation techniques and in establishing the situation or environment in which such types of organization can persist in equilibrium.

More could be done at this point to discuss the problems of leadership in underdeveloped countries which served as the introduction of the paper. Most of the implications should, however, be reasonably clear and will for the present be left as they were presented—the initiating stimulus for undertaking the study. The important problem was to provide the model or "structure" which could then be adapted for application to these specific situational problems. The same statement could be made with regard to the applications to participative management.

## SUMMARY

A model was developed showing how certain situational forces develop to produce shifts between democratic and authoritarian forms of leadership. It was established that where group goals assume greater importance than do individual goals and there are ambiguities obscuring the path to attaining these goals, an authoritarian leadership will be sought to reduce these ambiguities. Where ambiguities are not of a stress-creating nature, that is, not standing in the way of goal attainment, and the attainment of group goals is not seen as a necessary *prior* event to the attainment of individual goals, a more democratic leadership will be sought.

## REFERENCES

Back, Kurt W., "Influence through Social Communication," in E. Maccoby, T. M. Newcomb, and E. L. Hartley (eds.), *Readings in Social Psychology* (New York: Holt, 1958).

Coffin, T. E., "Some Conditions of Suggestion and Suggestibility: a Study of Some Attitudinal and Situational Factors Influencing the Process of Suggestion," *Psychological Monographs,* 241 (1941).

Cohen, A. R., "Situation Structure, Self-esteem, and Threat-oriented Reactions to Power," in D. Cartwright (ed.), *Studies in Social Power* (Ann Arbor, Mich.: Institute for Social Research, 1959).

Gerard, Ralph, Unpublished study reported in D. Cartwright and A. Zander (eds.), *Group Dynamics.* 2d. ed (Evanston: Row, Peterson, 1960).

Hamblin, Robert L., "Leadership and Crises," *ibid.*

Hertzler, J. O., "Crises and Dictatorship," *American Sociological Review,* 5 (1940), pp. 157–169.

Hook, S., *The Hero in History* (New York: John Day, 1943).

Lewin, K., *Field Theory in Social Science* (New York: Harper and Brothers, 1959).

Luchins, A. S. and Luchins, E. H., "Previous Experience with Ambiguous Stimulus under Various Social Influences," *Journal of Social Psychology*, 42 (1955), pp. 249–270.

March, J. G. and Simon, H. A., *Organizations* (New York: John Wiley, 1958).

Smock, C. D., "The Influence of Stress on the 'Intolerance of Ambiguity,' " *Journal of Abnormal and Social Psychology*, 50 (1955), pp. 177–182.

Sussman, Marvin B., "The Calorie Collectors: a Study of Spontaneous Group Formation, Collapse and Reconstruction," *Social Forces*, 34 (1956), pp. 351–356.

Torrance, E. P., "The Behavior of Small Groups Under Stress Conditions of 'Survival,' " *American Sociological Review*, 19 (1954), pp. 751–775.

Waring, E. S., Dwyer, F. M., and Junkin, E., "Guidance: The Case of Ronald," *Cornell Bulletin for Homemakers*, 418 (1939), pp. 1–112, in K. Lewin, *Field Theory in Social Science* (New York: Harper and Brothers, 1951).

Weitz, J. "Job Expectancy and Survival," *Journal of Applied Psychology*, 40 (1956), 245–247.

White, Ralph K. and Lippitt, Ronald, *Autocracy and Democracy: an Experimental Inquiry* (New York: Harper and Brothers, 1960).

Wispe, Lauren G. and Lloyd, Kenneth E., "Some Situational and Psychological Determinants of the Desire for Structured Interpersonal Relations," *Journal of Abnormal and Social Psychology*, 51 (1955), pp. 57–60.

# 7 Values

## A Theory of Organization and Change
## Within Value-Attitude Systems[1]

MILTON ROKEACH

My purpose . . . is to present a first report of an ongoing research program broadly concerned with the relations existing among values, attitudes and behavior. In the first part of this paper, I will consider the functional and structural role which attitudes, values and value systems play within a person's total system of belief (Rokeach, 1960), some conditions which might lead to enduring change in values, and some consequences which might be expected to follow from such change. In the second part of this paper, I will briefly describe our approach to the measurement of values and value systems, and I will report some results relevant to several facets of the theoretical formulations discussed in the first part of this paper.

Unlike other cognitive approaches in contemporary social psychology which focus attention on attitude organization and change, we are focussing our attention primarily on value organization and change. This shift of focus from attitude to value evolves from certain second thoughts that I would like to share with you about the central position which the attitude concept has held in social psychology.

It is now exactly half a century since Thomas and Znaniecki (1918) first proposed that the study of social attitudes should be the central problem of social psychology. In the intervening years the attitude concept has indeed occupied a dominant place in theory and research, and it has been assigned prominent space in the textbooks and handbooks of

Milton Rokeach, "A Theory of Organization and Change Within Value-Attitude Systems." *Journal of Social Issues,* XXIV, No. 1 (1968), pp. 13–33.

[1] Presidential address to the Society for the Psychological Study of Social Issues, the American Psychological Association, September 2, 1967. The work reported here was supported by a grant from the National Science Foundation. I would like to express my appreciation especially to Charles Hollen, Robert Beech and Joseph Bivins for their contributions to the research reported herein.

social psychology. "The concept of attitudes", Allport has written in one of these handbooks, "is probably the most distinctive and indispensable concept in contemporary American psychology. No other term appears more frequently in the experimental and theoretical literature" (1935, 798).

Now, half a century later, the time is perhaps ripe to re-open the question as to whether the attitude concept should continue to occupy the central position it has enjoyed for so long. In raising this question, I do not mean to suggest that it is no longer important nor that it is any the less important now than it has been in the past, but only to ask whether there is now, and indeed whether there always has been, an even more deserving candidate for this central position.

## The Value Concept

Several considerations lead me to place the value concept in nomination ahead of the attitude concept. First, value is clearly a more dynamic concept than attitude having a strong motivational component as well as cognitive, affective and behavioral components. Second, while attitude and value are both widely assumed to be determinants of social behavior, value is a determinant of attitude as well as of behavior. Third, if we further assume that a person possesses considerably fewer values than attitudes, then the value concept provides us with a more economical analytic tool for describing and explaining similarities and differences between persons, groups, nations and cultures.

Consider, finally, the relative ubiquitousness of the value and attitude concepts across disciplines. While attitudes seem to be a specialized concern mainly of psychology and sociology, values have long been a center of theoretical attention across many disciplines—in philosophy, education, political science, economics, anthropology and theology, as well as in psychology and sociology. All these disciplines seem to share a common concern with the antecedents and consequents of value organization and value change. Around such a shared concern we may more realistically anticipate genuine interdisciplinary collaboration.

It might seem somewhat paradoxical, in view of the more central theoretical status generally accorded the value concept, that we should have witnessed over the years a more rapid theoretical advance in the study of attitude rather than value. One reason for this, I suspect, was the more rapid development of methods for measuring attitudes, due to the efforts of such men as Bogardus, Thurstone, Likert and Guttman. A second reason, perhaps, was the existence of a better consensus on the meaning of attitude than value. A third possible reason is that attitudes were believed to be more amenable to experimental manipulation than values. In any event, the ready availability of quantitative methods for measuring attitudes made it only a matter of time before experimentally-minded social psychologists would seek to determine whether the attitude variable could be fruitfully fitted into the classical pretest-treatment-posttest paradigm. And upon finding that attitudes were indeed susceptible to experimental influence, a demand was created for theories of attitude organization and change to explain the results rather than for theories of value organization and change.

I would like to draw special attention to one consequence of the fact that it was the attitude rather than the value variable which thus came into the experimentalist's focus. Bypassing the problem óf values and their relation to attitudes, we settled perhaps a bit too hastily for studies that I will call problems of persuasion to the neglect of what I will call problems of education and re-education. We emphasized, for example, the persuasive effects of group pressure, prestige, order of communication, role playing and forced compliance on attitudes. But we neglected the more difficult study of, say, the more enduring effects of socialization, educational innovation, psychotherapy and cultural change on values.

It was, therefore, our hope that in shifting from a concern with attitudes to a concern with values we would be dealing with a concept which is more central, more dynamic, more economical, a concept which would invite a more enthusiastic interdisciplinary collaboration and which would broaden the range of the social psychologist's traditional concern to include problems of education and re-education as well as problems of persuasion.

## DEFINITIONS OF ATTITUDES, VALUES AND VALUE SYSTEMS

The discussion thus far has proceeded on the assumption that the conceptual boundaries between an attitude and a value, and between a value and a value system, are clear and widely understood. This assumption is surely unwarranted. Since I plan to employ these concepts in distinctively different ways, I am obliged to first define them and to try to spell out the main distinctions I see among them.

An attitude is an organization of several beliefs focussed on a specific object (physical or social, concrete or abstract) or situation, predisposing one to respond in some preferential manner.[2] Some of these beliefs about an object or situation concern matters of fact and others concern matters of evaluation. An attitude is thus a package of beliefs consisting of interconnected assertions to the effect that certain things about a specific object or situation are true or false and other things about it are desirable or undesirable.

---

[2] For a fuller discussion of the nature of attitudes see Rokeach (1968).

## Instrumental and Terminal Values

Values, on the other hand, have to do with modes of conduct and end-states of existence. To say that a person "has a value" is to say that he has an enduring belief that a specific mode of conduct or end-state of existence is personally and socially preferable to alternative modes of conduct or end-states of existence. Once a value is internalized it becomes, consciously or unconsciously, a standard or criterion for guiding action, for developing and maintaining attitudes toward relevant objects and situations, for justifying one's own and others' actions and attitudes, for morally judging self and others and for comparing oneself with others. Finally, a value is a standard employed to influence the values, attitudes and actions of at least some others, for example, our children's.

This definition of value is highly compatible with those advanced by Clyde Kluckhohn (1951), Brewster Smith (1963) and Robin Williams (1968). So defined, values differ from attitudes in several important respects. While an attitude represents several beliefs focussed on a specific object or situation, a value is a single belief which transcendentally guides actions and judgments across specific objects and situations and beyond immediate goals to more ultimate end-states of existence. Moreover, a value, unlike an attitude, is an imperative to action, not only a belief about the preferable but also a preference for the preferable (Lovejoy, 1950). Finally, a value, unlike an attitude, is a standard or yardstick to guide actions, attitudes, comparisons, evaluations and justifications of self and others.

The distinction between preferable modes of conduct and preferable end-states of existence is a more or less familiar one in the philosophical literature on values: it is a distinction between values representing means and ends, between instrumental and terminal values (Lovejoy, 1950; Hilliard, 1950). An instrumental value is therefore defined as a single belief which always takes the following form: "I believe that such-and-such a mode of conduct (e.g., honesty, courage) is personally and socially preferable in all situations with respect to all objects". A terminal value takes a comparable form: "I believe that such-and-such an end-state of existence (e.g., salvation, a world at peace) is personally and socially worth striving for". Only those words or phrases that can be meaningfully inserted into the first sentence are instrumental values, and only those words or phrases than can be meaningfully inserted into the second sentence are terminal values.

Consider next the concept of value system. Many writers have observed that values are organized into hierarchical structures and substructures. Operationally speaking, the concept of value system or hierarchy suggests a rank-ordering of values along a continuum of importance. And given the distinction which I have just drawn between instrumental and terminal values, two separate value systems may be posited—instrumental and terminal—each with a rank-ordered structure of its own, each, no doubt, functionally and cognitively connected with the other, and both systems connected with many attitudes toward specific objects and situations.

It is often the case that a person is confronted with a situation in which he cannot behave in a manner congruent with all of his values. The situation may activate two or more values in conflict with one another. For example, a person may have to choose between behaving compassionately or behaving competently, but not both, between behaving truthfully or patriotically, but not both. Similarly, in a given situation a person may have to choose between such terminal values as self-fulfillment and prestige, between salvation and a comfortable life. A person's value system may thus be said to represent a learned organization of rules for making choices and for resolving conflicts—between two or more desirable modes of behavior or between two or more terminal states to strive for.

Given a reasonably sizeable number of values to be arranged in a hierarchy, a large number of variations are theoretically possible. But it is extremely unlikely that all such value patterns will actually be found. Many social factors can be expected to restrict sharply the number of obtained variations. Similarities of culture, social system, caste and class, sex, occupation, education, religious up-bringing and political orientation are some of the major variables which are likely to shape in more or less similar ways the value systems of large numbers of people. We may thus expect that while personality factors will give rise to variations in individual value systems, cultural, institutional and social factors will nevertheless restrict such variations to a reasonably small number of dimensions.

## MENTAL ORGANIZATION OF VALUE-ATTITUDE SYSTEMS

The conceptual distinctions I have drawn between attitudes and values, between instrumental and terminal values and between values and value systems suggest that there are different numbers of attitudes, instrumental values and terminal values within a person's total system of beliefs. The distinctions suggest that a grown person possesses thousands and perhaps tens of thousands of attitudes toward specific objects and situations, but only several dozens of instrumental values and perhaps only a few handfuls of terminal values. Such a difference in numbers immediately points to the presence of a hierarchically connected system of attitudes and values. Let us suppose that the thousands of attitudes within a person's total belief system are all in the service of and cognitively connected with perhaps a few dozen instrumental values, and that the instrumental values are, in their turn, functionally and cognitively connected with an even fewer number of terminal values.[3] We can further suppose that this value-attitude system is more or less internally consistent and will determine behavior, and that a change in any part of the system will affect other connected parts and that it will lead to behavioral change.

It is now possible to discern the outlines of at least four separate subsystems within the value-attitude system just described, and we may concern ourselves with problems of measurement, organization and change within any one of these subsystems considered separately. First, several beliefs may be organized together to form a single attitude focussed on a specific objection or situation. Second, two or more attitudes may be organized together to form a larger attitudinal system, say, a religious or political system. Third and fourth, two or more values may be organized together to form an instrumental or a terminal value system.[4]

This description of a person's value-attitude system is incomplete, however, unless we also represent within it at least three additional kinds of cognitions or beliefs that are continually fed into the value-attitude system, in order to provide it with the raw materials for growth and change. Coordinated with the four subsystems just mentioned there are, fifth, the cognitions a person may have about his own behavior (or commitments to behavior), sixth, the cognitions he may have about the attitudes, values,

---

[3] Woodruff and DiVesta (1948) were perhaps the first to clearly formulate the idea that attitudes are functionally and cognitively connected with values. The kinds of values which these authors and others (Smith, 1949; Peak, 1955; Rosenberg, 1956; and Carlson, 1956) apparently had in mind were terminal values. Scott (1959, 1965), on the other hand apparently had instrumental values in mind. The present formulation attempts to go beyond these formulations to propose an operational distinction between terminal and instrumental values, to propose that there are many attitudes, fewer instrumental values, and even fewer terminal values and to propose that attitudes, instrumental and terminal values are all functionally interrelated.

[4] As already indicated, the major portion of our combined research efforts have been directed primarily toward measuring and gaining a better understanding of organization and change in the first and second subsystems of the more inclusive value-attitude system—single and multiple attitude organizations. But what seems to have received considerably less systematic attention thus far are problems of measurement, organization and change which are directly focussed on the third and fourth subsystems as such—the instrumental and terminal value systems—and problems of organization and change in the more inclusive value-attitude system containing all four subsystems. Nevertheless, a number of studies have moved significantly to one degree or another in this direction. In addition to the studies already cited the following are especially relevant: the study of terminal value patterns by Hunt (1935), Smith's work on value as a determinant of attitude (1949), White's approach to value analysis (1951), Morris' formulation of 13 Ways (1956) and Kluckhohn and Strodtbeck's cross-cultural study of value orientations (1961).

motives and behavior of significant others, and, seventh, the cognitions he may have about the behavior of physical objects. All such cognitions may be experienced by a person as being consistent or inconsistent to varying degrees with one another or with one or more of the attitudes or values within his value-attitude system.

## CHANGE IN VALUE-ATTITUDE SYSTEMS

We not only seek to describe the manner in which value-attitude systems may be organized but also how they may change. In common with other balance formulations the present theory also postulates a motivation for consistency, but consistency is defined, primarily, as consistency with self-esteem (Deutsch, Krauss and Rosenau, 1962; Malewski, 1962; Frentzel, 1965) and, secondarily, as consistency with logic or reality. While a person will typically strive for both kinds of consistency, consistency with self-esteem is probably a more compelling consideration than consistency with logic or reality.

But we seek to go beyond contemporary consistency theories to articulate systematically all the combinations of elements or subsystems of elements that can conceivably be brought into an inconsistent relation with one another. In our efforts to formulate a theory of organization and change within value-attitude systems we are groping toward a theory of dissonance-induction as well as a theory of dissonance-reduction. We ask: How many different types of inconsistent relations might a person experience naturally, or might he be induced to so experience? Are there theoretical grounds for supposing that certain types of inconsistent relations are more likely to be psychologically upsetting than other types? Will certain types of inconsistent relations lead to larger and more enduring change than other types? And are certain types of inconsistent relation likely to have more far-reaching consequences for cognition and behavior than other types?

Let us posit that a person strives for consistency within and between each and every one of the seven subsystems that I have just represented within the value-attitude system. If we label these subsystems A to G we can then produce a matrix, shown in Table 1, of all the possible relations which a person might experience or might be induced to experience as inconsistent.

The matrix suggests at least 28 relations which may be experienced as cognitively inconsistent. The diagonals represent seven such possibilities *within* each of the subsystems: AA represents an inconsistent relation between two or more beliefs within a single attitude organization; BB represents an inconsistent relation between two or more attitudes within an attitude system; CC represents an inconsistent relation between two or more instrumental values within the instrumental value system; and so on. The remaining 21 relations shown in Table 1 represent possible experiences of inconsistency *between* subsystems. Type CD, for example, represents an inconsistent relation between a terminal and instrumental value,

**Table 1.** Matrix of Inconsistent Relations Possible Within the Value-Attitude System

| Cognitive Organization of | A | B | C | D | E | F | G |
|---|---|---|---|---|---|---|---|
| A. Attitude | $X^1$ | x | x | $x^2$ | $x^3$ | $x^4$ | x |
| B. Attitude system | | $X^5$ | x | x | x | $x^6$ | x |
| C. Instrumental value system | | | X | x | x | x | x |
| D. Terminal value system | | | | X | x | x | x |
| E. Cognitions about own behavior | | | | | X | x | x |
| F. Cognitions about significant others' attitudes, values, motives, or behavior | | | | | | X | x |
| G. Cognitions about behavior of non-social objects | | | | | | | X |

[1] McGuire (1960)
[2] Abelson and Rosenberg (1958)
[3] Festinger (1957)
[4] Sherif (1965); Hovland, Janis and Kelley (1953, 1957); Janis, *et al.*, 1959); McGuire (1964)
[5] Osgood and Tannenbaum (1955)
[6] Heider (1958) and Newcomb (1961)

as when a person discovers that he places a high value on salvation but a low value on forgiveness; Type AC represents an inconsistent relation between an instrumental value and an attitude, as when a person discovers that he places a high value on tenderness but favors escalating the Vietnam war.

If we now scrutinize contemporary theories of balance and attitude change through the lattice-work of this matrix we may compare them with one another for comprehensiveness of formulation or extent of overlap. Osgood, for example, who is concerned with incongruities between two attitudes linked together by an assertion, is apparently dealing with inconsistencies of Type BB; Festinger, who is typically concerned with inconsistencies between an attitude and a cognition about behavior, is apparently dealing with inconsistencies of Type AE. I have tried to locate within the matrix the specific types of inconsistencies which various balance and attitude change theorists have been mainly concerned with, and you may wish to inspect these more closely at your own leisure. My analysis suggests that each of these theoretical approaches is studying a different part of the elephant, concentrating on different kinds of inconsistent relations, as represented within different cells of the matrix. It also suggests that a majority of all the possible experiences of consistency and inconsistency, especially those implicating the more central parts of the value-attitude system, still remain for the most part unexplored.

The intriguing question now before us is which of the 28 types of inconsistency are likely to lead to the greatest pay-off in magnitude and enduringness of change, in effects on other parts of the system and in effects on behavior. A look at the matrix suggests that the greatest pay-off should come about by bringing into an inconsistent relation the most central elements of the system, those conceived to have the most direct functional and structural connections with the rest of the system. Attention is thus drawn especially to Type DD in the matrix—an inconsistent relation between two or more terminal values—and close behind, to other types combining D with A, B, C, E, F, or G. Since these terminal values are the most centrally located structures, having many connections with other parts of the system, we would expect inconsistencies which implicate such values to be emotionally upsetting and the effects of such inconsistency to dissipate slowly, to be long-remembered, to endure over time, to lead to systematic changes in the rest of the value system, to lead to systematic changes in connected attitudes and, finally, to culminate in behavior change.

I would next like to propose three main methods for inducing a state of inconsistency between any two of the elements shown in Table 1. The first two are well-known, and the third is perhaps new.. First, a person may be induced to engage in behavior which is inconsistent with his attitudes or values. Second, a person may be exposed to new information from a credible source which is inconsistent with information already represented within his value-attitude system. A third way, which to the best of my knowledge has not been employed thus far, and which I hope will open the door to an experimental study of problems of education and re-education, is to expose the person to information about states of inconsistency already existing within his own value-attitude system. What I am proposing here is somewhat analogous to the effects which may be generated by showing a person undergoing a medical examination his X-ray revealing previously unsuspected and unwelcome medical information. It may be assumed that in every person's value-attitude system there already exist inherent contradictions of which he is unaware for one reason or another —compartmentalization due to ego-defense, conformity, intellectual limitations or an uncritical internalization of the contradictory values and attitudes of his reference groups. In other words, feelings of inconsistency may be induced not only by creating it but also by exposing to self-awareness inconsistencies already existing within the system below the threshold of awareness.[5] I will return to this issue shortly.

---

[5] Stotland, Katz and Patcher (1959) have reported some incidental evidence that subjects whose attitude was at variance with their values were more likely to change their attitude in order to bring it into a consistent relation with their values. The functional approach of Katz and his co-workers is, however, somewhat different from the approach discussed here. First, the theoretical approach of these investigators, like that of others, is primarily focussed on the problem of attitude change and

## SOME RESEARCH FINDINGS

I would now like to describe some findings from our current research program that bear on the theory just presented. Our first problem was to find a way to measure value systems, and our approach to this problem was extremely simple. Initially, we collected a dozen instrumental values (e.g., broadminded, clean, forgiving, responsible), another dozen terminal values (e.g., a comfortable life, equality, freedom, salvation), alphabetized each set of values, and simply asked our subjects to rank-order them in order of importance. In a matter of a few minutes we were thus able to obtain data on the relative importance our subjects attached to 24 values—12 instrumental and 12 terminal.

I do not have time here to go into the details of how we initially selected these values, how we improved upon them in successive versions or to discuss the results we obtained along the way. I hope it will suffice to say here that the rank-orderings of instrumental and terminal values seem to be reasonably stable over time: Form A, our initial form composed of 12 instrumental and terminal values, had test-retest reliabilities in the .60's after a seven week period; Form D, our fourth and final version composed of 18 instrumental and terminal values, had test-retest reliabilities in the .70's after 7 weeks. In the course of developing these scales we and terminal values of many groups—college, high school and grade managed to obtain data on the similarities and differences in instrumental school students, various occupational groups, and various religious and political groups. We also obtained data on the factorial dimensions along which instrumental and terminal values are organized, both separately and together, on the relation between instrumental and terminal values, between values and attitudes and between values and behavior.

Especially relevant to the validity of our approach to the theory and measurement of value systems are the results we obtained on the relation between values and behavior, and between values and attitudes. In this connection, let me cite some statistically significant findings concerning religious and political values. We find that the rank-ordering of one terminal value alone—*salvation*—highly predicts church attendance. College students who go to church "once a week or more" rank *salvation* first on the average among 12 terminal values. But other groups—those who attend church "once a month," "once a year," or "never"—typically rank *salvation* last among 12 terminal values.

---

not on value change. Second, they have approached the problems of attitude change by attempting to give their subjects insight into the psychodynamics of their attitudes. In contrast, the present approach skirts the problem of underlying psychodynamics and instead merely attempts to give the subjects insight into whether certain relations within their systems are or are not consistent.

Table 2 shows significant relationships between two distinctively political terminal values—*equality* and *freedom*—and attitude toward civil rights demonstrations. Those who report they are "sympathetic, and have participated" in civil rights demonstrations rank *freedom* first on the aver-

Table 2. Composite Rank-Order for Freedom and Equality and Attitude Toward Civil Rights Demonstrations[a]

|  | Yes, and Have Participated N = 10 | Yes, but Have Not Participated N = 320 | No, not Sympathetic N = 114 | p[b] |
|---|---|---|---|---|
| Freedom | 1 | 1 | 2 | .01 |
| Equality | 3 | 6 | 11 | .001 |

[a] All cell entries are based on the rank-ordering of median scores obtained for 12 terminal values. All references in the remainder of this paper to "composite rank order" are similarly defined.
[b] Obtained by Kruskal-Wallis one-way analysis of variance.

age and *equality* third among 12 terminal values; those who are "sympathetic, but have not participated" rank *freedom* first and *equality* sixth; and those who are "unsympathetic" rank *freedom* second and *equality* eleventh.

A second kind of data we are collecting has a purely descriptive purpose, to determine the extent to which fundamental similarities and differences among various groupings can be meaningfully and economically described solely in value terms. Some of these descriptive data are predictable in advance on the basis of various considerations, thus providing us with additional validity data. For example, *salvation* was found to rank first among 12 terminal values by Lutheran ministers, by students attending a Calvinist college and by Catholic and Lutheran students attending a midwestern university. But *salvation* is typically ranked last by Jewish students and by those expressing no religious preference.

Our descriptive data, however, also provide us with many surprises which cannot be altogether predicted in advance. Consider, for example, some contrasting patterns of findings on *freedom* and *equality* shown in Table 3.

Table 3. Composite Rank-Order for Freedom and Equality for Four Samples

|  | 50 Policemen | 141 Unemployed Whites | 28 Unemployed Negroes | 75 Calvinist Students |
|---|---|---|---|---|
| Freedom | 1 | 3 | 10 | 8 |
| Equality | 12 | 9 | 1 | 9 |

Fifty policemen from a medium-sized midwestern city rank *freedom* first on the average and *equality* last, showing a value pattern even more extreme than that of college students who are unsympathetic with civil rights demonstrations. Unemployed whites applying for work at a state employment office show a similar pattern, though not as extreme as that of policemen. Unemployed Negroes applying for work show a reverse value pattern—*freedom* is ranked tenth, and *equality* is ranked first. Finally, Calvinist students show yet another pattern: both *freedom* and *equality* are ranked relatively low in their hierarchy of terminal values.

All these data on *freedom* and *equality,* as well as other considerations which I do not have time to discuss here, seem to point to the presence of a simple, nonetheless comprehensive two-dimensional model for describing major variations among various political orientations. Picture, if you will, the four points of a compass. I will represent at the north pole those groups that place a high value on both *freedom* and *equality,* such as the liberal democrats, socialists and humanists; at the south pole, I will represent those groups that place a low value on both *freedom* and *equality,* such as the fascists, Nazis and KKK; to the east, on the right, I will represent those groups that place a high value on *freedom* and a low value on *equality,* such as the John Birch Society, conservative Republicans and followers of Ayn Rand; finally, to the west, on the left, I will represent those groups that place a low value on *freedom* and a high value on *equality,* such as the Stalinist or Mao type Communism.

Data supporting this model have recently been obtained in a study carried out in collaboration with James Morrison. We selected 25,000-word samples from political writings representing the four poles, and counted the number of times various terminal and instrumental values were explicitly mentioned. Samples were taken from socialist writers like Norman Thomas and Erich Fromm, Hitler's *Mein Kampf,* Goldwater's *Conscience of a Conservative* and Lenin's *Collected Works.* Table 4 shows the results obtained for the two terminal values, *freedom* and *equality.*[6]

The socialists mention *freedom* favorably 66 times and they mention *equality* favorably 62 times. For the socialists, *freedom* turned out to rank first and *equality* second in relative frequency among 17 terminal values. Employing these same 17 terminal values, analysis of Hitler's *Mein Kampf* revealed that *freedom* was ranked 16th and *equality* 17th. In Goldwater's hierarchy of values, *freedom* ranked first and *equality* 16th; and in Lenin's the results were the other way around, *freedom* ranking 17th and *equality* first. All in all, these data seem to fit the two-dimensional model almost perfectly.

---

[6] A fuller report on all the values—instrumental and terminal—will be presented in a separate report.

**Table 4.** Frequency of Mention and Rank-Order of Freedom and Equality in Writings by Socialists, Hitler, Goldwater and Lenin

|  | Socialists | | Hitler | | Goldwater | | Lenin | |
|---|---|---|---|---|---|---|---|---|
|  | Freq.* | Rank | Freq. | Rank | Freq. | Rank | Freq. | Rank |
| Freedom | +66 | 1 | −48 | 16 | +85 | 1 | −47 | 17 |
| Equality | +62 | 2 | −71 | 17 | −10 | 16 | +88 | 1 |

\* Number of favorable mentions minus number of unfavorable mentions.

While I do not have time here to elaborate further on this model or to consider its implications, I do want to raise the question of possible inconsistencies within a person's value-attitude system which might involve *freedom* and *equality*. One of the advantages we gain in asking our subjects to rank-order a set of positive values for importance is that the subject, having little or no awareness of the psychological significance of his responses, has little or no reason to disguise them. In this sense, our value scales function like projective tests. All the values we employ, considered in isolation, are socially desirable ones in our culture and, in the final analysis, the subject has only his own value system to guide him in rank-ordering them. Thus, a subject who ranks *freedom* first and *equality* last (or who ranks, say *salvation* first and *a comfortable life* second) is not apt to be aware of the possibility that he may be revealing something about himself that others might interpret as anti-democratic or logically inconsistent, or, even, as hypocritical. But some of our subjects, upon having their attention drawn to the fact that they ranked *freedom* and *equality* in a highly discrepant manner or that they ranked both *freedom* and *equality* relatively low seemed embarrassed by their ratings. I would suggest that embarrassment is one overt behavioral manifestation of cognitive imbalance.

This discussion of possible inconsistencies lurking below the threshold of awareness brings me back to the matrix of dissonant relations previously discussed and presented in Table 1. I have already suggested that a felt state of inconsistency in relation between two values or between a value and an attitude or between one's values and a reference group's values should lead to persistent dissonance effects, which, to alleviate, would require change to make them more consistent with one another. I would now like to report briefly on the results of an experiment designed to test these expectations.

Three groups of subjects, Control Group A and Experimental Groups B and C, first filled out an attitude questionnaire concerning equal rights for the Negro, equal rights for other groups, and American policy in Vietnam. A week later all three groups rank-ordered the 12 terminal values shown in Table 5. Experimental Group B was then presented with information in the form of "Table 1" showing the composite rank orders actually obtained by 444 Michigan State University students for these same 12 values. To arouse feelings of inconsistency between two terminal values the experimenter drew attention to "one of the most interesting findings shown in Table 1" namely, that the students, on the average, ranked *freedom* 1 and *equality* 6. "This suggests," the experimenter continued, "that Michigan State students in general are more interested in their own freedom than they are in freedom for other people." The subjects were then invited to compare their own rankings with those shown in "Table 1."

The procedure with the subjects in Experimental Group C was identical with that for Group B except for the fact that they were shown "Table 2" in addition to "Table 1." The purpose of "Table 2" was to induce an additional dissonant relation between a value and an attitude. "Table 2" showed the relationship between civil rights attitude and average rankings of *freedom* and *equality* (the same results shown herein in Table 2). The experimenter discussed these results in some detail and then concluded: "This raises the question as to whether those who are against civil rights are really saying that they care a great deal about *their own* freedom but are indifferent to other people's freedom. Those who are *for* civil rights are perhaps really saying they not only want freedom for themselves, but for other people too." The subjects were then invited to compare the results shown in "Table 2" with their own previously-recorded responses to the same civil rights question and with their own previously-recorded rankings on *freedom* and *equality*.

Posttests on values and attitudes were administered three weeks later and three to five months later—to the two experimental groups as well as to the control group, which had received no information. The overall results are shown in Table 5.

Control Group A showed small and generally non-significant changes in values three weeks later and three months later. Note that there was a significant change in *freedom* three months later, but that it is in a negative direction. But Experimental Group B shows significantly positive increases in *equality* and in *freedom* three weeks later. Three to five months later we still find sizable increases in *equality,* which is significant, and in *freedom,* which is not significant. For Experimental Group C we observe significant positive changes on both *equality* and *freedom*—three weeks later as well as three to five months later.

Along with these experimentally-induced increases in the importance of *equality* and *freedom* we also observe systematic changes in the rest of the value system. Other social values—*a world at peace* and *national security*—consistently increase in importance, while personal values —*a comfortable life, a meaningful life, maturity, salvation, true friendship*

**Table 5.** Mean Changes in Rank-Order of 12 Terminal Values for Control and Experimental Groups 3 Weeks and 3 Months Later

|  |  | Group A | Group B | Group C |
|---|---|---|---|---|
|  |  | N = | | |
|  | 3 wks | 47 | 135 | 178 |
|  | 3 mos | 32 | 93 | 120 |
| A comfortable life | 3 wks | .17 | −.48* | −.34 |
|  | 3 mos | .09 | −.57 | −.61* |
| A meaningful life | 3 wks | −.23 | −.39 | −.29 |
|  | 3 mos | .25 | −.44 | −.20 |
| A world at peace | 3 wks | .34 | .61* | .18 |
|  | 3 mos | .19 | .62* | .30 |
| Equality | 3 wks | .79 | 1.47*** | 1.72*** |
|  | 3 mos | .44 | 1.47*** | 1.68*** |
| Freedom | 3 wks | −.47 | .78** | .70*** |
|  | 3 mos | −1.19** | .48 | .46* |
| Maturity | 3 wks | −.04 | −.10 | −.13 |
|  | 3 mos | 1.16 | −.10 | −.17 |
| National security | 3 wks | .36 | .41 | .55** |
|  | 3 mos | .31 | .65 | .54* |
| Respect for others | 3 wks | .11 | .16 | −.11 |
|  | 3 mos | .75 | −.03 | .33 |
| Respect from others | 3 wks | .13 | −.09 | −.11 |
|  | 3 mos | .03 | −.52 | .14 |
| Salvation | 3 wks | .15 | −.21 | −.48** |
|  | 3 mos | .09 | −.27 | −.53* |
| True friendship | 3 wks | −.83* | −1.06*** | −1.05*** |
|  | 3 mos | −.72 | −.52* | −1.12*** |
| Wisdom | 3 wks | −.55 | −.99*** | −.61** |
|  | 3 mos | −.28 | −.72* | −.90** |

* $p < .05$   ** $p < .01$   *** $p < .001$, t test for correlated measures.

and *wisdom*—consistently decrease in importance. Many of these changes are statistically significant, and the value changes are evident not only three weeks later but also three to five months later. And the magnitude of the systematic changes observed is on the whole greater for Experimental Group C than for Experimental Group B.

Experimental Groups B and C not only showed enduring changes in values but also in attitudes. We observed enduring changes in attitude toward the two most salient issues in contemporary American life—equal rights and Vietnam. Table 6 shows the nature of the attitude and value changes obtained in four Group C subgroups. The first column shows the results for those subjects who had initially ranked *equality* high and, consistent with this value, were procivil rights in attitude. This subgroup showed no changes in attitudes—either three weeks or three months later—and

**Table 6.** Mean Changes in Values and Attitudes in Four Group C Subgroups

| | | Ranks Equality High and Is | | Ranks Equality Low and Is | |
| | | Procivil Rights | Anticivil Rights | Procivil Rights | Anticivil Rights |
| --- | --- | --- | --- | --- | --- |
| | | N = | | | |
| | 3 wks | 55 | 14 | 70 | 39 |
| | 3 mos | 40 | 8 | 49 | 23 |
| A comfort- | 3 wks | .58 | −.07 | −1.10** | −.36 |
| able life | 3 mos | .13 | .50 | −1.41** | −.57 |
| A meaningful | 3 wks | −.25 | −.50 | −.17 | −.46 |
| life | 3 mos | .28 | −.50 | −.47 | −.35 |
| A world at | 3 wks | .44 | 1.79 | −.27 | .05 |
| peace | 3 mos | .18 | 1.75 | .16 | .30 |
| Equality | 3 wks | .36 | .00 | 3.16*** | 1.67*** |
| | 3 mos | −.23 | −1.13 | 3.71*** | 1.65** |
| Freedom | 3 wks | .82** | .29 | .80* | .49 |
| | 3 mos | .60 | −.50 | .39 | .70 |
| Maturity | 3 wks | −.05 | .57 | .06 | −.85 |
| | 3 mos | −.48 | .63 | .02 | −.30 |
| National | 3 wks | .44 | .86 | .53 | .64 |
| security | 3 mos | .20 | .50 | .73 | .74 |
| Respect for | 3 wks | −.38 | .71* | −.17 | .08 |
| others | 3 mos | .45 | .75 | .29 | .09 |
| Respect from | 3 wks | −.13 | .00 | −.73* | 1.00* |
| others | 3 mos | .68 | −.13 | −.37 | .39 |
| Salvation | 3 wks | −.67* | −.14 | −.57* | −.15 |
| | 3 mos | −.65 | .25 | −.80 | −.04 |
| True | 3 wks | −.58 | −1.57* | −1.30*** | −1.05* |
| friendship | 3 mos | −.33 | −1.25 | −1.43* | −1.78** |
| Wisdom | 3 wks | −.69 | −1.93 | .03 | −1.15* |
| | 3 mos | −1.00* | −.88 | −.86 | −.83 |
| Equal rights | 3 wks | −.47 | 4.57* | .09 | −1.95 |
| for Negroes | 3 mos | .80 | 9.25** | 1.80 | −.30 |
| Equal rights | 3 wks | −.11 | −.43 | .20 | −2.44 |
| for others | 3 mos | .23 | 2.88 | 4.33** | −.26 |
| Vietnam | 3 wks | −1.09 | .36 | .60 | −1.59 |
| | 3 mos | −.83 | .75 | 1.63* | .74 |

\* p < .05    \*\* p < .01    \*\*\* p < .001, t test for correlated measures.

they showed virtually no enduring changes in values. The second column shows the results for those subjects who although initially high on *equality* were nevertheless anticivil rights in attitude. Three months later their values remained unchanged, but notice what had happened to their attitude toward equal rights for the Negro. Three weeks after the experiment their attitude toward equal rights for the Negro increased significantly by a mean of 4.57 in the liberal direction; and three to five months later the mean increase had grown to 9.25. The other two attitudes—equal rights for others and Vietnam—did not change for this group.

The third column shows the results obtained for those subjects whose initial attitude was also inconsistent with their value for *equality*. They had ranked *equality* low but had nevertheless expressed sympathy for civil rights demonstrations. Three weeks and three months after the experimental session they showed sizeable and highly significant increases in *equality*, thereby bringing *equality* into alignment with their procivil rights attitude, and they also showed significant decreases in two personal values, *a comfortable life* and *true friendship*. And this group, already pro-Negro in attitude, became significantly more favorable in their attitude toward equal rights for others and significantly more dove-like in their attitude toward the American presence in Vietnam. These attitude changes were not evident three weeks after the experimental session, but they were clearly evident three months afterward—a "sleeper" effect.

Consider, finally, the fourth column which shows the results for those subjects who consistently ranked *equality* low and were anticivil rights. Three months later these subjects valued *equality* significantly more and *true friendship* significantly less. But we found no changes in attitudes for this group.

All these results are reasonably consistent with the now widely accepted proposition that a necessary condition for change is a state of cognitive inconsistency. We have independently measured this state of inconsistency by asking our subjects at the end of the experimental session to tell us whether they felt "satisfied" or "dissatisfied" with what they had found out about the way they had ranked the several values. We found that variations in these intervening states of satisfaction-dissatisfaction were significantly related to variations in discrepancy between values, objectively determined. In turn, these intervening states of dissonance, assessed at the end of the experimental session, significantly predicted the changes in values which were observed three weeks and three months after the experimental treatment.

## IN CONCLUSION

As I conclude this paper I become acutely aware of at least a few questions which should be raised about the methods and findings reported here. Do the various value terms have the same meaning for different subjects? What ethical precautions are especially necessary in research on value change? Are the systematic and the sleeper effects value and attitude changes reported here genuine changes or are they artifacts of the experimental situation? Can we expect behavioral changes to follow from such value and attitude changes? Is it just as consistent for a person to move *freedom* down to *equality,* as to move *equality* up to *freedom?* Under what conditions will values change to become more consistent with attitudes, and will attitudes change to become more consistent with values? Can each of the different kinds of inconsistent relations represented in the matrix be experimentally isolated and their relative effects tested? What are the implications of our formulations and findings for education, therapy and for other areas of human concern which necessarily engage people's values?

For lack of time I must defer considerations of these questions and deal with them in a fuller report on a later occasion. Instead, I would like to return to the main theme stated in the opening to this paper, namely, that there are grounds for arguing in favor of a shift of focus away from theories of attitude organization and change toward more comprehensive theories of value organization and change. The empirical findings I have reported in the latter part of this paper now embolden me to advocate even more strongly the desirability for such a recentering within the discipline of social psychology.

## REFERENCES

Abelson, R. P. and Rosenberg, M. J., "Symbolic Psychologic: a Model of Attitudinal Cognition," *Behavioral Science,* 1958, 3, pp. 1–13.

Allport, G. W., "Attitudes," in C. Murchison (ed.), *A Handbook of Social Psychology* (Worcester: Clark University Press, 1935).

Carlson, E. R., "Attitude Change Through Modification of Attitude Structure," *Journal of Abnormal and Social Psychology,* 1956, 52, pp. 256–261.

Deutsch, M., Krauss, R. M. and Rosenau, Nora, "Dissonance or Defensiveness?" *Journal of Personality,* 1962, 30, pp. 16–28.

Festinger, L., *A Theory of Cognitive Dissonance* (Evanston: Row, Peterson, 1957).

Frentzel Janina, "Cognitive Consistency and Positive Self-concept," *Polish Sociological Bulletin,* 1965, 1, pp. 71–86.

Heider, F., *The Psychology of Interpersonal Relations* (New York: John Wiley, 1958).

Hilliard, A. L., *The Forms of Value* (New York: Columbia University Press, 1950).

Hovland, C. I., Janis, I. L. and Kelley, H. H., *Communication and Persuasion* (New Haven: Yale University Press, 1953).

Hovland, C. I. *et al., The Order of Presentation in Persuasion* (New Haven: Yale University Press, 1957).

Hunt, Alice McC., "A Study of the Relative Value of Certain Ideals," *Journal of Abnormal and Social Psychology,* 1935, 30, pp. 222–228.

Janis, I. L. *et al., Personality and Persuasibility* (New Haven: Yale University Press, 1959).

Kluckhohn, C., "Values and Value Orientations in the Theory of Action," in

T. Parsons and E. A. Shils (eds.), *Toward a General Theory of Action* (Cambridge: Harvard University Press, 1951).

Kluckhohn, Florence R. and Strodtbeck, F. L., *Variations in Value Orientation* (Evanston: Row, Peterson, 1961).

Lovejoy, A. O., "Terminal and Adjectival Values," *Journal of Philosophy,* 1950, 47, pp. 593–608.

Malewski, A., "The Influence of Positive and Negative Self-evaluation on Post-decisional Dissonance," *Polish Sociological Bulletin,* 1962, 3–4, pp. 39–49.

McGuire, W. J., "A Syllogistic Analysis of Cognitive Relationships," in M. J. Rosenberg et al. (eds.), *Attitude Organization and Change* (New Haven: Yale University Press, 1960).

McGuire, W. J., "Inducing Resistance to Persuasion," in L. Berkowitz (ed.), *Advances in Experimental Social Psychology,* Vol. 1 (New York: Academic Press, 1964).

Morris, C. W., *Varieties of Human Value* (Chicago: University of Chicago Press, 1956).

Newcomb, T. M., *The Acquaintance Process* (New York: Holt, Rinehart and Winston, 1961).

Osgood, C. E. and Tannenbaum, P. H., "The Principle of Congruity in the Prediction of Attitude Change," *Psychological Review,* 1955, 62, pp. 42–55.

Peak, Helen, "Attitude and Motivation," in M. R. Jones (ed.), *Nebraska Symposium on Motivation* (Lincoln, Nebraska: University of Nebraska Press, 1955).

Rokeach, M., *The Open and Closed Mind* (New York: Basic Books, 1960).

Rokeach, M., "The Nature of Attitudes," in *International Encyclopedia of Social Sciences* (New York: Macmillan, 1968).

Rosenberg, M. J., "Cognitive Structure and Attitudinal Affect," *Journal of Abnormal and Social Psychology,* 1956, 53, pp. 367–372.

Scott, W. A., "Cognitive Consistency, Response Reinforcement, and Attitude Change," *Sociometry,* 1959, 22, pp. 219–229.

Scott, W. A., *Values and Organizations* (Chicago: Rand McNally, 1965).

Sherif, Carolyn W., Sherif, M. and Nebergall, R. E., *Attitude and Attitude Change: the Social Judgment-Involvement Approach* (Philadelphia: Saunders, 1965).

Smith, M. B., "Personal Values as Determinants of a Political Attitude," *Journal of Psychology,* 1949, 28, pp. 477–486.

Smith, M. B., "Personal Values in the Study of Lives," in R. W. White (ed.), *The Study of Lives* (New York: Atherton Press, 1963).

Stotland, E. Katz, D. and Patchen, M., "The Reduction of Prejudice Through the Arousal of Self-insight," *Journal of Personality,* 1959, 27, pp. 507–531.

Thomas, W. I. and Znaniecki, F., *The Polish Peasant in Europe and America,* Vol. 1 (Boston: Badger, 1918–20).

White, R. K., *Value Analysis: the Nature and Use of Its Methods* (Glen Gardner, N.J.: Libertarian Press, 1951).

Williams, R. M., "Values," in *International Encyclopedia of Social Sciences* (New York: Macmillan, 1968).

Woodruff, A. D. and DiVesta, F. J., "The Relationship Between Values, Concepts, and Attitudes," *Educational and Psychological Measurement,* 1948, 8, pp. 645–660.

# 8 Setting

## Ten Developmental Stages of Society

KAZUMA TATEISI, MITITAKA YAMAMOTO, AND ISAO KON

In the progress and development of human society, science and technology have made a great contribution in drastically changing the structure and course of society, which is recognized as "Technological Innovation."

Technological Innovations have occurred discontinuously and thoroughly changed the social structure being promoted by economic factors. Their accumulated and accelerated momentum is ever more threatening the deepest roots and fundamental structures of our very existence, the values of our human society and culture.

We will introduce SINIC theory—an approach to the future.

SINIC is an abbreviation for Seed-Innovation & Need Impetus Cyclic Evolution of Technological Innovation, being accidentally analogous to the CYNIC theory of the Greek philosophers' school which held that the essence of virtue is self-control.

SINIC theory consists of exploring and forecasting what society presumably, at least with a high plausibility, might be bound to appear, if the autonomous forces now at work in social history were going to proceed in a possible, desirable and realized way.

## INTERRELATION AMONG SCIENCE, TECHNOLOGY AND SOCIETY

Looking back on the history of technological innovation, it is noted that technology makes rapid progress with great spinning off heteronomously by

Kazuma Tateisi, Mititaka Yamamoto, and Isao Kon, "Ten Developmental Stages of Society: SINIC Theory." Excerpts from a paper entitled "SINIC Theory—An Approach to the Future" presented at the International Future Research Conference, Kyoto, Japan, April 10–16, 1970, and included in the "Proceedings of the International Future Research Conference," Vol. 2, published by Kodansha Ltd., 1971, Tokyo, Japan.

## FIGURE 1 SINIC DIAGRAM

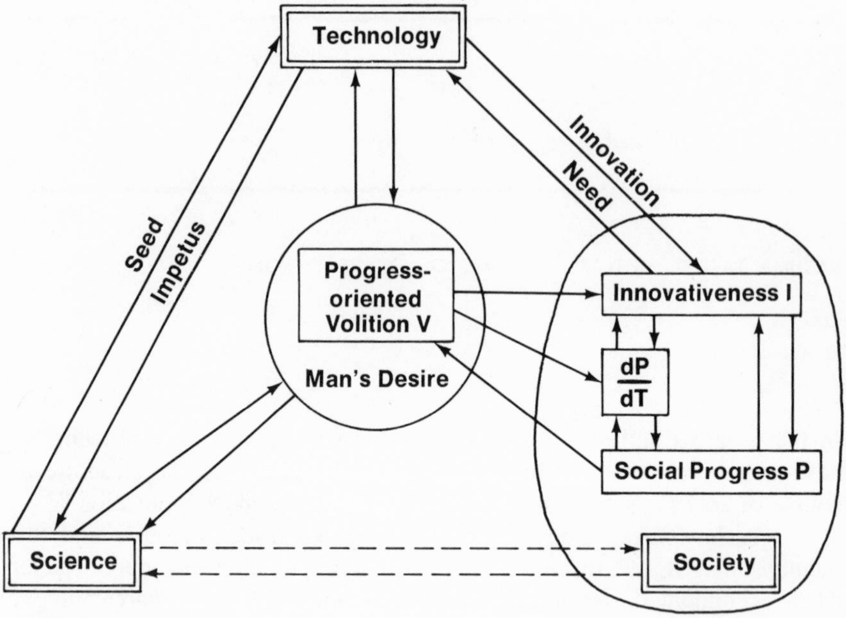

receiving Seed from science and Need from the society, while technology in turn causes Innovation in the society and gives necessary Impetus to science. Accordingly, the evolutive interrelation among science, technology and society could be understood, as shown in Figure 1, to be the Seed-Innovation & Need-Impetus Cyclic Evolution of Technological Innovation—that is, the SINIC theory.

## TEN DEVELOPMENTAL STAGES OF SOCIETY

GNP per capita for the most advanced society at each era would be assumed to be the standard for dividing the development of the human society into ten different stages, together with considerations of epoch-making historical events and normative predictions of the future society.

### 1. Primitive Society (1000M B.C.–12M B.C.)

GNP per capita: Less than $50.

Man came to exist on the earth. He started to ask questions, explore his enjoyment possibilities and wanted to determine his own fate, while keeping the highest place of dignity and motivation power in harmonious balance and fixed order. He surrendered to any experience as ultimate proof of truth with everything including himself.

Man's greatest scientific discovery, the use of fire, and his greatest invention, language, go far back in this prehistoric time. Furthermore, bows and arrows, manufactures of earthenware and so on were invented.

## 2. Collective Society (12M B.C.–700 B.C.)

GNP per capita: $50–$100.

The transition of food gathering to food growing is the main feature of this society. That is, raising of domestic animals, cultivation of land, and construction of stone buildings were introduced. The social form developed from the family community into a clan. This change is called "Socialization." And, the four greatest civilizations rose. Exact observation and recording of nature started the development of the primary sciences in such fields as astronomy, mathematics, metallurgy and astronomy.

## 3. Agricultural Society (700 B.C.–1302)

GNP per capita: $100–$170.

This period saw widely spread agriculture, and the rise of new commercial and industrial classes with the appearance of a monetary economy. Athenian civilization was at the zenith of prosperity, when ancient science developed amazingly since the beginning by Thales in the seventh century B.C. In addition to Roman civilization, the frequently undertaken crusades between the years of Mediaeval Age 1096 and 1291 intensified the development with such general effects as greater awareness of the surrounding world, the greater demand for improved traditional technics, and the increased circulation of coinage.

## 4. Handicraft Society (1302–1765)

GNP per capita: $170–$300.

This period marks a transition from Agricultural Society to Industrialization Society. The inventions of a mariner's compass, gun powder and printing paved the way for the development of handicraft. The Renaissance period witnessed the development of various branches of fundamental science necessary to provide technology for the next Industrialization Society. Leonardo da Vinci took the role of pioneer of modern science and technology. Later on, modern science was established by Galileo, Newton and others.

In the meantime, after the discoveries of the New World and the Indian route, England enjoyed maritime superiority all over the world with the first modern joint stock company. Within the country, the civil revolutions such as the Puritan Revolution and the Glorious Revolution removed the restriction on production exercised before by guilds, and established the freedom of the industrial bourgeois thereby opening the main road for capitalism.

## 5. Industrialization Society (1765–1876)

GNP per capita: $300–$700.

The Industrial Revolution (1760 to 1830) involved the substitution of machinery for hand tools, the introduction of the factory system and the rise of mass production.

As more and more manufacturers began to turn to steam power to run their machines, the Industrial Revolution gained momentum, and mass production became more prevalent, which accelerated the growth of the modern capitalistic society. In 1825, the first cyclic depression occurred that is a sign of a highly developed capitalistic society. In 1857 the first financial panic on a world-wide scale started.

The 18th and 19th centuries saw three major revolutions, i.e., the Industrial Revolution in England, the political revolution in France and the philosophical revolution in Germany.

## 6. Mechanization Society (1876–1945)

GNP per capita: $700–$2,500.

Advances in scientific knowledge have led to advances in technology. From 1870 to 1920 took place the second Industrial Revolution especially in the electric power, automobile, machinery and chemical industries; in addition to the existing traditional light industries, expansion and strengthening of heavy chemical industries were seen. The rise of these new industries resulted in the creation of millions of new jobs. At the same time in Germany, a renovation of the patent system and a systematization of education were carried out as one program for promotion of science and technology, which reflected the mounting competition among capitalistic countries. Furthermore, the research activities by giant monopolistic enterprises gradually became organized.

In the United States, the National Research Council was established after the end of World War I as a permanent organ to solve various technological problems arising as a result of the war. Under the Council, large-scale research organizations such as colleges, state or private research institutes were established.

To cope with such new developments of various kinds of industrial equipment, a new big stride in the progress of technology was essential: more precise production techniques and mass production of machine tools. It was for such mass production purposes that a scientific method of production control was developed by Taylor. Meanwhile, the way for automation was being paved by the systematization of machine techniques and development of automatic machines.

In the 20th century, Einstein established his mass-energy equation, which in later days resulted in technology whereby a huge amount of energy condensed in the form of mass can be released.

## 7. Automation Society (1945–1974)

GNP per capita: $2,500–$5,000.

Remarkable technological innovations took place from 1940 to 1960, the features of which may be summarized as follows: growth of concentrated science type of industries (such as chemical, electronics, aeronautics and nuclear power industries); wide-spread use of synthetic materials; introduction of N C (numerical control) machine tools and electronic control technology with computers; development of systematic method (system engineering); and promotion of big R & D projects by the government.

Automation which had stemmed from mechanization became widely used in industries as mechanical automation, business automation and process automation by means of computers having feed-back control function.

The economy became more and more international and the activities of world enterprises became further intensified. In business, stress shifted from the conventional stable market to the continuous development of new products. Consequently, the concept of a business field also shifted to the widest definition—a system aiming at a function, as Dr. Shon says, which is more particularly described as follows: gigantic products of which the number of component parts exceeds the order of $10^5$ (such as large-size computers, jet planes, rockets, etc.); and system industries having complicated sub-systems (such as educational system, data processing system, ocean exploitation system, city development system).

## 8. Cybernation Society (1974–2005)

GNP per capita: $5,000–$15,000.

In the social background described below, the human beings in this society will be freed from such disregard of humanity as were necessarily found in the Mechanization and Automation Societies and will establish their subjectivity and responsibility.

This will be a creative period where we can find a life worth living, as follows: the importance of informational functions will be greatly increased resulting in the enhancement of selective functions; approach to and practical application of quantification of evaluative standards under ever changing value systems; optimization of knowledge as a result of combination of logic and sentiment; popularization of higher education; diversification of individual consumption; advancement of the service economy; diversification of the activities of big businesses prompted by social requirements; practical application of such intellectual technology as will enable "controlled experiments" and "plans highly likely to be a success" in the social, economic, industrial, managerial and other fields; generalization of new soft technological systems, such as coding and systematization beyond the level of conventional individual technology; introduction of automation plants relieving man from simple labor; generalization of man-machine systems for mechanization in the solution of typical problems; and wide application and development of cybernetics in connection with life science, that may be tentatively called bio-cybernetics, i.e., bionetics.

### 9. Optimization Society (2005–2025)

GNP per capita: $15,000–$40,000.

In this society, individual and social desires of men and women will change, and a function of finding out the best route to satisfy much desires will be developed.

Thus, increased selective functions for optimal information will enable man to find the most suitable and pleasant job, according to his own individual ability.

This will lead to the optimization of the whole society. Subsequently, a method will be invented and put into practical use wherein all men and women (including those whose knowledge level is so low as to be well replaced by machines) can be given a job which will make them feel worthy under the social circumstances of reviving the arts and crafts and of making personal services more respectable.

The individual and the society are in what may be called a dualistically monistic relation. In terms of systematics, total system and sub-system are well balanced in their respective directions toward optimization. We should like to call this an optimal combination of optimization. In this society, the nature of knowledge itself which has passed through the preceding Cybernation Society will undergo a major change and knowledge will come to occupy the most important position for everybody.

Thus, the development of techniques for optimization of the entire social system will make the whole society more normative and with the help of highly advanced science and technology will enable control of natural and human environments, and even human nature itself.

Particularly, mental phenomena would be treated within the field tentatively called psycho-bionetics, i.e., psychonetics.

10. Autonomous Society (2025–2033)

GNP per capita: more than $40,000.

This society represents a transition from the societies of conscious control beginning with the Collective Period to the Natural Society of non-control.

The human beings who live in this society are required to have undergone a real change, since otherwise there is a fear that they may be enervated in such an orderly world where there is no real struggle for existence. This is because through the long history of mankind they have been much indebted for their progress to their resistant power evinced in the face of three struggles mentioned by B. Russell; the struggle with nature, the struggle with other humans and the struggle·with themselves. What may serve as motivation stimulus and reward in a permanently affluent leisure society?

Thanks to the highly advanced super-psychology and related fields that may tentatively be called Metapsychonetics, each member of the society will be able to act autonomously without being troubled by actualized controls from the society or by himself. The latter case could be dimly seen in the grown-up being able to operate with the maximum use of his power potential, partly because he has realized its rough limitations. Values will reside only in the creation of something new and the members of the society will be able to live beyond their natural span of life.

The clarification of super-psychological phenomena will tremendously increase human capabilities and as a still higher society, a natural society will be sought after as the Utopia for mankind. By that time any temporary confusion caused by super-technological innovations to cope with such super-psychological phenomena may have been overcome. The technique of face-to-face communication between individuals will reach the highest stage of development where they can even communicate in some telepathic manner.

Due to such human revolutions, human society will emerge out of the miserable and atrocious dark eras where ignorance and greed dominated and will be entirely transformed into a society where wisdom and goodwill of man prevail and peace and human life are of supreme importance. Thus what we call the Autonomous Society will be realized.

NATURAL SOCIETY (the future after 2033)

Human society will develop from the village community in the Optimization Period to the clan in the Autonomous Period and further to the family community in this Natural Society. It is noted that the form of human society cyclically comes back to that of the primitive society, though these two forms of society are on different planes.

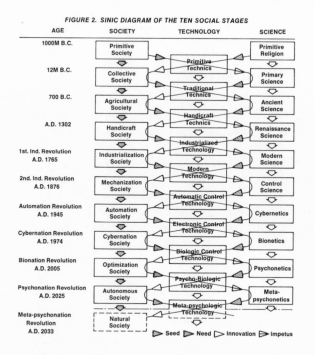

FIGURE 2. SINIC DIAGRAM OF THE TEN SOCIAL STAGES

In the dualistic monistic relationship between mind and matter, and time and space, vitality springs up and the pleasure of life is sought after.

As is clear from the above explanation, the Autonomous Society which is positioned at the end of one cycle in the Cyclic Evolution is now just around the corner.

At present, such spiritual or psychological phenomenon as telepathy or appearance of a ghost is considered to be something remote from science. In the near future, however, such phenomena will present very important problems for us. Figure 2 shows the ten developmental stages of the society and the related science and technology.

## CONCLUSION

According to Marxian general theory, all history is a history of class struggle, and all historical changes are ultimately determined by changing relations of production due to changes in technical conditions.

In correspondence with this, we could rather say that all history is a history of rising GNP per capita and all historical changes are ultimately determined by the innovativeness of society, which is spurred by the development of technology.

In order to make certain of an even-progressing society, the pursuit of rationality should be conducted so as to raise "mental productivity" as well as "material productivity." This is because the pursuit of "real" rationality requires a dual approach. . . .

# Part Three

## Some Strategies of Inquiry

### INTRODUCTION

A constantly improving repertoire of research skills will be required to advance the study of political leadership. These skills may be adapted from methods being developed in the socio-behavioral sciences and other disciplines or may be invented to meet the special needs of political leadership studies. Both adaptation and invention should constantly spur progress in this field.

An inevitable interaction can be expected to occur between the perfection of research methodologies and conceptualization of the nature of political leadership. New research methods will suggest new questions to be asked about political leadership behavior. Conversely, new questions will stimulate efforts to seek innovative ways of obtaining more adequate answers. Furthermore, pluralism in research methods is to be welcomed since it offers alternative ways of confirming the validity of findings and alternative avenues of escape from methodological entrapment. Not all researchers in the study of political leadership will command all the necessary research skills, but among the scholarly community as a whole the necessary skills should be represented so that a sharing of multi-faceted findings can occur.

The objectives of Part Three are to call attention to some strategies of inquiry that are available for the study of political leadership, to illustrate four of them, and to invite consideration of the potential contribution of research methods to the advancement of knowledge in this field.

As a point of departure it may be helpful to recall that the behavior of political leaders is probably the most abundantly recorded of all men who have lived, even though it may also be one of the least subjected to scientific inquiry. Consider all the oral epics, songs, plays, poems, paintings, diaries, letters, memoirs, speeches, state papers, autobiographies, biographies, photographs, films, sound recordings, historical accounts, journalistic observations, and contemporary public appearances that are relevant for political leadership studies. While elections may take place only at an interval of several years, and while legislatures may meet only for a period of several months each year, the behavior of political leaders as a whole takes place constantly. Obviously the sun never sets on examples of political leadership behavior. It is true that no historical record is ever complete, and that existing records are riddled with intentional or unintentional distortions, but the fact remains that the records available for the study of political leadership, as compared with those available about other areas, are enormous. Furthermore, it is likely that future advancements in audiovisual recording devices, in methods for reproducing printed documents, and in the freedom that associates of leaders feel in writing about them, will make even greater amounts of information available.

The observed and the observers may be one or many. The objects of inquiry may be individual leaders; comparative, cooperative, or competitive dyads; co-acting aggregates such as politburos, councils, factions, party congresses, and legislatures; dispersed aggregates such as sample surveys of village chiefs, mayors, governors, and party leaders; and various combinations of the foregoing. The observer may be an individual of varying disciplinary or professional training or a research team composed of persons possessed of different research skills and experiences, including political leaders themselves. Consider the insights that might emerge from the study of political leadership in a given community by an effectively functioning research group that included first-rate talents from fields such as political science, history, personality psychology, social psychology, sociology, anthropology, entrepreneurial economics, journalism, and experienced political leadership.[1]

Among the methods that may be applied in the study of political leadership are: observation, interview, content analysis, biography, the case study, comparison, aggregation, and experimentation.

### Observation

The study of political leadership can benefit from two advantageous conditions facilitating observation: the fact that political leadership roles usually require a certain amount of public visibility; and the emergence of an increasingly sophisticated sociobehavioral science rationale for observational research methods.[2] Seven observational techniques merit application and further development in political leadership studies: *self-observation,* in which a cooperative leader is asked to keep a record for scientific purposes of the nature and frequency of certain behavior; *peer observation,* in which political leaders are asked to observe the behavior of other leaders in circumstances where they interact; *associate observation,* in which staff members or other persons, such as journalists, who work closely with political leaders help to record their behavior; *participant observation,* in which the scientific researcher himself takes up an associate observation position or another active role in direct relation to the observed leaders; *laboratory observation,* in which leaders carry out their activities in a laboratory setting with full understanding that their behavior is being observed for scientific purposes;[3] *field observation,* in which the scientific observer gains acceptance as a non-participating recorder of behavior under natural conditions such as decisional meetings and caucuses; and *non-reactive observation,* in which observations are made in a way or upon materials such that leaders are unaware that a scientific study is being made of their behavior.[4]

Observational methods are useful to supplement or substitute for other research methods. Sometimes hypotheses reached by other means can be checked by observation; sometimes observations suggest questions to be answered in other ways. The categories for observing verbal and non-verbal leadership behavior include frequency, sequence, duration, relation, omission, gesture, expression, and the reactions of others to the leader's presence. A single researcher may act as the observer or the observational group might be expanded to include hundreds of observers who could study either the behavior of a single leader or of many leaders simultaneously.

### Interview

The interview is the most direct and may be the most powerful research tool of contemporary political leadership studies. For help in answering many research problems why not ask experienced political leaders directly? After all, the interview method is the heart of journalism that seeks to describe and explain the contemporary world of public affairs; also it is the core of psychiatric efforts to understand the significance of individual life experiences.

There are different types of interview: the introductory meeting to build mutual rapport, the reconnaissance interview to explore major problems that may be subjected subsequently to precise examination, the detailed depth interview, the reconfirmation interview to clarify understandings and to fill in missing information, and the termination interview to bring to a close the research relationship.[5] The most important interview problems that scientific students of political leadership must overcome will be to gain acceptance for their distinctive interviewing role and to formulate theory-relevant research questions that are both interesting to the leaders and scientifically productive. Most political leaders are highly skilled at answering questions and have had enormous interview experience. The more competitive the political system, the more competitive and diversified the communications media, and the more open to foreign journalism the society, the greater the expected question-answering experience of political leaders in the direction of public policy defense or offense. For a political leader, every question offers the possibility of strengthening or weakening his public position. The task of scientific researchers will be to establish their reputation as seekers after truth and to differentiate themselves from images as journalists, opponents, supporters, or psychiatrists. Among ways of doing this will be partly the same ways employed by some journalists and psychiatrists: to take a non-judgmental position, to respect confidences, to translate sensitive particulars into general statements that express the truth, and to report back to the cooperating leaders insights gained that may be useful to them.

Among interviewing innovations that merit further exploration are the group interview in which a number of experienced leaders respond collectively[6] and the peer interview in which one experienced political leader interviews another. Indirect interviews from any one of the observational standpoints noted above merit consideration.

### Content Analysis

This method involves the qualitative and quantitative study of symbols that appear in documentary, visual, or oral materials.[7] The high rate of symbol production by political leaders provides many opportunities for this type of analysis. While it is relatively easy to describe content patterns and contemporaneous correlations, it is less easy to establish antecedent causal factors or subsequent causal connections. Thus content analytic research in the study of political leadership should be conducted within a framework that attempts to provide a general overview of leadership behavior. It is not just a question of establishing that a political leader produces a quantifiable pattern of symbols but rather of interpreting it as part of a political leadership process.

A pioneering content analytic inquiry into political leadership values is represented by Ralph K. White's comparative study of the wartime propaganda of Hitler and Franklin D. Roosevelt.[8] Comparing speeches of the two leaders under sixty-two values, White found that the two leaders were similar in (1) their verbal emphasis on "peace and conventional morality," (2) their ideas of "national grandeur," and (3) their usage of "black vs. white dichotomy." Hitler differed from Roosevelt in his greater emphasis upon "ideas of persecution" and "strength and morality." Roosevelt showed greater stress on "economic values," "means-ends analysis," and "concern for the welfare of others." Another pioneering example of content analysis is contained in an unpublished study by Margaret G. Hermann of videotaped press conference materials.[9] The period was the 1965–66 New York City transit strike. The main actors were Mayor John V. Lindsay, the president of the Transit Workers Union, the chairman of the Transit Authority, and a mediator. Periods of high and low stress in the negotiations were taken as independent variables and the filmed behavior of the four individuals was studied to determine the characteristic styles by which each coped with these conditions. Hermann employed two uncertainty measures (articulation rate and "Ah" ratio), four anxiety measures (type token ratio, sentence change, repetition, verbal rate), and four measures of defensive behavior (allness terms, ambivalent constructions, negatives, and self and other references). One finding was that Mayor Lindsay's speech patterns indicated that he was less confident about the outcome of the negotiations than he wanted to appear.

As the informational or cybernetic society unfolds around us in the near future the perfection of ways for monitoring and analyzing the symbolic production of political leaders promises to be of increasing importance as a research strategy.

### Biography

Various forms of biographical inquiry have long been employed to increase understanding of individual lives and to provide penetrating insights into larger historical events. Already there are indications in the work of Lewis J. Edinger (Selection 9) and others that the study of biography will be conducted with increasing theoretical relevance for the study of political leadership. Basically, biography involves an attempt to recreate the life cycle of an individual, or some significant portion of it, in order to describe and explain the contribution and responses of the person to the manifold circumstances of his surroundings.

Whether political leaders' lives are approached as a cumulative process of generalization of past learning into new situations or as a self-driven process of becoming, as a product or creator of circumstance, or as a likely combination of all of these, biography offers an opportunity for gaining an integrated overview of what it means to be a political leader. Biographical studies can uncover problems for more intensive analysis in such areas as: the effects of early identifications with political leaders; the persistence and variations of personality style; patterns of role seeking and performance; organizational problems; task selection and task effectiveness; the emergence of value attachments, relative value strengths, and the effect of values on other aspects of behavior; setting relevancies and influences; and overall patterns of engagement, performance, and disengagement in political leadership life. From a theory-building standpoint biographies of minor local leaders can be as important as those of national figures.

In considering biography as a mode of inquiry, the advice of John A. Garraty,[10] a leading student of the subject, merits attention. Garraty pronounces the successful biography to be "the product of a harmonious mixture of writer, subject, and surrounding circumstance." [11] He emphasizes that the researcher should be truly interested in his subject and should follow Cromwell's advice to the artist, "Paint me, warts and all." Garraty urges also that the biographer should be self-conscious about his motives in order to control biasing distortions as best he can. Some motivations he mentions are filial piety, to find oneself in the life of another, money, contractual obligation, and to earn an academic degree. We might suggest two more, although these do not exhaust the possibilities and actual motives are mixed: curiosity and desire to achieve theoretically relevant insights. Garraty suggests also that the best biographer is likely to be a person whose skills and experience most closely match those of the subject. This idea has many implications for political leadership studies including enhanced appreciation for biographical sketches written about leaders by other leaders[12] and the possibility of specialist team collaboration in the study of political leaders with professional backgrounds in such fields as medicine, engineering, law, industry, agriculture, and the military.

One of the most outstanding examples of political biography in recent political science is the study of Woodrow Wilson by Alexander L. George and Juliette L. George.[13] Tracing his life from childhood through the presidency of Princeton to the presidency of the United States, they advance the hypotheses that Wilson's drive toward political leadership was motivated by a need to compensate for damaged self-esteem and that his inability to compromise was provoked by situations which threatened the mechanisms by which he sought compensatory gratifications. Emphasizing personality factors, the Georges explain the utility of biographical method as follows: "The complexity of personality organization, the important role of ego functioning, and the variety of ways in which given personality factors express themselves in a political leader's behavior—all these emerge only when the career as a whole, not merely a few isolated episodes from it, is examined in detail." [14]

## Case Study

If biography in political leadership studies is considered to be analogous to the novel, then the case study can be considered as a short story. Or if the former is a documentary film, then the latter is an X-ray photograph. Another way of expressing it is that the case study is the surgical instrument of political leadership research methods. It provides a sharp, penetrating insight into a part of political leadership behavior over a relatively short period of time.

For scientific theory-building purposes a case study may be defined as a set of statements at a relatively low level of abstraction which describes something to be explained (the referents of dependent variables) and contains references to those factors and events hypothesized to be potentially relevant for the desired explanation (referents of independent variables).

Case studies in political leadership may be conducted in order to clarify any aspect of an emerging conceptual framework: for example, to explore the influence of personality, to explicate a role, to illuminate organizational relationships, to reveal task properties, to clarify value influences, and to show setting relevancies. Or they may be accomplished to show all of these variables in short range interaction. A basic problem of case study method, as of biographical method, will be to make it possible for research to be cumulative, comparative, and contributive to the building of initially intermediate and eventually general theories of political leadership behavior.

Examples of case studies that reveal political leadership behavior under one type of task situation (an international crisis) are provided by Elie Abel's description of President Kennedy's response to the emplacement of Soviet missiles in Cuba in 1962 [15] and the present writer's study of President Truman's response to the invasion of the Republic of Korea in 1950.[16] Both these studies reveal the President as the final decision maker, contributing strongly to the power, affective, instrumental, and associative dimensions of group behavior. Both studies also show clearly the emergence of a task or instrumental leader who served as the main initiator or catalyst in formulating the action alternatives among which the president had to decide: Attorney General Robert F. Kennedy, the president's brother, in the Cuban case; Secretary of State Dean G. Acheson in the Korean case. Both studies show remarkably similar *ad hoc* organizational characteristics (fourteen to sixteen deliberating officials) and the noticeable influence of values ("no American Pearl Harbor" in Cuba and "no appeasement of aggression" in Korea).

While further exploration of political leadership behavior in international crises (and extension to comparison with domestic crises) is definitely required, case inquiry also needs to be extended to encompass both more routine events and more varied problem areas; e.g., political leadership relationships with poverty and the poor, with different ethnic groups, and with problems of economic development and environmental pollution.

### Comparison

The objective of comparison is to search for variation in a framework of understanding that cannot be observed in a single case.[17] The more varied the cases considered the less adequate a given conceptual framework or emergent theory is likely to be, but the more some expectations are confirmed across cases, the greater the meritable confidence in their validity. Approaches to comparative inquiry may range from relatively unstructured scanning for salient similarities and differences (no specific hypotheses) through semi-structured inquiry (some hypotheses, other potential relevancies left open) to fully structured investigation (only hypotheses are tested).

An ancient contribution to comparative analysis in political leadership studies—still unsurpassed and worthy of rediscovery and modern methodological development—is contained in Plutarch's paired comparisons of Greek and Roman leaders.[18] An example is his comparison of the Greek Demetrius and Antony, the Roman. According to Plutarch, Demetrius inherited power, while Antony achieved it; his marriage was advantageous, while Antony's union with Cleopatra was considered disgraceful; Demetrius preserved liberties among a people accustomed to kingly rule while Antony crushed freedom after Rome's emancipation from Caesar's domination; in crisis, Demetrius abandoned dissipations for battle, while Antony sacrificed potential victories in infaturated pursuit of Cleopatra. In conclusion, Plutarch tells us,

> The achievements of Demetrius are all his own work. Antony's noblest and greatest victories were won by his lieutenants. For their final disaster they have both only to thank themselves; not, however, in an equal degree. Demetrius was deserted, the Macedonians revolted from him; Antony deserted others, and ran away while men were fighting for him at the risk of their lives. The fault to be found with the one is that he had entirely alienated the affections of his soldiers; with the other that he abandoned so much love and faith as he still possessed. We cannot admire the death of either but that of Demetrius excites our greater contempt. He let himself become a prisoner and was thankful to gain a three years' accession to life in captivity. He was tamed like a wild beast by his belly, and by wine; Antony took himself out of the world in a cowardly, pitiful and ignoble manner, but still in time to prevent the enemy from having his person in their power.[19]

Two recent studies that are reminiscent of the Plutarchian tradition are comparisons by Louis E. Lomax of Malcolm X and Martin Luther King, Jr.,[20] and by Tom Wicker of Presidents Kennedy and Johnson.[21] Lomax advances the thesis that if the two black leaders had not been assassinated they would have moved toward greater convergence: Malcolm X toward more tolerance; Martin Luther King, Jr., toward greater militance. Wicker concentrates upon Kennedy's loss of Congressional support and Johnson's loss of consensus as "stories of men who tried to govern and found their own personalities and circumstances not the least of their trouble." [22]

To advance the study of political leadership it will be helpful to have inquiries that compare personalities, roles, organizations, tasks, values, and settings both within and across cultures and political systems. Comparison offers political leadership studies an opportunity to escape from parochialism.

## Aggregation

Aggregative studies represent an extension of comparative method. The computer revolution now means that it is increasingly possible to analyze more answers to more questions by more leaders more quickly than ever before. The data-gathering instrument is usually an oral interview schedule or written questionnaire containing both open-ended and checklist-type items.

The advantage of aggregative methods is that they facilitate the study of political leadership conceptualized as a collective phenomenon. By way of illustration consider all the political leaders, incumbent and aspirant, in a small society such as the State of Hawaii. Aggregative methods make it possible to make statements about the personalities, roles, organizations, tasks, values, and settings that characterize this group of leaders as a whole and to portray the range of variation that exists among them. Aggregative methods thus offer the promise of a final summation of the nature, impact, and potential variation of political leadership in a total society. They will be as adequate and valid as the information about any individual leader that can be contributed to them; they will be as significant for the explanation of political and other social phenomenon as the theoretical bridges that link them.

Several types of leadership aggregates merit study: the macroaggregate (the total political leadership population of a society); the co-acting aggregate (the membership of a leadership group such as a politburo, council, or legislature); the dispersed aggregate (e.g., all governors, mayors, party cell leaders, or precinct captains); the cross-role aggregate (a subset containing examples of two or more different political leadership roles); and the sample aggregate (sub-sample of leaders selected so as to permit inferences about the characteristics of any of the foregoing as a whole). In terms of temporal attention aggregative studies may focus upon present configurations, changes over past time, time panel comparisons, or future projections.

Among the purposes that can be served by aggregative analysis are the following: the discovery and analysis of typological variations; exploration of the limits of variation in leadership characteristics; comparison of aggregate characteristics with inferences or evidence about inputs to or outputs from political leadership behavior; and the exploration of political leadership subsystems.

A major criticism that has been directed against aggregative studies, especially as they have focused upon socio-economic background characteristics of political elites, is that they have not yet convincingly demonstrated linkages between properties of the aggregate and other significant aspects of political behavior such as attitudes.[23] There are several ways in which the study of political leadership can contribute to removal of this indeterminacy. The most important is to gain greater conceptual clarity about the behavioral properties of political leadership as opposed to the more structurally defined and sociologically rooted concept of political elites. This will mean increased clarity about who political leaders are, what background characteristics are most significant for predisposing their behavior, what kinds of immediate antecedents of behavior are significant as triggering stimuli, and what kinds of overt acts form the significant output characteristics of political leadership behavior. As Searing's[24] incisive methodological critique suggests, the barriers to advances in aggregative studies lie now not in the capacity for sophisticated multivariate analysis, but rather in the need for better conceptualization and operationalization of the nature of political leadership.[25] Temporarily, methodological capability has outrun conceptual precision and theoretical imagination in the study of political leadership. But as promised by both voting studies and analyses of roll call behavior in legislatures, where dependent variables are clear and where there is an opportunity to experiment with aggregative background predictors, higher levels of accurate anticipation are possible.

Aggregative studies, including the mapping of influence networks and career patterns[26] in political leadership systems, promise opportunities for students of political leadership to think big. They can envision the impact of an entire political leadership collective (complete with internal conflicts and tensions) upon a whole society. They can compare leadership collectivities within and across societies and can envision intersocietal coalitions and antagonisms. Taking the globe as a whole, they can aspire eventually to describe and analyze with precision the origins and impact of political leadership on world development.[27]

### Experiment

One of the most promising approaches to theoretical advancement in the study of political leadership, and one of the least developed, is the application of experimental methods.[28] Experiments may be conducted under natural field conditions or contrived in a laboratory. If in a laboratory they may attempt to "simulate" [29] natural conditions or may concentrate upon theoretical questions without direct reference to replicated reality. They may seek to vary personality, role, organization, task, values, or setting while holding other variables constant. They may focus upon the person and human relationships or they may seek to examine the influence of factors outside the immediate situation through the introduction of symbolic representations of them. The subjects for experimental inquiry may be incumbent, aspiring, or retired political leaders; persons especially knowledgeable about political leadership behavior such as staff associates and journalists; persons having leadership characteristics (e.g., persons matched on certain personality variables with known characteristics of actual political leaders); or persons of known characteristics on any variable whose response to changes in other variables can be measured. Progress in the study of political leadership will require mutually supportive interplay between two types of experiments: those that concentrate upon showing the complex interrelationships of variables in a conceptual framework or emergent theory, and those that select out pairs (or otherwise limited sets) of variables for partial but precise analysis.

A pioneering quasi-experimental study is illustrated by James D. Barber's inquiry into leadership behavior that emerged in elected school boards when they were confronted with the laboratory task of cutting to a minimum their most recently approved budget.[30] One finding was that the formal chairmen of these groups differed significantly in the degree of their activity or passivity.

Another recent example of the application of experimental method in political research is the study by Charles F. Hermann[31] of the decision-making behavior of Navy petty officers when three crisis variables (surprise, decision time, and threat to values) were manipulated. Hermann's principal finding was that the simultaneous occurrence of surprise, short decision time, and high threat to values produced the more significant crisis behavior responses as compared with partial combinations of only two of the three variables. Still another pioneering experimental effort is the computer simulation of Congressional behavior reported by Cherryholmes and Shapiro.[32]

The future development of experimental inquiry into political leadership should seek to overcome one shortcoming of much of the social psychological literature on leadership. That is, political leadership should be treated more as a dependent variable rather than as an independent variable for the purpose of developing causal theories of why it emerges and functions as it does. Even the "classic" leadership experiment by White and Lippitt[33] is focused more upon follower responses to experimentally manipulated leadership styles (authoritarian, democratic, and laissez-faire) than upon the determinants of the leadership styles themselves. Of course, a fully developed theory of political leadership will have to encompass both perspectives in explaining patterns of emergence, maintenance, functioning, decline, and disengagement.

One of the advantages in approaching the study of political leadership in terms of an explicit conceptual framework is that research methods that have been created previously for the constituent components of the framework may be adapted for inquiry into the new subject. Several examples of useful research methods may be cited for the concepts introduced in Part Two: Bloc's California Q-set for the study of personality;[34] the Ohio State checklist for ideal role behavior;[35] Bales' observational categories for small group research;[36] an adaptation of Flanagan's critical incident technique for task analysis;[37] Kilpatrick and Cantril's self-anchoring scale for value analysis;[38] and Jonassen and Peres' application of factor analysis to delineate the dimensions of a community setting for political leadership behavior.[39]

Some other research techniques that deserve further exploration in political leadership studies—by no means an exhaustive listing—are the following: the techniques devised by McClelland and associates for measuring personality need for power, achievement, and affiliation;[40] an operationalization of Banton's conception of role as "a set of rights and obligations" for role analysis;[41] the methods for organizational research mentioned in the recent survey by Barton;[42] the problem analysis diagram proposed by Bennis and others for task research;[43] the "semantic differential" developed by Osgood and others for value analysis;[44] and the ecological study techniques developed by Barker for setting analysis.[45]

The important point to recall is that the conceptual framework suggested here invites application in political leadership studies of whatever future methods of research that may be created for inquiry into personality, role, organization, task, values, and setting.

The essays reproduced in this section have been selected to illustrate four major strategies of inquiry: biography, comparison, aggregative analysis, and experiment.

Lewis J. Edinger (Selection 9) presents the most complete conceptual framework now available to guide biographical inquiry in the study of political leadership. It is strongly influenced by the role analysis model of Neal Gross and others.[46] Also it is reminiscent of the ideas about the reduction of cognitive dissonance associated with the work of Leon Festinger and his associates: e.g., where there is a perceived discrepancy between actual and ideal states of affairs, under various conditions, the subject moves (1) to change the actual to conform to the ideal, (2) to change the ideal to fit the actual, or (3) to withdraw from the disturbing situation.[47] Edinger also clearly distinguishes three analytical viewpoints—those of the actor, significant other, and outside observer.

As biographical studies advance in political leadership research it is likely that they will be benefited by inclusion also of the perspectives concerning the life cycle development of the individual person represented by the work of such scholars as Erikson,[48] Lidz,[49] and Buhler.[50] Biographical studies will also be benefited by introduction of social learning perspectives as illustrated by the work of Bandura and Walters.[51]

Edwin Shneidman's comparative essay (Selection 10), in the tradition of Plutarch, is of special interest for several reasons: the application of an explicit framework for comparative analysis compounded of both logical and psychological elements, the utilization of mass media materials produced naturally by the political process, and the prominence of his subjects (1960 presidential candidates Kennedy and Nixon, both later to become president). Shneidman's work suggests four categories of analysis that should be of continuing interest in political leadership studies: "idiologic," the way a leader actually thinks; "contralogic," the kinds of assumptions which, if made, would make the leader's pattern of thought entirely reasonable; "psychologic," the kind of personality a leader must have in order to think that way; and "pedalogic," the approach to communicating with the leader that is likely to be the most effective given prior analysis of his idiologic, psychologic, and contralogic.

An example of aggregative analysis is provided by the study of Jerome Davis of the background political socialization experiences of 163 early Russian Commuinst leaders (Selection 11). Although the study was conducted in 1929 and lacks the multivariate sophistication of more recent statistical analyses, it is nevertheless of enduring interest, not only in terms of substance, but also because it attempts to focus attention upon some specifically political experiences in the backgrounds of the leaders. Often aggregate studies of this nature rely upon standard socio-economic categories and do not probe deeply into political background factors. Davis seeks to describe who the Communist leaders were, to discover "some of the stimuli that caused them to become revolutionaries," and to determine factors that contributed to their rise to leadership. He does not proceed to the further step of attempting to associate the background characteristics with ongoing performances in political leadership roles and their implications for variance in the political system. This remains a continuing challenge for aggregative analysis and for the study of political leadership as a whole.

The Davis study illustrates other continuing problems of aggregative analysis: the intimate connection between data sought and a guiding theory or conceptual framework; the empirical constraints of available data; the dependence upon imaginative hypothesis to discover fruitful correlations in multivariate analysis; the tendency not to probe deeply into deviant cases that do not fit dominant aggregative profiles; and the loss of focus upon significant individuals who disappear in aggregate categories (e.g. Stalin). The study also illustrates some of the benefits of aggregative inquiry: an appreciation of range of variation and a sense of modal tendencies.

The last essay in this selection by Robert D. Meade (Selection 12) illustrates the application of experimental method in leadership studies. It reports on a cross-cultural replication of a famed leadership experiment by Ronald Lippitt and Ralph K. White. The essay is of special interest because it extends a reversal of earlier experimental findings; i.e., Lippitt and White first found that American subjects performed best under a "democratic" style of leadership; Meade later showed that Indian subjects responded best to an "authoritarian" style; finally, the present comparative study of Chinese and Chinese-Americans shows that propensities to respond to leadership styles are socially learned and that followers may acquire a varied repertoire.[52] Among problems of experimental method raised by this example are: the use of student surrogates versus experienced political leaders as subjects, the possibility of extrapolating experimental findings into natural political behavior, the comparative utility of field versus laboratory experimentation, and the need for experiments that explore the determinants of leader behavior as well as the nature of follower responses. Finally the Meade experiment serves as a reminder for the entire field lof political leadership studies, from initial concept formation to the most highly sophisticated experimental inquiries, that cultural and sub-cultural biases require constant scientific efforts to bring them into awareness and subsequently under control.

Having suggested briefly some modes of inquiry that may be employed to advance knowledge of political leadership behavior, we turn in Part Four to consider problems of political leadership education.

# Notes

to Part Three: Some Strategies of Inquiry

1. Three principal results are to be expected from such collaboration: (1) a broader range of perceived relevancies as compared with that produced by a less diverse group; (2) the elaboration of more extended hypothetical chains of causal relationships; and (3) a greater sense of the validity of common findings reached from different theoretical and methodological viewpoints. The convergent effects of team research are described by Richard T. Morris and Melvin Seeman, "The Problem of Leadership: An Interdisciplinary Approach," *American Journal of Sociology,* LVI (1950), pp. 149–155. The convergent validity potentials of diverse approaches are discussed by Donald T. Campbell and Donald W. Fiske, "Convergent and Discriminant Validation by the Multi-trait Multi-method Matrix," *Psychological Bulletin,* LVI (1959), pp. 81–105.

2. Eugene J. Webb, Donald T. Campbell, Richard B. Schwartz, and Lee Sechrest, *Unobtrusive Measures: Nonreactive Research in Social Science* (Chicago: Rand McNally, 1966).

3. A pioneering example of this type of research with quasi-experimental qualities has been contributed by James D. Barber, *Power in Committees: An Experiment in the Governmental Process* (Chicago: Rand McNally, 1966). Barber persuaded twelve local government budget-making committees to meet in the Yale University Interaction Laboratory.

4. Chadwick F. Alger, for example, observed U.N. delegates from the press gallery. He recorded "who talked to whom, who initiated the conversation, and how long it lasted." See "Interaction and Negotiation in a Committee of the United Nations General Assembly," *Papers of the Peace Research Society* (International), V (1966), pp. 141–159.

5. Some useful insights into interviewing problems are contained in Harry Stack Sullivan, *The Psychiatric Interview* (New York: Norton, 1959); Alexander Heard, "Interviewing Southern Politicians," *American Political*

*Science Review,* XLIV (December 1950), pp. 886–896; Erwin O. Smigel, "Interviewing a Legal Elite: The Wall Street Lawyer," *American Journal of Sociology,* LXIV (September 1958), pp. 159–165; and Lewis A. Dexter, *Elite and Specialized Interviewing* (Evanston: Northwestern University Press, 1970).

6. An example of this is the study by Charles L. Clapp of congressional roles. Eight dinner meetings of two separate party groups (19 Democrats and 17 Republicans) were held. An agenda for discussion was circulated in advance of each meeting. As a side effect, participants reported that they learned a great deal from one another. Charles L. Clapp, *The Congressman: His Work as He Sees It* (Garden City: Anchor Books, 1964).

7. Robert C. North *et al., Content Analysis* (Evanston: Northwestern University Press, 1963) and Ole R. Holsti, *Content Analysis for the Social Sciences and Humanities* (Reading: Addison-Wesley, 1969).

8. Ralph K. White, "Hitler, Roosevelt and the Nature of War Propaganda," *Journal of Abnormal and Social Psychology,* XLIV (April 1949), pp. 157–174.

9. Margaret G. Hermann, "Indirect Methods of Assessing Defensive Behavior and Affect of Stress: I. Use of Spontaneous Verbal Material from Press Conferences," Princeton, Educational Testing Service, mss., n.d.

10. *The Nature of Biography* (New York: Vintage Books, 1964).

11. *Ibid.,* p. 155.

12. E.g., Woodrow Wilson, *George Washington* (New York: Harper, 1897), and Herbert C. Hoover, *The Ordeal of Woodrow Wilson* (New York: McGraw-Hill, 1958).

13. *Woodrow Wilson and Colonel House* (New York: Dover Publications, 1964).

14. *Ibid.,* p. 318.

15. *The Missile Crisis* (New York: J. B. Lippincott, 1966).

16. Glenn D. Paige, *The Korean Decision: June 24–30, 1950* (New York: The Free Press, 1968).

17. An important recent examination of issues in comparative method is presented by Adam Przeworski and Henry Teune, *The Logic of Comparative Inquiry* (New York: John Wiley, 1970).

18. With rare exceptions, as in the Clausen edition, Plutarch's comparisons tend to be omitted in paperback selections from his work. Thus several full-scale translations of his works need to be studied to appreciate the range and quality of his method; e.g., Bernadotte Perrin, trans., *Plutarch's Lives* (Cambridge: Harvard University Press, 1914–26), 11 volumes.

19. Wendell Clausen (ed.), *Lives of Nine Illustrious Greeks and Romans* (New York: Washington Square Press, 1964), pp. 415–416.

20. Louis E. Lomax, *To Kill a Black Man* (Los Angeles: Holloway House, 1968).

21. Tom Wicker, *JFK and LBJ: The Influences of Personality Upon Politics* (Baltimore: Penguin Books, 1969).

22. *Ibid.*, p. 21.

23. The major methodological critique of elite social background analysis is Donald D. Searing, "The Comparative Study of Elite Socialization," *Comparative Political Studies,* I (January 1969), pp. 471–500.

24. *Ibid.*

25. The leadership background data called for in the early study by Jerome Davis (Selection 11), for example, contains some items that seem much more directly pertinent to specific political leadership socialization than many of those available to Searing.

26. A pioneering study of leadership career patterns in the United States is contained in Joseph Schlesinger, *Ambition and Politics* (Chicago: Rand McNally, 1966).

27. For example, comparison of the decision making groups involved in American international crises (Korea 1950, Cuba 1962) reveals that about 15 officials—including only one elected leader—participated directly in them. Furthermore, the politburos of communist countries seem to be about the same size. Assuming a world of 150 nations with 15-man crisis decision making groups in each, that would give us a world crisis-coping aggregate of 2,250 high officials. This is not analytically unmanageable; neither, with improved computer capacities, would be a hundred-fold increase to permit monitoring routine world political leadership behavior.

28. An excellent overview of this subject may be found in Donald T. Campbell, *Experimental and Quasi-Experimental Designs for Research* (Chicago: Rand McNally, 1966).

29. Harold Guetzkow (ed.), *Simulation in Social Science: Readings* (Englewood Cliffs, New Jersey: Prentice-Hall, 1962); and William D. Coplin, *Simulation in the Study of Politics* (Chicago: Maskham, 1968).

30. James D. Barber, *Power in Committees: An Experiment in the Governmental Process* (Chicago: Rand McNally, 1966).

31. Charles F. Hermann, *Crises in Foreign Policy: A Simulation Analysis* (Indianapolis: Bobbs-Merrill, 1969).

32. Cleo H. Cherryholmes and Michael J. Shapiro, *Representatives and Roll Calls* (Indianapolis: Bobbs-Merrill, 1969).

33. Ralph K. White and Ronald O. Lippitt, *Autocracy and Democracy: An Experimental Inquiry* (New York: Harper, 1960).

34. Jack Block, *The Q-Sort Method in Personality Assessment and Psychiatric Research* (Springfield, Ill.: Charles C. Thomas, 1961).

35. The Ohio State Leadership Studies, "Ideal Leadership Behavior," (Columbus: Ohio State University Center for Business and Economic Research, Division of Research, 1957), 3 page checklist.

36. Robert F. Bales, "Interaction Process Analysis," in David I.

Sills (ed.), *International Encyclopedia of the Social Sciences* (New York: Macmillan, 1968), Vol. VII, pp. 465–471.

37. John C. Flanagan, "The Critical Incident Technique," *Psychological Bulletin,* LI, No. 3 (July, 1954), pp. 327–358. For an application see K. N. Singh and T. Sen Gupta, "Measuring Effectiveness of Village Level Workers," *Indian Journal of Public Administration,* XI (January–March, 1965), pp. 42–55.

38. F. P. Kilpatrick and Hadley Cantril, "Self-Anchoring Scaling, A Measure of Individuals' Unique Reality Worlds," *Journal of Individual Psychology,* XVI (November 1960), pp. 158–173.

39. Christen T. Jonassen and Sherwood H. Peres, *Interrelationships of Dimensions of Community Systems: A Factor Analysis* (Columbus: Ohio State University Press, 1960).

40. David C. McClelland *et al., The Achievement Motive* (New York: Appleton-Century-Crofts, 1953).

41. Michael Banton, *Roles: An Introduction to the Study of Social Relations* (London: Tavistock Publications, 1965).

42. Allen H. Barton, "Organizations: Methods of Research," in David Sills (ed.), *International Encyclopedia of the Social Sciences* (New York: The Free Press, 1968), Vol. XI, pp. 334–343.

43. Warren G. Bennis, J. W. Thomas, and M. C. Fulenwider, unpublished mimeographed materials on the Problem Analysis Diagram (PAD) entitled "Bennis Project #1," n.d. Basically this method involves classifying a problem, then listing and weighing "increasing" and "restraining" forces that relate to problem solution. These forces are compared and correlated with such things as estimated probability of problem-solving success.

44. Charles E. Osgood, George J. Suci, and Percy H. Tannenbaum, *The Measurement of Meaning* (Urbana: University of Illinois Press, 1957).

45. Roger G. Barker, *Ecological Psychology: Concepts and Methods for Studying the Environment of Human Behavior* (Stanford: Stanford University Press, 1968).

46. Neal Gross *et al., Explorations in Role Analysis* (New York: Wiley, 1965).

47. Leon Festinger, *A Theory of Cognitive Dissonance* (Stanford: Stanford University Press, 1962).

48. Erik H. Erikson, "Eight Ages of Man," in *Childhood and Society* (New York: W. W. Norton, 1963), pp. 247–274.

49. Theodore Lidz, *The Person: His Development Throughout the Life Cycle* (New York: Basic Books, 1968).

50. Charlotte Buhler, "The Curve of Life as Studied in Biographies," *Journal of Applied Psychology,* XIX (1935), pp. 405–409.

51. Albert Bandura and Richard K. Walters, *Social Learning and Personality Development* (New York: Holt, Rinehart and Winston, 1963).

52. Meade's essay may also be read profitably in conjunction with Korten's essay on stress (Selection 6). Is it possible that the introduction of stress as a variable might lead to greater tendencies toward "authoritarianism" in democratic cultures, but in movement toward "democratization" in basically authoritarian cultures?

# 9

## Political Science and Political Biography

LEWIS J. EDINGER

In the remainder of this article I shall endeavor to put forward an approach to the study of individual leadership which I have found useful for a case study of Kurt Schumacher, post-war chairman of the German Social Democratic party. This approach can claim to be no more than one possible form of analysis, and it is to be hoped that other suggestions may be forthcoming.[1]

The nature of leadership has been variously defined. Most writers seem to agree that leadership is characterized by varying degrees of ability to influence the behavior of others in a social relationship.[2] At the same time,

Lewis J. Edinger, "Political Science and Political Biography, II." *The Journal of Politics,* XXVI (August 1964), 648–676.

[1] See *Kurt Schumacher: A Study in Personality and Political Behavior* (Stanford: Stanford University Press, 1965). The method I have employed owes a great deal to the work of Harold Lasswell and some of his students in the area of political personality studies, as well as to developments in role theory, particularly by Neal Gross, Ward S. Mason, and Alexander W. McEachern in *Explorations in Role Analysis: Studies of the School Superintendency Role* (New York: John Wiley, 1958). For another attempt to utilize latter study for political analysis, see John Wahlike, Heinz Eulau, William Buchanan, and LeRoy Ferguson, *The Legislative System: Explorations in Legislative Behavior* (New York: John Wiley, 1962), particularly the theoretical discussion by Wahlke, pp. 3–28.

[2] The following observations on the study of leadership are based, *inter alia,* on discussions of the subject in Sidney Verba, *Small Groups and Political Behavior* (Princeton: Princeton University Press, 1961); Bernard M. Bass, *Leadership, Psychology, and Organizational Behavior* (New York: Harper and Row, 1960); Ernst Bornemann, "Sozialpsychologische Probleme der Führung," *Kölner Zeitschrift für Soziologie und Sozial Psychologie* xiv, 1 (1962), 105–122; Cecil Gibb, "Leadership," in Gardner Lindzey (ed.), *Handbook of Social Psychology,* II (Cambridge, Mass.: Addison, Wesley, 1954), pp. 877–920; Alvin W. Gouldner (ed.), *Studies in Leader-*

the literature also reveals the difficulty of trying to establish clear conceptual boundaries between leaders and non-leaders, partly because the difference between leaders and followers is judged to be one of degree, rather than kind, partly because individuals may be leaders in one situation and followers in another. Another analytic difficulty arises from attempts to apply the findings of small-group studies to large-scale groups like political organizations and communities. For heuristic purposes, one can assign the various concepts of leadership to three major categories of definition:

## 1. The Positional-Ascriptive Definition

Including a range from more or less circular descriptions to highly formalistic institutional definitions, this approach in general conceives leadership in terms of certain objectivity identifiable positions, offices, tasks, or functions which are explicitly or implicitly associated with assumed power and influence in various formal and informal groups of any size. This version of leadership has been the traditional one in political science, and is sufficiently familiar to warrant no further elaboration.

## 2. The Behavioral-Descriptive Definition

Here the emphasis falls on performance rather than position; that is, on what individuals identified as high influencers do and how they do it. Leadership is seen as the ability to guide and structure the collective behavior patterns of a given group in a desired direction, so that the decision of the leader is implemented by group action. Some social scientists define leadership and attempted leadership explicitly in terms of a stimulus-response relationship: The potential leader generates stimuli which, if they are to elicit the desired positive responses from members of a group, must coincide with their pattern of expectations. Under the behavioral-descriptive definition a leader is followed because he is loved, admired, respected, or feared, because he can coerce, persuade, or manipulate group members, because he can promise psychic as well as material rewards and punishment, or because

---

ship (New York: Harper, 1950); Harold D. Lasswell, *Power and Personality* (New York: Norton, 1948); Johannes Stemmler, "Führertypen," *Kölner Zeitschrift für Soziologie*, vi (1953/54), 533–562; Max Weber, *The Theory of Social and Economic Organization* (New York: Oxford, 1947); W. Olmsted, *Social Groups, Roles, and Leadership*, East Lansing, Mich.: Institute for Community Development, Michigan State University, 1961); Gerth and Mills, *Character and Social Structure;* and various essays in C. G. Browne and Thomas S. Cohn, *The Study of Leadership* (Danville, Ill.: Interstate, 1958), and Petrullo and Bass (eds.), *Leadership and Interpersonal Behavior.*

compliance with his wishes is sanctioned by habit, tradition, or legal-rational behavior norms.[3]

### 3. The Cognitive-Attitudinal Definition

While the above categories of definition center on social interaction, the question of who or what is a leader might also be established in terms of an individual's subjective perception. That is, regardless of objective relationships, leadership may exist as an attitudinal phenomenon in the mind of an actor who ascribes it to others, to himself, or both, and responds accordingly to stimuli from his social environment. He may aspire to lead because he considers himself a leader, he may follow or want to follow others or delegate authority to them because he attributes leadership qualities to them. In this sense, leadership is subjective orientation to a situation, rather than actual behavior. An individual may be an "inner-directed" person—in Riesman's terminology—who perceives himself as an intellectual or religious leader without actually exercising or even aspiring to leadership in contemporaneous interpersonal relations. He may, for instance, see himself as providing leadership to future generations in his writings. The belief that one has a mandate from God or history to give guidance to others may either precede efforts to attract followers or be accompanied by relative indifference to contemporaneous popularity. His interpretation of a situation may induce him to pursue an unpopular course of action and to ignore or cast aside the reactions of others, although their responses may at the same time either reinforce or weaken his conviction that his views are correct, especially in the case of a political actor.[4]

The evaluation of leadership acts by the investigator depends on his definition of leadership and the behavior model which he chooses to employ. When the rational-behavior model is used, success as a leader is measured by the achievement of certain objectively posited goals, and failure by an inability to achieve them. Functionality and dysfunctionality of an actor's behavior here is perceived by the investigator in terms of manifest end values which may be achieved by bargaining, persuasion, or coercion. Using

---

[3] Obviously, I have sought to include here a vast number of definitions of leadership, including the Weberian typology as well as various conceptualizations which strive to make a distinction between permissive and coercive, authoritarian and democratic, responsive and irresponsive, responsible and irresponsible leadership on the basis of behavioral responses. The question of specific leadership traits, whether static and universal or dynamic and particularistic, tends also to be considered in terms of such behavioral phenomena.

[4] See David Riesman, The Lonely Crowd (Garden City, N.Y.: Doubleday, Anchor Books, 1953), p. 245.

the group-behavior model, functionality and dysfunctionality of a leader's actions is evaluated according to means rather than ends. Functional leadership is that of an individual who satisfies group-approved goals and performs group-approved tasks effectively. He is influential in structuring collective group behavior because the group's members are more or less strongly motivated to follow him because of his perceived ability to deny or satisfy certain of their wants. In both instances, functionality and dysfunctionality of leadership behavior is assessed according to means and ends related to social interaction rather than to the actor's individual personality needs.

Where an actor-centered personality model is used, functionality and dysfunctionality must be evaluated in terms of the individual's personality needs, such as ego satisfaction and tension reduction. The functionality of his behavior is equated with satisfaction of subjective personal goals—conscious and unconscious—which may or may not correspond to rationally posited or group-oriented goals and norms. Here a particular action or the achievement of a specific end is a matter of personal need-gratification and may, in fact, appear highly dsyfunctional in terms of either the group- or rational-behavior model. For example, a leader's aggressive responses may be tension-reducing and thus serve his personal needs, though they seem to be dysfunctional to others under the objective circumstances if he does not thereby show some overt progress toward an apparently rational goal. Or the repetition of a particular behavior pattern may be highly satisfying to a compulsive individual, although it may be quite ineffectual in terms of his professed goals as a leader or an aspirant to leadership.

These remarks are not intended to imply that in the study of individual leadership we should focus on an actor's personality to the exclusion of situational variables. Rather, they are meant to call attention to the interactions between an actual or aspiring leader and his social and political environment which appear particularly relevant in this sort of analysis. In particular, it seems important to note the cognitive processes—the subject's perception of himself and the situation, and the perception others have of him and the situation, and their interrelationship. The extent to which the participants share such perceptions is a key factor in the analysis of individual leadership. Role analysis seems to be particularly adapted to encompassing the various aspects of leadership activity, and to relating an actor's personality characteristics to his behavioral responses in a given setting. Before elaborating on this point, however, we must settle on a definition of leadership and, specifically, political leadership.

For the purposes of this analysis, let us define leadership as a position within a group which is characterized by the ability of its incumbent to guide and structure the collective behavior pattern of the group members in a direction dictated by his personal values. Thus, leadership may be both an objective phenomenon and a subjectively perceived condition; it may be a more or less abstract aspirational goal as well as a fact. Leadership behavior, in this sense, may be objectively described and analyzed by an non-participant observer as well as perceived by participants in the relationship. By a group is meant a collection of individuals having in common a process of structured social interaction, interdependence or function, and certain shared in-group traits which distinguish them from non-members. The word "group," like leadership, may be used to designate an existential object, such as a formal organization, as well as a subjectively-perceived association which need not exist outside the mind of a participant or particular observer.[5] By "small group" I mean a group characterized by direct, face-to-face interpersonal relations, and by "large group," one that includes both direct and indirect relations between its members.

What concerns us here, of course, is political leadership, as distinguished from leadership in general. Political leadership focuses on what Easton has called the authoritative allocation of values in a community and involves both the attempt to exercise and the actual exercise of power to make policy-choices between alternative courses of action affecting this allocation of values.[6] In particular political leadership is concerned with the distribution of influence over authoritative policy-decisions in the multi-functional, large-scale, geographically identifiable group known as a political community. Political conflict in such a community revolves around who should have a say in decision-making, whose interests should be satisfied, how, and how much. The study of political leadership thus involves the analysis of the interaction between the decision-makers and those who are subject to the decisions, as well as the struggle of individuals and groups for direct or indirect influence over these decisions as a means to realizing certain of their values and interests. In short, it deals not only with relations between leaders and followers, but also with the interaction between different leaders, between the leaders of one political group and the members of another, between potential leaders and potential followers, and between actual and inspiring leaders.[7]

Political leadership is thus a position or—in the language of the cognitive approach to role analysis—the location of an actor or actors in a

---

[5] For example, a national community may be objectively identified by certain geographic, legal, social, and political criteria, but—like a social class—it may also exist only as an ideal in the minds of a single or a few persons. On this and related matters, see Karl W. Deutsch *et al., Community in the North Atlantic Area* (Princeton: Princeton University Press, 1957).

[6] David Easton, *The Political System* (New York: Knopf, 1953), p. 130ff. See also Gabriel A. Almond, "A Functional Approach to Comparative Politics," in Almond and James S. Coleman (eds.), *The Politics of Developing Areas* (Princeton: Princeton University Press, 1960), pp. 5–58.

[7] See Seligmann, *op. cit.,* pp. 181–182.

group, characterized by the ability of the incumbent to guide the collective behavior of this group in the direction of a desired authoritative distribution of values in a political community.[8] The political leader, in this sense, is a *central actor* occupying a *focal position* which relates to various *counter positions* in a particular *role-set*. As the incumbent of such a position, the central actor is perceptually related to the occupants of these counter-positions in terms of reciprocal expectations and evaluations associated with these positions. He perceives himself, and may be perceived by other relevant actors, as playing one or more roles oriented toward the exercise of decision-making authority in a political community by himself and/or other members of his particular group.[9]

The striving for and the exercise of political leadership may accordingly be described and analyzed in terms of behavior patterns resulting from reciprocal and interacting cognitive expectations and evaluations in a given political context. The participating actors in a perceived role-set—be they potential or actual leaders or followers, be the relationships internalized or externalized—hold certain expectations about the qualities and/or behavior of the incumbents in a relationship involving a perceived leadership position

---

[8] In general, the following discussion of the role of a political leader and that of his counter-players will rely on the terminology and concepts developed by Gross *et al.*, in *Explorations in Role Analysis* on the basis of earlier work by Theodore Newcomb and Talcott Parsons. I have also found useful an unpublished manuscript by Bruce J. Biddle, "Roles, Goals, and Value Structures in Organizations," prepared for presentation to a Conference on Organization Research at the Carnegie Institute of Technology on June 22, 1962. See also Olmsted, *op. cit.*, and Theodore R. Sarbin, "Role Theory," in Gardner Lindzey (ed.), *Handbook of Social Psychology*, I (Cambridge, Mass.: Addison-Wesley, 1954), pp. 223–258.

[9] The cognitive approach to role analysis uses the concept of role to interpret interpersonal behavior in terms of phenomena which are assumed or inferred to take place in the minds of the actors in a system of social relationships, and which are seen as mediating between situational stimuli and behavioral responses. In this sense, *role* means a set of expectations applied to the incumbent of a position in a social relation, *expectations* means an evaluative standard applied to the incumbent, and *role behavior* is the perceived performance of the incumbent, which can be referred to an expectation for an incumbent of such a postition. Such expectations may relate to attributes, behavior, or both. An individual may hold such expectations concerning the incumbent of a particular perceived position against which he evaluates what he sees as the actual behavior and qualities of the incumbent. He may himself occupy the perceived position, in which case comparison of expected and actual attributes and/or performance takes the form of self-evaluation, or he may evaluate the incumbents of other positions in terms of his expectations. He may also hold expectations and make evaluations about how other actors should and do perceive him. In short, the attributes and behavior of the incumbent of any particular perceived position in a social relationship are evaluated by the participant observer in terms of conformity with or departure from the expectations which he associates with such a position.

*Figure 1.   The Relationship between Individual Personality and Role in a Specific Role-Set\**

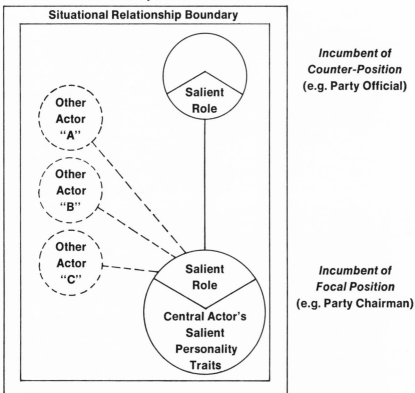

\*Adapted from Gross *et al., Explorations in Role Analysis,* p. 51.

and evaluate the relevant counter-players in accordance with these expectations. Responding to stimuli from the general political context and, more particularly, from his counter-players, the subject or central actor will pattern his behavioral responses on the basis of evaluations which relate to his own position in the perceived relationship as well as those of other actors (see Figure 1).

When we speak of such cognitive images it is necessary to distinguish between normative and non-normative behavioral expectations. The former are expectations of the incumbent of a position in terms of how the observing actor thinks the incumbent *should* act, the latter in terms of how he thinks the incumbent *will* act. Both types of expectations relate to the observer's own actions as well as to the actions of others. An actor in a political role-set may perceive his own prospective or actual behavior as consistent or proper in terms of the expectations he has come to hold for his position, but judge the behavior of his counter-players as inconsistent or improper. For example, a revolutionary may believe that the cause he sees himself as serving gives him the right to destroy those he feels stand in his way, but consider it highly illegitimate for his opponents to use force against him. In this case his expectations and evaluations of role behavior are normative. On the other hand, he may see himself locked in a savage struggle for power in a political community in which all actors can be expected to use every means at their disposal to gain their ends—like soldiers locked in battle—in which case his expectations and evaluations may be considered more or less non-normative. A citizen may dislike the actions of his governors but expect no better from them and, accordingly, either pay or strive to evade his taxes. But a voter may expect great things from the representative he sends to the legislature, only to be disappointed in his expectations by the behavior of his man in office. Browning's well-known commentary on the "Lost Leader"

> Just for a handful of silver he left us,
> Just for a riband to stick in his coat—
> Found the one gift of which fortune bereft us,
> Lost all the others she lets us devote;

reflected his disappointed normative expectations when Wordsworth switched his political allegiance from the Liberals to the Tories in Britain. Hitler's denunciation of the German people at the end of his regime as unworthy of their *Führer* was an evaluation in normative terms of relative roles and role behavior by a man who perceived his position as that of the all-knowing leader who should be obeyed unquestioningly by his counter-players.

Political leadership conceived as a cognitive role rather than as an office or behavior permits us to analyze it as an aspiration as well as a function, and to compartmentalize different segments of an individual's political activities in terms of relevant role-sets. The same person may simultaneously hold expectations relating to his exercise of political leadership in one political context and his aspirations for political leadership in another. For example, a politician may perceive himself as functioning as a leader in his party and strive for leadership in the larger political community, or a governor in the United States may see himself as occupying a leadership position in his state while, at the same time, seeking to become president (see Figure 2).

Let us also remember that when we speak of a leadership role in terms of expectations concerning the incumbent of a perceived political position, an individual who sees himself as occupying such a position may be more or less alone in his belief and the expectations associated therewith —even if he holds a formal leadership office. That is, position in this sense must not be confused with office. The "neutralist" prime minister who sees

## Figure 2. The Relationship Between Individual Personality and Specific Role-Sets in Various Political Situations*

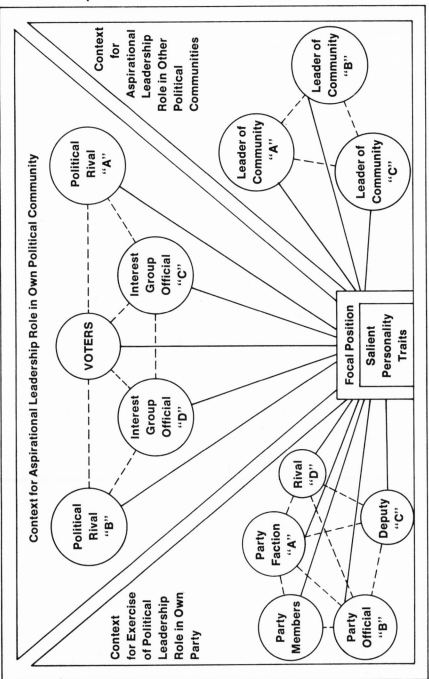

*Adapted from Gross et al., Explorations in Role Analysis, p. 55.

himself as the leader of a "third-force" may discover that his own expectations do not coincide with those of other statesmen: the king who considers himself responsible to God alone may pay with his life for his indifference to others' expectations; the general who believes that his position requires his taking political action may find himself dismissed by a president who does not agree with this view. On the other hand, the onetime deviant may come to command a following when others come to share his perception of his role as "the man of the hour." A maverick back-bencher like Churchill may then become prime minister, a minor general like de Gaulle become leader of a liberation movement, and a once obscure megalomaniac like Hitler ascend to the position of Chancellor of Germany.

The test of successful and effective political leadership would seem to be apparent congruence of the aspiring or actual leader's role perception with those of his counter-players in a relevant role-set. An individual may be able to translate his aspirations into fact and wield the power he attaches to the position he seeks or holds if most of the members of his party, or the voters in his community, or other influential actors in a political setting are ready to accept if not share his role assignments. Such a person may be sustained in his role behavior in a particular role-set if his counter-players more or less share the legitimacy expectations he brings to his position, as in the case of the party bureaucrat sustained by organizational norms or the prime minister who is seen as achieving the satisfaction of the public interest. He may successfully perform in accordance with his expectations because the other actors believe he is effectively realizing group goals or reconciling the satisfaction of apparently conflicting sub-group and individual interests.[10] Sometimes such a person is called a great leader, sometimes an astute politician, sometimes a demagogue. Lack of congruence between his role perception and that of the others may be skillfully concealed— for a time at least—if such an individual can persuade other relevant actors that he shares their goals (when in fact he does not), that he is performing a sanctioned role in a legitimate fashion, or that the king can do no wrong. Despite actual incongruence, the exercise of leadership at this point is still functional in terms of the incumbent's efforts to direct the collective behavior of his group.

---

[10] Thus, Harold Laski's suggestion to Clement Attlee that he hand over the Leadership of the British Labor Party to someone who had "more of the essential gifts" required for the position was not shared by the mass of the party's membership. Attlee's reply that he had "neither the personality nor the distinctiveness to tempt [him] to think that [he] should have any value apart from the party in which he served" reflected the membership's general expectations regarding the party leader's position which gave the leadership to Attlee rather than to a more "charismatic" type such as Laski seemed to have in mind. See W. L. Guttsman, "Changes in British Labour Leadership," in Marvick, *Political Decision-Makers*, p. 130.

When expectations and role performance manifestly conflict and the other relevant actors in a role-set actually perceive the central actor's expectations and actions as incongruent with their own expectations, the behavior of the person attempting to exercise political leadership becomes dysfunctional in terms of such interpersonal relations. The threat and application of sanctions on his part, divisive tactics, and weakness of the opposition may perhaps for a time continue to sustain his role performance—but not for long, if historical experiences and the findings of small-group experiments may be taken as guides. The central actor's attempts to induce others to agree to his role assignments, to accept him as their leader, will be frustrated unless role congruence is restored by (1) changes in the situational determinants, (2) changes in his role performance, or (3) both. In the case of persistent incongruence, the voters will retire the central actor, a revolution overthrow him, his formal subordinates fail to execute his orders. In the case of restored congruence, cognitively perceived stimuli emanating either from the central actor or the political situation act to change the counter-players' expectations once more in his favor—even if his behavior does not change, as in the case of General de Gaulle's return in 1958. Variations in expectations and role behavior produced by environmental determinants have received considerable attention in the literature on political leadership and social structure; adjustments in the role performance of the central actor, however, have been given far less consideration. The possibility of the latter appears to be primarily a matter of personality characteristics, and it is to these that we shall now turn because they seem particularly important for the study of individual political leadership.

In the actor-centered personality model, the self is the intervening variable between situational stimuli and the individual's response in role-choice and role behavior.[11] An actor's choice among roles and actions is a function of his orientation to the situation in terms of his conscious and unconscious motives, dispositions, and values. He will define and select his role and that of his counter-players according to his personality, choose for himself roles which are most congenial to his personality, and base his actions in any particular perceived situation on his desire to achieve the

---

[11] Role analysts, insofar as they deal with personality variables, tend to be rather ambiguous in making operationally useful distinctions between "the self" and other elements of an individual's personality. It is usually posited that the self is only a part of personality, some writers identifying it as the socially oriented aspects of personality, others as dynamic organization of attitudes and feelings as distinguished from a more permanent component called "the ego." Because the distinction strikes me as rather vague, I will take the liberty of using both the terms "self" and "personality" to describe characteristics associated with environment in which he functions (including other actors and their personality characteristics).

Figure 3.    The Relationship Between Situation, Personality, and
             Political Behavior

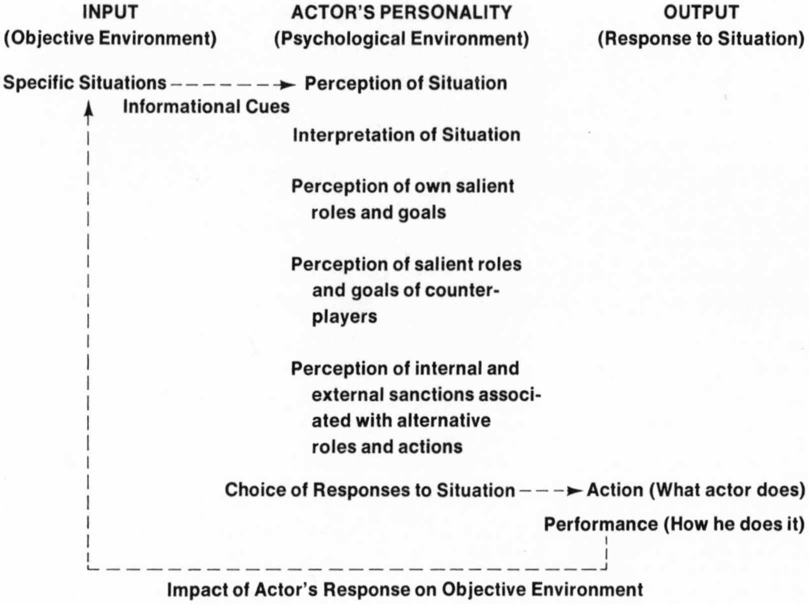

| INPUT | ACTOR'S PERSONALITY | OUTPUT |
|---|---|---|
| (Objective Environment) | (Psychological Environment) | (Response to Situation) |

Specific Situations – – – – – –➤ Perception of Situation
    ▲    Informational Cues

                        Interpretation of Situation

                        Perception of own salient
                           roles and goals

                        Perception of salient roles
                           and goals of counter-
                           players

                        Perception of internal and
                           external sanctions associ-
                           ated with alternative
                           roles and actions

        Choice of Responses to Situation – – –➤ Action (What actor does)

                                        Performance (How he does it)

Impact of Actor's Response on Objective Environment

gratification of certain goals and avoid the denial of others. Role and personality thus interact in the development of the self as well as in its maintenance (see Figure 3):

> Thus, a person's *self-conception* does or does not make him "psycho-
> logically eligible" *in his own eyes* for the assumption of certain roles,
> so that he imaginatively projects himself into certain roles . . . in a
> selective manner. Conversely, the self-picture is provided with con-
> tinuous reinforcement by what a person does, and by the reaction of
> others, as he fills a given role.[12]

In the light of the importance of temperamental differences in the
choice and evaluation of roles, it seems all the more surprising that "the
study of political roles has not been planned or extended to the consideration
of the total personality structure of a politician, or its developmental history,"
as Lasswell observed some years ago.[13] Indeed, many social scientists have
been aware of the significance of personality characteristics in the analysis
of leadership behavior, but the current attitude seems to be that there is

---

[12] Olmstead, *op. cit.,* p. 29. Italics added.
[13] "The Selective Effect of Personality," in Christie and Jahoda, *op. cit.,*
p. 202.

too little known on the subject to allow precise "scientific" statements to be made about it. A "really satisfactory theoretical formulation" of the complex interaction between personality and situational variables" does not exist at this time, one social psychologist has observed.[14] Reliable techniques for the description and measurement of personality characteristics are said to be lacking. However, shortcomings in theory and method are peculiar reasons for abandoning a whole area of study. Where necessary, we must— for the time being at least—rely on the eclectic application of imaginative if less precise methods to fill the present gap.

When we seek to examine the interrelationship between personality, role, and political setting, we assume that it is possible to distinguish between the objective and the psychological environment. The objective environment is how a non-involved, non-participant observer sees a situation and the behavior of the actors involved in it; the psychological environment is how an involved, participating actor perceives them. The investigator must preserve an explicit distinction between what he feels in his own "objective" evaluation of a situation and the "subjective" perceptions of the actors he is studying. Moreover, he must guard against projecting his own standards into the minds of his actors, for acts that he, as a non-involved observer, considers irrational and inconsistent may seem quite consistent and rational to the participating actors. And behavior which appears to him as having no utility in the achievement of an actor's manifest goals may in fact be functional in terms of the actor's latent personality needs.

I would like to stress the above caveats at the risk of belaboring the obvious, for the distinction between various types of rationality is frequently not very clear in studies of political leaders.[15] Despite the impressive efforts of Weber, Mannheim, Simon and others to make explicit distinctions between various forms of rationality, the term remains highly ambiguous in contemporary political science literature. It has proven difficult to make opera-

---

[14] Gibb, "Leadership," in Lindzey, *Handbook*, II, p. 914.

[15] For those who implicitly or explicitly employ the rational behavior model, a political decision is considered correct "in fact" when it meets given "objective standards of rationality." For our purposes this will not do. The psychological environment of an actor or group of actors may make actions seems rational to them that seem irrational to others, including the investigator. For example, the actors may have access to information which, according to the rational behavior model, should increase the likelihood that they will act "objectively rationally." However, they may factor out such information because it does not fit their orientation to the situation: Thus, Stalin apparently ignored Churchill's warnings in 1940 that a German attack on the Soviet Union was imminent. Hitler, in 1941, ignored the leak of American war plans to the press three days before Pearl Harbor, though they made it plain that Germany would be the United States' primary objective. In each instance, the information available to the decision-maker apparently did not fit into his perception of the situation and was, therefore, factored out.

tionally useful distinctions between rationality of means and rationality of ends, and between "normative" and "scientific" rationality, as it has to avoid circular reasoning. In particular, the fact that the goals of an actor may not be manifest has complicated the task of identifying "rational" political behavior which will advance his achievement of them. For our purposes at least, the distinction between objective and psychological environments seems more adequate for the task at hand.

Naturally, the socio-political environment limits considerably the individual's freedom to choose political roles and actions. Political socialization imposes certain role expectations and evaluations upon him from childhood on, which more or less direct his actions, interpretations, and choice of means and ends in political situations. In particular, society and culture define the attributes and behavior for institutionalized roles in a political system or sub-system—the "good citizen," the "honest official," and the "responsible ruler"—which, in most instances, the individual accepts as valid for the role behavior and decision-making in his political community. Thus, a politician's role conception in a comparatively stable political system is influenced by the institutionalized expectations of that system—particularly if he wants to maintain the system or sub-system in which he is engaged in role interactions.[16] This is strikingly evident in Britain, for example, where the exercise of political roles is highly circumscribed by institutionalized expectations toward incumbents of parliamentary and ministerial positions. To pursue a political career an aspirant must conform to a recruitment process which rather rigidly prescribes his role behavior as a candidate for parliament, as a back-bencher, and a member of the ministry. In other political systems role performances prescribed by traditional or legal-rational rules of political behavior may not be as explicitly rigid, but nonetheless provide stability for the system. The rules of the game must be observed more or less if the political system is to function efficiently. The deviant who violates them must be prepared to pay the penalty. However, when the institutionalized patterns break down and affective interpersonal relationships predominate, the political leader or aspirant is far less subject to such restrictions.

At such times the deviant may become an innovating leader, particularly if he can substitute a charismatic for an institutionalized role.

Institutionalized roles tend to structure reality for the central political actor by defining to a large extent his expectations, and allowing him to predict the behavior of his counter-players with some accuracy. In addition,

---

[16] This point is particularly well brought out by Wahlke, *et al.* in *The Legislative System* and by Nathan Leites in *On the Game of Politics in France* (Stanford: Stanford University Press, 1959), and, with Constantin Melnik, in *The House Without Windows: France Chooses a President* (Evanston, Ill.: Row, Peterson, 1958).

they help to structure his "super-ego content" by providing general normative standards for evaluating his own role-behavior and that of others.[17]
Whether he accepts or rejects these standards, however, is again a matter
of personality. The deviant—the fanatic or the dedicated revolutionary—
rejects them because of components in his personality which prove stronger
than the norms required through political socialization.

Insofar as role definitions constitute "the individual's attempt to
structure his social reality, to define his place within it, and to guide his
search for meaning and gratification," as a social psychologist has expressed
it, they constitute "an ego achievement."[18] That is, he strives to satisfy
personality needs through the assumption and performance of certain roles.
Thus, a political actor's orientation to a situation, his opinions and style of
role behavior are shaped by the interplay of personality characteristics and
the perceived demands of his political environment. This applies in particular
to how he perceives and reacts to sanctions, the primary significance of
which is gratificational-deprivational in terms of expectations and behavior.[19]
Consciously or unconsciously, the actor chooses, performs, and reacts to
certain roles in order to gratify some needs or to avoid denial of their
satisfaction. The extent of his conformity with "legitimate" role expectations
will be in proportion to the extent to which he is prepared to accept or reject internal sanctions (i.e., those sanctions that he applies to himself) and
external sanctions (i.e., those which someone else appears in a position to
apply to him) and how willing he is to accept or postpone gratification
to further his goals (i.e. perceived and desired future states of affairs).
Within as well as beyond the boundaries of societal norms for political role
performance, a number of roles may thus appear available to the aspirant
for political leadership. Which of these he chooses to play and how he chooses
to play them is at bottom a matter of his personality characteristics.

In their study of American state legislators, Eulau and his associates
assumed that the course of a politician's career and his perspectives are
circumscribed by his "sense of reality." That is, the individual who lacks
sufficient cognitive sensitivity to political circumstances "as they really are"

---

[17] See Talcott Parsons, "Psychoanalysis and the Social Structure," reprinted
from *The Psychoanalytical Quarterly,* Vol. 19, No. 3 (1950) in Hendrik M. Ruiten-
beek (ed.), *Psychoanalysis and the Social Sciences* (New York: Dutton, 1962), pp.
48f.

[18] Daniel J. Levinson, "Role, Personality, and Organizational Structure in the
Organizational Setting," *Journal of Abnormal Psychology,* Vol. 58 (1959), p. 177.
See also Heinz Hartmann, *Ego Psychology and the Process of Adaptation* (New York:
International University Presses, 1958).

[19] Gross *et al., op. cit.,* pp. 65f. See also Talcott Parsons and Edwards, Shils,
"Values, Motives, and Systems of Action," in *Toward a General Theory of Action*
(New York: Harper Torchbook, 1962), pp. 47–158.

is likely to experience considerable personal frustration in his attempts to play political roles.[20] The political system or sub-system demands that he adjust his career-oriented behavior to the expectations of the salient counter-players who can facilitate or frustrate his externalized personal drives. As the Georges found in their study of Woodrow Wilson, and as I have found in my own study of Kurt Schumacher, the individual who cannot make the requisite adjustments in his behavior is likely to meet with severe frustrations which, in turn, affect his personality and subsequent behavior. In their more extreme form, such inflexible behavior patterns may lead to self-denying prophecies as the individual fails to obtain the gratification he seeks for per-sonal needs in the public sphere because he cannot make the necessary behavioral adjustments or misinterprets behavioral clues from the situational environment. Thus, insofar as the individual actor's personality needs demand gratification through personal success in the political arena, such rigid be-havior patterns may prove dysfunctional in terms of his personality needs as well as the effectiveness of his group.

Men like Franklin Roosevelt and Konrad Adenauer, as different as they may appear to the casual observer, have in common a keen "sense of reality" which enables them to adjust their behavior to the expectations of their salient counter-players and thus to acquire and exercise political leadership. Their personality characteristics apparently permit sufficient out-ward orientation to satisfy their personal needs as well as the expectations of those who could facilitate or block their desire for political leadership.

The successful leader may thus be an individual whose role inter-pretations are accepted by the salient counter-players because he satisfies their expectations, or he may be a person who so clearly comprehends the political context that he can adjust his behavior to meet the expectations of these relevant others. The great leader, as Lucien Pye has concluded from Erik Erikson's work on Luther, settles some of his own inner problems by not only adapting to the expectations of others, "but in turn changing and controlling his surroundings." Striving to find his own identity, he strikes out against his environment and succeeds in stimulating a satisfying response in the public arena because he is the right man at the right time.[21]

In the last analysis, therefore, we must concern ourselves intensively with the personality of our leading actor and, specifically, with those variables which appear to be salient to his political motivation, attitudes, and responses to specific situational stimuli. His orientation to the political environment and his perception of the specific situation is conditioned by psychological

---

[20] Eulau *et al., op. cit.,* in Marvick, *Political Decision-Makers,* pp. 206–261.

[21] Pye, *op. cit.,* in Marvick, *Political Decision-Makers,* pp. 303–308, 310. See also Daryl deBell, "Of Man, Magic, and Motives," in *ibid.,* pp. 331–332, as well as the Erikson study, *Young Man Luther* itself.

factors, and these images in turn determine his response to environmental cues. Such perceptions structure his attitudes and behavior according to his hierarchy of values, his recognition of the saliency of particular actions of others, and his possible rewards or punishments. The internalized belief system—the images of the perceived salient past, present, and future—as well as the externalized response to environmental cues need be studied in the light of explicit psychological behavior models as we seek to relate the attitudes and behavior of present or past political leaders or aspirants to their underlying motivation. By studying manifest attitudinal and behavioral patterns in terms of hypotheses derived from such models we may be able to indicate possible explanations of past behavior and, in the case of contemporary actors, perhaps, predict future behavior.[22]

The individual's degree of self-orientation, as against his sensitivity to the values of other relevant actors in a political relationship, appears to have a considerable influence upon his role choice and role behavior when he seeks or exercises leadership. Speaking in terms of ideal-types, Bass distinguishes between self-oriented individuals who are concerned above all with the personal rewards of leadership, task-oriented individuals who seek or exercise leadership principally because a group's actions seem attractive, and interaction-oriented individuals who are drawn to positions of leadership in the belief that they can derive satisfaction from effective interpersonal relations within a group.[23] The self-oriented actor who is motivated by personality needs related to a striving for status, esteem, or some other self-assertive compensation for low self-esteem may tend to distort or be indifferent to cues about the expectations of others and ruthlessly pursue his personal goals even when they manifestly injure group effectiveness. The leader who leads his group to destruction seems to fit this type of which Hitler is an example. On the other hand, the task-oriented actor may seek or exercise leadership determined to "get things done" even if it means subordinating personal and group rewards to the perceived task—this type is often associated with party bureaucrats. Finally, the interaction-oriented actor may be preoccupied with the expectations of other political actors to the point of extreme self-abnegation in favor of perceived group effectiveness, avoiding leadership when he thinks it is likely to disrupt a satisfactory interaction pattern. Thus, a leader may resign to preserve "party harmony" or a candidate withdraw for the sake of "national unity" in time of crisis.

---

[22] Some of these points are raised in a fine study of John Foster Dulles by Ole R. Holsti, "The Belief System and National Images: A Case Study" in *The Journal of Conflict Resolution*, 6, 3 (September 1962), 244–252, as well as by Sidney Verba in his excellent discussion of the "Assumptions of Rationality and Non-Rationality in Models of the International System," in *World Politics*, 14, 1 (October 1961), 93–117.

[23] Bass, *Leadership*, pp. 449–451.

An individual's personality characteristics may drive him to seek psychic satisfaction by behavior which is highly dysfunctional in terms of the objective logic of the situation and even his own conscious goals. He may unconsciously invite defeat or other deprivational sanctions to satisfy guilt feelings or masochistic needs. Or he may so crave esteem or other rewards that he is driven to choose and perform roles which promise immediate gratification of these desires at the expense of more distant rewards or task or group demands. Verba has suggested that the greater the personal involvement an actor feels in a situation, the more ambiguous the cognitive and evaluative aspects of the situation will be to him, and the less situationally structured his role behavior, the greater likelihood that personality variables will assert themselves in determining his responses.[24] Max Weber's well-known distinction between individuals who live *off* politics and those who live *for* politics is also relevant here, since personality characteristics are related to each type of behavior.[25] So, also, is Lasswell's distinction between the power-seeking "political type" and individuals who voluntarily give up positions of authority for "the woman I love," or for religious meditation or scholarly work, for example.[26]

But how are we to examine an actor's personality? On this point I find myself in agreement with Alexander and Juliette George: "The complexity of personality organization, the important role of ego functioning, and the variety of ways in which given personality factors may express themselves in a political leader's behavior . . . emerge only when the career as a whole, not merely a few isolated episodes from it, is examined in detail." [27] We lack as yet, and may never have, a comprehensive and satisfactory conceptual model for the study of the political personality and are compelled to make eclectic selections among relevant propositions and hypotheses in the ever-growing literature of personality theory.

---

[24] Verba, "Rationality and Non-Rationality," pp. 99–103.

[25] Max Weber, *Politik als Beruf* (Munich and Leipzig: Duncker and Humblot, 1919), p. 12.

[26] Lasswell, *Power and Personality,* pp. 20–22, 38, 57.

[27] *Woodrow Wilson and Colonel House,* p. 318. In addition to this very suggestive study, based on Lasswell's explorations in developmental biography, I have found the following works particularly useful for a consideration of the function of personality characteristics in the determination of political leadership behavior: Lasswell, *Power and Personality,* especially Chapter III, and "The Selective Effect of Personality in Political Participation" in Christie and Jahoda, *op. cit.;* Gardner Murphy, *Personality: A Biosocial Approach to Origins and Structure* (New York: Harper and Brothers, 1947); Brewster Smith, Jerome S. Bruner, and Robert W. White, *Opinions and Personality* (New York: John Wiley, 1956); and James McGregor Burns, *Roosevelt: The Lion and the Fox,* particularly pp. 481–487 ("A Note on the Study of Political Leadership").

For our purposes, a holistic approach to the dynamics of personality development and expression which gives consideration to antecedent as well as contemporaneous events, to psychic as well as somatic factors, to the "inner man" as well as the impact of socio-political "outside" variables in the patterning of behavioral characteristics seems most appropriate. With the data available and—where they are inadequate—imaginative theorizing, we must trace the growth of the biological organism and its degree of maturation at various stages in the individual's political career, as well as somatic factors which may have had an important influence on his role and performance as, for example, stomach disorders, deformity, or long illnesses.[28] In considering the psychological development of our subject we must seek to examine not only formative childhood experiences, but personality development through adolescence and adulthood to the point of any particular political act, including traumatic experiences and other personality crises which may have significantly influenced subsequent behavior. Nor must we neglect the impact of socialization on personality development, the continuous process by which the individual adopts patterns of adjustment and responses to his social and political environmental stimuli.

The cumulative interaction between personality and external stimuli produce the political actor as experiences condition and reinforce his role identification, philosophy of life, and his way of recognizing and responding to environmental cues. Personality factors condition his perception of himself and others in a given situation and cause him to factor out some stimuli, distort others, and admit others intact. They shape his responses and choices among roles and courses of action, subject to the perceived limitations of group and societal norms and interests, and the information available to him.[29] The actor finds certain roles and decisions more gratifying than others, psychologically, and he seeks to satisfy some needs and avoid the denial of others. According to his personal inclinations and expectations, he adapts himself to his personality needs on the one hand and the demands of the situation on the other. The form which this inner-outer response-mix

---

[28] In this connection, see Gottfried, *Boss Cermak,* Appendix II, which attempts to bring the findings of psychosomatic studies to bear upon an analysis of a political personality, though with rather disappointing results (previously published under the title "The Use of Psychosomatic Categories in a Study of Political Personality" in *The Western Political Quarterly,* Vol. 8, pp. 234–247 and reprinted in Eulau *et al., Political Behavior,* pp. 125–132).

[29] See, Robert E. Lane, "Political Personality and Electoral Choice," *The American Political Science Review,* XLIX, 1 (March 1955), pp. 173f. Also, W. I. Thomas and F. Znaniecki, "The Definition of the Situation," in Theodore M. Newcomb and Eugene L. Hartley, *Readings in Social Psychology* (New York: Holt, 1947), p. 76; Simon, *Administrative Behavior,* pp. 95, 105; and Gibb, "Leadership," in Lindzey, *Handbook,* II, pp. 901ff.

will take varies with the relative influence of his basic impulses, socially-implanted values and expectations, and situational cues.

In politics, as in other interpersonal relationships, the degree to which an actor is inwardly or outwardly oriented is a function of his personality. His value hierarchy and his perception of the particular environment at any given moment—including such perceived counter-players as loyal followers and rivals, other leaders, and potential supporters—are internalized factors, which are externalized as specific behavior in accordance with the ratio of inward to outward orientation. Or, to use Lasswell's well-known formulation, private motives are more less displaced onto public objects and rationalized in terms of group interests.[30] His response to situational stimuli may be more or less automatic because his actions are narrowly circumscribed by the situational context or rigidly structured by his personality characteristics. But it may also result from a considered choice among the alternative responses open to him in the light of available information.

The extent of an actor's inward or outward orientation in a specific situation is of particular importance in the study of political leadership, as I have already noted. Whether the incumbent of a position which he perceives as promising potential or actual leadership makes a choice primarily in terms of future internal or external sanctions whether he sees immediate or future gratification or deprivation resulting from one alternative action or another is a matter of personality. The more sensitive he is to the immediately relevant external environment, the more readily he may adjust his style of performance to it and avoid behavior other relevant actors will consider deviant. The more atuned he is to personal, internalized motives and needs, the more difficult he may find it to make behavioral choices realistically in accordance with the demands of the external environment. In the one instance, we may have the interaction-oriented individual who leads by readjusting his performance to group demands—in the extreme case, the conformist who must follow because he must lead. Some would call such a leader opportunistic, others democratic. In the other instance, we may have the self-oriented individual who insists that others adjust their actions to his demands. Some would call him a dedicated idealist, others a self-willed autocrat.

It has been my contention that in studying an individual's efforts to exercise political leadership we must attempt to trace the dynamic patterns of interaction between personality, role, and setting. We can now try to bring together the various factors which I have sought to establish as relevant in a series of propositions:

---

[30] As first formulated in his *Psychopathology and Politics* (Chicago: University of Chicago Press, 1940), pp. 74–76.

1. Political leadership is a position in a particular situational setting involving decision-making for a political community.
2. Occupancy of such a position is a function both of the personality of the incumbent and the situation in which he finds himself.
   a. Different situations favor different types of leadership.
   b. A variety of passive and active, more or less salient expectations toward the incumbent of such a position combine to elevate some individuals to leadership, to maintain others as leaders, and to displace still others from positions of leadership.
   c. Functional role behavior for the actor aspiring to lead is behavior which is congruent with the expectations which most members of a group hold for the incumbent of a position associated with aspiring or actual leadership.
   d. The actor who can meet these expectations by emitting stimuli which make his behavior appear congruent with the expectations of those he wishes to lead is behaving functionally in terms of his aspirations to lead.
   e. Dysfunctional role behavior for the actor aspiring to lead is behavior which is incongruent with the expectations which most members of a group hold for the incumbent of a position associated with of aspiring or actual leadership.
   f. The individual who fails to meet these expectations by emitting stimuli which make his behavior appear incongruent with the expectations of those he wishes to lead is behaving dysfunctionally in terms of his aspirations to lead.[31]
   g. The type of stimuli emitted by an individual who wishes to lead in response to a specific situation is a function of his personality characteristics and is conditioned by:
      1) His orientation to the situation and his perception of situational stimuli.
      2) His cognitive sensitivity ("sense of reality") to the objective situation.[32]
      3) His inclination to maintain or modify previous behavior patterns in the light of his interpretation of the new situational stimuli.
   h. The relevance of individual personality factors varies with the situation in which an individual endeavors to exercise leadership and the more highly structured the situation, the less play there is for such factors.

---

[31] "One becomes a leader, others are characterized as mad, and the essential difference is not alone in the stimulus individual, but rather in the attitudes and beliefs of the stimulated persons, which determines the latter's response to the stimulus." Gibb, "Leadership," in Lindzey, *Handbook,* II, p. 915.

[32] On this, see Heinz Eulau *et al.,* "Career Perspectives of American State Legislators," in Marvick, *Political Decision-Makers,* p. 261.

i. If we can determine some of the specific functional demands and limitations placed on an individual seeking to exercise political leadership in different designated situations and if, at the same time, we can ascertain some of the salient personality characteristics of such an individual, we may be able to establish behavior patterns which help explain past, present and, perhaps, even future performance of such an individual in terms of interaction between situational and personality variables.[33]

3. When role and role behavior based on personality needs more or less correspond to role and role behavior demanded by situational requirements, an individual's efforts to acquire and/or exercise political leadership will be functional, both in terms of the personality needs and the group needs.

4. When role and role behavior based on personality needs more or less conflict with role and role behavior demanded by situational requirements, an individual's efforts to acquire and/or exercise political leadership may be dysfunctional in terms of his personality needs (e.g., internalized conflict), or the group needs (e.g., externalized conflict), or both. For example, enforced conformity with rigidly institutionalized roles may produce severe personality crises, and compulsive personality drives may bring about severe interpersonal conflicts between the individual and the group which will prove frustrating to both.

5. In general, the more inwardly-oriented the individual, the more difficult he may find it to acquire and/or exercise political leadership.

6. In general, the more outwardly-oriented the individual, the more successful he may be in acquiring and/or exercising political leadership.

7. An individual's expectations and role behavior may be congruent with the expectations of his counter-players in one role-set and simultaneously incongruent with the expectations of counter-players in another role-set. For example, a party official may act in a manner approved by some or all the members of his party and, at the same time and by the same actions clash with the expectations of non-party members in the larger political community in which his party operates.

8. In a situation perceived as constituting a crisis condition by the members of a political group, an inwardly-oriented individual's role perceptions may come to be shared by salient counter-players so as to facilitate his drive for and/or exercise of leadership in the group.

9. In a situation perceived as a non-crisis situation by the members of a political group, an inwardly-oriented individual is likely to be less successful in acquiring and/or exercising leadership than more outwardly-oriented individuals.

Our focus in such an investigation is on the central actor, the subject of our study, and his interaction with various situations that arise in the

---

[33] Adopted, with considerable modification, from a statement in Bass, *op. cit.*, p. 21.

course of his endeavors to exercise political leadership. That is, we seek to study his patterns of political behavior over time by examining his specific behavioral responses to particular situations. To guide us in such an analysis, I have sought to outline below the variables which appear to me particularly relevant:

I. The Central Actor
  A. Salient Background Variables
    1. Personal (Non-Political) History
      a. Biological factors (e.g., sex, age, health)
      b. Socio-psychological factors
        1) Social background (e.g., family, community, culture, society)
          a) Acculturation and socialization (e.g., normative-deviant traits)
        2) Personality Characteristics
          a) Attitudinal Patterns (e.g., dogmatism)
          b) Behavioral Patterns (e.g., nature, extent, and style of social intercourse)
    2. Political History
      a. Recruitment into political activity (i.e., when, why, how)
      b. Political experiences (i.e., nature, extent of commitment to politics, career, successes and failures, stability of allegiances, etc.)
  B. Salient Contemporaneous Factors
    1. The Objective Setting for Political Activity
      a. The Political System and/or Sub-systems (e.g., party, state)
      b. Nature and Conditions for Political Participation (e.g., extent of political mobility and access to policy-making offices)
    2. The Objective Location of Central Actor in Terms of Political System
      a. Group memberships (e.g., dominant elite, revolutionary underground organization)
      b. Politically relevant offices (e.g., prime minister, deputy, voter)
      c. Manifest evidence of political power (e.g., dictator, voter)
    3. Central Actor's General Orientation to Contemporary Political Context
      a. Motivation for Political Activity (e.g., personality needs, material reward)
      b. Self-image and orientation (i.e., how he believes he fits into context)
        1) Self-, task-, interaction-orientation
      c. Images of Political Environment
        1) Attitudes Toward In-group
          a) What group does he identify with, if any (e.g., community, party)

b) Orientation to perceived group goals

c) Extent of identification of personal with perceived group goals

d) Orientation toward other group members

2) Attitudes Toward Non-group Members

a) Identification of salient others

b) Evaluation of salient others

II. Political Performance of Central Actor

A. Objective Environment for Performance of Specific Roles by Central Actor

1. Specific Political Situation

2. Relevant Counter-Players in Specific Role-Sets

a. Identity, positions, tasks, activities, values, goals, behavioral characteristics, orientation

b. Relationship to Central Actor

1) Structural in terms of political system or sub-system (e.g., institutional, formal, social)

2) Cognitive

a) Attitudes (e.g., affection, hostility, indifference)

b) Respective role definitions and assignments

c) Expectations concerning Central Actor's Role Attributes and Behavior (e.g., sanctioned, non-sanctioned)

B. Communication Links Between Objective Environment and Psychological Environment of Central Actor

1. Nature and Intensity of Situational Stimuli

C. Central Actor's Psychological Environment for Performance of Specific Roles

1. Perception of Political Situation

a. Definition of situation in terms of perceived informational cues and their saliency; who and what is involved (e.g., counter-players, values)

b. Evaluation of Situation in terms of central Actor's salient values and expectations: what needs to be done? What can be done?

2. Role Definitions

a. Own role in specific situation: what he should do

1) Conflicting Roles

2) Alternative Role Choices

b. Role of perceived counter-players: what they should do or will do

3. Expectations About Attributes and Behavior

a. Own role: what he can go (e.g., in terms of internal sanctions)

b. Perceived counter-players: what they can or will do in response to actor's own behavior (e.g., external sanctions)

D. Central Actor's Role Performance
  1. Behavioral Response to Situational Stimuli
     a. Nature of action: what he does (e.g., automatic response)
     b. Nature of performance: how he does it
E. Appraisal of Central Actor's Role Performance
  1. By Himself
     a. In terms of personal gratification-deprivation
     b. In terms of gratification-deprivation for others
     c. In terms of impact on attitudinal patterns for future action
        1) His own
        2) Salient other actors (e.g., voters)
  2. By Participant Observers
     a. In terms of congruency-incongruency with their expectations
     b. In terms of approval-disapproval (e.g., efficient, honest, effective)
     c. In terms of impact on attitudes toward central actor and his role relative to future behavior toward actor
        1) Modification of previous attitudes
        2) Maintenance of previous attitudes
  3. By Non-participant Investigator
     a. Functional-dysfunctional in terms of manifest values of actors
     b. Functional-dysfunctional in terms of latent needs of actors.

As I conceive it, our task is to attempt to write political biographies, of dead as well as living individuals, which will increase our understanding of their actions both as aspirants to and incumbents of positions of political leadership. Using as our guide an outline such as I have put forward, we may be able to proceed, with the most adequate means available, to seek answers to questions such as these:

1. What are generally the objective conditions under which our central actor engages in political activities: For example, does he operate in a stable or unstable political system?
2. From the point of view of the investigator, what roles seem to be available to our central actor in various situations? For example, does a particular situation severely restrict his choice or does it give him a wide latitude?
3. What roles does the central actor appear to see open to him in various situations and how does he seem to evaluate them? For example, does he consistently appear to perceive only one "honorable" part which he can play in the light of the apparent behavior of his counter-players?
4. What roles does the central actor choose to play in various situations and how does he perform them? For example, does he constantly

readjust his role choice to new situations, or does he consistently choose roles which he professes have served him well enough in previous situations?

5. Why does the central actor choose to play some roles rather than others which seem available to him? For example, is there evidence that organizational or personality patterns induce him to make particular choices?

6. What roles does the central actor appear to perceive as available to other salient actors and how does he evaluate them? For example, does he seem to expect members of his group to obey him unquestioningly and react violently when his expectations are disappointed?

7. How does the central actor evaluate his own performance and that of other salient actors? For example, does he seem to feel he always does the "right" thing, but others do not?

8. What is the effect of the central actor's role choice and performance on participant observers and how do they evaluate these in terms of their own expectations? For example, do they reelect him to office because they believe he has consistently satisfied their needs, or do they deny him their support because they judge that his past performance augurs ill for their own interests?

9. What means does the central actor employ to induce others to accept his role assignments, both for himself and them, in a particular role-set? For example, does he deliberately offer emotional or material satisfaction of certain of their needs?

10. What induces the central actor's salient counter-players in various situations to accept or reject his role assignments? For example are they bound to him by ties of affection (e.g., charisma) or rational-legal norms?

One purpose of political biography, is to allow us to understand not only what our chief actor did or does, but why. But a political biography is also a case history which, together with similar investigations of other men, should move us toward comparative generalizations about the success or failure of similar individuals in different situations and different individuals in similar situations. In studying one person, we strive to identify salient personality and situational variables which may allow us to classify political actors striving for leadership in terms of personality types, behavior, and the context in which they operate. For example, compulsive individuals may be effective crisis leaders because the "abnormal" man fits "abnormal" times, while the "well-adjusted" individual may make a good caucus chairman but an ineffectual revolutionary. Secondly, such case studies may have a predictive value and lead toward probabilistic predictions about the future behavior of a single individual, about the behavior of a class of actors with similar characteristics in similar situations, and about the type of individual most likely to achieve positions of leadership in various situations.

In studying the interaction of personality, role, and setting we are dependent upon conceptual models and data, as well as empathy. The subject actor's performance can be more or less accurately determined empirically. His role perceptions we can ascertain only imperfectly; here we must largely rely on imaginative reconstruction. Finally, the identification of salient personality characteristics requires reliance on personality models which allow us to make meaningful connections between motivation and behavior on the strength of available data.

To a certain extent, this sort of analysis gives an unbalanced and even distorted picture of the individual being studied. Because we are interested only in those factors which seem relevant to his political behavior, we are likely to slight those aspects of the "whole man" which would interest the descriptive or creative biographer. We seek explanations at a different level and in a different form from the humanistically-oriented men of letters. By committing ourselves to explicit constructs or models we sacrifice *a priori* some of the concrete and unique aspects, and slant our investigation toward those aspects of the subject's activities which can be isolated for comparative purposes. If we are to achieve our purpose, this seems as unavoidable as it is justifiable. Our concern is not the whole man, but the political actor and the factors which seem to bear upon him as such. Accordingly, the political scientist writing political biography strives not to displace the humanist man-of-letters, but to bring his particular interests and skills to bear upon those aspects of a man's life which will illuminate his political behavior and, through it, that of others like him or unlike him.

# 10

## Comparison of Nixon and Kennedy: The Logic of Politics

EDWIN S. SHNEIDMAN

When significant political figures speak nowadays, people listen. Our common sense tells us that we are living in a time of political activities of such extreme importance that national and international decisions can affect not only the subtle tenor of our lives but indeed whether or not we shall survive at all. If this time is, as it has been called, "the age of anxiety," it is probably fair to say that the burden of that anxiety revolves around political actions and political crises—and their implications for global destruction.

Of the many attributes of political speeches (or any kind of verbalization, for that matter) which might be the focus for analysis, one avenue of investigation which has been relatively neglected (but which nonetheless might prove to be extremely important) relates to the *cognitive* aspects and the psychological concomitants of these cognitive aspects. We apply the label "psychologic" to the joint analysis of the logical and psychological elements of a text. We propose to outline a specific method for psychological analysis of the stimulus materials and to illustrate the application of that new method of analyzing political thinking by using materials from some particularly interesting examples.

We are a nation of millions of television sets; we are a nation of almost constant political elections and of intense political interests. We are also living in a world where the other nations include both tangible friends and potential foes. Television influences our elections and our international relationships, and it is extremely important for us to know more about the

Edwin S. Shneidman, "The Logic of Politics." *Television and Human Behavior*. Edited by Leon Arons and Mark A. May. New York: Appleton-Century-Crofts, 1963, 178–199. Copyright © 1963 by Television Bureau of Advertising, Inc. Reprinted by permission of Appleton-Century-Crofts, Educational Division, Meredith Corporation, and the author.

television stimuli that our own political leaders transmit and the "impact" which they produce at home and abroad. We must also learn more about the "meaning" (and implications to us) of the televised materials from our international brethren—especially those with keen sibling rivalry.

The purpose of this essay is to present the outlines for a logical model, a model which might be employed in any one of several settings and which would provide a conceptual scheme for translating the logical elements contained in verbal stimuli into their related psychological attributes. Assuming that each individual has—along with his universal and culturally common ways of thinking—some idiosyncratic ways of thinking, the purpose of this paper is to set up a system whereby one can convert these into their psychological attributes. The implication here is that the important impact of the logical aspect of the verbal stimulus is not in the logic which it portrays, but rather in the personality attributes which it implies. A second purpose of this essay is to give content to this notion by way of example and, further, to suggest (in the last section of this paper) some experiments which would be required to test the appropriateness and fruitfulness of the model itself.

The framework of suppositions contained in this essay can be stated in terms of the following:

1. That, given the typescript of a televised speech (address, debate, program, etc.) of a specific political personage, it is possible to analyze meaningfully the unique logical elements or styles of thinking which are latently contained within it.

2. That, given this cognitive analysis, it is then possible systematically to infer specific personality or psychological characteristics that accrue to that individual. The assumption here is that the style of a man's thinking is directly related to other aspects of his personality and that meaningful inferences as to personality or psychological traits can be made from an analysis of an individual's thinking patterns.

3. That, further, in an election situation, given the two candidates' logical styles (and their inferred psychological characteristics), it may be possible to make specific predictions over and above chance expectations as to the impact of the two candidates upon television audiences.

4. That those voters who are television viewers are influenced not entirely by what a candidate says (in that it may be confusing or essentially similar to what the other candidate says), or by what a candidate looks like, but in some significant part by the candidate's "personality" (the kind of person he "is"), which they (consciously or unconsciously) infer in part from his styles of thinking.

5. That most voters have in mind the "kind of person" they would like to see occupy a particular office at a particular time, and they will tend to vote for that candidate whose "projected" personality (as inferred in part from the candidate's styles of thinking, etc.) comes closest to the average "model" that the voters have in mind.

6. That a basis for making predictions of the outcome of elections is available through "matching" candidates' personalities with voters' personality models.

## RELEVANT GENERAL BACKGROUND AND PHILOSOPHIC ASSUMPTIONS

There are several diverse sources of materials which are relevant to this essay.

1. Behavioral Analysis. There are respectable numbers of previous psychological researches which relate styles of thinking to psychological (or behavioral) variables. Examples would include the investigations of the effects of various experimental variables on the logical styles of *normal* subjects. Along these lines are studies of the effects on syllogistic reasoning of drugs,[1] of anxiety,[3] of negative premises,[28] etc. Also there are investigations of the developmental aspects of styles of thinking. In this connection, the work of Piaget[17] and Werner[26] on the development of different types of reasoning in people of various ages immediately comes to mind. There is extensive literature on the investigation of the styles of thinking of *aberrant* persons, limited largely to schizophrenic and brain-damaged patients. In this connection, one would want to make reference to the work of Goldstein,[10] Kasanin,[12] Vigotsky,[24] von Domarus,[25] Arieti,[2] Cameron,[5] Sullivan,[23] and Rapaport.[19] The work on the "logic of suicide" by Shneidman[21] in which are analyzed various attributes of logical thinking in genuine and simulated suicide notes also furnishes relevant background.

2. Content Analysis. Also directly related to this essay are important works in the area of content analysis, which have been concerned with the description of the stimulus pattern in communication. In this connection, reference should be made to the work of Berelson in communications research,[4] of Lasswell in "the language of politics,"[13] of George in propaganda analysis,[8] of Osgood and his semantic differential,[15] and of the volume of content analysis edited by Pool.[18]

3. Thematic Apperception Analysis. Most directly related are the stimulating concepts from Murray[14] and his host of followers[20] in the tradition that is called thematic apperception test analysis—a

tradition which encompasses a large variety of approaches applicable to the analysis of verbal responses to pictorial stimulus materials.

4. Concern with the Importance of the Stimuli. Our problem reflects our general need to "understand" (and to predict) behavior better than we do. In behavioral science, a basic formulation is that of "stimulus-organism-response" (S-O-R). There has generally been too little systematic study of the properties of the stimulus.[9] This is true not only in television research but throughout psychological science as well. Cornell Professor James J. Gibson has stated the following about the stimulus in psychology: "It seems to me that there is a weak link in the chain of reasoning by which we explain experience and behavior, namely, our concept of the stimulus. . . . Enough has been said to show that in the twentieth century we have inherited a mixed batch of ideas about the stimulus. We constantly use the term but seldom define it. We take it for granted. We have behavior theory in full bloom, and perception theory in ripened complexity, but who ever heard of stimulus theory?" [9]

There is great need to understand the potentiating properties of the television stimulus. The current study ties in with the growing interest in the psychology of the stimulus and the growing general awareness that understanding the nature of the stimulus is particularly important for understanding the operation of mass communication, especially for television.

5. Philosophic Background. The notion that there are different logical styles (or different styles of thinking) is given intellectual permissiveness particularly by the writings of the American philosophers Charles Sanders Peirce,[16] William James,[11] and John Dewey,[7] especially in those parts of their works which relate to logical systems. For this writer, the philosophic father of this notion is Peirce. In order for the reader better to follow the subsequent analyses, it will be useful, at the outset, to indicate some general suppositions which underlie the argument in this paper. It is assumed that:

(a) Thought is common to all. All individuals—possibly excluding neonates and unconscious persons—mentate, reason, cerebrate, deduce, induce, come to conclusions, etc. Thought is not too good for common people.

(b) Individuals think in various ways. There is not one way of thinking, but many ways. In this paper we are not talking about "correct" thinking, but just thinking. People think as they do, often believing they are thinking aright. People do not just make mistakes; there are good reasons for their seeming to be unreasonable. In this paper, we are interested in the *processes* of "concludifying" * which the individual thinker traverses. We wish to recapitulate the "concludifying" so that we can infer (from the individual's patterns of concludifying) the psychological "reasons" (or personality variables) which, for him, are consistent with his being "unreasonable" (that is, reasoning as *he* does).

(c) The concept of "error" in relation to modes of thinking has, in the past, been applied somewhat narrowly, if not superciliously. "Error" has ordinarily implied a departure from a particular (theoretical) standard of thinking, usually that attributed to Aristotle when he was thinking about thinking. Our position is that a madman's thinking or a feebleminded person's thinking is as bona fide as the thinking of a genius, and further, is as "reasonable"—given the thinker's premises and accepting his modes of thinking as possible modes of thinking. (It is not implied for a moment that thoughts are of equal value.) The marriage between an individual's patterns of thinking and other aspects of that individual's personality is binding whether "in sickness or in health." We are interested in how people do think, not in how they ought to think. "Reasoning," to quote William James, "is always for a subjective interest."

(d) This "nonevaluative" point of view toward thinking provides a lever to understand (rather than to score or evaluate) the reasoning of the other individual. The main point of this approach is that the thinking of an individual is best understood by assuming that the other person's thinking is logical for that person doing the thinking. Then one is in the position to cast about to see what logical assumptions—no matter how "illogical" from our point of view—would have been made for that individual to have thought as he did.

(e) After one has identified the "idiosyncratic logical position" of the individual thinker, he may then proceed to inquire as to what kind of psychological state in that individual would be consistent with (or even, so to speak, compel) that individual's adopting the logical position which he apparently assumed.

(f) By supplying these intervening variables of idiosyncratic logical position and concomitant psychological status, one can better understand aberrant or unusual thinking in terms of psychological

---

* "Concludifying" is the author's term and refers to the logical maneuvers, the logical gambits, the sequences of logical activities, etc., by which an individual reasons, thinks, mentates, cognizes, or arrives at a conclusion. An example of this process, with the illustrious Samuel Johnson as the thinker—in which he first asserts a belief, then points out a distinction, then accepts another's objection as an unavoidable consequence of his own position, etc.—is given on page 6 of Susan Stebbing's *A Modern Introduction to Logic,* 2nd ed., New York, Harper and Bros., 1933.

states, and aberrant or unusual psychological states in terms of ways of thinking. A bridge between these offers a most-interesting road to explore.

(g) A word of caution is in order. The way that a man thinks on occasion is not necessarily the way that he must think at all times. Specific idiosyncratic ways of thought need not be globally characteristic of an individual, but may occur only with specific content or in specific situations, so that there may well be intraindividual variations in ways of thought which might account, within that individual, for the "logic of prejudice," the "logic of neurosis," the "logic of suicide," etc. Intensive idiographic (intrapersonal) studies would be important in pursuing this approach.

(h) It is believed that this approach to the analysis of the stimulus, if consistently carried out, could clarify a number of problems in the psychology of thinking, which purely logical or purely experimental approaches cannot handle. We would hope that data could be analyzed to obtain meaningful findings about human psychology.*

## BRIEF OVERVIEW OF PROPOSED METHOD AND ILLUSTRATIVE MATERIALS

If different individuals may have different ways of reasoning, what becomes of paramount importance is the development of a system or procedure for delineating the specific characteristics of a man's logical styles, and then, in some manner explicating the specific psychological characteristics that would be consonant with a particular logical style. In line with this approach (and with our general concern with the nature of the stimulus), three concepts, which are basic to the development of this essay, must be defined. They are as follows:

1. The *idiologic* or "styles of thinking" represent the latent stimulus in this approach, that is, therein is contained the individual patterning and arrangement of logical nuances (in, for example, the political speech coming out of the television set) which serve as the basis (after appropriate conversion to other forms described below) of the listener's response. In this essay, the word "idiologic" is used as roughly synonymous with individual "styles of thinking." Every human (except perhaps newborns and some severe neurological cases) thinks. Individuals think differently. They have different styles of

---

* A more extensive discussion of the rationale of this method is presented in the author's chapter in Kagan and Lessor's recent book.[21] The application of this approach to a psychological case study is given in "The Case of El." [22]

thinking. There are many individual idiosyncratic ways of cognizing, mentating, intellectualizing, inferring, deducing, inducing, reasoning, cerebrating—*thinking*. Idiologic refers to all those things which can be said—given the text of a speech, etc.—about the syllogistic structure, the idiosyncrasies of either induction or deduction, the form or the content of the (explicit or implied) premises, the gaps or unwarranted conclusions, etc.—indeed, anything that a logically oriented investigator who understood the approach propounded in this paper might wring from a manuscript if he put his mind to it. The idiologic properties of the stimulus are made up of idiosyncrasies of reasoning and cognitive maneuvers, both described later.

2. The *contralogic* or "method of rationalizing logical idiosyncrasies" is our technique for clarifying the latent stimulus. Briefly described, the speaker's contralogic would be that theoretical logical system (which might be operating unconsciously in the mind of the speaker) which would serve to undo or rectify or make reasonable the apparent idiosyncrasies of the speaker's logical positions. Its purpose is to permit us to see what is required—what the speaker must implicitly believe—to logically "explain" the speaker's own special logic. This concept of contralogic will be elaborated and illustrated later.

3. The *psychologic* or "psychological traits relevant to styles of thinking" correspond to the psychological impact of the stimulus, that is, the psychological traits or portion of his "personality" which the speaker conveys or imparts by means of his particular logical styles or his ways of thinking. It is to this (implied) aspect of the logical stimulus that potential voters would primarily respond. Some of the specific psychological traits which can be inferred from styles of thinking will be listed and some examples given.

An impetus for the development of this presentation was the 1960 Kennedy-Nixon "Great Debates" and the possibility of analyzing these unique television exchanges. It seemed evident from viewing the debates that Kennedy and Nixon "thought" differently from each other, that they had different styles of thinking and were thus prone to different ranges and kinds of logical errors; also that these differences in logical styles could be systematically analyzed and that they carried with them substantially different personality impacts. As social science data, however, the debate materials raise questions. Are there meaningful methods for such analysis? What was the impact of the Great Debates? What did they tell us about the candidates? Could one have predicted the outcome of the election from an analysis of the Great Debates? Can one, having analyzed aspects of the thought processes of Kennedy and Nixon, now make predictions (better than chance) as to the manner in which each of these individuals would cognize (or think through) some present or future issue? In addition to the questions listed above for the Kennedy-Nixon debates, one might pose some additional general questions. Can one believe that the best prediction of a man's future behavior is an extrapolation from his past behavior in similar situations? Specifically, by knowing something about the manner in which, for example, Khrushchev or Castro thinks today, can we predict how either of these individuals will cognize or "solve" some conflict situation (that might inexorably involve us) tomorrow? And, are there specific techniques for predicting behavior which can be applied to leaders—helpful and hostile—on the international scene?

Results from the analysis of these debates are presented as illustrative material in the delineation of our method. The analysis itself made use of verbatim texts of two of the four debates (*The New York Times*, 9/27/60 and 10/8/60). The first two debates involved approximately 22,000 words of which approximately 20,000 were divided almost equally between Kennedy and Nixon. The numbers of separate, discrete statements (usually one or two paragraphs in length and in almost every case in response to a question by a member of the panel of newcasters) by the two main participants in the first two debates were 25 for Kennedy and 24 for Nixon. An analysis of the logical components of the first and then of the second debate indicated that the results for these first two debates were so similar that it was feasible to combine each participant's logical tabulations and to present the two debates as one unit.*

## THE IDIOLOGIC OR "STYLES OF THINKING"; THE LATENT STIMULUS

Idiologic has been described as the explication of the ways in which a specific individual cerebrates in his processes of coming to conclusions. With our approach, his idiologic is assessed by way of his (1) idiosyncrasies of reasoning and (2) his cognitive maneuvers.

*Idiosyncrasies of reasoning* are, essentially, an individual's deductive gambits or tactics. They are the styles of his reasoning, his ways of "syllogizing" and "concludifying" and include what would ordinarily be subsumed under "logical fallacies." Our list is an extension and a rearrangement of the currently "traditional" logical fallacies as might be found in any standard

---

* It is, of course, essential in analyzing a man's style of thinking (as recorded in his spoken thoughts) to be sure that it is *his* speech, and not his ghost writer's, that one is analyzing. In the case of the Kennedy-Nixon materials it was fairly obvious that although both participants had been briefed—with the exception of the opening statement in the first debate which *could* have been ghost-written or group written and memorized by the speaker—the material was extemporaneous and unrehearsed.

**Table 1.** Idiosyncrasies of Reasoning

| | Per Cent Kennedy | Nixon |
|---|---|---|
| I. Idiosyncrasies of Relevance. Those features of the argumentative style involving the intrusion of conceptual elements extraneous to the argument. | | |
|    A. *Irrelevant premise.* Premise is irrelevant to the conclusion it is purportedly instrumental in establishing. | 9 | 5 |
|    B. *Irrelevant conclusion.* Conclusion is irrelevant to the major body of premises which purportedly establish it. | 7 | 3 |
|    C. *Argumentum ad baculum.* Appeal to force or fear in one or more premises where the conclusion in question does not involve these concepts. | 2 | 0 |
|    D. *Argumentum ad hominem.* Appeal to real or alleged attributes of the person or agency from which a given assertion issued in attempting to establish the truth or falsity of that assertion. | 1 | 4 |
|    E. *Argumentum ad misericordium.* Appeal to pity for oneself or for an individual involved in the conclusion where such a sentiment is extraneous to the concepts incorporated in the conclusion. | 1 | 0 |
|    F. *Argumentum ad populum.* Appeal to already present attitudes of one's audience where such attitudes are extraneous to the concepts incorporated in the conclusion. | 3 | 12 |
|    G. *Argumentum ad vericundium.* Appeal to authority whose assertions corroborate or establish the conclusion where no premises are asserted to the effect that the authority is dependable or sound. | 2 | 0 |
|    H. *False cause.* Falsely judging or implying a causal relationship to hold between two events. | 1 | 4 |
|    J. *Complex question.* A premise or conclusion of an argument contains a qualifying clause or phrase the appropriateness or adequacy of which has not been established. | 0 | 2 |
|    K. *Derogation.* A premise or conclusion contains an implicit derogation of an individual or group, where the concepts expressing derogation are neither relevant nor substantiated. | 1 | 5 |
| II. Idiosyncrasies of Meaning. | | |
|    A. *Equivocation.* The use of a word or phrase which can be taken in either of two different senses. | 7 | 2 |
|    B. *Amphiboly.* An unusual or clumsy grammatical structure obscuring the content of the assertion incorporating it. | 5 | 3 |
|    C. *Opposition.* The phrasing indicates an opposition or disjointedness of elements which are in fact not opposed or disjointed. | 3 | 1 |
| III. Enthymematic Idiosyncrasies. Argument contains suppressed premises or conclusion. | | |
|    A. *Contestable suppressed premise.* A suppressed premise, necessary for rectifying initial invalidity of argument, is contestable. | 5 | 4 |
|    B. *False suppressed premise.* A suppressed premise necessary for rectifying initial invalidity of argument is false, either logically or empirically. | 3 | 3 |
|    C. *Plausible but not obvious suppressed premise.* A suppressed premise necessary for rectifying initial invalidity of argument is plausible but not obvious. | 4 | 2 |

**Table 1.** (Continued)

|  | Per Cent Kennedy | Nixon |
|---|---|---|
| D. *Suppressed conclusion.* The conclusion, while determined by the context of discussion, is never explicitly asserted, so that the point allegedly established by the argument is not brought clearly into focus. | 0 | 1 |
| IV. Idiosyncrasies of Logical Structure. |  |  |
| A. *Stranded predicate.* A predicate occurs in a premise which occurs neither in the remaining premises nor in the conclusion, the function of such recurrence being to bind or relate the isolated predicate to other predicates. | 6 | 7 |
| B. *Novel final predicate.* A predicate occurs in the conclusion which does not occur in any premise. | 7 | 6 |
| C. *Stranded term.* A term occurs in a premise which occurs neither in the remaining premises nor in the conclusion. | 5 | 5 |
| D. *Novel final term.* A term occurs in the conclusion which does not occur in any premise. | 4 | 4 |
| E. *Top-heavy predicate structure.* Stranded predicates outnumber novel final predicates. | 6 | 3 |
| F. *Bottom-heavy predicate structure.* Novel final predicates outnumber stranded predicates. | 1 | 2 |
| G. *Balanced predicate structure.* Number of stranded predicates equal to number of novel final predicates. | 2 | 3 |
| H. *Top-heavy term structure.* Stranded terms outnumber novel final terms. | 5 | 3 |
| J. *Bottom-heavy term structure.* Novel final terms outnumber stranded terms. | 1 | 1 |
| K. *Balanced term structure.* Number of stranded terms equal to number of novel final terms. | 3 | 5 |
| V. Idiosyncrasies of Logical Interrelations. |  |  |
| A. *Truth-type confusion.* A confusion between unquestionable assertions on the one hand (logically true assertions, definitions, and "bald" empirical truths), with empirically questionable assertions on the other hand. | 2 | 6 |
| B. *Inconsistency.* Making conflicting or contradictory assertions. | 1 | 1 |
| C. *Identification of conditional with its antecedent.* Treating an assertion of the form $A \rightarrow B$ (if A, then B) as equivalent to A. | 0 | 2 |
| D. *Illicit distribution of negation.* Treating an assertion of the form $\sim(A \rightarrow B)$ (it is false that if A, then B) as equivalent to $\sim A \rightarrow B$ (if it is false that A, then B). | 1 | 0 |
| E. *Illicit derivation or normative from descriptive.* Attempt to derive an assertion of the form I(P) (it is imperative that P—usually occuring as "Therefore we should . . ." "Therefore we must . . . ," and the like) from assertions not of that form—in effect, from assertions not incorporating imperatives. | 2 | 1 |
| Total | 100 | 100 |
| N | (229) | (267) |

textbook on logic, such as Copi.[6] A brief description of each idiosyncrasy, and the percentages for Kennedy and Nixon in the first two debates are presented in Table 1.

*Cognitive maneuvers* relate to the manner of development of thought, and describe the linear flow of the argumentation. The cognitive maneuvers, so to speak, deal with the interstices between the specific idiosyncrasies of reasoning. Table 2 lists these cognitive maneuvers with percentages for Kennedy and Nixon in the first two debates.

### Resumé of the Idiologic of Kennedy

Kennedy's logical style is meandering and loose-knit and tends to be top-heavy (IV-E–IV-K)* and impulsive (I-A, I-B, V-E). He is somewhat prone to irrelevancies, both with respect to the premises and conclusion (I-A, I-B), but the distinctive feature of his irrelevancies is that whole sentences tend to be irrelevant rather than isolated concepts in otherwise relevant sentences (I-A, I-B, IV-A–IV-E). In effect, on occasion, the whole conceptual framework can be "off-base" rather than isolated details. His style is abundant, prolix, and comprehensive. It is spontaneous, natural, and relatively unvaried. (When restricted to cohesive arguments, the drop in idiosyncratic features is considerably less marked than with Nixon.) Again, it is straightforward, undevious, and impersonal (I-D–I-K). There is a marked idiosyncratic proneness toward ambiguity, a proneness toward double meanings and overlapping meanings of concepts (II). He thinks in a many faceted continuous, "both-and," inclusive style (II), that is, in terms of qualitative continua rather than in terms of discrete concepts (II, V-D–V-F). He thinks in broad terms and tends to overlook small structural details (I-A, II, V-D–V-F).

### Resumé of the Idiologic of Nixon

In general, Nixon's logical style is cohesive, balanced, and univocal (I-A, I-B, II). His style is cerebral, controlled, and deliberate—capitalizes on emotive potentialities (I-D–I-F, I-K) offered by discursive argumentative contexts, but his style changes abruptly in cohesive argumentative contexts —hence he also displays great variety in style (depending on whether the context is cohesive or discursive). His style is detailed and balanced, with some emphasis on economy of concepts (I-A, I-B, IV, V). He is prone to invoking considerations about special circumstances in attempting to establish a conclusion (I-D, I-E), and also, appeals "to the gallery," that is, makes

---

* References are to Table 1.

**Table 2.** Cognitive Maneuvers

|  |  | Kennedy | Nixon |
|---|---|---|---|
| 1. | Switch from a normative to a descriptive mode. | 0 | 1 |
| 2a. | Switch from a descriptive to a normative mode. | 0 | 1 |
| b. | Switch from descriptive to emotive or personal mode. | 7 | 5 |
| 3a. | Switch from an emotive or personal mode to a descriptive one. | 5 | 3 |
| b. | Switch from an emotive or personal mode to a normative one. | 0 | 1 |
| 5.* | Enlarge or elaborate the preceding, relevantly or irrelevantly. | 8 | 6 |
| 7. | Use an example, relevantly or irrelevantly. | 3 | 3 |
| 8. | Deduce or purport to deduce from the preceding. | 3 | 3 |
| 9. | Change emphasis, with continuity or warrant or without continuity or warrant. | 2 | 2 |
| 10. | Make a distinction between two preceding notions, a preceding notion and a new notion, or between two new notions, with or without warrant, justification, relevance. | 4 | 6 |
| 11. | Branch out. | 4 | 3 |
| 12. | Synthesize or summarize. | 4 | 3 |
| 14. | Obscure or equivocate by phrasing or context. | 7 | 5 |
| 16. | Smuggle a debatable point into a context which is semantically alien to it. | 6 | 8 |
| 17. | Paraphrase or otherwise render as equivalent statements which, in general, are not to be taken as syntactically identical, with or without warrant. | 2 | 2 |
| 21. | Give a premise or assumption for a statement explicit or implicit in the preceding. | 5 | 6 |
| 25. | Be irrelevant. | 7 | 10 |
| 26. | Repeat or rephrase. | 2 | 1 |
| 28. | Allege but not substantiate. | 4 | 6 |
| 31. | Deny or reject with or without warrant. | 3 | 3 |
| 35. | Agree with the whole but take issue with a part, implicitly or explicitly. | 1 | 1 |
| 39. | Accept conditionally. | 3 | 2 |
| 41. | Render another's assertion stronger or weaker by paraphrase. | 1 | 2 |
| 42. | Digress. | 1 | 2 |
| 42a. | Initiate discontinuities. | 4 | 2 |
| 44. | Perpetuate or aggravate discontinuities. | 2 | 1 |
| 46. | Go toward greater specificity. | 5 | 6 |
| 47. | Go toward greater generality. | 1 | 1 |
| 48. | Transfer or attempt to transfer authority or responsibility. | 2 | 1 |
| 50. | Attack. | 4 | 4 |
|  | Total | 100% | 100% |
|  | N | (725) | (678) |

\* Not all numbers are represented because items in which neither Kennedy nor Nixon had any tabulations are omitted in this present list.

statements with "mass appeal" incorporating popular or "folksy" phraseology (I-F). He is prone to derogating his opponent without establishing the alleged charge—usually by innuendo or suggestion (I-K). He shows propensities toward irrelevancies of an emotive nature which influence the listener's acceptance of an argument. While his thinking style is detailed (II, V-F) and balanced (I-A, I-B, IV-G, IV-K), there is considerable idiosyncratic confusion about logical and causal interrelationships (V-A, V-C, I-H) and a hestitancy in drawing consequences from a position or situation (V-C). Tends to be "either-or" rather than "both-and" (II).

## THE CONTRALOGIC OR THE METHOD OF RATIONALIZING LOGICAL IDIOSYNCRASIES

The process of converting the idiological properties into *psychological* attributes is accomplished by means of the contralogic. To follow the presentation of this idea, the reader is asked to refer to the illustrations in Table 3.

**Table 3.** Illustration of Method of Logical Analysis

| Column I—Idiologic. | Column II—Contralogic. | Column III—Psychologic. |
|---|---|---|
| Sample of specific way of thinking, in terms of idiosyncrasies of logic | Logical conditions under which the logical idiosyncrasy is rationalized | Psychological state concordant with contralogic |
| Example taken from von Domarus, and Arieti: "Switzerland loves freedom; I love freedom; therefore I am Switzerland." Fallacy: identification in terms of attributes of the predicate (or undistributed middle). III-B, IV-G, IV-K. | If one supplies the implicit premise that Switzerland is the *only* member of the class of freedom-lovers (and if I loved freedom), then it would follow, without logical error, that I would *have* to be Switzerland. | The reasoning reflects a psychological state in which the range of attention is constricted and narrowed (to one member of a class). Psychological symptoms: intense concentration, oblivion to ordinary stimuli, hypesthesia, acute withdrawal, and, at its extreme, catatonia. |

In the first column, idiologic, appear individual idiosyncrasies of reasoning as defined above and listed in Table 1. The second (and pivotal column, contralogic, involves one's taking the position that all logical formulations can be thought to demonstrate some sort of straightforward reasoning (for that individual who is doing the reasoning) if one will only supply the logical conditions under which the apparent error would be "true" (i.e., in effect the "new" logic would neutralize or rationalize the error). In the third column, psychologic, are those psychological and psychiatric conditions which are concordant with the contralogic advanced in Column II (i.e., psychological states which would be involved, if this "new" logic is to make psychological sense).

The following presents for Kennedy and Nixon a hypothetical tailor-made set of constructs developed from our analysis of the first two Great Debates. These constructs may be said to represent the private, covert logical-system assumptions—the contralogic—which were operating (most likely unbeknownst to the persons themselves) in the minds and thinking processes of these two principals.

It should be stated that these resumés of the contralogic of the two men are not meant either to represent the ways these individuals think, nor in any way to imply a "clinical description" of these individuals, but rather, the purpose is to describe what could be the latent or unspoken or "unconscious" epistemological and metaphysical positions—"philosophies of life" —of these two individuals which would be consistent with the idiologics which they manifested.

The mental or psychological characteristics that one could infer from these particular constellations of contralogic are indicated in the next section.

### Resumé: Contralogic of Kennedy

Everything is related to everything else (I-A)* and, furthermore, related in a dynamic sense. There being many things that can bear a given relation to a given thing (II-A), the world allows extensive change and permutation by man. There are no boundaries or limitations to action—the universe can be manipulated by the will of man, and desire and actuality can be made to accord with that will (II-A, V-E). The means appear incidental and have value primarily as they efficiently implement the desired ends (I-A, IV-E). Reality is given, i.e., is independent of what men think or desire it to be, but that reality can be manipulated and changed to accord with man's desires (I-D, I-F). It is important to know the causal laws operating in that world (I-H).

### Resumé: Contralogic of Nixon

Subjective desires and attitudes are identified with the objective world (I-D, I-F, I-K). Value statements have cognitive import (I-D, I-K, V-A). The world is what each man legislates that it is (V-A). The implementation of goals is not important (I-H, V-C)—one projects his subjective feelings and desires onto the world. The emphasis is not on causal relationships operating in the outside world, but on perfecting the inner subjective self (I-H, V-C). Truth is man-made—there are no objective conditions (I-D, I-F). Acceptability to man is the criterion for truth; argumentation is developed to influence others' acceptance to one's subjective desires and attitudes (I-D, I-F).

---

* References are to Table 1.

## THE PSYCHOLOGIC OR PSYCHOLOGICAL TRAITS RELEVANT TO STYLES OF THINKING/THE PSYCHOLOGICAL IMPACT OF THE STIMULUS

We have developed a set of thirteen relevant psychological traits or dimensions with our method; these appear in Table 4. Two observations concerning the nature of these traits will be clarifying. First, it should be noted that these do not encompass the entire spectrum of psychological traits which are part and parcel of human personality, but rather are limited to those aspects of personality having to do with ways of thinking. For example, some persons tend to be more-or-less dichotomous, discrete, binary, "either-or" in their thinking, as opposed to others who appear more or less neutralistic, looking for middle ground and compromise, believing in the possibility of "both-and." These are psychological dimensions, *and* they influence styles of thinking—as anyone who has ever contrasted the "logic" of Khrushchev and Nehru would readily see. The traits listed, thus, are extrapolations from the individual's thinking patterns, and refer to the cognitive or intellective or mental aspects of the individual's personality and do not necessarily imply anything about other aspects of his personality.

Second, since we are presenting essentially a theoretical logical model, the personality attributes of the individuals described will be "theoretical" descriptions in the sense that the descriptions indicate how these individuals might think (and act) if they were left entirely to their own thinking devices. With a prominent public figure we can assume that there will be little opportunity, at least in his public life, to manifest uncensored impulse or officially to speak or act without a great deal of forethought, discussion, and consultation with advisers. However, the point can be made that such individuals may tend to choose advisers who are largely psychologically compatible and that even after consultation, the individual himself may well proceed in his own logically idiosyncratic way.

And finally, one may ask why we infer psychological characteristics from the contralogic (Table 3: Column II) rather than directly from the manifest idiologic (Table 3: Column I). The apparent psychological characteristics of an individual may be different than when inferred from the contralogic. The contralogic, moreover, seems a more powerful method. It enables the psychologician to make meaningful statements about the individual's psychological states, frequently when the manifest logic is cryptic. Once converted into the contralogic, however, one can see what must have been going on in that person's mind, what that person's logical systems must have been in order that the way he was thinking would make sense to him.

The contralogic and the psychological characteristics derived thus are basic to our method.*

In the following we present the psychological characteristics which can be derived for Kennedy and Nixon, from the particular constellations of contralogic inferred from the logical analysis of the two debates. The traits are primarily in terms of the attributes listed in Table 4. The references included with the descriptions are to particular logical idiosyncrasies (Tables 1 and 2), from which the contralogic itself was derived.

**Table 4.** Psychological Traits Relevant to Patterns of Thinking

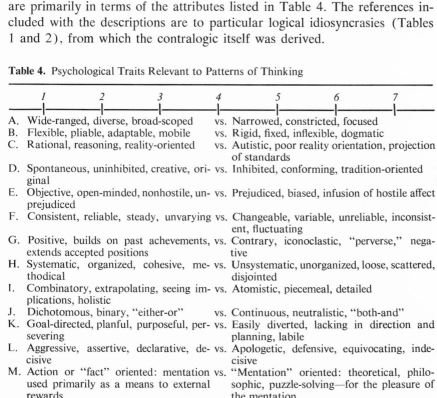

|   | 1 | 2 | 3 | 4 | 5 | 6 | 7 |
|---|---|---|---|---|---|---|---|

A.  Wide-ranged, diverse, broad-scoped vs. Narrowed, constricted, focused

B.  Flexible, pliable, adaptable, mobile vs. Rigid, fixed, inflexible, dogmatic

C.  Rational, reasoning, reality-oriented vs. Autistic, poor reality orientation, projection of standards

D.  Spontaneous, uninhibited, creative, original vs. Inhibited, conforming, tradition-oriented

E.  Objective, open-minded, nonhostile, unprejudiced vs. Prejudiced, biased, infusion of hostile affect

F.  Consistent, reliable, steady, unvarying vs. Changeable, variable, unreliable, inconsistent, fluctuating

G.  Positive, builds on past achevements, extends accepted positions vs. Contrary, iconoclastic, "perverse," negative

H.  Systematic, organized, cohesive, methodical vs. Unsystematic, unorganized, loose, scattered, disjointed

I.  Combinatory, extrapolating, seeing implications, holistic vs. Atomistic, piecemeal, detailed

J.  Dichotomous, binary, "either-or" vs. Continuous, neutralistic, "both-and"

K.  Goal-directed, planful, purposeful, persevering vs. Easily diverted, lacking in direction and planning, labile

L.  Aggressive, assertive, declarative, decisive vs. Apologetic, defensive, equivocating, indecisive

M.  Action or "fact" oriented: mentation used primarily as a means to external rewards vs. "Mentation" oriented: theoretical, philosophic, puzzle-solving—for the pleasure of the mentation

## Resumé: Psychologic of Kennedy

Our analyses suggest that in the cognitive sphere, Kennedy tends to be impatient (I-A, I-B, II), spontaneous (note the great difference in idiosyncrasies

---

* It would, of course, be theoretically possible to construct different contralogics from any one given idiologic. These different contralogics could be made from the point of view of different major language-logic orientations, such as standard average European,[27] Chinese, Hopi, Eskimo, and even Russian, as opposed to American. In this present approach we limit our contralogic to the standard average European (SAE) point of view.

when restricted to cohesive arguments). He appears goal-oriented but disdainful of details (I-A, I-B, II, IV-E, IV-H, V-E), apparently regarding achievement of goals to be important and unmindful of incidental consequences resulting from their achievement (I-A, I-B, II, V-D, V-E). In effect, he is goal-oriented but not analytic. He seems willing to take risks (I-A, IV-E, IV-H). He is relatively nonintrospective. (Again note the great difference in idiosyncrasies when restricted to cohesive contexts). In many of his relationships he is impersonal (I-D, I-E, I-F, I-K). His orientation is toward realistic facts (I-H, V-A); he is objective, open-minded (I-D, I-K). For him considerations of psychic economy appear unimportant, in that he wants to bring everything to bear in achieving a goal. There seems no undue anxiety regarding failure or waste of effort (I-A, I-B, IV-E, IV-H). Certain courses of action are mandatory when given states of affairs prevail—he feels each man has a unique destiny to fulfill (V-E). He feels he must drive himself to his own. He tends to see things on a qualitative continuum: he is continuous, "both-and" (II), but not especially compromising (I-F). He seems to prefer to use all means available for instrumenting a goal rather than take time to seek out the most effective solution (I-A, IV-E, IV-H). He appears constructive (I-K) but somewhat iconoclastic (V-D, V-E)—forceful, impulsive, driving (II, V-E). He is not troubled by conflict, and he functions well under pressure; he is persevering, energetic, driven (II, I-D).

### Resumé: Psychologic of Nixon

Nixon can be described as systematic, organized, methodical, planful (as indicated in marked drop in idiosyncrasies in cohesive arguments (I-A, I-B, II, IV-E–IV-K, V). However, he seems to have limited scope (II, V-C, V-E), and gives more attention to details of manner of execution of an act and to its peripheral consequences than to the over-all efficacy of that act (I-A, I-B, I-H, IV-E–IV-K, V-A, V). He has some anxiety about making decisions—apparently feeling that decisions involve a commitment to one extreme or another (IV-G, IV-K, V-C). He tends to be concerned about consequences and prefers to have his position judged for its intrinsic merits rather than for what may follow from that position (V-C). He seems to value compromise, balance, equilibrium (IV-E–IV-K), and is painstaking, cautious, piecemeal, inhibited, (I-A, I-B, IV, V-C, V-E, V). He tends to fear imbalance (IV-E–IV-K) and direct attack, but he himself attacks indirectly by innuendo and suggestion (I-D–I-F, I-K, especially I-F). He appears labile, opportunistic (I-D, I-F, I-J, I-K, also note marked drop in idiosyncrasies in cohesive arguments). He dichotomizes the universe into "good" and "bad," "we" and "they" (I-D, I-F, I-K). He dislikes conflict and prefers to resolve it quickly (II, IV-G, IV-K, V-S, V). He is apt to react personally to criticism (I-D, I-F, I-K). He is analytic, intelligent, but sensitive emotionally—easily diverted (I-D, I-F, I-K). He emphasizes economy of concepts and orderliness rather than action and effectiveness (II, IV, V-E, V).

Whereas Kennedy's image came through as a "doer," albeit he might impulsively do some "wrong" things, Nixon's image came through as a man who might "deliberately" do the wrong things, but they would be done with careful attention to detail.

## SOME RESEARCH PROPOSALS

The chief value of all theoretical models is that they serve as stimuli and guides for research. In our case we have a model directed largely toward the properties of the *stimulus* in the basic S-O-R formulation of behavioral science. We are concerned with cognitive aspects—styles of thinking—and have developed a rationale for translating the manifest logical structure of verbal stimulus material (idiologic) into latent psychological characteristics (psychologic) conveyed by the speaker, through a mediating contralogic.

As we have pointed out, the model was developed in connection with political debates, and we shall propose empirical tests with voting behavior. First, however, we wish to present certain methodological considerations.

### Methodological Considerations

It is important that there be a high order of consistency or concordance among psychologicians in the outcomes obtained when applying the method. While there should be little difficulty in training persons who have appropriate backgrounds, concordance should be checked, particularly in connection with the contralogic and psychologic.

The stability of patterns of logical style over time, should be investigated. While our analysis of patterns shown by Kennedy and Nixon revealed that results were very similar for the first two debates, we have little knowledge of how much stability we can normally expect over a period of time, and the conditions which make for greater or less stability. This is important in connection with the problem of selecting "representative" material for experimentation, as well as for other problems.

If the impression a person conveys to others is not alone a matter of what he says, but also of how he goes about saying it (his logical style), it should be possible to validate this experimentally. One approach which comes to mind would be to adapt the thirteen psychological traits (Table 4) for use with experimental Ss. Experimental materials might be obtained, for example, from intercollegiate debate scripts. From these, one which showed definitely contrasting patterns of logical style on the part of the debaters would be selected. An experimental script would be derived, restricted to a manageable number of debaters.

The resulting script would be videotaped (or filmed), using performers who were not known to the Ss. In preparing the tapes the performers' roles would be rotated to control for other personal factors (i.e., appearance and other visual and auditory nonverbal cues). Ss would be assigned at random to the experimental groups, one group for each version of tape. To provide a control, each experimental tape would be preceded by a brief "neutral" (taped) interview of each of the performers. Ss would check scales for each performer at the conclusion of the interview, and then told they would have an opportunity of seeing these persons in action. Ss would check scales again at the conclusion of the experimental tape. Pretests should be done on the adaptation of the scales, and to determine procedures more precisely. For example, it might be desirable to separate the control and experimental sessions, or to include an additional criterion—one which more nearly approaches the behavioral in character. If the experiment were conducted at a university, the experiment might be placed in a mock voting context, and the Ss required to vote (for an official in the local community government, president of student government, etc.). Since the psychological impressions conveyed by logical style may not be readily verbalizable by members of an audience, a behavioral criterion could have great value.

### Empirical Field Tests—Voting Behavior

The studies indicated below are illustrative of a larger number which can be related to our model. They involve the following hypothesis: The winner will be the candidate whose psychological profile (derived from logical analysis of spontaneous verbal campaign material) comes closest to the "personality style" appropriate for the time and place. In times of comparative tranquility we would expect the winners to have profiles of psychological traits (Table 4) close to the average or midpoints of the scales. However, in times of great crisis (war, economic upheaval) the winners would be those candidates whose profiles reflect qualities toward the extremes deemed necessary by the electorate to meet the particular crisis situation.

1. As one test of our major hypothesis, we propose a three-wave field test, making use of a panel of representative adults. The first wave of interviewing would take place very early in the campaign. Respondents would be questioned on the candidate for whom they expected to vote, knowledge of the candidates, and extent of exposure to speeches (very few at this time) or other material on the candidates. In addition, an appropriate adaptation of the psychological characteristics scale would be used to secure the respondent's evaluation of

each candidate and of the requirements for the office itself "in times like these." The second wave of interviewing (three to four weeks before election day) and the final wave (during the week after the election) would cover essentially the same ground, except that in the postelection interview, respondents would be asked whether they had voted and the candidate for whom they voted. The standard household and personal characteristics information would be secured, together with party affiliation and other information usual in political polls. Appropriate pretesting of the questionnaires and procedures would be necessary.

Concurrently, speeches of the candidates would be analyzed for the psychological characteristics revealed by styles of thinking. These results would be related to those of the survey. Their relation to the extent of exposure to candidate speeches should be particularly interesting. In addition to serving as a test of our hypothesis, the study data should provide methodological insights, for example, the stability of candidate profiles, of voter evaluation (and reliability of our scales), and the interrelations of the two.

2. A second study could be restricted to cases in which the same candidate ran (successfully or unsuccessfully) for the same office two or more times. Here again, one would relate the nuances and differences in psychological patterns manifested by the same candidate in different campaigns with the differences in voting patterns at the times of those respective elections. The approach employed would generally parallel the first study except that only one wave of interviewing would be required. New representative samples would be drawn for each election in such a longitudinal study. This study could throw considerable light on why it is that mayors, governors, and other officials manage to get elected time after time.

The foregoing studies by no means exhaust the possible uses of the theoretical model for generating empirical research not only in the field of political behavior but in other areas as well—mass communication, advertising, education, in fact in any area in which it is important to learn more about how behavior in general can be influenced through projection of more effective verbal stimuli.

## REFERENCES

1. Andrews, T. C., "The Effect of Benzedrine Sulfate on Syllogistic Reasoning," *Journal of Experimental Psychology,* 26:423–431, 1940.

2. Arieti, S., *Interpretation of Schizophrenia* (New York: Robert Bruner, 1955).

3. Beier, E. G., "The Effect of Induced Anxiety on Flexibility of Intellectual Functioning," *Psychological Monographs,* Vol. 65, No. 9, 1951.

4. Berelson, B., *Content Analysis in Communication Research* (New York: The Free Press, 1952).

5. Cameron, N., "Reasoning Regression and Communication Schizophrenia," *Psychological Monographs,* 50:1–33, 1938.

6. Copi, I. M., *Introduction to Logic* (New York: Macmillan, 1953).

7. Dewey, J., *Logic: The Theory of Inquiry* (New York: Henry Holt, 1938).

8. George, A. L., *Propaganda Analysis: A Study of Inferences Made from Nazi Propaganda in World War II* (Evanston: Row, Peterson, 1959).

9. Gibson, J. J., "The Concept of the Stimulus in Psychology," *American Psychologist,* 15:694–703, 1960.

10. Goldstein, K., "Methodological Approach to the Study of Schizophrenic Thought Disorder," in Kasanin, J. S. (ed.), *Language and Thought in Schizophrenia* (Berkeley: University of California Press, 1944).

11. James, W., *Pragmatism* (New York: Longmans, Green and Company, 1907).

12. Kasanin, J. S., "Disturbance of Conceptual Thinking in Schizophrenia," in Kasanin, J. S. (ed.), *Language and Thought in Schizophrenia* (Berkeley: University of California Press, 1944).

13. Lasswell, H. D., Leites, N. *et al., The Language of Politics* (New York, G. W. Stewart, 1949).

14. Murray, H. A., *Explorations in Personality* (New York: Oxford University Press, 1938).

15. Osgood, C. E., Suci, G. J., and Tannenbaum, P. H., *The Measurement of Meaning* (Urbana: University of Illinois Press, 1957).

16. Peirce, C. S., *Philosophic Writings of Peirce* (New York: Dover Publications, 1955).

17. Piaget, J., *The Language and Thought of the Child,* 2nd ed. (London: Routledge and Kegan Paul Limited, 1932).

18. Pool, I. de S. (ed.), *Trends in Content Analysis* (Urbana: University of Illinois Press, 1959).

19. Rapaport, D. (ed.), *Organization and Pathology of Thought* (New York: Columbia University Press, 1951).

20. Shneidman, E. S. (ed.), *Thematic Test Analysis* (New York: Grune and Stratton, 1951).

21. ———, "Psycho-Logic: A Personality Approach to Patterns of Thinking," in Kagan, J., and Lessor, G. (eds.), *Contemporary Issues in Thematic Apperceptive Methods* (Springfield: Charles C. Thomas, 1961).

22. ———, "The Logic of El: A Psycho-Logical Approach to the

Analysis of Test Data," *Journal of Protective Techniques,* 25:390–403, 1961.

23. Sullivan, H. S., "Language of Schizophrenia," in Kasanin, J. S. (ed.), *Language and Thought in Schizophrenia* (Berkeley: University of California Press, 1944).

24. Vigotsky, L. S., "Thought in Schizophrenia," *Archives of Neurology and Psychiatry,* 31:1063–1077, 1934.

25. Von Domarus, E., "The Specific Laws of Logic in Schizophrenia," in Kasanin, J. S. (ed.), *Language and Thought in Schizophrenia* (Berkeley: University of California Press, 1944).

26. Werner, H., *Comparative Psychology of Mental Development,* rev. ed. (New York: International Universities Press, 1957).

27. Whorf, B. L., *Language, Thought and Reality,* John B. Carroll (ed.) (New York, John Wiley, 1956).

28. Woodworth, R. S., and Sells, S. B., "An Atmosphere Effect in Formal Syllogistic Reasoning," *Journal of Experimental Psychology,* 18:451–460, 1935.

# 11

## A Study of One Hundred and Sixty-three Outstanding Communist Leaders

JEROME DAVIS

In this study I am trying, first, to find out some of the characteristics of Russian Communist leaders; second, to discuss some of the stimuli which caused them to become revolutionists; third, to ascertain any facts regarding the causes of their leadership. I had access to considerable material, all in Russian. This included the biographical sketches in the *Kalendar Kommunista* for 1926 and 1927, the *Nastolny Slovar,* and *Albom Deyateley V K P.* The year at which the various leaders joined a party was taken from the records of the various party congresses when it was not clearly stated elsewhere. When individual pamphlets giving autobiographical sketches were available, I have used them also, although this was done in only five cases. The population of the cities and towns in which the revolutionists were born is based on the census of 1897 as given in the *Russky Kalendar* (Suvorin) for 1917.

This study, however, is based primarily on the biographical sketches in the seventh edition of the *Encyclopaedia* published by the Russian Bibliographical Institute Granat. This *Encyclopaedia* contains 245 sketches, of which 131 are autobiographical, 27 are authorized biographies, and 87 are merely unauthorized sketches. I used all the autobiographical sketches and all the authorized biographies. With the exception of 5, I omitted all the unauthorized sketches because the data did not in all cases seem comparable and because many of these were so brief as to be of small value. The 5 selected were leaders about whom I had other printed biographical material and every one of whom I had personally interviewed and questioned. This means that I have used over 66 per cent of all the Communist leaders in the three-volume *Encyclopaedia,* and since these three volumes include prac-

---

Jerome Davis, "A Study of 163 Outstanding Communist Leaders." *American Sociological Review,* XXIV (1929), pp. 42–55.

tically all the outstanding Communist leaders, we have an adequate statistical proportion. The length of each sketch varied a great deal, some being less than a page and one running to more than ten thousand words.

The reader should guard against drawing any sweeping conclusions from the data presented. In the first place, the facts themselves are limited and cover a rigidly-selected group. They deal with leaders and outstanding leaders only. Every leader must have been included in the Communist *Encyclopaedia,* and this means that nearly all of them (over 98 per cent) were Communists. In any case, they were selected for inclusion by a Communistic group, but to some degree this makes all the more significant facts which are contrary to Communist theory. Some of the facts desired were not given in every autobiography, which means that uniformity in all the 163 sketches was impossible. In our tabulation we were rigidly limited by whatever facts the leader thought wise to include. This is the reason for differences in the totals in any tables presented. This is a study of what Communist leaders say about themselves. Some of the most important stimuli may have been consciously or unconsciously omitted by the revolutionists. It is, of course, obvious that the numbers involved are so small that no general conclusions can be drawn about the characteristics of Russian revolutionary leadership outside the Communist ranks, nor can the data be applied to situations in other countries. In any statement which the writer makes these limitations must be borne in mind. It is hoped that the data presented here may be but one study of many which in the end may give us a more complete scientific picture of revolutionary leadership.

The statistical tables giving the facts as collected are given herewith.

## 1. Place of Birth

It has often been said that revolutions are led by leaders from subject nationalities. It is therefore interesting to see whether the proportion of Communist leadership from Poland, Finland, and Turkestan, for example, has been greater or less than one would expect from the relative population of those districts. See Table 1.

It will be noted that Finland has none, Poland only five, and Turkestan three; this is less than their quota according to the population in these districts in 1897.[1] On the other hand, the Caucasus has a greater proportion of leaders than the average. Possibly this may be due to the fact that the present leader of the Communist party is a Caucasian and more leaders from that district have been included.

When, however, we consider the data in Table 2, we have a slightly different picture.

---

[1] *Russky Kalendar 1889,* p. 107.

**Table 1.** Place of Birth

(*Districts as Under the Tsar's Régime*)

| | |
|---|---|
| 1. Russia proper . . . . | 89 |
| 2. Ukraine . . . . . | 27 |
| 3. Siberia . . . . . . | 6 |
| 4. Caucasus . . . . . | 14 |
| 5. Poland . . . . . . | 5 |
| 6. Finland . . . . . . | 0 |
| 7. Baltic Provinces | |
|              Latvia 7 | |
|              Esthonia 1 | 8 |
| 8. Lithuania . . . . . | 3 |
| 9. Turkestan . . . . . | 3 |
| 10. Bessarabia . . . . . | 1 |
| 11. Crimea . . . . . . | 3 |
| 12. Abroad . . . . . . | 2 |
| Total . . . . . | 161 |

It will be noted that the total of Polish revolutionists, including those of Polish descent, rises considerably and the Lettish group furnishes six. On the basis of the nationality of the father, the subject groups would now seem to have more than their proportion. It is probable that the numbers involved

**Table 2.** Race or Nationality of Father

| | |
|---|---|
| 1. Russian . . . . . . . . . . . . . . . | 80 |
| 2. Ukrainian . . . . . . . . . . . . . . | 9 |
| 3. Caucasian nationalities . . . . . . . . . . | 14 |
| 4. Polish or Polish descent . . . . . . . . . . | 11 |
| 5. Jewish . . . . . . . . . . . . . . . | 28 |
| 6. German extraction including German Baltic barons . . . | 11 |
| 7. Lettish . . . . . . . . . . . . . . . | 6 |
| 8. Minor Mongolian tribes . . . . . . . . . . | 3 |
| 9. Bulgarian . . . . . . . . . . . . . . | 1 |
| Total . . . . . . . . . . . . . . | 163 |

are so small that the calculations in regard to the percentage of revolutionary leadership to population are without much significance. Based on the census of 1897 in this study, we have one revolutionist for every 854,055 of the population of all the Russian empire. Since the Jews in Russia at the beginning of the twentieth century were estimated to number about seven million,[2] they had one revolutionist for every 250,000, or over three times their quota. On the other hand, it is my opinion that the Jewish race in Russia usually were successful above the average, that perhaps even their

---

[2] *American Jewish Yearbook, 1917–18* (Philadelphia, 1917), p. 409. It is probable that this estimate is high rather than low.

intellectual capacity and their education were above the average. We should expect, therefore, that they would produce more than their quota of leaders. It has frequently been charged in America that the Communist movement is largely Jewish in its inception and leadership. That this theory is false so far as the outstanding leaders of Communism are concerned, this study apparently demonstrates. Only 17 per cent of the total number of leaders were Jewish.

## 2. Present Address

As might be expected, the Revolution concentrated the leadership of the Communistic party in the new capital at Moscow. A few leaders were sent abroad in the diplomatic service, but the dangers of bureaucracy are clearly evident.

**Table 3.** Present or Last Address

| | | | |
|---|---|---|---|
| 1. Moscow | 96 | 9. Esthonia | .. |
| 2. Russia proper outside of Moscow | 9 | 10. Lithuania | 1 |
| 3. Ukraine | 10 | 11. Turkestan | 3 |
| 4. Siberia | 1 | 12. Bessarabia | .. |
| 5. Caucasus | 8 | 13. Crimea | .. |
| 6. Poland | .. | 14. Abroad | 12 |
| 7. Finland | .. | Total | 140 |
| 8. Latvia | .. | | |

**Table 4.** Population of Birthplace

| | |
|---|---|
| 1. Up to 2,500 | 62 |
| 2. 2,501–5,000 | 4 |
| 3. 5,001–10,000 | 5 |
| 4. 10,001–50,000 | 18 |
| 5. Over 50,000 | 56 |
| Total | 145 |

According to the 1897 census only 13 per cent of the Russian population lived in cities.[3] At the time of the birth of the majority of the revolutionists, the proportion was undoubtedly even less. In spite of this fact cities of more than fifty thousand population furnished over 38 per cent of the leaders and cities of more than ten thousand gave over 50 per cent. From our data we might conclude that in any thousand of the population the Communist revolutionary leader is most likely to be born in a city of more than ten thousand, and in any event in order to achieve leadership, he usually

---

[3] *Encyclopaedia Britannica* (11th ed.), p. 873.

must have been able to move to a city to secure his major education and training.

## 3. Sex

Out of the 163 biographies studied only 5 were those of women. Whether this is because of the hang-over of a male superiority complex or because, as the Communists say, our culture has always discriminated against the weaker sex and unfitted her for leadership, or whether it is because of sex differences which make leadership in a revolutionary movement difficult, is not indicated. The writer suspects that, although historical and traditional cultural forces have played their part, nevertheless the result is partly due to biological differences.

## 4. Age Distribution

Table 5 gives the present age of those studied.

**Table 5**

| | | | | |
|---|---|---|---|---|
| Under 30 | 0 | 55–59 | 23 |
| 30–34 | 4 | 60–64 | 11 |
| 35–39 | 18 | 65-69 | 2 |
| 40–44 | 42 | 70 and over | 0 |
| 45–49 | 30 | Total | 158 |
| 50–54 | 28 | | |

When it is considered that twelve years have already elapsed since the Bolsheviks assumed power and that almost all these leaders had had long records of revolutionary struggle prior to 1917, it will be realized that Communism is largely a youth movement. Over half were under thirty-seven at the time of the Bolshevik capture of the Russian government, and the largest age group—forty-two—were between the ages of twenty-eight and thirty-two even at that time. The youth character of Communism is even more clearly shown in Table 6. Here the reader will note that more than

**Table 6.** Age on Joining Some Revolutionary Party

| | | | | | | |
|---|---|---|---|---|---|---|
| 13 | 1 | 21 | 10 | 29 | 2 |
| 14 | 2 | 22 | 8 | 30–34 | 7 |
| 15 | 4 | 23 | 11 | 35–39 | 6 |
| 16 | 10 | 24 | 4 | 40–44 | 2 |
| 17 | 15 | 25 | 6 | 45–49 | 2 |
| 18 | 15 | 26 | 5 | Total | 149 |
| 19 | 16 | 27 | 1 | | |
| 20 | 21 | 28 | 1 | | |

half the leaders were twenty or less when they first joined a revolutionary party, and over 82 per cent were twenty-five or less. Apparently if one does not join a revolutionary party in the early twenties the chances of becoming a leader in the radical movement are appreciably lessened.

Although 87 per cent of the population in 1897 was rural, as we have already noted, peasant fathers furnished less than 19 per cent of the leaders under consideration. On the other hand, the working class did furnish more than their quota, providing 21 per cent of the total. The intellectuals and professional classes probably furnished an even greater proportion of leaders. The teachers alone gave 13, or 9.4 per cent, and including the professional classes furnished 23, or 16.7 per cent. As a matter of fact, the peasants and workers together comprising perhaps 93 per cent of the Russian population provided only 40.8 per cent of the revolutionary leaders studied. Possibly,

**Table 7.** Occupational Status of Father

| | |
|---|---:|
| Laborers | 30 |
| Peasants. | 26 |
| Teachers, 13; intellectuals, 4; priests, 2; doctor; lawyer; editor; engineer | 23 |
| Minor government officials or clerks | 16 |
| Important government officials | 3 |
| Recorded simply as very wealthy | 11 |
| Proprietors of estates or factories | 11 |
| Nobles | 8 |
| Business men | 6 |
| Officers (including one general) | 3 |
| Total | 137 |

if the revolutionists from the other parties were included, these results would be changed. On the other hand, it is possible that the so-called upper classes after all do furnish the leadership for the overthrow of their own class institutions. It is apparently true that a revolution cannot be successful without winning over a substantial group of the masses, but the early antagonism and hostility of Communism toward all classes except those of the workers and peasants would seem in some measure to overlook their own revolutionary background.

The tremendous value of education, even that provided by the Tsar's régime, for revolutionary leaders is shown in Table 8. Over 60 per cent

**Table 8.** Education

| | |
|---|---:|
| None | 2 |
| Primary school or its equivalent | 34 |
| High school (Gymnasia) or its equivalent | 23 |
| University incomplete | 48 |
| University graduates | 51 |
| Total | 158 |

had taken work in the university, although a much smaller number had been graduated. At least sixteen of the autobiographers specifically mentioned being expelled for revolutionary work or for participation in student organizations. How many others were dismissed for this cause who did not so state is problematical. Only 22.7 per cent who had not had high-school training or its equivalent succeeded in being included in this group of leaders. Apparently education is just as valuable for revolutionary leadership as for any other, and, in spite of the charge that education under the Tsar was reactionary and inadequate, it did make its contribution even to Communism.

**Table 9.** Age of First Radical or Revolutionary Action

| | | | | |
|---|---|---|---|---|
| 11 | . . . . . . | 1 | 23 . . . . . . | 8 |
| 12 | . . . . . . | 0 | 24 . . . . . . | 2 |
| 13 | . . . . . . | 0 | 25 . . . . . . | 4 |
| 14 | . . . . . . | 3 | 26 . . . . . . | 3 |
| 15 | . . . . . . | 11 | 27 . . . . . . | 1 |
| 16 | . . . . . . | 13 | 28 . . . . . . | 1 |
| 17 | . . . . . . | 22 | 29 . . . . . . | 0 |
| 18 | . . . . . . | 22 | 30–34 . . . . . | 3 |
| 19 | . . . . . . | 19 | 35–39 . . . . . | 2 |
| 20 | . . . . . . | 17 | Above 40 . . . . | 0 |
| 21 | . . . . . . | 10 | | |
| 22 | . . . . . . | 6 | Total . . . . | 148 |

In comparing the figures in Table 9 with those in Table 6 "Age on Joining Some Revolutionary Party," it will be noted that revolutionary activity definitely preceded joining a party. The largest group of leaders took revolutionary action at seventeen and eighteen years of age, but they did not join the party until nineteen or twenty. This can be seen in its full significance if one compares one table with the other.

Almost 80 per cent of the total for which we have data began their revolutionary activity by the time they were twenty-one years of age, and over 95 per cent had begun actual revolutionary activity by the time they were twenty-six. Apparently if in Russia the environmental forces had not forced the individual into revolutionary work by the time he was twenty-six years of age, there was an extremely slight chance that he would become a Communist leader later on.

As might be expected, the largest number began their activity by taking some radical action while still studying. Nevertheless, over 36 per cent took action in helping a labor group and only 32 per cent assisted in radical activity for students. Of these, 38 individuals helped to organize secret student circles, 17 took part in student political demonstrations, while 6 actually organized student strikes. It should be noted also that all of the types of activity recorded were against the rules of an educational institution or they were definitely illegal at the time they were committed. The theo-

**Table 10.** Character of Early Radical or Revolutionary Activity (In Some Cases Two Lines of Activity Inaugurated About the Same Time Were Recorded)

| | |
|---|---:|
| Assisting a workers' circle | 53 |
| Definitely organizing a labor union | 5 |
| Organizing or assisting in a strike | 11 |
| Organizing a peasant revolutionary group | 1 |
| Assisting in a student circle | 38 |
| Assisting in a student demonstration | 17 |
| Assisting in a student strike | 6 |
| Propagandizing soldiers | 3 |
| Writing a revolutionary pamphlet or book | 4 |
| Editor of a revolutionary periodical | 6 |
| General propaganda and lecture-work | 16 |
| Participation in revolutionary outbreak | 4 |
| Distribution of illegal literature | 8 |
| Miscellaneous | 18 |
| Total | 190 |

retician who kept within the law during the Tsar's régime did not graduate into an outstanding Communist leader. One leader was expelled from the high school at sixteen for making a speech in a revolutionary Jewish organization; another student started an illegal revolutionary library; still another refused to swear allegiance to the Tsar while he was in military school. The latter attributes this act solely to his own thought regarding political conditions and not to any outside influence. One of the workers refused to salute a police officer when he visited the factory, and so was discharged. Nearly all of these leaders showed that they were willing to rebel against authority. Some of those in the revolutionary group were even more radical. One kept arms for a revolutionary group; another, while still a boy, bought a revolver and practiced shooting so that he would have the glory of killing the Tsar or

**Table 11.** Number of Arrests Recorded

| | | | | |
|---|---:|---|---|---:|
| None | 17 | 8 | | 4 |
| 1 | 26 | 9 | | 2 |
| 2 | 26 | 10 | | 1 |
| 3 | 26 | 11 | | 1 |
| 4 | 24 | 12 | | .. |
| 5 | 15 | 13 | | 1 |
| 6 | 9 | Total | | 163 |
| 7 | 11 | | | |

some other official when he grew up. Still another joined a fighting group which participated in raiding expeditions against the rich and powerful landlords. In these trips they would even go to the extent of robbery, arson, or murder. It seems probable that the unconscious drives to some of these types of action may have been not so different from that which leads the

American boy to join gangs of all types. It is impossible to tell how far the egoistic impulse was partially responsible for revolutionary work. Certainly it provided a good opportunity for adventure and recognition. The evidence of these biographies seems to indicate that achievement is a dynamic spur to further achievement. Once the individual had done work which he considered successful, this in itself was a powerful spur to further achievement in the same direction.

Only 17 out of the 163 failed to record any arrests, and in some cases the biography started immediately with the revolution which means that in all probability arrests had not been included. There is no guaranty that all the arrests were noted in any of these accounts. Indeed, in some cases the writer said that he was frequently arrested in the course of several years. In those few cases I recorded the number of arrests as three, although there were probably more. Therefore, it is probable that the number of arrests were more rather than less than here recorded. Using the foregoing data, these leaders were arrested on the average 3.3 times each up to the revolution. It is, therefore, apparent that most of them had courage and willingness to endure hardship, and persistence in the face of difficulties. It should be recognized, however, that to some extent an arrest in the Tsar's régime was considered by the Communists a badge of honor and a mark of success. Hence a prison experience might be a decided drive to further revolutionary activity. A concrete instance of this is given in one autobiography, which quotes from the letter of a father, of a revolutionist who had been arrested, saying, "In Russia all great leaders in their youth pass through the jail." It also seems possible that the very severity of the Tsar's binder of circumstantial pressure may have in the end acted as a stimulus, but this we shall consider under the next table.

### 5. Recorded Stimuli Influential in Making the Individual a Revolutionist

It is obvious that in recording the stimuli influential in the making of revolutionists, the sociologist is open to subjective bias. I have tried to guard against this by recording so far as possible *all* stimuli which the revolutionist himself thought were influential. Even so, I think it is probably true that if this analysis was repeated by some other sociologist the statistical summary would be slightly different. It is also true that the revolutionists may have omitted some of the most important stimuli. The drives to thought and action are usually disguised. It is quite possible that the chief stimulus to revolutionary action may have been what Dr. Thomas has called the desire for a new experience, the desire for response, and the desire for recognition, which would not necessarily have been stated in an autobiography.

It would be perfectly possible to analyze these cases also from a psychiatric standpoint. How did the individual get the revolutionary "complex"? It is conceivable that the desire for recognition in the Russian social environment was blocked in a number of directions by caste and property limitations. The individual then would be subject to conflict and repression, and it would be quite understandable if he seized the revolutionary method to satisfy his natural desires. To some extent the revolutionist is also prone to phantasy and daydreams. For he builds himself an ideal state in imagination. To be sure, he then tries to build that state in reality, but he is always prone to think it will come too quickly and too ideally. The number of Communist revolutionists who have committed suicide are indicative of disappointed hopes of one sort or another. Space limitation forbids an analysis from the psychiatric standpoint, but it is hoped that such an examination will some time be made. Let us consider the detailed data as we found them (Table 12).

**Table 12**

| | |
|---|---|
| 1. Influence of revolutionary parents or grandparents | 8 |
| 2. Sacrifice and idealism of father, or his revolutionary ideas | 17 |
| 3. Father's harshness, immorality, or narrowness | 9 |
| 4. Sacrifice and idealism of mother or her revolutionary ideas | 12 |
| 5. Influence of older brother | 8 |
| 6. Revolutionary literature, books, and periodicals | 66 |
| 7. Racial discrimination | 5 |
| 8. Cruelty of Tsar's officials or jail experience | 9 |
| 9. Hardships of family or injustice of landlords against family and others | 15 |
| 10. Hardships of peasants | 9 |
| 11. Hardships of workers | 15 |
| 12. Repression of school authorities or expulsion | 14 |
| 13. Influence of fellow-students | 45 |
| 14. Influence of fellow-workers | 20 |
| 15. Influence of teachers | 13 |
| 16. Influence of general revolutionary group | 10 |
| 17. Direct influence of exiles or contact with those in jail | 3 |
| 18. Participation in revolutionary activity itself | 3 |
| 19. Revolution of 1905 | 15 |
| 20. Assassination of Alexander II | 3 |
| 21. October Revolution, 1917 | 3 |
| 22. Witnessing strikes | 5 |
| 23. Experiences while a resident abroad | 2 |
| 24. Disillusionment about religion really translating its ideals into life | 3 |
| 25. Miscellaneous: World War, witnessing student uprisings, etc. | 5 |
| Total | 317 |

It will be noticed that the influence of the family, including grandparents, father, mother, and brother, were responsible for a total of 54 cases, or 17 per cent of the total. However, this includes 9 cases in which the individual reacted against the strictness or unsocial attitudes of his father to desire a revolution in general. Books and periodicals were noted as influential in 66 cases, or 20.8 per cent of all. The experience of the individual himself as shown in items 7, 8, 9, and 12 was responsible for forty-three stimuli, or 13.5 per cent. It should be remembered, however, that some of the items under 10 and 11 were also partially experienced by the individual, and so this factor is actually higher. In this connection it is interesting to record that several stated that their jail experience was the final stimulus which caused them to become Communists. For instance, one said that the prison "was the best university in his whole life." Several said that reading aroused merely a theoretical interest in radicalism, but that it was practical work which made the deepest impression. Another said he read Karl Marx's *Capital* merely as a theoretical assignment and it made no impression on him. It was the practical work which made him decide on a revolutionary career.

The hardships of others were influential in at least 24 cases, or 7.8 per cent, and may have been influential in nearly all since the revolutionists almost took for granted that conditions under the Tsar's régime were so unfavorable that the masses were suffering. It is possible, therefore, that they did not record this stimulus in their biographies to the extent that it really was influential.

The influences of teachers, fellow-students, or fellow-workers were the most important of any one group, totaling seventy-eight stimuli, or 24.6 per cent. If to these are added the influence of general revolutionary groups and exiles, it makes a total of ninety-one stimuli, or 29.6 per cent of all that came directly from individuals outside the home.

The influence of larger outside revolutionary events (items 19, 20, 21, and 22) acted as a stimulus in 28 cases, or 9.7 per cent of all.

As far as this analysis is indicative, it would seem to show that the home is not quite as influential as is commonly supposed, at least in the recorded attitudes of Communist leaders. Books and periodicals and the influence of others outside the home were much more powerful. Here again, however, it is quite possible that the subtle and unrecorded influence of the home may have been very influential in nearly all these cases. Teachers and those who write should receive encouragement from the fact that literature and teachers have been so influential.[4]

---

[4] It is to be regretted that a series of graphic charts which were used to illustrate the statistical material in this address had to be omitted owing to space limitations.

# 12

Leadership Studies of Chinese and Chinese-Americans[1]

ROBERT D. MEADE

Most empirical studies of leadership effectiveness have been conducted within the framework of the American culture where democracy has had a rather long history of well-established traditions. Experimental studies such as those of Lippitt and White (1940) which were conducted within the American culture demonstrated that democratic leadership of boys' club activities resulted in higher morale and less aggressiveness than did authoritarian leadership. This same study showed evidence that productivity was higher when work was carried out under democratic leadership than when done under authoritarian leadership. Another study that was carried out for a much shorter period of time with college students by Shaw (1955) found that followers in an authoritarian atmosphere did better in terms of productivity but had lower morale than followers in a democratic atmosphere. A survey by Greer (1953) reported that individuals who are more equalitarian or democratic are more likely to be nominated for leadership by their neighborhood than are authoritarian individuals. A survey by Hollander (1954) in a military setting showed a negative correlation between authoritarianism and leadership nomination.

The studies reported above have concentrated on the personality characteristics of the leader with followers essentially being chosen randomly. An extensive study by Sanford (1950) found that individuals who are high in authoritarianism prefer leaders who have status, are strongly directive and who talk in terms of "power." Haythorne, Couch, Haefner, Langham, and Carter (1956) have presented evidence that shows authoritarian leadership

Robert D. Meade, "Leadership Studies of Chinese and Chinese-Americans," *Journal of Cross-Cultural Psychology,* Vol. 1, No. 4 (December 1970), pp. 325–332. Copyright © 1970 by the Center for Cross-Cultural Research.
[1] This work was supported by a contract between the Office of Naval Research and Western Washington State College.

is effective when the followers have scored high on a test of authoritarianism. They found a tendency for increased morale, more effective communication and increased cooperation when both leaders and followers are authoritarian. Results such as these suggest that in cultures which have traditions that are more authoritarian than those in America, authoritarian leadership would prove to be more effective than democratic leadership.

Meade and Whittaker (1967) have reported data from college students in several cultures which show cultural variation in authoritarianism. One of the cultural groups scoring high was India and these findings are supported by data reported by Ghei (1966) which indicate that both male and female Indian college students score higher on the deference scale of the Edwards Personal Preference Schedule than do Americans. Studies by anthropologists and sociologists who have investigated family, religious, school, and social relationships in India also report the general authoritarian nature of the culture. Using this information as background, Meade (1967) predicted that authoritarian leadership would prove to be more effective in India than would democratic leadership. Using a boys' club atmosphere such as that employed earlier in America by Lippitt and White (1940), Meade found that both morale and productivity were higher when leadership was authoritarian than when it was democratic. In addition, he found that the quality of production was also judged to be superior for the authoritarian groups. He explained his results with the assumption that Indian boys were more accustomed to authoritarian leadership in all spheres of their activities and hence were better able to adjust to such leadership in the experimental situation. Conversely, since they had had little experience with activities which are carried out in more democratic situations there was considerable difficulty in gaining satisfaction in that kind of an atmosphere. Authoritarian needs, then, are more likely to be met with authoritarian leadership whereas in America democratic needs are more dominant and more likely to be satisfied with a democratic leadership atmosphere.

The present study was conducted on two other cultural groups which have also been described as having a higher level of authoritarianism than is found among Americans generally. One of the groups was Chinese college students who have grown up with their parents in Hong Kong or mainland China. The second group was Chinese-American college students who have grown up in Hawaii but whose parents had grown up in China prior to immigration to the United States. The study is based on an experimental technique reported by Preston and Heintz (1949) who found that participatory leadership resulted in greater cohesiveness of judgment among their American subjects than did supervisory leadership. Their participatory leadership resembled the democratic atmosphere described by Lippitt and White (1940) while supervisory leadership resembled the laissez-faire atmosphere used by the same investigators.

In addition to leadership atmosphere this study has a number of other concerns. One of these is a comparison of responses to different leadership atmospheres of individuals who have lived totally in the traditional authoritarian atmosphere both outside as well as inside the home with those whose parents grew up in authoritarian traditions but who themselves have had [democratically] oriented atmospheres outside the home. The Chinese-Americans fit the latter category. Finally, in Chinese culture as well as Asian cultures generally, males are usually considered to enjoy a greater status and greater degree of dominance than females. The present study then attempts to evaluate the relative effectiveness of male and female leaders on cohesiveness of group judgments in the two cultures.

## METHOD

### Subjects

One hundred forty-four Chinese students at the Chinese University of Hong Kong and 144 Chinese-American students at the University of Hawaii participated in the study as respondents to a student opinion survey.

### Materials

Mimeographed lists of nine issues of importance to university students in the two cultures were used. These issues were developed by group discussion with students and student leaders in the universities concerned. A criterion for selection was that every issue had to be of importance to all students; thus providing a guarantee that all issues would be considered by the subjects. In Hong Kong the issues were:

  (a) provision for adequate housing for students
  (b) making a greater number of courses available to students
  (c) provision for expanded and improved library facilities
  (d) major changes in the degree examination
  (e) establishing the Chinese University of Hong Kong as a "Chinese University"
  (f) provision for removal of aged and ineffective teaching staff
  (g) increase in effectiveness of student union
  (h) provision for student voice in academic affairs, and
  (i) abolition of intermediate examinations.

In Hawaii the issues were:

  (a) making a greater number of relevant courses available to students
  (b) making changes in requirements for graduation

(c)  improving the grading and examination system
(d)  improving the food services offered to students
(e)  providing more adequate housing for students
(f)  hiring a more effective teaching staff
(g)  allowing more student voice in academic affairs
(h)  providing for expanded and improved library facilities, and
(i)  improving the transportation and parking facilities.

### Procedure

In both cultures two male and two female leaders were selected from behavioral science majors who had had some experience in conducting research projects. They were given six weeks' training and practice in leading small discussion groups under the three leadership atmospheres described by Lippitt and White (1940).

Each leader conducted two sessions using each of the three leadership atmospheres in groups consisting of three male and three female subjects. None of the subjects was known personally to the leader in any session.

At the beginning of the session the leader distributed mimeographed lists of the issues to all subjects. The list of issues appeared at both the top and bottom of the page which was folded so that only the top list was visible. Subjects were asked to read over all of the issues and decide which was the most crucial issue facing the university at the present time, which was second most critical, etc., and rank the issues from one to nine in order of importance. Five minutes were allotted for this initial individual ranking.

During the following 50 minutes a group discussion was held on the relative importance of the nine issues with the object being to arrive at a group consensus in the form of a group ranking. It was during this discussion period that the leader maintained one of the atmospheres, authoritarian, democratic, or laissez-faire. At the end of the discussion period in the democratic conditions, if no one had suggested that a vote be taken on the importance of the issues, such a vote was suggested by the leader and the result written on the blackboard. In both the laissez-faire and authoritarian conditions, the leader announced what appeared to him to be the group consensus and wrote this on the blackboard. Finally, subjects were asked to turn over the folded mimeographed sheet to where the same issues were duplicated and rank them once again on an individual basis.

### RESULTS

Preston and Heintz (1949) assessed the extent to which group discussion under different types of leadership affected judgments of individuals in the groups by correlating the rankings of the group judgments with the individual's final rankings. Where these correlations were higher, it was assumed that the group discussion had favorably affected the final judgments of individuals more than in those cases where these correlations were lower. This procedure was followed with data collected in the present investigation, the Chinese and Chinese-American data being considered separately. Since the data from each of the male leaders did not differ significantly from that of the other male leader in each nationality, their results were pooled. The same was true for female leaders. The average rank-difference correlations for the three leadership atmospheres and sex of leader for the Chinese subjects are presented in Table 1. The data for the Chinese-American subjects are presented in Table 3.

**Table 1.** Average Rank-Difference Correlation Coefficients between Group and Final Ratings for Chinese (Hong Kong) Students

| Leader | Leadership Atmosphere | | |
| | Laissez-faire | Authoritarian | Democratic |
| --- | --- | --- | --- |
| Female | .35 | .24 | .31 |
| Male | .14 | .74 | .46 |

For purposes of analyzing these data, the individual rho correlations were converted into Fisher's $Z$ correlations, and the transformed values treated by analysis of variance. The analysis of variance for the Chinese data is presented in Table 2 while that from the Chinese-American phase of the study are presented in Table 4.

**Table 2.** Analysis of Variance of Fisher's $Z$ Coefficients for Sex of Leader and Leadership Atmosphere for Group-Final Rankings for Chinese Subjects

| Variable | Mean Square | df | F |
| --- | --- | --- | --- |
| Sex of leader | 18.97 | 1 | 36.48* |
| Leadership atmosphere | 15.30 | 2 | 29.42* |
| Sex x atmosphere | 28.29 | 2 | 54.69* |
| Within cells | .0052 | 138 | |

* $p < .01$

Considering the data resulting from the encounters between Chinese leaders and followers it appears that male leaders are generally more effective than female leaders in producing cohesiveness of judgment among the followers. One notable exception, however, is to be found in the case of the laissez-faire atmosphere where the female leadership condition appeared to have produced a greater cohesion. The $t$ value of 2.03 between the male and

**Table 3.** Average Rank-Difference Correlations between Group and Final Rankings for Chinese-American (Hawaii) Subjects

| | Leadership Atmosphere | | |
|---|---|---|---|
| Leader | Laissez-faire | Authoritarian | Democratic |
| Female | .19 | .14 | .24 |
| Male | .24 | .64 | .67 |

female leadership effectiveness in the laissez-faire condition is significant at the .05 level of confidence. This discrepancy is believed to be due to an unexpected event that took place in two of the four laissez-faire sessions conducted by the female leader in which one of the followers emerged as a

**Table 4.** Analysis of Variance of Fisher's $Z$ Coefficients for Sex of Leader and Leadership Atmospheres for Group-Final Rankings for Chinese Subjects

| Variable | Mean Square | df | F |
|---|---|---|---|
| Sex of leader | 6.28 | 1 | 11.59* |
| Leadership atmosphere | 1.28 | 2 | 57.09* |
| Sex x atmosphere | 1.16 | 2 | 10.55* |
| Within cells | .11 | 138 | |

*$p < .01$

self-appointed leader. In both cases these subjects who assumed leadership were males. There were no incidents of such assumption of leadership roles in any of the sessions conducted by the male leaders. It appears, then, that while no one was willing to challenge the seemingly nondirective and unproductive male leaders characteristic of laissez-faire atmospheres, such challenge did take place when there was a female leader. This finding may be taken as further evidence of differences in respect enjoyed by the different sexes while playing leadership roles.

Although the laissez-faire condition with female leadership appeared to result in a greater cohesion of judgment, there was no reliable difference between the three leadership atmospheres for female leaders. Among the male leaders, however, there was significant variation as is indicated by the interaction between the sex of leader and leadership atmosphere $F$ value. By far, the authoritarian leader was the more effective ($t = 5.54$, $p < .01$) and laissez-faire leadership seems to have had little effect in producing cohesion of judgment.

Considering the data from the Chinese-American subjects, male leaders again appear to be more effective than did females. While there is no significant difference between the leadership atmospheres as practiced by the female leaders, male leadership does show significant variation between the three conditions. Both authoritarian and democratic leadership appeared to be equally effective ($t = .69$, and not significant) while laissez-faire leadership was considerably less effective.

When both cultures are considered and contrasted, there was no reliable difference between the results from male authoritarian leaders ($t = 1.14$ and not significant). However, male democratic leadership was more effective among Chinese-Americans than it was with Chinese ($t = 3.69$, $p < .01$). While there appears the possibility that female leaders are more effective generally among Chinese than among Chinese-Americans, this was confounded by the assumption of leadership by followers in the laissez-faire conditions and no meaningful evaluation can be made.

## DISCUSSION

The data presented here have illustrated a number of ways in which responses to leadership atmospheres have been conditioned differentially by culture. The first of these is the relatively high correlation between group and final rankings in the case of authoritarian conditions of leadership for both cultures examined here. By contrast, however, while democratic leadership is less effective among Hong Kong Chinese, it is as effective as authoritarian leadership among the Chinese-Americans when practiced by male leaders. The apparent equal effectiveness of democratic and authoritarian leadership among the Chinese-Americans may be explained by the fact that these $S$s have learned at home to respond to authoritarian atmospheres but have also learned outside the home to respond equally well to democratic situations. On the other hand, the learning experiences of the Chinese as provided by their acculturation is likely to be more exclusively authoritarian outside as well as inside the home. As a result, their ability to respond in a way which is satisfactory to them in a democratic situation is somewhat less.

Since the male has traditionally played the more dominant role in Chinese culture, it is not surprising that response to male leadership was greater than it was to female leadership. That female leadership enjoys a lower status than that of the male is also evidenced by the fact that leadership of female leaders in the laissez-faire condition was challenged by male followers while that of the male laissez-faire leader was not. Since laissez-faire leadership appears to be basically nondirective and unproductive, the need to accomplish the task may have appeared to be thwarted by the leader. But when the leader was male, the respect for the appointed leader was apparently stronger than the desire to overcome the resulting frustration of lack of direction and accomplishment.

While it was not possible to obtain meaningful statistical evaluation of the overall differences between female leadership in the two cultures, the fact that in both the democratic and authoritarian conditions, Chinese female leaders were more effective than their counterparts in the Chinese-American groups raises some question. There is a possibility that simply being a labeled "leader" brought about a tendency for the leader to be more effective in bringing about cohesion of judgment in the Chinese subjects. In the Chinese-American culture the role of "leader" may not carry with it as much status or prestige and consequently provide less effect on the followers. In any event, when compared to male leaders, the effectiveness of females is considerably less and this raises the question of sex differences in leadership in other cultures as well.

While no direct comparison can be made between the findings of the present investigation and that of Preston and Heintz (1949), it can be concluded that response to leadership has been demonstrated, in part, by cultural conditioning. While laissez-faire or supervisory leadership resulted in less group cohesion of judgment in both Chinese and Chinese-American subjects than did democratic or participatory leadership as was true for Caucasian-American Ss tested by Preston and Heintz, authoritarian leadership atmosphere was of equal or greater effectiveness for both Chinese and Chinese-Americans. These findings suggest the importance of considering how learning and acculturation has affected the ways in which needs of followers are met in different cultural settings.

## REFERENCES

Ghei, S., "A Cross-Cultural Study of Need Profiles," *Journal of Personality and Social Psychology*, 1966, 3, 580–585.

Greer, F., "Neighborhood leaders," in D. Courtney, F. Greer, J. Masling, & H. Orlans (eds.), *Naval, Neighborhood and National Leaders* (Philadelphia: Institute for Research in Human Relations, 1953).

Haythorne, W., Couch, A., Haefner, D., Langham, P., & Carter, L., "The Effects of Varying Combinations of Authoritarian and Equalitarian Leaders and Followers," *Journal of Abnormal and Social Psychology*, 1956, 53, 210–219.

Hollander, E., "Authoritarianism and Leadership Choice in a Military Situation," *Journal of Abnormal and Social Psychology*, 1954, 49, 365–370.

Lippitt, R., & White, R., "An Experimental Study of the Effect of Democratic and Authoritarian Group Atmospheres," *University of Iowa Studies in Child Welfare*, 1940, 16, 43–195.

Meade, R., & Whittaker, J., "A Cross-Cultural Study of Authoritarianism," *Journal of Social Psychology*, 1967, 72, 3–7.

Meade, R., "An Experimental Study of Leadership in India," *Journal of Social Psychology*, 1967, 72, 35–43.

Preston, M., & Heintz, R., "Effects of Participatory versus Supervisory Leadership on Group Judgment," *Journal of Abnormal and Social Psychology,* 1949, 44, 345–355.

Sanford, F., *Authoritarianism and Leadership* (Philadelphia: Institute for Research in Human Relations, 1950).

Shaw, M., "A Comparison of Two Types of Leadership in Various Communication Nets," *Journal of Abnormal and Social Psychology,* 1955, 50, 127–134.

# Part Four

## Education and Political Leadership

INTRODUCTION

The subject of education deserves an important place in the study of political leadership. Education means broadly how persons learn and how others intervene in the learning process. As applied to political leadership, there are three principal groups of learners (political leaders, other citizens, and professional students of leadership behavior), two main processes of learning (natural socialization and contrived experience), and three major emphases of concern (research on both processes for all three groups, teaching as experimentation with contrived experience, and learning as both seeking and responding to experience). Viewed from an educational standpoint, the study of political leadership broadly involves inquiring into how leaders learn to lead, how other persons in society learn about their behavior, and what effects accompany experimental change in either of these learning processes. There is an obvious overlapping of concern with that field of political science known as "political socialization" of which learning about political leadership is a part, but the concept of "education" deserves retention because it calls attention to the possibility of very active and deliberate intervention in the learning processes from the most casual general exposure to the subject of political leadership in educational curricula right up to the most intense, specialized, leadership cadre training. Some professional students of political leadership indeed may wish to become specialists in educating political leaders as well as other persons about leadership behavior in addition to doing research and tutoring research apprentices.

The objectives of this introductory essay are to call attention briefly to four of the main problem areas that challenge the study of political leadership: (1) natural processes of political leadership socialization, (2) comparative experience with deliberate efforts at political leadership training, (3) the problem of leadership education for other members of society who are not themselves political leaders, and (4) the possibility of beneficial interventions in political leadership learning processes on a societal or even global scale from a futuristic perspective.

There are at least four modes by which political leaders "naturally" learn about how to be a political leader; these range along the life cycle from childhood,[1] through pre-recruitment aspirant experience, through incumbent leadership role performance, and through role disengagement processes into post-retirement reflections. These modes include: political leadership modeling behavior with four variations (copying, model-guided learning, critic-guided learning, and vicarious learning),[2] transference of leadership concepts and skills learned in a different area into political leadership role performance (e.g., military, business, or trade union leadership experience), trial and error learning (feedback experienced from the leader's own decisions), or *ad hoc* anticipatory learning (self-directed or tutor initiated pre-decisional inquiry by a political leader to assist him in coping with immediate or expected future problems).

Some illustrations of these are in the following. First, consider the four forms of modeling behavior. Copying is illustrated by the tendency of some associates of leaders to imitate their mannerisms. For example, it was reported that an American visitor (Secretary of the Interior Stewart L. Udall) to the Soviet Union in 1962 met a Siberian leader (Irkutsk Oblast Chairman Ivan V. Gritsenko) whose style was strongly reminiscent of that of the then Soviet premier Nikita Khrushchev: "Mr. Gritsenko," reported *The New York Times,* "a tall, burly man with a sense of humor similar to Premier Khrushchev's, frankly told his guests that he had tried to copy the relaxed, jovial atmosphere that usually surrounds the Premier." [3] This example also, of course, involves the possibility of critic-guided as well as model-guided learning. A clear example of vicarious learning is provided by the series of case studies of especially courageous American politicians written by the then Senator John F. Kennedy. As explained in the preface to his book *Profiles in Courage:* "Since first reading—long before I entered the Senate—an account of John Quincy Adams and his struggle with the Federalist party, I have been interested in the problems of political courage in the face of constituent pressures, and the light shed on these problems by the lives of great statesmen." [4] Another illustration of vicarious learning is contained in Mao Tse-tung's recollection, shared with Edgar Snow in 1936, that in his youth he had been impressed by an article on the American Revolution which contained a sentence like: "After eight years of difficult war, Washington won victory and built up his nation." Mao also told Snow that he had read about "Napoleon, Catherine of Russia, Peter the Great, Wellington, Gladstone, Rousseau, Montesquieu, and Lincoln." [5] In fact, so common are examples of modeling behavior in political leadership careers from the most conventional to the most revolutionary, that a major research effort on the subject seems definitely desirable. On a long-range time dimension it should be possible to map "family trees" of model leader influences both within and across political communities at the local, provincial, national, and international levels.

Another source of natural learning about political leadership lies in the transference of leadership skills learned in other professions into politics. A good example of this, not yet subjected to systematic analysis,[6] is the contribution to political leadership role orientations that derives from prior military leadership experience. Some of the characteristics of military leadership that may contribute to political leadership styles are dedication to mission, paternalistic concern for the welfare of the troops, respect for superiors, expected subordinate obedience, a sense of proper "channels," standard procedures for operational planning, procedures for inspection and supervision, and so forth. A frank admission that his major preparation for service as mayor of the City of Philadelphia came from administrative experience as an Air Force officer has been given by Joseph S. Clark, later Senator from Pennsylvania. "Without the Air Force, I would have been lost in the mayor's chair," he has written.[7] Inquiry into the leadership concepts and skills of professions other than the military that contribute to the natural socialization of political leaders also is needed; this would include the analysis of leadership training in such fields as business, labor, religion, sports, and social organizations as well.

Learning by observation of political leadership models and by transference of leadership skills from other areas are probably second in importance only to direct trial and error learning experience. Positive affirmation of the value of such experiences is given by the emphasis upon the development of leaders out of "struggle" that is characteristic of the writings of Lenin and Hitler. Basically the same assumption underlies faith in the efficacious educational benefits of immersion in electoral battles and on-the-job learning that characterize competitive democracies such as Britain and the United States. Even where emphasis is placed upon the necessity for the "summing up" of direct action experience in terms of its relevance for an ideological framework such as is stressed in "the thought of Mao Tse-tung," [8] ideally the basis for actual learning is located in practice. As Mao explained in *On Practice,* "Knowledge starts with practice, reaches the theoretical plane via practice, and then has to return to practice." [9] In such contexts doctrinal mastery is portrayed as a necessary but not sufficient condition for education in political leadership. Much the same emphasis holds for less ideologically self-conscious political communities where politicians commonly assert that academic political scientists "do not know anything about politics." The response of students of political leadership should be to welcome such statements with the invitation, "Then teach me," so that the nature of trial and error learning in political leadership education may be better understood. Perhaps intensive analysis of actual examples of political leadership decisions and the introduction of a rigorous case study method can produce a reasonable academic equivalent of actual trial and error learning.[10] For example, the failure of the Bay of Pigs invasion attempt upon Cuba in 1961 was a trial and error learning experience for President Kennedy, as was the Cuban missile emplacement failure for Premier Khrushchev in 1962. Might not these two experiences be transformed into useful "academic" learning experiences for other aspiring political leaders?

A further natural process of political leadership education is represented by *ad hoc* learning. This may be either self-initiated or thrust upon the leader by aspiring tutors. This is not only represented by common interest in reading political biographies that we have mentioned under modeling behavior, or in reading history, but also by more specific inquiries into task-related matters. A good example of this is contained in the education in economics that President Kennedy sought and obtained while in the White House. As a Harvard undergraduate he had taken only one introductory course in the subject for which he received a C. Subsequently he had shown little interest in economic theory. But as President he soon found that he had to become far more knowledgeable in order to decide among often conflicting alternatives proposed by his circle of economic advisers. Thus he combined reading, intense questioning of economic experts, and the personal tutelage of "outside" advisers like economics professor Paul Samuelson until he advanced to a position where another economist, friend, and adviser, professor Seymour Harris, concluded, "He is now by far the most knowledgeable President of all times in the general area of economics." [11] Similarly, Cuba's Premier Fidel Castro is said to have become an acknowledged expert on agriculture through reading.[12]

A second major object of inquiry in leadership education consists in the study of deliberately contrived programs for ensuring that leaders have the required skills and background knowledge deemed necessary in a particular society. It is likely that all societies with identifiable leadership roles have some form of purposive program for the education of potential or actual role incumbents. Deliberate education or specialized training for leadership may occur at several stages of the life cycle of an aspirant or incumbent: during periods of general socialization or pre-occupational educational orientation, during the process of recruitment into political leadership roles, and later in specialized efforts to improve role performance throughout a leadership career. Examples of contrived educational efforts range from the training of chiefly successors in tribal societies, through the tutelage of princes in hereditary monarchies, to the purposive programs of leadership training that characterize some modern political parties (e.g., the Communist party of the Soviet Union). Where there are no comprehensive programs for career-long leadership training, there may be short-range, *ad hoc* efforts to deliberately facilitate leader performance. Examples of this in the United States include the campaign seminars often held under the auspices of the Democratic and Republican parties to introduce candidates to successful electoral strategies and the pre-legislative session briefings that are sometimes arranged for newly elected state legislators to prepare them for their responsibilities. While in office, the attempts made by lobbyists, newspaper editors, diplomats, staff associates, and others to provide background information and frameworks of analysis for political leaders also have some quasi-educational qualities. The advisory circle of intellectual advisers and consultants frequently assembled by leaders, such as the group that met at Senator Robert F. Kennedy's home with subsequent fame as "Hickory Hill University," may also be regarded as deliberately structured *ad hoc* efforts at political leadership education.

Some persons in a society may be trained especially for political leadership roles or an attempt may be made to provide all members with skills required for performance as leaders. This is the hypothesis advanced by the anthropologist Henry Selby after a survey of elite education in several historical societies (including the Chuckchee of Siberia, the Inca, Aztecs, the Iatmul of New Guinea, and the American Plains Indians). He writes,

> To the degree that a society recruits members for elite positions from a restricted group of individuals (immobile societies), special training, separate ritual functions, special knowledge, and distinctive deportment will be emphasized in the training of the young. And conversely, to the degree that a society recruits members for elite positions from all the people (mobile societies), training will be directed at instilling elite values in all; but separate-but-equal roles may be provided for those who do not make the grade.[13]

Selby's hypothesis calls attention to a third major object of educational inquiry in political leadership studies: study of the nature of education about political leadership received by members of society who are not themselves leaders. The search for answers to this question should lead in contemporary societies to study of the political leadership content of textbooks at all educational levels, the mass media, and peer tutelage by word-of-mouth "underground education." Like leaders themselves, followers learn about political leadership in two principal ways: by deliberate education, training, or indoctrination, as in school curricula or party-led leadership study groups, and by less structured natural means. Less contrived learning about leadership may occur during societal crises and during electoral contests among aspiring leaders where these are permitted. We need to inquire simply into how other members of society learn about the nature of political leadership.

A fourth area of attention in political leadership studies needs to focus on educational experimentation. We need to explore different ways in which leaders and followers can be introduced to knowledge about political leadership and must evaluate the effects of such educational efforts. Existing literature reveals a variety of findings of educational interest to students of political leadership. Whereas political scientists usually have reported that they have found no correlation between political activism and regular university education in political science,[14] social psychologists have often discovered that deliberate programs to provide leadership training have resulted in significant behavioral changes at least temporarily in the specific areas concerned.[15] These findings suggest that if political science experimented with methods for explicit political leadership education both inside and outside the university, measurable influences might also be observed.

Some of the questions to which political science might address itself include: Can the study of political leadership contribute new knowledge and skills to (1) persons aspiring to become leaders, (2) persons who will play supportive or subversive roles as followers, and (3) persons who may become professional scientific researchers on the subject? Can the study of political leadership presented in a professional extension-type way benefit persons who are already active in political leadership roles throughout their careers? And can the diffusion of better scientific knowledge about political leadership throughout a society have a measurable effect upon its functioning? Is it possible that the higher the quality of scientific knowledge about political leadership in a society the more realistic the demands placed upon the leadership roles, the more constructive the followership, and the more probable the deliberate engineering of such roles to enhance capacities for societal problem-solving?

Among educational experiments that merit further exploration are such things as the study of political leadership biographies by leaders, students, and other citizens (the academic extension of a natural political leadership learning process); the extension of efforts to simulate political leadership role performance;[16] the creation and evaluation of alternative ways of conveying knowledge about political leadership at all educational levels from the primary to the most advanced;[17] and the exploration of alternative modes of political leadership education for citizens outside the formal educational system including films, radio, television, drama, street theater, songs, poetry, and discussion groups involving political leaders in ways that differ from usual campaign or incumbency defense confrontations.

In conclusion, it is important that a special field of political leadership studies approach educational problems from a broad societal perspective, from a historically and cross-culturally sensitive viewpoint, and with a keen sense of the future. In 1970 it is said, for example, that the next

thirty years of human development toward the year 2000 are likely to include more scientific advances and technological breakthroughs than have
characterized *any past several centuries* put together.[18] It is also commonly
argued that mankind faces catastrophe in the form of overpopulation, over-
pollution, and overkill in the same period. However one views it, either
as a period of unprecedented promise or of unprecedented peril, it is likely
to be a period of turbulent, multi-faceted change characterized by problems
with complex global ramifications. For incumbent political leaders, other
aspirants, and educators alike the same educational questions arise. How
can persons aspiring to or incumbent in political leadership roles—as well
as scholarly specialists in political leadership—be assisted in preparing themselves for coping with onrushing changes of the future as they affect their
chosen vocation. One suggestion is that future-oriented political leadership
seminars be formed that include experienced political leaders, young aspirants, and intellects with a keen sense of the future under catalytic
scholarly leadership.

The essay by Yehezkel Dror (Selection 13), one of the scholarly
leaders in the effort to develop a future-oriented policy science, contains a
bold proposal for the education of political leaders in developing countries
that is just as relevant for leaders in "advanced" societies. This essay is an
unusual one in the academic literature on development because it is based
on explicit recognition of the importance of purposive political leadership
and frankly seeks to explore ways to assist politicians in their tasks through
advanced education. Dror deals realistically with the taboos and political
sensitivities connected with his proposal. The ideas he presents can serve
as a prototype for many variations related to the education of incumbent
leaders, aspiring leaders, and ordinary persons who must deal with leaders.
To the eleven different types of teaching methods that he mentions might
be added emphasis upon biography as a subject for guided reading and
utilization of films, recordings, and drama as "lecture" materials.

The second essay in this section by Warren H. Schmidt (Selection 14)
reports on an unusual effort at bi-partisan political leadership education by
the University of California at Berkeley. The basic idea could be extended to
cover less-established political groups. The more the university becomes a
tool of reactionary or repressive forces or of revolutionary or subversive
ones, the less it can function as a creator and transmitter of scientifically
valid knowledge about political leadership, whether ideologically palatable
or not. As an ideal goal, the university should make the scientific study
and teaching of political leadership open to persons who hold right (conservative), middle (liberal), and left-wing (radical) values at the undergraduate, graduate, and adult education levels. This notion will be rejected

by partisan ideologues and will be impossible to achieve in most contemporary political societies, but it still offers a desirable goal for world political leadership education.

This issue leads us to consider problems related to alternative social roles that may be available to or created by students of political leadership. This is the subject of the essays presented in Part Four.

# Notes

to Part Four: Education and Political Leadership

1. E.g., see Fred I. Greenstein, *Children and Politics* (New Haven: Yale University Press, 1965).

2. Copying means simple imitation of a political leader's behavior by an emulator. Model-guided learning means that the emulator is in the position of an apprentice to a political leader who directly reinforces his behavior. Critic-guided behavior means that the emulator receives instruction from a third party who is in a position to observe both his own and the leader model's behavior. Vicarious learning means self-reinforcement of behavior by an emulator based on the direct or indirect observation of a model of political leadership behavior. I have adapted these ideas from two major works on modeling behavior: Neal E. Miller and John Dollard, *Social Learning and Imitation* (New Haven: Yale University Press, 1941); and Albert Bandura and Richard H. Walters, *Social Learning and Personality Development* (New York: Holt, Rinehart and Winston, 1963).

3. *The New York Times,* September 9, 1962, p. 5.

4. John F. Kennedy, *Profiles in Courage* (New York: Harper and Row, 1967), p. xv.

5. Edgar Snow, *Red Star Over China* (New York: The Modern Library, 1944), p. 134.

6. While American political scientists have been especially interested in exploring the effects of legal training and experience on political leadership role performance [e.g., Heinz Eulau and John D. Sprague, *Lawyers in Politics* (Indianapolis: Bobbs-Merrill, 1964)], they have not given adequate attention to the effects of military socialization on American political leadership styles despite the apparently high proportion of former military commissioned and non-commissioned officers in executive and legislative roles since World War I.

7. Joseph S. Clark, "Notes on Political Leadership," *Harper's Magazine,* CCXVI (June 1958), p. 27.

8. John W. Lewis, *Leadership in Communist China* (Ithaca: Cornell University Press, 1963).

9. Mao Tse-tung, *Selected Works* (New York: International Publishers, 1954), Vol. I, p. 29.

10. This assumption seems to have been accepted, for example, for business leadership training in the famed case study program of the Harvard Business School.

11. Theodore C. Sorenson, *Kennedy* (New York: Bantam Books, 1966), p. 444.

12. Herbert Matthews, *Fidel Castro* (New York: Simon and Schuster, 1969), p. 240.

13. Henry Selby, "Elite Selection and Social Integration: An Anthropologist's View," in Rupert Wilkinson (ed.), *Governing Elites: Studies in Training and Selection* (New York: Oxford University Press, 1969), p. 22.

14. A study at New York University during 1953–63 concluded that students of a two-semester government course as compared with a three-semester social science sequence did not significantly differ in their attitudes toward politicians, political views, and political participation. See Marvin Schick and Albert Somit, "The Failure to Teach Political Activity," *American Behavioral Scientist,* VI, No. 5 (January 1963), pp. 5–8.

15. The effective retraining of recreation leaders to employ more democratic practices is reported by Alex Bavelas and Kurt Lewin, "Training in Democratic Leadership," *Journal of Abnormal and Social Psychology,* XXXVII (January 1942), pp. 115–119.

16. For example, see Marvin G. Weinbaum and Louis H. Gold, *Presidential Election: A Simulation with Readings* (New York: Holt, Rinehart and Winston, 1969); Leonard Stitelman and William D. Copland, *The Congressman at Work* (Chicago: Science Research Associates, 1969); and Andrew M. Scott and Trudie M. Lucas, *Simulation and National Development* (New York: John Wiley, 1966).

17. James A. Robinson *et al.,* "Teaching with Inter-Nation Simulation and Case Studies," *American Political Science Review,* LX (March 1966), pp. 53–65.

18. This point was made by Charles W. Williams, vice-president of the World Future Society and deputy director of the National Goals Research Staff, White House, during the Governor's Conference on the Year 2000, State of Hawaii, Honolulu, August 5–8, 1970.

# 13

## The Improvement of Leadership in Development Countries

YEHEZKEL DROR

### I. DEVELOPMENT THEORIES AND DEVELOPMENT POLICIES

Examination of present trends in theories of development on one hand and in applied development policies on the other hand reveals an increasing gulf between these two, which threatens to become an abyss. Increasingly, the complexities of modernization processes and their dependence on deep-rooted and multidimensional variables is recognized by modern theories of development.[1] No longer do we believe in any simple devices which will result in some dramatic "taking-off," which assures continuous and fast modernization. Instead, modern theories of modernization tend to identify clusters of critical "modernization crises," [2] successful mastering of which is presented as an essential (though not necessarily sufficient) condition for accelerated modernization. Often highly sophisticated, modern theories of development clearly constitute an important first step forward in our understanding of modernization processes. But as yet they provide very poor guidance for operational development policies. Certainly, there is little relation, if any, between modern theories of development and actual development policies as practised in the development countries themselves and as encouraged and furthered by international and inter-state aid arrangement.

Modern theories of development point out the critical importance of complex and multi-dimensional factors such as, for instance: levels-of-aspira-

---

Yehezkel Dror, "The Improvement of Leadership in Development Countries." *Civilisations*, XVII, No. 112 (1967), 72–79. Reproduced with permission of the International Institute of Differing Civilizations, Brussels.

[1] One of the best presentations of modern theories of development is Benjamin Higgins, *Economic Development* (New York: W. W. Norton, 1959).

[2] E.g., see Lucian W. Pye, *Aspects of Political Development* (Boston: Little Brown, 1966), pp. 62–66.

tions; political participation; population balance; societal communication networks; economic and political entrepreneurship; identification with the state; assurance of order and peace; mobility of elites; changes in bases of legitimations; and quality of public policymaking. Insofar as we accept these theories as approximate indicators of at least some of the realities of development processes, our strategy for development-policies should be to try and identify variables which satisfy two conditions: (a) they are operational, that is, they can be influenced by conscious action; (b) they are significant, that is, they have significant impact on actual development processes through changing the basic relevant factors as identified by modern development studies. (To be more exact, a third condition should be added, namely efficiency in terms of benefits-costs. But at the present state-of-the-art, when most policies are ineffective, this is perhaps too sophisticated a requirement—though I think it should be kept in mind.) In fact, development policies tend to concentrate on variables which are more related to the visible outer façades of underdevelopment than to the hard core of development-processes and their basic factors, and which, therefore, tend not to meet the condition of significance (nor, in many cases, the conditions of operationability).

Leaving aside, as deserving separate analysis, concrete physical projects such as steel mills, water systems and road networks, the following oversimplified picture presents much of contemporary development policies: The external layers of underdevelopment reveal many shortcomings which seem to cry for speedy action. These include, for instance: lack of technical know-how and dearth of professionals; low levels of nutrition and health; slums near the urban centers; absence of investment capital; weaknesses of administrative structures and personnel; soil erosion; tendencies towards local separations; and often some types of insurgence. These shortcomings are well recognized and receive intense treatment through international aid and through efforts by the involved development countries themselves—with little results in terms of the basic development processes. This is not to say that action directed at these and similar shortcomings has no effect whatsoever. Medical facilities are improved; teachers are trained; agricultural technologies are changed and so on. But often these results are isolated islands, which at best change little, are often eroded away by the stormy waves of deeper processes, and sometimes even aggravate the situation (for instance, by increasing the net birth rate beyond any possible rate of increases in G.N.P. or by creating a strata of school graduates who cannot be usefully employed).

A number of possible conclusions can be drawn from this diagnosis. One possible view is that in view of the complexities of modernization processes and the limitations of our knowledge and other resources—the best we can try to do is to engage in some incremental improvements, as is done to some extent in reality. These incremental improvements at least provide some help, promise better modernization-policies for the future to be arrived at through learning from accumulating experience, and may perhaps achieve in the aggregate a critical mass effect which will result in changes in more basic features of society. Another possible view is that the best we can try to do is to expose underdeveloped societies to a series of less or more intense shocks, through radical changes in a number of easier accessible variables—hoping that at best the shocks may stimulate movement in the direction of modernization, while at worst no real harm can result. A third possible view is that new modernization policies should be designed on the basis of modern theories of development, policies which should aim at the critical factors through influencing variables which satisfy the conditions of operationality and significance (and, later on efficiency) as explained above.

Among these three views, the third has much to recommend itself. The risk is not high because present policies will continue till the search for new policies identifies alternatives with a higher expectation of desirable results. And the gulf between modern theories of development and most contemporary modernization policies, taken together with the niggardish results of most contemporary modernization policies—clearly justify very intense efforts at designing new modernization policies.

I am leaving for another occasion a broad examination of required changes in meta-policymaking (that is, policies on how to make policies) in respect to modernization policies.[3] In this paper I want to demonstrate the necessity and feasibility of innovations in modernization-policies by exploring one such proposal, namely, improvement of leadership.

## II. THE NEED FOR IMPROVEMENT OF LEADERSHIP

One of the most critical resources for modernization is the high-level political elite, that is leadership. The "nation building" aspects of modernization, the need for widespread active popular participation and enthusiasm, the necessary broad scope of governmental activities—all these (and additional) needs combine to make the role of political leadership in "avant-garde" development countries[4] a critical one and a very difficult one. The qualities required for successful leadership in development countries are much more demanding than those needed in modern states, in which the

---

[3] For a broader study of contemporary policymaking and its improvement see Yehezkel Dror, *Public Policymaking Re-examined* (San Francisco: Chandler, 1967).

[4] For this concept and some characterization of the weaknesses of political elites in development countries, see Yehezkel Dror, "Public-Policy-Making in Avant-Garde Development States", *Civilisations,* Vol. XIII, No. 4 (1963), 395–405 (esp. pp. 398, 403–404).

political elite does not attempt far-going directed social change, and in which the political elite is only one component of a highly developed social guidance cluster.[5] At the same time, conditions in development countries are hardly conducive to spontaneous growth of a political elite having the required qualities. The resulting inadequacies constitute one of the most difficult barriers to modernization, which frustrate most contemporary modernization policies.

This diagnosis is well recognized both by modern theories of development and by development advisors and development-encouraging agencies. Nevertheless, practically nothing is being done to try and improve leadership in development countries.

Three of the main reasons for this serious omission in development-aiding activities are not difficult to identify.

1. *A taboo effect.*   In Western Democratic countries, the political elite is not regarded as a legitimate subject for conscious shaping and development. Any efforts to interfere with the spontaneous processes shaping the political elite are regarded as contradicting basic democratic values and are therefore outside the scope of legitimate alternatives for public policy. There is some experience available on training for political elites in Western Democratic countries, especially in labor parties which often had no ready-made supply of suitable prepared candidates for leaderships. But this experience is spotty and has made no impact on the taboos surrounding discussions of the subject.

2. *Political sensitivity.*   Training for leadership constitutes a much more sensitive interference with the politics of development countries than, say, training of engineers or technical assistance for improvement of administrative management. Necessarily, such training deals with highly controversial non-technical issues and can easily be misused for indoctrinization and brainwashing, rather than leadership development. Participation in leadership-training can easily stamp a politician as belonging to one or another "camp" which provided him with training and can have disastrous results for his political career. International agencies are naturally weary of initiating such highly suspect activities, which can easily get them involved in acute political controversies. Aid-giving countries are similarly cautious, or are more

---

[5] This very useful concept is developed in Bertram M. Gross, "The Management of National Economic Change" in R. C. Martin (ed.), *Public Administration and Democracy: Essays in Honor of Paul H. Appleby* (Syracuse: Syracuse University Press, 1965), esp. pp. 101–127, and Bertram M. Gross, *The State of the Nation: Social System Accounting* (London: Tavistock Publications Ltd., 1965), esp. pp. 72–74.

interested (or at least suspected as being more interested) in gaining political support and "selling" their values.

3. *Lack of methods.*   Improvement of leadership is at best a difficult and hard process, requiring much effort and a long-range point-of-view. Few ready-made methods are available and much learning through trial-and-error is necessary. New types of teaching material must be developed or adjusted from different uses. Even after optimal action, many sceptics will doubt the benefits of the improvement efforts which will be very difficult to evaluate and prove.

The lack of reliable methods compounds the taboo effect and political sensitivity, resulting in the contemporary lack of action for improvement of leadership for development countries. Thus, one of the more serious omissions in development policies is not very difficult to explain and understand. But explaining an omission is one thing, while justifying and continuing that omission is another. As long as an optimistic view of the prospects of accelerated modernization was justified by events—there was perhaps some sense in trying to help modernization through more conventional types of aid. But now the futility of many types of aid, if unaccompanied by changes in the political processes of the development countries, is quite clear. Therefore, incrementalism and "muddling through" in development-policies loses its justifications and more innovating, more imaginative, and even more daring action becomes necessary. Concerted action for improvement of leadership is in no way a panacea and not too much should be expected from it. Nevertheless, improvement of leadership, if feasible, is relevant to basic development processes, and thus satisfies the earlier presented condition of significance. If feasible at all, improvement of leadership is probably also highly efficient—maximum costs being quite small in comparison with expected benefits. What we still have to examine is whether and to what extent improvement of leadership in development countries is feasible.

## III. POSSIBILITIES FOR IMPROVEMENT OF LEADERSHIP

Recruitment to the political elite and advancement in it involves a large number of stages. Most of these are not susceptible to directed improvement within medium and intermediate time periods. Motivation to engage in politics, finding a patron, building a first power-base, passing various screening and selection mechanisms—these and other critical stages are shaped by a large number of constantly changing variables which seem in the main, in development countries, non-operational for purposes of directed, improvement-oriented, action. Furthermore, overt interference with selection and advancement of political elites—even when feasible—is too dangerous a tool and too value-sensitive a tool to be encouraged for systematic use.

What we are looking for are ways for improving leadership and not a totalitarian *Kaderpolitik*[6] which necessarily defeats modernization by stifling innovation and smothering political entrepreneurship. Therefore, by necessity and by choice, improvement of leadership will have to be a post-entry activity, directed at persons who are already active in politics. Directing improvement-efforts at already active politicians is also time-saving by promising faster impact on political behavior and more efficient by concentrating on persons who have already passed some tests of practical politics.

My suggestion is to establish courses for politicians, where they will spend between four to twelve months and undergo a very intensive experience designed to improve their performance as political leaders. Tentatively, some main features of such leadership-improvement courses can be summed up as follows:

1. *Participants.* The courses are designed for practising politicians. Optimal participants are bright politicians who still occupy junior positions (and thus are able to leave their jobs for an extended period) and who show promise for advancement to senior positions. The term "politicians" is used broadly, as covering the wide spectrum of political positions in development countries—including parties, trade unions, military officers in countries with military regimes, political civil service positions, etc.

2. *Main objectives and curriculum.* The overall goal of the courses is to improve political leadership capacities and qualifications. More specifically, the course is directed at better preparation for the main types of political activities, including, *inter alia:* (1) policy-making and decisionmaking; (2) support-recruitment, coalitions-building and conflict-treatment; (3) interpersonal relations; (4) management of organizations and broader systems. Improvement of these activities requires educational efforts directed at all levels of human capacities and qualification, including, *inter alia:* (a) intellectual capacities; (b) explicit knowledge; (c) tacit knowledge and patterns of behaviour; (d) personality and values. By cross-tabulating these two main dimensions, we get a matrix of training objectives which permits us to identify the main components of the curriculum and organize them according to purpose. This is done on a tentative basis in Table 1 (See Table 1.—Suggestive Main Objectives and Curriculum of Courses for Improvement of Leadership in Development Countries).[7]

---

[6] A fascinating and alarming description of such a totalitarian *Kaderpolitik* is Joachim Schultz, *Der Funktionär in Der Einheitspartei* (Stuttgart: Ring-Verlag, 1956).

[7] Parts of this matrix were first prepared for presentation at the International Planning Conference held in Warsaw by the International Group for Studies in Na-

**Table 1.** Suggestive Main Objectives and Curriculum of Courses for Improvement of Leadership in Development Countries (With Reference to Main Relevant Teaching Methods)

| Types of Activities | Levels of Capacities and Qualifications | | | |
|---|---|---|---|---|
| | (a) Intellectual Capacities | (b) Explicit Knowledge | (c) Tacit Knowledge and Patterns of Behavior | (d) Personality and Values |
| (1) Policymaking and Decisionmaking | (1a) Abstract thinking; conceptualization; detachment from wishful thinking; data processing and evaluating capacities; analysis of complex situations; capacities for realistic appraisal of emotional situations. (Main teaching methods: C, D, E, F, J.) | (1b) Decision-theory, planning studies; policy-science; economics; intelligence studies; knowledge of involved society. (Main teaching methods: A, B, D, E, I.) | (1c) Intuition; feeling for the possible; tacit knowledge of involved society; capacity for teamwork. (Main teaching methods: C, F, G, H, I.) | (1d) Creativity; high energy level; high tolerance of ambiguity; high propensity to change and learning capabilities; "realistic idealism"; moral integrity; patience; self-confidence. (Main teaching methods: G, H, I.) |
| (2) Support-Recruitment, Coalition-Building and Conflict-Treatment | (2a) As in (1a). | (2b) Social sciences and especially development studies, political science, psychology; coalition theory and conflict studies; knowledge of power structure of involved society. (Main teaching methods: A, B, D, E, F, G, I.) | (2c) As in (1c) *plus:* Rhetoric abilities; tactical skills; capacity to know and understand others. (Main teaching methods: as in (1c) *plus* K.) | (2d) As in (1d) *plus:* Charisma; trust-evoking; tolerance for others. (Main teaching methods: as in (1d).) |
| (3) Interpersonal Relations | (3a) As in (1a). | (3b) Psychology; organization theory, group dynamics. (Main teaching methods: A, B, C, D, E, I.) | (3c) Empathy; "human relations" skills; capacity to "know others." (Main teaching methods: G, H, I.) | (3d) Charisma or "pleasant personality." (Main teaching methods: F, G, H, I.) |
| (4) Management of Organizations and Other Systems | (4a) As in (1a). | (4b) Administrative sciences; systems theories. (Main teaching methods: A, B, C, D, E, I.) | (4c) As in (3c) *plus:* Group-dynamic skills. (Main teaching methods: as in (3c) *plus* F.) | (4d) As in (2d). |

Key to Teaching Methods (including training and personality-development methods):

A = Lectures
B = Guided Reading
C = Case Studies
D = Individual and Group Reports
E = Projects
F = Political Gaming
G = Role Playing
H = T-Groups and Sensitivity Training
I = Individual Counselling and Tutoring
J = Special Subjects (e.g. mathematics, logics)
K = Special Exercises (rhetorics)

3. *Teaching methods and material.* Teaching methods and teaching material must be adjusted to the unique objectives and participants of the courses. Much can be learned from modern courses for government-administration, business-executives, senior military officials, planners, etc. But in the main the teaching methods and teaching material must be specially designed for the course. The lack of academic background by the participants, the need to unlearn a lot and the necessity to influence various levels of capacities and qualifications—these are some of the characteristics which require a special mix of conventional and new teaching methods and teaching material. In addition to variations of more conventional passive and active teaching methods (such as lectures, guided reading, case studies, and individual and group reports), a number of more novel methods must be utilized. These include, for instance, complex projects, political gaming, T-Groups and sensitivity training, and individual counselling. A number of subjects may also have to be taught not as an integral part of the curriculum, but as auxiliary tools (e.g. fast reading) or as a training tool (e.g. mathematics and logics). The relationship of different teaching methods to the various elements of the curriculum are indicated in Table No. 1, in brackets in each cell of the matrix.

4. *Work load and course-culture.* In order at least to move in the direction of the objectives of the course, more is required than specially designed and well-prepared curricula, teaching methods and teaching material. The courses have to achieve a break-through into quite deeply rooted assumptions, opinions, perception-sets and dogmas of hardened politicians, who will initially be on the defensive. This requires an intense and focused impact to be achieved by a "total learning experience." The work-load should be maximal, taxing the participants to the utmost. By mixing different teaching methods, fatigue can and should be controlled. Also, efforts must be made to adjust demands to the individual participants and to minimize negative feed-back resulting from drop-out during the course. But each participant must be worked to the utmost. This requires residential arrangements, with special attention to the families who should accompany the participants for longer courses. (It may be a good idea to arrange some training for the wives of the participants, both to gain their assistance in the intense effort demanded from the latter and to prepare the wives better for their supporting roles for the political

tional Planning in April 1965 and devoted to "The Development of National Planning Personnel," and for presentation at the Seminar on Productivity for Directors of Productivity Institutes from South America, held in Tel Aviv in November 1965.

activities of their husbands.) The course-culture should be one of intense co-operative effort and high intellectual tension, with hard give-and-take between the instructors and the participants and among the participants themselves. Frustrations, periods of self-despair, steep drops in the learning curve—all these are natural parts of such a course which the participant should be helped to handle and which will become an important and much-cherished part of his learning experience.

5. *Faculty.*    The proposed courses require a top faculty, which works for an extended period on the preparation and running of the courses. No fast collection of experts and university teachers brought together for a short period will do. For some subjects guest-lectures can be used, but a permanent, high-quality core-staff is essential. This is indeed the most scarce resource needed for the course, which may prove to be very difficult to get. The necessity to get together a top quality staff, which also enjoys political and academic credibility among prospective participants, constitutes a specific constraint which must be carefully taken into account when the organizational set-ups and locations of the courses are determined.

Beyond these six features, many problems remain to be faced and many details must be filled in. But these are of secondary importance. First, it is necessary to recognize the need for improvement of leadership in development countries as an essential part of realistic and innovating policy for accelerated modernization (and as an illustration of possibilities for designing new development-policies, which are operational, significant and efficient). Then it is necessary to accept in principle the idea to establish courses for politicians from development countries[8] to work out basic principles for these courses and to mobilize the necessary resources. Only at that stage should a more detailed program for action be elaborated by a work-shop, with the participation of experts in relevant disciplines and selected outstanding politicians from development countries.

---

[8] This is not to say that courses and other improvement activities are not needed for politicians in modern countries. But this is a different subject requiring separate treatment. See Yehezkel Dror, *Public Policymaking Reexamined, op. cit.,* Chapter 17.

# 14

## Developing a University Bi-Partisan Political Program

WARREN H. SCHMIDT

What educational services can a state university provide for leaders of the two major political parties? Under what circumstances can a state university cooperate with the two major parties without jeopardizing its non-political status? How can a university initiate the exploration of educational interests which might be held in common by leaders of both political parties?

These questions occupied the attention of some administrators of the University Extension program at the University of California in the late spring of 1959. Plans were already under way for launching a political education program for the general public—dealing with political issues and political processes during the coming presidential election year. Then the question arose, "Is there something which could be done directly with political party leaders and workers?" Since educators and politicians do not generally fraternize too easily and comfortably, considerable thought was given to the desirability of direct work with political parties before action was taken. On the one hand, University Extension officials had a deep conviction that whatever strengthens and enriches political party operation contributes to the effectiveness of our democratic process. On the other hand, many individuals within and without the university warned that dealing with the two parties was fraught with some danger.

Since officials in other tax-supported universities and colleges may have a similar ambivalence, this article is designed to describe the way in which one university—the University of California—undertook a program of education for the two major political parties and established an on-going relationship with them.

---

Warren H. Schmidt, "Developing A University Bi-Partisan Political Program," *The Journal of Social Issues*, XVI (1960), 48–52.

First Step—An Exploratory Conference (Aug. 7–8, 1959);
Testing Readiness

The chairmen of the Democratic and Republican State Central Committees were asked to nominate leaders to discuss a possible educational program with political party leaders and workers. The Dean of University Extension then invited these leaders to a two-day meeting. The conference participants unanimously agreed that to advise on program selection, development and implementation, a Continuing Committee should be established, consisting of five Republicans, five Democrats, and five officers from University Extension. Each party delegation would include the Chairman of the State Central Committee. The Dean of University Extension was to function as chairman of this committee.

Second Step—Initial Meeting of the Joint Continuing Committee
(Oct. 12, 1959); Collaborative Planning

At this initial meeting, the committee reviewed the various suggestions from the conference and decided to give priority to two kinds of programs during the first year of operation: (1) Training Programs for leaders; and (2) Residential Seminars for party leaders. Two kinds of training programs were seen as desirable—training in conference and discussion leadership and training for public speaking. Residential Seminars were proposed for dealing with such topics as "Party Organization," "Election Code," and "The Public Image of Parties and Politicians."

The decision was made to conduct a Residential Seminar on Party Organization as the first activity. In order to make this seminar of practical value to the party leaders, it was agreed that a series of personal interviews would be conducted to determine what kinds of problems were seen as important by leaders occupying different positions within the party organizations. Each State Central Committee Chairman agreed to furnish a list of individuals to be interviewed.

Third Step—Interviews With Party Leaders (Nov., Dec., 1959);
Fact-finding for Program Development

Twenty-one leaders from both parties were interviewed, including National Committeemen and Committeewomen, leaders of the State Central Committees, legislators, county chairmen, professional staff workers, leaders of women's party organizations, leaders of the volunteer party organizations and several other influential leaders.

**Fourth Step—Meeting of Continuing Committee (Jan. 5, 1960);
Completion of Plan**

The committee reviewed plans for the Residential Seminar and the leadership Training Programs. The summary of interviews formed the basis for planning the seminar. The committee also viewed, modified, and accepted proposed plans for two simultaneous leadership training institutes to be held in Northern and Southern California, each to be attended by both Democrats and Republicans. Party leaders accepted responsibility for identifying individuals to be invited to the institutes and the University accepted responsibility for designing and staffing the program. Each participant in the institutes would pay a registration fee to cover meals and conference materials.

**Fifth Step—Residential Seminar on "Party Organization
in California" (Feb. 26–27, 1960)**

This residential conference (Friday evening to Sunday noon) brought together 35 top leaders from the two major political parties. Political scientists from the University of California and out-of-state universities participated as resource people describing patterns of party organization in Colorado, Connecticut, Indiana, and New York, to provide a background for consideration of party organization in California.

Questions raised by the previously-conducted interview study were considered in two bipartisan seminar groups led by University discussion leaders and their findings and recommendations were reported back to the total group. In this final session, the participants urged the University to initiate the study of a number of problem areas, ranging from methods for increasing participation in party activity through problems of clarifying the size and roles of State and County Central Committees. Party leaders offered their full support for such studies. One specific recommendation for a change in the California Election Code was adopted unanimously, and the legislators in the group agreed to bring the matter before the State Legislature.

**Sixth Step—Leadership Training Institutes for Political Party Leaders
(March 12–15, 1960)**

A total of 125 leaders from both the Republican and Democratic parties participated in two week-end leadership training institutes conducted in northern and southern California. These institutes combined lecture presentations by University social scientists and workshop sessions. The topics in-

more easily discuss their inter-party suspicions, concerns, and hopes, enabling them to operate more securely in the bipartisan meetings.

7. *Careful preparation for all meetings.* Considerable University Extension staff time went into the preparation of the exploratory conference, the committee meetings, as well as the seminar and leadership training institutes. Because of this preparation, the objectives of all meetings were clearly defined and plans for achieving these objectives were carefully considered.

8. *Keeping the initiative with university officials.* Although the programs undertaken represented the thinking and planning of the tripartite committee, the initiative for program implementation stayed with the University Extension staff. This arrangement seemed to be very acceptable to leaders of both parties, and gave continuity to the committee activity.

9. *Selection of appropriate topics for initial programs.* The kind of topic chosen for the first programs proved to be most important. The institutes on "leadership" were well-received; the Seminar on Party Organization was judged to be less useful. Upon reflection, it seemed to some members of the Committee that "Party Organization" was too sensitive and guarded an area to explore in a joint conference. The problems of leadership, however, could be discussed without exposing internal party stresses to the view of the opposition.

It is our belief that the experience now opens the way for a continuing full-scale program to bring the resources of both the University and the parties to bear on the basic problems of American politics in a period of rapid change.

# Part Five

## Social Roles for Students
## of Political Leadership

What kinds of contributions might one make to human life on the basis of specialized study of political leadership? This question, or something similar that raises issues about the social relevance of inquiry, will be important to consider as the study of political leadership develops on a local, national, international, and world scale. At least eight types of roles, or principal modes of orientation, each with many possible variations and potential overlaps, are initially discernible.

### Active Political Leadership

Some students of the subject will wish to pursue careers as professional political leaders. Their intent will be to help shape the direction of society by pursuing active political leadership careers. Their study of political leadership should help them in such ways as widening their appreciation of alternative models of behavior, increasing their capacity to empathize with other leaders whose socialization experiences are different from their own, enabling them to view their own career development in the context of similar experiences of others, providing them with frames of reference which they can creatively adapt on the basis of concrete experience, broadening their sense of alternative strategies and tactics of problem-solving behavior so that they can choose most appropriately in a given context, and providing them with a sensitivity for research so that they can initiate studies of leadership that will assist them in solving their own problems. Above all, political leadership education for professional leadership aspirants should seek to achieve a negative goal, not to trap the student in a prison of dogma. For political leaders, ideological incarceration should be self-imposed, if at all. In the course of their careers, potential leaders may anticipate varied experiences such as failure, ascendance to a dominant leadership position, limitation to subordinate leadership roles, crises, and revolutionary action. Throughout the career cycle, not only during student days, continued study of political leadership undoubtedly would contribute to more successful or satisfactory coping with such experiences. The study of political leadership may therefore be considered as a life-long activity of usefulness for professional political leaders themselves.

### Political Leadership Associates

Students of political leadership may also serve as close associates of active political leaders. They may serve as advisers, consultants, secretaries, staff assistants, and intimate supporters (such as campaign workers or as members of a guerrilla band). Working closely with political leaders on a day-to-day basis, they have remarkable opportunities to assist and observe political leadership behavior. It is likely that the more such persons understand the range of considerations involved in political leadership roles, the more likely they will be able to serve in the roles of "constructive followers."

### Political Leadership Observers

Some social roles involve the close observation of political leadership behavior, although incumbents in them may not be direct associates or partisan supporters of the leaders concerned. Examples may be found in journalism, diplomacy, and political research roles in government, political parties, industry, labor, and other socio-economic organizations. Observational roles such as these range from the public observation and reportage of journalism to the clandestine operations of political surveillance. It is true that the processes and results of such observation may contribute to good or evil; but it is also probable that continued study of political leadership would assist incumbents of such roles to attain greater validity, a deeper sense of significance, and a broader sense of relevance in their inquiries. This is based on the assumption that it is better for both public and private recipients of political leadership information to have more accurate rather than less accurate knowledge.

### Political Leadership Negotiators

Many social roles involve interaction and negotiation with political leaders by persons who are not political leaders themselves, nor close associates, nor professional observers of them. Examples include the representations that are often made to political leaders by leaders in agriculture, labor, business, religion, education, science, the arts, and other professions as well as others with needs to elicit political leadership action. All such persons whose interest it is to secure action on their behalf or to respond appropriately to leadership initiatives could benefit from the study of political leadership.

### Ordinary Citizens

The study of political leadership can also enrich the life of the ordinary citizen who is called upon to evaluate, support, and oppose various leaders throughout his citizen life cycle. This is true both within and across cultures as the world of improved transportation and communications moves toward a global community. Doubtlessly all citizens of the world could benefit in more ways than are now predictable from enhanced knowledge of the entire range of political leadership relevancies.

### Teaching

Some students of political leadership could also contribute as teachers in roles ranging from that of general political socialization at primary and secondary levels to highly specialized concentration upon the diffusion of political leadership knowledge at the college, university, and adult education levels, either in the classroom or via mass media of communication. A pioneering challenge is offered by the opportunity to teach oncoming generations and inquiring minds of any age about the nature, potentialities, and limitations of political leadership revealed by research as one aspect of the human condition.

The teacher will have to decide upon the degree of partisanship or neutrality in his presentations and his special responsibilities to students as compared with his general responsibilities as a citizen. He will also have to cope with student and community pressures to shape his discussions of political leaders in ways considered acceptable to them.

### Scholarly Research

Some students of political leadership may wish to pursue careers emphasizing scholarly research on the subject. They may be motivated by considerations ranging from sheer curiosity to desire to help solve political leadership problems. They will have to decide such questions as how to gain acceptance by contemporary leaders, what research problems should be pursued, how to report research results so that the scientific truth is preserved without harm to individuals, how research should be financed, and what limitations, if any, should be placed on the publication of research findings. Researchers also will have to decide whether they will accomplish studies for private sponsors or whether they will do research only of a world public nature in which the results are made available to the scientific community. One of the problems that frankly they may have to face is the problem of possible violations of political leadership confidences by persons working under their direction.

### Scholarly Consultation

Some students of political leadership may serve as consultants to political leaders or to other persons or organizations having interests in dealing with them. An issue here is whether the scholar should make his special knowledge known to private sponsors on a confidential basis (e.g., join a campaign strategy or revolutionary group to support a particular political leader) or should make it available to all persons or groups in the community on a non-partisan basis, either privately or publicly. An alternative possibility is not to engage in community consultation or advice-giving for the purposes of influencing political leadership behavior or aiding others in its study and interpretation beyond the bounds of the academic community (classroom teaching and published research).

As indicated by the diversity of roles and associated problems mentioned above, it will not be an easy task to develop appropriate social roles for students of political leadership—especially the academic ones of teaching, research, and consultation. Diversity will be both inevitable and usually helpful. A world community of scholars specializing in the study of political leadership will have to emerge, assist, and support each other in solving the various problems. In some circumstances there is no accepted role of the objective sociobehavioral scientist; in others where it has arisen, the concept of scholarly detachment is under constant assault. In many circumstances the behavior of political leaders is regarded as a taboo area immune to outside inquiry; in these, the understanding cooperation of political leaders will have to be won. In other situations research on political leadership problems may be possible, but only under controlling political sponsorship which tends sometimes to distort and suppress knowledge. In still other circumstances it may be possible to conduct research relatively independently of direct political controls, but with the danger that research and consultation about results may be biased in directions favorable to the financial sponsors of such research. In many circumstances scholars may be subjected to biasing pressures from governments; military organizations; intelligence agencies; parties; economic, social, and cultural organizations; communications media; students; and other scholarly colleagues. They may expect demands for commitment or disengagement from the ideological right, middle, and left. Politics is a serious human concern and concentrated inquiry into its very heart cannot be expected to be a casual matter.

In the face of such difficulties, hope for continually advancing scientific knowledge about political leadership for the benefit of all mankind lies fundamentally in the integrity of the individual scholars, in the vision of outstanding political leaders of all persuasions, in the wisdom of supportive members of society, and in the strength of the institutional contexts in which they work. Whatever roles now exist or eventually emerge, it is hoped that the role of the non-partisan scholar, seeking scientific knowledge with painstaking deliberate efforts to control ideological biases both within and across cultures, will be an accepted one of fundamental importance. It is not that such a scientist should have no values but that he should be open to the conduct of political leadership research from a variety of different value positions. The initial stimulus to research and the final interpretation of research findings may have a value basis but the conduct of the inquiry and the demonstration of finding should exemplify scientific methods. For the emergence and development of such a role the understanding and support of a world scholarly community and of far-seeing world political leaders at every level will be essential.

The essays included in this final section are intended to elicit discussion about appropriate roles for students of political leadership. One essay is about active political leadership; another is about research; and three others suggest problems confronting scholars in different political settings—the Soviet Union, the Chinese People's Republic, and the United States of America.

The portrait of the political leader given by Stimson Bullitt (Selection 15), an experienced candidate for elective office, is based primarily upon American competitive electoral experience, but his deep sense of history and breadth of intellect gives his portrayal a classical quality that seems to transcend parochial boundaries. It would be a great contribution if the study of political leadership could produce comparable portraits of active political leadership in different political systems (and in sub-cultures of any given society)—non-competitive single party and oligarchical ones as well as different competitive systems. Based upon such inquiries, the similarities and differences of active political leadership roles could be better appreciated and the empirical grounds upon which persons might choose to pursue leadership careers would be strengthened.

In summing up the satisfactions of political leadership, Bullitt describes them as being "the pleasure of working with people, the fascination of work with ideas, the challenge of problems important to all the world, and the satisfaction of fulfilling a central function of world society." The first of these accords well with the spontaneous response by a governor of Pennsylvania when asked by two Princeton undergraduates what he would miss most if he left politics. "People," he replied instantly, "all kinds of people."

The essay by the noted biologist Hans Selye (Selection 16) conveys some of the excitement that pervades scientific research. It is as pertinent to the socio-behavioral sciences as to natural science. In the contemporary age of insistent demands that research be "relevant" to the solution of societal problems, Selye's reminder of the precious nature of freedom of scientific curiosity for its own sake as well as for its unforeseen practical benefits deserves thoughtful consideration. Also important for the development of political leadership research is his portrayal of a small group of basic researchers whose mutual scientific respect transcends parochial prejudices and reaches toward a global scientific community. Selye's discussion of the influence of scientific heroes is reminiscent of the emulation processes characteristic of political leaders themselves. This is perhaps one link to greater understanding among scholars and political leaders, for both are only human.

The essay by F. Burlatskii (Selection 17) constitutes a plea for the establishment of a discipline of political science in the Soviet Union. The definition of the discipline he proposes implies strong concern for the study of political leadership. Burlatskii explains, "The object of this science is to provide answers to basic questions related to the perfection of forms and methods of leadership by society, the precise delineation of its functions, the rights and obligations among all levels of the administrative apparatus, and the problem of the selection and training of cadres." Putting stress on the applied usefulness of scientific political research and urging development of contemporary as well as historical inquiry, Burlatskii attributes the past failure to establish an intellectual community between political leaders and scholars as located in the "commandism" of the former and the irrelevance to immediate problems of the latter. Burlatskii's caveat that political science should not be regarded as coping satisfactorily with problems that should be treated by the social sciences as a whole suggests also that the study of political leadership will not encompass satisfactorily all problems of interest to political science. His conclusion that within the Soviet context "scientific institutions engaged in political science can develop successfully only under conditions where they are closely linked to party and state organs, where they have the necessary information at their disposal, and where they can rely on a broad base of practical workers" illustrates both realistic understanding that leadership research must gain the acceptance of contemporary leaders and the potential limitations of partisan control.

The essay by Chinese scholar Chou Yang (Selection 18), written before the Cultural Revolution, presents a call for the combined commitment of scholarly energies to revolutionary studies and revolutionary action. Chou argues that scholars must embody a proletarian class standpoint, serving the interests of workers and peasants. Facts are to be highly valued. There should be a strong relationship of mutual learning between "professional theoretical workers" and "practical workers" who are united in the creative application of Marxist-Leninist principles to concrete problems as pioneered by the examples of Mao Tse-tung. If these ideal views of the interaction of scholars and active political leaders are carried into action, then we should be able eventually to look to Communist China for profound empirical studies of political leadership behavior with special reference to organizational relationships with workers and peasants, the tasks of revolutionary change, and the effects of Maoist values within the setting of the world's most populous society. The portrait of the Chinese Communist scholarly specialist on political leadership implied by Chou Yang's essay is thus a person who is both "red and expert," a devoted revolutionary who combines both practical political leadership experience and theoretical knowledge. He is a theoretical worker who seeks to transform particular competence into general relevance with the assistance of more experienced political leaders.

In contrast to both the Soviet and Chinese essays, the concluding article by the child psychiatrist Paul L. Adams (Selection 19), written from a pacifist value position, depicts a wide variety of professional orientations to social action that are possible in contemporary American society: six types of uninvolved professors and five types of professional activists (including two kinds of "revolutionists"—the "haters" and the "lovers"). It is unlikely that even these encompass all the possibilities. One type of non-involvement not mentioned that might be considered by students of political leadership is what might be termed "constructive non-involvement"—that is, vigorous efforts to conduct research on political leaders of the radical right, radical left, and moderate middle for the purpose of gaining accurate information about all three, but avoiding partisan commitment to any one of them. Analogously there is an additional form of "constructive activism" that might be considered: positive commitment to the preservation and enhancement of human values that over-arches and seeks to heal the wounds and oversights that result from the collisions of the "reactionists," "issue protestors," and "revolutionists." Perhaps this might best be viewed as a kind of political leadership scholarly Red Cross active on the field of combat and requiring the kind of compassion for which Adams expresses admiration.

As we come to the end of this book it is well to remember that it is really not an end, but a beginning. In order to advance the study of political leadership, successive generations of scholarly students in cooperation with political leaders of all persuasions will have to return repeatedly to basic questions about concepts of political leadership, conceptual frameworks, propositional linkages, theories, research methods, education, and social relevancies. We shall have to be willing to begin anew, to salvage, to reconstruct, to extend, and to perfect. The line of development has not been, and will not be, linear. But hopefully men everywhere will have available more scientific knowledge about political leadership on a global scale than is now available to us.

# 15

## Politics as a Calling

STIMSON BULLITT

To enjoy politics one must enjoy people; it helps if one likes them as well. A politician wants and tries to like people. He must be with them, and a friendly relationship makes it easier for him to satisfy and please. He meets and works with every kind. He is enabled to associate with the best, and compelled by duty and circumstance to spend time with some of the worst. Near the centers of government, which has come to reach us all, he is invited to open almost any door; and the universal franchise makes him practice unrestricted social intercourse. His uncommon relationship to people requires him to develop a singular attitude toward them. He must be sensitive to all aspects of their personalities, including their changing opinions of him, yet be numb to the pain of their rebukes.

A politician should feel at home in both the abstract and the concrete. He needs to think along the boundary between the general propositions of the schoolroom or the cloister and the specific problems of the business office or the shop. To get along in politics a man's inclinations should be balanced between people and ideas. A man too concerned with people may lack judgment in his decisions of public policy, and campaign for office as though he were in a popularity contest. One who puts too much emphasis on issues tends to forget his fellow citizens, each of them, whose welfare is the object of his work. Free from the facts of human needs, here and now, he risks becoming dogmatic. His grand designs may so enchant him that he forces others to accommodate themselves to the symmetrical perfection of his program. Countries like China, France, and Russia in their periods of revolution tend to be afflicted by those hard men who try to impose a plat-

Stimson Bullitt, *To Be a Politician* (Garden City, N.Y.: Doubleday & Company, Inc., 1961), 3–18. Copyright © 1959, 1961 by Stimson C. Bullitt. Reprinted by permission of Doubleday & Company, Inc.

form as an iron frame, while America suffers from the men who would rather be loved.

It is impossible to master or even learn a great deal about all the subjects to be tackled—war, peace, education, money, labor, preservation of national monuments, disposition of useless papers . . . It would take a universal genius to be expert in all. An able politician is neither an amateur nor a specialist. He is a general practitioner.

There is less difference now between a politician's work and the work of those who manage society in other fields. In antiquity, the skills and functions of the military, business, and government were united in one man, as in some Roman leaders who in one career would manage farms, administer a province, negotiate a treaty, judge disputes, collect rents, debate laws, and march on Antioch at a legion's head. Then for a long time these skills and functions were apart. The Confederacy's performance was impaired by combining in Jefferson Davis both military and political strategy. Conversely, their separation benefited the Union, whose generals either admitted or demonstrated their unfitness for politics. Now these functions are merging again. The change tends to be more drastic for the officer and executive than for the politician, who has long been attending to a little of everything. This extension of his range has made a politician's knowledge even broader and more shallow. Having children and trying to answer their questions is a good preparation for a politician, who must deal with many things he does not understand.

In the political world the grasp of abstract ideas is better than it is in business, but not so good as in the university. Among politicians the comprehension of specific problems is also intermediate, not so good as it is among businessmen but better than it is among academics. Writing of politicians, Macaulay declared: "The perfect lawgiver is a just temper between the mere man of theory, who can see nothing but general principles, and the mere man of business, who can see nothing but particular circumstances." Although the average politician's mentality is below that in some other professions, in politics one can acquire a better comprehension of the forest, together with its trees, than in any other field.

An American politician does a job and plays a part. He serves as both a craftsman and a symbol. The higher public offices bear more moral and emotional color in the public eye than other occupations, except perhaps that of the clergy.

A superior politician combines two contrasting qualities: In the details of his work he is flexible, yet the outlines of his personality are definite. The flexibility is necessary to do justice under the democratic process, and also to permit him to survive in politics. His nature must be clearly enough defined for him to know who he is, so that his policies may be guided by some rational framework of principles as well as for his satisfaction with himself.

Few great public men have differed from this pattern, and in none of them was it reversed—none was without direction or identity yet stiff in execution of detail. But the proportion of those in politics who have a well-defined character is exaggerated in the public mind, because a visible sign is often mistaken for proof of an inward grace. Evidence only, and often overrated, is a forelock, a brown derby, red suspenders, or an underslung pipe.

A constituent's patriotic idealism or self-esteem is shown by his disappointment at a politician's failure to meet the standards of merit which the constituent thinks deserved by his country, his community, or himself. But from this falling short of an ideal standard, for the citizen to presume his representative's inferiority to politicians of another time or place (whose merits he has heard of or imagined) is to confuse an expectation with a wish. If his clay-footed Senator is one of the Senate's best, he should recognize the depressing fact. To appreciate comparative worth among politicians is to face reality and to give them their due, as did André Gide when the foreigner asked, "Who is France's greatest poet?" and he replied, "Victor Hugo, alas."

Because politicians are regarded as necessary evils, both their conduct and existence are condoned. It is thought that by the necessities of his profession a soldier must kill and a politician lie. Most American citizens are given better government than they realize, and most politicians are better public servants than many people think. The more complete and accurate information which citizens now receive about candidates and their records tends to eliminate the worst knaves and fools from among elected officials. In general, as in other fields, the quality has improved as the profession has grown more competitive, although the magnitude of the problems has increased faster than the average quality of the membership has risen.

One cause of the disparity between popular belief and fact is ignorance of how much a politician is affected by his instinct of workmanship and his desire to be liked, respected, and re-elected. People are confused by their contradictory attitudes toward public leadership: On the one hand there is the notion that most politicians are rascals, based partly on substantial evidence of it in the period following the Civil War; on the other hand is the admiration for institutions of government, compounded of reverence for tradition and pride in the merits of the city, state, or nation as symbolized in its government. It is not generally realized that politicians are steeped in the same patriotic myth that is common to all other citizens who grew up in this country. The mansions and temples of government in state capitals and in Washington encourage upright conduct as well as vanity.

The most dramatic demonstration of the influence on politicians of this patriotic myth is the Presidency. On entering it, a man will raise the level of his performance sharply, unless he does not clearly understand what is expected of him. Not only is he inspired to surpass himself but also he is free from concern about self-preservation and, on the whole, from temptation to promote immediate selfish aims. This is by reason of the sign which could be displayed above the White House door: "Banish hope of further advancement (except in the history books) ye who enter here."

To enter politics at the bottom is easy and good sense. Competition is mild, and one may practice in an arena where unseasoned judgment is not fatal. Among professionals, however, the game is played for keeps. Survival depends on quick resourcefulness and judgment which come partly from experience. A few people in public life but not in politics can, like Mrs. Roosevelt, make up for lack of cunning by common sense and purity of heart. The danger line is crossed when a man starts to appear in the papers. From then on he will be saddled with his record and penalized for his unpopular companions or unfortunate remarks. On the Congressional level the players are skilled, most of them seasoned by years in minor leagues. The only way to learn the system well is to see its whole range. Those who enter politics late in life, and start in high office, are led by ignorance into errors which are avoided by those who realize the nature and significance of the work done by people down the line.

The most important reason for starting as a part-time apprentice is that one may at the same time learn politics and another trade. The risk is slight that one will stay an amateur so long that he becomes a dabbler. The choice does not matter much, but a private calling is essential to the politician who is brave and wishes to be free. Like Cincinnatus, he should have a plow standing ready for him in a field at home. This goes for everyone, despite the independence of his means. A strong-willed politician's flesh is too weak not to be chilled by the prospect of a long drop. Without a happy alternative, an acrobat's net, he cannot afford the independent judgment which he must have to do his duty. Through the window he sees the old men sitting on the courthouse lawn; unless he can afford to lose he may think, "There . . . go I," and keep a wetted finger in the air. Such service to constituents is less than they deserve, although they may be given what some of them demand. And on those terms politics is not worth its price. The Book of Common Prayer addresses God, "whose service is perfect freedom." But base obedience to others' whims dissolves a man's identity by his immersion in the mass.

To succeed in American politics, one must win the acceptance of many people and the approval of some, but compared to other fields the approval needs to be more widespread and need not be as strong. As always, success depends both on circumstances of background and situation, and on personal qualities. But the balance has shifted to favor personal qualities. Accidents of prejudice or birth are smaller factors now, except for a Negro or a Roosevelt. A distinguished origin, such as a Mayflower ancestor or a log cabin, is worth less now than it was before, while qualities of ability and personality and experience common to the voters are worth more. Scandal among one's kin is not much of a handicap except for a candidate for local office in a small town.

Some people have substantial advantages available to them in the form of status, connections, or inherited wealth, factors not a part of their own personality or the result of their own efforts. In many situations, if one's gifts of privilege are used to further personal aims, one's talents atrophy because they are not whetted on other people's skills. On the other hand, if a person's outward gifts are used either not at all or only toward ends unconnected with his career, he misses the chance to put himself closer to a spot where his inner gifts will be most effective. In fact, the time spent in diversions to collateral ends is a handicap in competition with those who focus on a single goal. A person who uses money for play, status for security, and connections for social pleasure, tends to lose out to one who has none of these but puts all his time on his career's advance.

And where is the line to be drawn? For the son of a general or the child of a successful doctor or lawyer who follows the same profession it seems the correct course to avail himself of all such outside advantages. A man who stays within the shelter of his family business is not likely to develop unless he runs the firm, rather than working for it, and unless it must compete, instead of being just a collection of investments. In politics it is wise to make full use of those advantages which are outside one's self and which mankind has chosen to applaud so much less than those gifts which happen, equally by chance, to be located within us. Politics is so competitive that there is no risk that a person's powers will decay if he employs his outward gifts to help him toward success.

Among politicians one finds cowardice, dishonesty, and pride, but little sloth, lust, cruelty, or greed. Contrary to popular fiction, Americans eminent in the management of affairs make poor symbols of evil. We refuse to elevate Caligulas and Borgias, who "drink iniquity like water." Although some politicians have colorful personalities, few successful ones have lurid faults.

In politics, voluptuaries are even more uncommon than ascetics. Ambition makes most successful politicians impose on themselves disciplined habits of restraint from vicious pleasures. They have little time for self-indulgence. Even when they have a moment with nothing to do but degrade themselves, they generally can resist temptation because they prefer success to pleasure. To obtain the secrecy necessary for vice is often more inconvenient for them than for obscure men. However, some high-ranking politicians are promiscuous with women. After long neglect, their wives tend to cool toward them. They are away from home much of the time and often drink enough to forget some of their duties when an opportunity comes to hand. Because they are celebrated figures the flattery shown by their favor is a substitute for time-consuming preliminary pursuit. Some female campaign workers combine frustration with hero worship. But the main cause, these men's driving egos, overshadows the supplemental causes. They take women not for pleasure but as one of the signs of success, like exclusive club memberships and addressing big shots by their first names. Their practice proves the narrowness rather than the breadth of their interests. Denied the ancient privilege of pushing underlings around and the chance to take revenge on peers, these men would feel they were missing out if they did not indulge in the surviving prerogatives of rank which remind them of their success.

Some people mistakenly think politics endurable only for a puritan who likes to show off. They see the politician as a person exposed to the sight of all and held to the level of rectitude of a schoolteacher in a small town or a man of the cloth, while subject to derisive criticism which is even harder to take than the insulting condescension accorded teachers and parsons. But in fact the public insistence on observance of domestic moral rules is not strict. Neither divorce nor the frequent commission of adultery wins a politician any votes, but neither one is a crippling handicap any longer, even for the highest positions, unless the circumstances are openly scandalous. In such matters, most voters condemn a politician not for private immorality but for lowering the dignity of his office.

The speech of politicians tends to be as drab as their sins. As in politics, few men successful in the management of affairs in private life have clear-cut individuality, and in each field their character type tends to be uniform. A major reason which does not apply to politicians is the increase in specialization. A man bent on success would fall behind in his race if he were to spend time learning things in many fields. He could not acquire more than a superficial knowledge of each. Of course, it is a drawback if one's knowledge and skill are narrower than the limits of the job, and the limits do widen at each higher level. If in competition in a narrow field a man can achieve enough superiority to rise to the broader levels, then he can effectively employ what broader outlook and knowledge he may have but did not use. Yet even up there most of the world's knowledge is still outside.

Many of these able Americans in private life are dull in speech because their attention tends to be kept within the immediate limits of their work. Politics makes dull men but for a different cause. Burke said that the law sharpened a man's mind by making it narrow. Politicians' minds are rarely narrow but often flat. Most are full of fascinating experience. But a politician is inhibited by the hazards of his profession. Seldom are his comments on the world amusing or clear-cut. Distrustful even of an audience of friends because he knows that every sentence from his mouth may be taken some day by itself and used to harm him, he is bound to the formula for dullness: accuracy and completeness about details and vagueness about general ideas. His talk of facts is constricted to banality by his need to be correct. For the sale of stocks and bonds it is almost impossible to draft a prospectus in language which at the same time will be eloquent yet satisfy the SEC. Ogden Nash's poem contrasting accuracy and wit contains the line, "If it's right, it's trite." Yet when a politician gives his own opinions he shuns exactitude. His words have rounded edges for he knows he may be understood. Clarity is perilous unless transfigured by enchantment, a blend given only to those who speak with the melodic line of a Mozart. And even they dare not sing out for fear some unresolved chord will be plucked from the score and used against them. An ex-politician no longer fears to fascinate but often is too old to learn.

For men who manage affairs in private life and for politicians as well, the daily life of incessant work toward a single goal tends to be the result of an egocentric nature and the cause of a dull one. On their way upward in a hurry, these men have no time for reflection or idle curiosity. Although some of their faculties are highly developed, they tend to be indistinct in personality. An important cause is the intensity of competition, partly due in turn to the horizontal and vertical extensions of opportunity—to choose one's vocation and to rise in it. Christopher Fry has Moses say, "The golden bear Success hugs a man close to its heart, and breaks his bones." Except for a few whose remarkable qualities enable them to retain their identities, politicians lose their sharp edges on the way to the summit, a table top covered with ivory billiard balls. Thomas Mann wrote: "In an age that affords no satisfying answer to the eternal question of 'Why?' 'To what end?' a man who is capable of achievement over and above the average and expected modicum must be equipped either with a moral remoteness and single-mindedness which is rare indeed and of heroic mould, or else with an exceptionally robust vitality."

A man who wishes to excel as a lawyer should forswear politics. As in any other competitive field, an almost exclusive attention is essential both to pre-eminence and to first-rate performance. But for one to be competent in his practice, political activity is compatible, even congenial, with law. To look at this another way, if politics is his main interest, law is a good home base. Although this factor is overrated, a legal background is a help in the performance of a politician's job, because the work experience of a lawyer, even a specialist, covers such a wide variety of facts in his community.

  In a way, one is better prepared for politics by a background in business than by a background in law because business and political decisions both deal with possible future events, while arguments before a court look mainly to the past. (There are partial exceptions: to law, a request for an injunction; to politics, a campaign.) Also, in appeal to voters, a background in small business probably ranks above one in law, which is a less popular profession in this century than it was in the last. However, although in some ways the practice of business seems to be a good preparation for politics, experience has shown that business life does not produce superior politicians. The deficiency of business in its preparation for politics seems to be its concreteness and lack of necessity to consider abstractions, even though it deals with intangibles such as money and price.

The practice of law is a castle which a man can leave for a venture in politics. When the fortunes of war or his own taste require, he can return to it more easily than to most other lines of work. "During my various excursions into public life," Henry Stimson once declared, "I always felt that I remained a lawyer with a law firm waiting as a home behind me, to which I could return on the completion of my public task and where I could always find awaiting me congenial friends and collaborators in the law."

And law is a worthy and satisfying alternative to politics. A man in public life can afford to take a more upright course if he is aware that his constituents lack the power to banish him to anything worse than the conditions of a lawyer's life.

To use politics as a means to increase one's law practice is not very effective, although a fairly innocent motive. It makes a man well known but not in his capacity as a lawyer. If his political activity makes his practice flourish, he finds that he has ceased to practice law; he is retained not for his skill with the lawyer's tools of analysis, debate, and scholarship, but either for his "connections," whom he tries to persuade in matters where the official decision is to be made by standards which are mainly subjective, or for his knowledge of the maze through which he guides his masters. He is a salesman or a seeing eye. The only resemblance which his work bears to that of a lawyer is the title under his name on the office door.

A businessman rarely gets his money's worth from "influence" peddlers, who foster his delusion that they know the passwords. Most people have as much success if they approach an official without an intercessor's help. To get an audience with a politician, no matter how august, you do not need to be his friend. High public officials are easier to approach than other busy men. It is no handicap that your closest contact with important politicians may be no more than a handshake with Kefauver or a signed picture from Ike.

Some lobbyists are paid a lot because they know important men and are thought to have their ear, but a lobbyist's power is less in those he knows than in those he represents. Few are like the Pope in having power without any armored divisions. The effective ones are those who marshal the things which influence politicians; vocal constituents, campaign contributors, and persuasive information about the matter to be decided. Without this leverage behind him, a lobbyist coaxes and appeals to old acquaintanceship in vain. He is known to be an agent for pay. A politician may yield to evidence, logic, temptation, or pressure, but he will not do much wrong to help the money-making of a friend.

The devices used to influence political decisions are spread across a moral spectrum. At one end are bribes and blackmail; dispassionate argument and information are at the other. As persons, the types range from criminals to upright citizens who exercise their right of petition to improve their government or to protect another right. The steps between are neither high-principled effort nor statutory crime. They include threats, promises, eloquence, entertainment, telegram avalanches, desk-pounding delegations and investment tips. Whether using them is a breach of civic duty or whether yielding to them is abuse of public trust depends on the degree of three things: the irrationality and force of the methods; their use by other contending parties so as to compel their adoption by all in order for each to hold his own; and the existence of an objective standard by which the choice can be made in the public interest so that reasonable men can agree on a single course.

A government official who is hired by another person has been bribed to use his power against the public interest. If his power is real even though his position is private in form, like a party chairman, a different law applies, but the morals are the same. If, like Senator Bricker, his excuse for his retainers from a railroad is his sincere belief in railroads' right to preference in public policy, even if he is telling the truth he still foregoes the right to change his mind. On the other hand, he cheats his customers if, like Lord Chancellor Francis Bacon, he takes money and then does the right thing or, if the matter is one of opinion, follows his own best judgment.

To enter politics costs a person little in his vocational progress. The return is the rub. The likelihood that they cannot recover their former private stations deters many good men from a whirl at politics. On returning, a person tends to be set back further in his private career than if his time away from it had been spent in some neutral occupation such as the armed forces, although not as far as if he had been in jail.

He may have to enter some new line of work. Doors are slammed shut behind one who undertakes elective public service. It is feared that a teacher might corrupt the youth with evil mysteries which have been revealed to him. A man employed in business loses caste but usually is allowed to return so long as he has not opposed his employer's interests or contradicted his beliefs. A lawyer always can resume his practice, but he, too, is set back. Some people assume that he lacks judgment, or that his practice was so poor he ran for office in order to better himself. Others fear to entrust their substantial affairs to a man who may be orating on a platform instead of tending to business. In the time spent away from practice he falls behind his colleagues in attainment of learning and skill. Perhaps lawyers suffer less blame than others for entering politics because some people do not expect any more of them.

The prospect of the stony ground on which a politician tends to fall when he returns to private life keeps some inferior men in politics at the same time that it keeps good men out. Although it is well for the roles of citizen and politician to differ in texture and color so that each man may better know who he is, the transition between should not be hard. Except by change in public attitude there does not seem to be a way to lower the wall that impedes the healthy tidal flow between politics and private life. For three reasons a smaller sacrifice should be exacted from a man when he comes back from politics. Politicians more easily can be righteous if the cost of defeat is lower; they more easily can be wise if they are sometimes out of politics; and good men are encouraged to enter politics if the price to them on departure from it is not so high. (A politician should be able to say to himself what Burke wrote to his constituents, declining their offer to renominate him to Parliament in 1780: "By being returned into the mass of private citizens, my burthens are lessened; my satisfactions are not destroyed. There are duties to be performed, and there are comforts to be enjoyed in obscurity, for which I am not without a disposition and relish.")

A permanent career service in elective office, implied in the proposals for special training of prospective politicians, is impossible under our electoral system. It is also undesirable, as shown by the examples of England and, even more, of France. Not all the arguments for a permanent career apply as well to politics as to other work. After a time the public tires of a person who no longer has anything new to tell or give them. Perhaps this is right and not to be regretted. Since a man's effectiveness as a teacher and guide depends partly on his personality and approach to life, his power to contribute may be reduced after he has performed before the same audience for long. A politician's assets include outlook and character, as well as training and experience. Few men retain enough perspective without recurrent periods in private life. During the height of his career as chief of Israel, Ben Gurion left office to this end for a year on a farm. Theodosius did the same, to save skin rather than soul, until he was called to lead and rule the Roman Empire. Tiberius, more from prudence, ambition and taste, secluded himself for seven years before he reached the top.

For the purpose of this [essay] it will be enough to define freedom as the widest possible range of choice for each person through each moment of time. A more penetrating definition would add nothing here. As Fats Waller said to the young lady who asked him to define swing music, "If you gotta ask, you ain't got it."

A politician may try to make a free society as either a liberal or a conservative, whose doctrines are opposite sides of the same coin, like those of Jefferson and Hamilton. Without liberty, an orderly society can be stagnant and unanimous but not stable or harmonious. As an end in itself, order is futile and security ignoble, although both are indispensable conditions to political liberty which, in turn, is an essential means to a society of free men. It should not be forgotten that this, too, is not a final end, but it does no harm for politicians to treat it as one. Liberals and conservatives differ in emphasis only. They stand together against those who prefer the swerving road between tyranny and chaos. One's choice, liberal or conservative, depends on the shape of one's outlook and the needs of the time. As the latter may change, so, like Halifax, may a politician shift his own position if the liberal and conservative outlooks are blended in him. It is harder to do this where party boundaries are mainly ideological, so that a shift means a change of party, than it is in the United States, where at any given moment each party contains among its members almost every currently held political belief.

What are the rewards of this profession? It gives the pleasure of dealing with people, the fascination of work with ideas, the challenge of problems important to all the world, and the satisfaction of fulfilling a central function of human society. At a time and place more harsh than here today, Achad Haam declared:

> I live for the perpetuation and happiness of the community of which I am a member; I die to make room for new individuals who will mold the community afresh and not allow it to stagnate and remain forever in one position. When the individual thus values the community as his own life and strives after its happiness as though it were his individual well-being, he finds satisfaction and no longer feels so keenly the bitterness of his individual existence, because he sees the end for which he lives and suffers.

A politician of many years tends to find private life unsatisfying. Even after circumstances isolate him, his ties to politics remain intact. Few can retire and, like Diocletian or Garner, find their gardens more diverting. Politics holds the attention of most veterans to the end. Not until six months before Andrew Jackson died at seventy-eight did he feel that he could write a friend, "I can now say in truth like Simeon of old, 'Now let thy servant depart in peace' "—and even then he was rejoicing at the election of Polk.

# 16

## Why Should You Do Research?

HANS SELYE

It is not easy to explain why people want to do research, and not everybody has the same motivation. "Researchers" will work for money, power, social position, but there are more efficacious ways of getting all these rewards. True scientists are rarely motivated by them.

Nowadays, scientific accomplishments give you a great deal of recognition, and scientists need an occasional approving pat on the back just as much as anyone else—although, for some reason they are very reluctant to admit it.

Of course, it is not the decibels of applause that count, but what you are applauded for and by whom. Few scientists seek anonymity and many put up bitter fights to defend their priorities; but they want to be recognized by competent colleagues—and for a very special kind of accomplishment. They want the kind of acknowledgment that confirms them in their belief that they have really understood some hidden laws of Nature. They want to be able to say with the divine in Shakespeare's *Antony and Cleopatra:* "In Nature's infinite Book of Secrecy a little I can read." And many of them, especially the physicians, derive their greatest satisfaction from having relieved human suffering through this understanding. Of course, a lawyer may avert suffering by a clever defense of his client; a politician can do this on an even larger scale by helping to enact a law, and a general can save thousands of lives by a strategic move. But all these people protect man against man, often at the expense of other men. The gain is always temporary and limited to certain people. A secret of Nature, once revealed, permanently enriches humanity as a whole.

Hans Selye, *From Dream to Discovery; On Being a Scientist* (New York: McGraw-Hill Book Company, 1964). Chapter 1, 5–18. Copyright © 1964 by Hans Selye. Used with permission of McGraw-Hill Book Company and the author.

Yet, neither the glory science can bring nor its potential usefulness are its only charms—certainly not its usefulness as most people understand it. The principal "use" of basic research, like that of a rose, a song, or a beautiful landscape is that it gives us pleasure. Every scientific discovery reveals new harmonies in the lawfulness of Nature for our passive enjoyment. But research is not a mere "spectator sport," the scientist actively participates in the unveiling of the enjoyable, and this type of activity is as close as the human mind can come to the process of creation.

Of course, if you have not yet known this feeling, my description of it will not be very meaningful; if you have, it will not be very necessary. It has been said about the pleasure of a kiss that those who have never experienced it will not gain much by a verbal description, while those who have will hardly need it. But the instinctive anticipation of pleasure is there before the kiss, before the discovery, and all those who eventually became scientists must have felt it vaguely before, or else they would not have thought of making research their career.

If you are a young physician interested in science, the best my remarks can do is to help you analyze your own feelings. I thought that such an analysis might in itself be useful now, when you have to make that most important decision of your career: the choice between basic research and the practice of medicine. You may be a physician by temperament, and, if you decide for practice, your choice is not necessarily guided merely by material considerations; all true physicians enjoy direct contact with the patient. If you decide for basic research, you will never see the grateful eyes of a mother whose child you have saved; you will never be able to say that, unless you had been there, this man would have died. But if you are successful in the impersonal solitude of your laboratory, you will have the satisfaction of knowing that, had you not unveiled it, no practitioner could have applied the law of Nature that you found for the benefit of his patient.

To a young beginner, my remarks cannot have the same meaning as they have for me, but this is the way I can best explain why I am doing research. And if you were born to be an investigator, you will understand.

Yet scientists have very diverse incentives for doing research. We must now consider these in detail, for no advice I could give in these Notes is more important than to examine your motivation very frankly and determine whether this is really what you want to do. Misfits in science are pathetic creatures, and many are the maladjusted who drifted into research careers by mere accident.

Some of the incentives for scientific work are accepted by society as praiseworthy; others are frowned upon as disgusting. Let me not judge them on this basis, but merely say that, as far as I can see—whether they seem beautiful or ugly to you—the following have the necessary force to make an otherwise qualified man succeed and be happy in a career of basic research:

*Detached love of Nature and truth.*
*Admiration for the beauty of lawfulness.*
*Simple curiosity.*
*The desire to be useful.*
*The need for approval.*
*The glory of success.*
And, last but not least: *The fear of boredom.*

## DETACHED LOVE OF NATURE AND TRUTH

"Avoid, as you would the plague, a man of God who is also a man of business."–St. Jerome

"It is preoccupation with possession, more than anything else, that prevents men from living freely and nobly."–Bertrand Russell

"And then, despite their faults and vices, scientists have more or less the same kind of soul. They all profess the cult of truth in itself. For them science is a religion."–Charles Richet

"Probably, what characterizes all scientists, whatever they may be, archivists, mathematicians, chemists, astronomists, physicists, is that they do not seek to reach a practical conclusion by their work."–Charles Richet

It may seem odd that people should work so hard to unravel the truths of Nature without any practical aim in sight. But what is practical? As Benjamin Franklin said: "What is the use of a newborn baby?" Not everything important to us is practical in the accepted sense of the word. The recognized values of success—money, power, ever shorter working hours—are but the means to buy happiness, and often they bring only a very shabby form of it at that. The baby is not a poential token or currency with which to buy something else that makes us happy; the baby, itself, makes us happy. The generally accepted tokens of practical value are all only means to happiness. Why not skip the intermediates and reach out directly for the end? Pure art —a great painting, a piece of music—is useful since it lifts us beyond the preoccupations of everyday life; it brings us peace, serenity and happiness. Basic research, the study of natural laws, is often undertaken for the same reasons.

Certain things are good for something; others are good in themselves; still others are both good for something and good in themselves. Money is useful only because we can buy something with it; it has no value as such. The pleasure of listening to a great symphony or of enjoying an excellent cigar is good in itself, but we can buy nothing in exchange for it. On the other hand, most things that are good in themselves are also good for something: it is enjoyable to eat a good meal; in addition, we derive useful calories from it. Nature has cunningly spiced most things that are useful to its purpose with subjective feelings that in themselves are agreeable. This is true not only of nutrition and reproduction, but also of understanding. Discovery through basic research is enjoyable, irrespective of its possible practical applications. But sooner or later the knowledge thus acquired does become useful in that it increases our power over Nature.

It is remarkable that good things so often also act as tokens with which we can buy other good things that the distinction between means and aims may become difficult. The miser likes to fondle his gold—and, curiously, some (few) scientists actually enjoy writing their papers—because the mere handling of the means for credit evokes the pleasant feeling of its aim. These are not pretty thoughts, I am afraid, but to the scientist, even the ugliest truth is more beautiful than the loveliest pretense.

## THE BEAUTY OF LAWFULNESS

"The fairest thing we can experience is the mysterious. It is the fundamental emotion which stands at the cradle of true art and true science. He who knows it not and can no longer wonder, no longer feel amazement, is as good as dead, a snuffed-out candle."–Albert Einstein

"I do not know what I may appear to the world; but to myself I seem to have been only like a boy playing on the seashore, and diverting myself in now and then finding a smoother pebble or a prettier shell than ordinary, whilst the great ocean of truth lay all undiscovered before me."–Sir Isaac Newton

It is difficult to explain the beauty of the transition from mystery to lawfulness. The collector of stamps, matchboxes or butterflies, the solver of crossword puzzles, enjoys the feeling of having completed an orderly series, of having found the key according to which a large number of apparently dissimilar items can be arranged in a logical fashion. The more diverse, the more peculiar and puzzling the items are, the more satisfactory it is to detect the laws that permit us to put them into a manageable, harmonious arrangement that brings their manifold features closer to understanding.

As children we all have what it takes to enjoy wonderful and mysterious things. When a child points out something unusual which he has never seen before—a colorful butterfly, an elephant, or a sea shell—just watch his eyes as he cries out with enthusiasm, "Look, Daddy!" and you will know what I mean.

No sensitive person can look at the sky on a cloudless night without asking himself where the stars come from, where they go, and what keeps the universe in order. We ask the same kind of questions when we look at the self-perpetuating, eternal universe within the human body, or even just at that pair of sensitive and searching human eyes which constantly strives to bridge the gap between these two universes.

The capacity to contemplate the harmonious elegance of Nature, at least with some degree of understanding, is one of the most satisfactory experiences of which man is capable. This is a noble and gratifying aim in itself, quite apart from any material advantages it may offer. But actually it does help us in our everyday life, very much in the same way as a deep religious faith or a well-balanced philosophic outlook helps us. Looking at something infinitely greater than our conscious selves makes all our daily troubles appear to shrink by comparison. There is an equanimity and a peace of mind which can be achieved only through contact with the sublime.

But as time goes by, most of us—not all—lose this gift of pure enjoyment. When we have seen most of the things that are encountered in everyday life, custom begins to stale variety. The petty routine of daily problems also tends to blunt our sensitivity to the detached enjoyment of greatness and wonder. It is a pity that nowadays most people are so bent on being practical, on getting ahead in life, that they no longer find time to make sure where they really want to go. After a while, the prosperous businessman, the efficient administrator, begins to get that lost feeling of aimlessly drifting from day to day—toward retirement and death.

So many people work hard and intelligently for some immediate objective which promises leisure to enjoy life tomorrow; but tomorrow never becomes today. There is always another objective which promises even more leisure in exchange for just a little more work. That is why so few people in the usual walks of life retain that wonderful gift which they all possessed as children: the ability to really enjoy themselves. But it hurts to be conscious of this defect, so adults dope themselves with more work (or alcohol) to divert attention from their loss. The inspired painter, poet, composer, astronomer, or biologist never grows up in this respect; he does not lose the abstract treasures of his naïve innocence, no matter how poor or how old he may be. He retains the childlike ability to enjoy the impractical. And pleasures are always impractical; they can lead us to no reward. They are the reward. .

The really acquisitive person is so busy reinvesting that he never learns how to cash in. "Realistic people" who pursue "practical aims" are rarely as realistic and practical, in the long run of life, as the dreamers who pursue only their dreams. True scientists—even when they become very old—retain a certain romanticism, a dreamy, imaginative habit of mind; they continue to dwell on the adventurous, the picturesque, the unusual; they never cease to be thrilled by the heroic grandeur and infallible consistency of the laws that govern the harmony of Nature in and around man.

## CURIOSITY

"Every man ought to be inquisitive through every hour of his great adventure down to the day when he shall no longer cast a shadow in the sun. For if he dies without a question in his heart, what excuse is there for his continuance?"–Frank Moore Colby

There is a certain opprobrium attached to inquisitiveness but only because people tend to confuse curiosity and nosiness. The curious wants to know that which is of concern to him; the nosy inquires into the personal concerns of others. The true scientist thrives on curiosity; he could not live without it. Whenever an investigator loses this driving force—because his efforts have been too often frustrated, or because he has become complacently satisfied by "practical achievements"—he retires from science and takes refuge in self-commiseration or the smug enjoyment of his prosperity. But we need not say much about scientific curiosity in particular, for it is superimposed upon all the other motives.

## THE DESIRE TO BE USEFUL

"They know that perhaps because of them, some light will appear on the crests of the dark ocean in which humanity struggles frantically. And all scientists, all without exception, have this magnificent hope to sustain them in their hard labors, that they will be useful to their human brothers."–Charles Richet

"Young man, I say, If you want to discover a new truth, do not worry about its practical applications. Don't ask yourself how medicine, commerce or industry will profit by it; for, if you do, you will find nothing. You want to solve the problem that you consider important: embark on its solution without worrying about the consequences. Approach the question from its simplest side. Do not let the injunctions of journalists, hygienists, engineers, pharmacists, or physicians stop you. Let them talk. Go straight at your problem by the shortest route. Leave to the practitioners the cumbersome task of conclusions and industrial complications. *Veritas lucet ipsa per se.* Truth is self-sufficient." . . . "Where would we be if Galvani, instead of touching the legs of his frogs with iron and copper, had wanted to construct a telephone? Soubeiran, in discovering trichlorinated methane, which he called chloroform, did not at all try to find an anesthetic, no more than Röntgen had looked for ways to facilitate surgical operations."–Charles Richet

"The first step, the fashioning of a world picture from life, is a task of pure science. The second step, the utilization of the scientific world picture for practical purposes, is the task of technology. The first task is just as important as the other and, since each of them claims the whole man, the individual investigator, if he really wants to promote his work, must concentrate all his strength on a single point and leave aside meanwhile the thought about other implications and interests. Therefore, let us not scold the scientist too much because of his unworldliness and his lack of participation in the important problems of public life. Without such a one-sided attitude, Heinrich Hertz would not have discovered the wireless waves, nor Robert Koch the tubercle bacillus."–Max Planck

A former United States Secretary of Defense, Charles E. Wilson, said that basic research is "what you do when you don't know what you are doing." I cannot quite agree with this definition.

More commonly, basic research is thought of as the opposite of "practical" research, the kind that can be immediately applied. This suggests a disassociation from man's everyday problems. The development of weapons, television sets, or vaccines, is obviously practical. Studies of the inner temperature of distant stars, of the habits of infinitely small living beings, of the laws governing the inheritable coloration of pea blossoms, all seemed eminently impractical—at least when first undertaken. They were viewed as sophisticated pastimes, pursued by intelligent, but somewhat eccentric, maladjusted people whose otherwise excellent minds had been sidetracked by a queer interest in the farfetched and useless.

Of course, basic research is rarely undertaken with its practical applications in mind; indeed, these are never predictable. I still remember my own reaction in school when I was taught how astrophysicists estimate the inner temperature of distant stars. Cunning, I thought, but why should anybody want to know? When Louis Pasteur reported that germs might transmit diseases, he was ridiculed. Fancy a grown man worrying about being attacked by bugs so small no one could see them! When the Austrian monk, Gregor Johann Mendel, amused himself by observing the results of crossbreeding red- with white-flowering peas in the monastery garden, even his most farsighted contemporaries failed to imagine the momentous implications of his findings.

Yet, without basic knowledge of the behavior of distant stars, we would not be placing satellites in orbit today. Without knowledge about bacteria, there would be no vaccines, serums and antibiotics. And without those observations on the inheritance of color in peas, modern genetics—with all its importance to agriculture, animal breeding and medicine—could never have developed.

The more manifestly sensible and practical a research project, the closer it is to the commonplace we already know. Thus, paradoxically, knowledge about the seemingly most farfetched, impractical phenomena may prove the likeliest to yield novel basic information and to lead us to new heights of discovery. But usually this takes time, often much time. Basic research neither becomes nor ceases to be useful as soon as the applied kind.

Some insist that basic research must proceed in the same spirit as "art for art's sake," and should not be appraised by its practical applicability. Yet, in defending this view they usually argue that even the most abstruse research may eventually yield practical results. It is odd that the study of the impractical should have to be justified by its potential usefulness.

Whatever our motives for undertaking it, basic research certainly can become practically useful. But to the scientist, how important is the motive of being useful to others? Man is essentially an egocentric and egotistic creature. It is not within my province to question why he was thus created nor to explore whether it is strength or weakness that seems to make some people disinterested in themselves. In any event, such totally altruistic individuals are exceedingly rare in the general population and—as far as I have been able to establish—they do not occur among scientists. The basic research man sets his sights high; he believes in the inherent value of his interests and is prepared to make, and press others to make, great sacrifices for them. If this is egotism, he must admit to being an egotist. It would be incompatible with his sense of honesty and objectivity to bluff himself into believing that he has no thought for his own interests.

Egotism is the most characteristic, the most ancient, and the most essential property of life. All living beings, from the simplest amoeba to man, are of necessity closest to themselves and the most natural protectors of their own interests. I see no reason why we should expect someone else to look after us more conscientiously than after himself. Selfishness is natural, yet it is ugly; we are so much repulsed by it that we try to deny its existence in ourselves. It is also dangerous to society. We are afraid of it, because it harbors the seeds of fight and revenge. Yet, despite their egotism, many scientists, especially among physicians, are strongly motivated by humanitarian impulses.

I do not believe that these two apparently contradictory drives reflect a schizoid trait, a kind of double personality, in which the instinct for self-preservation constantly fights the wish to help others. To me, even altruism is a modified form of egotism, a kind of collective selfishness that helps the community. Unconsciously, we sense that altruism engenders gratitude. By awakening in another person the wish that we should prosper because of what we have done for him, we elicit gratitude which is perhaps the most characteristically human way of assuring our security (homeostasis). It takes away the motive for a clash between selfish and selfless tendencies. By inspiring the feeling of gratitude, we induce others to share with us our natural wish for our well-being. The less a person is conversant with the ecology of living beings, the more is he repulsed by this kind of reasoning. But the biologist is not called upon to question the wisdom of creation; he merely analyzes its structure.

Whatever their conscious motives, many scientists have a sincere wish to be useful to society. That is why, even among those who do basic research without any expectation of practical applicability, few are completely indifferent to the hope that their discoveries may help to relieve suffering and to promote happiness. One of the most important reasons for this desire is the need for approval.

## THE NEED FOR APPROVAL—THE THIRST FOR CREDIT—VANITY

"Xenophon says that there is no sound more pleasing than one's own praises."–Plutarch

"A friend once said to Cato the Elder, 'It's a scandal that no statue has been erected to you in Rome! I am going to form a committee.'
" 'No,' " said Cato, " 'I would rather have people ask "Why isn't there a statue to Cato?" than "Why is there one?" ' "–Thomas L. Masson

"All this shows how ambitious I was; but I think I can say with truth that in after years, though I cared in the highest degree for the approbation of such men as Lyell and Hooker, who were my friends, I did not care much about the general public. I do not mean to say that a favourable review or a large sale of my books did not please me greatly, but the pleasure was a fleeting one, and I am sure that I have never turned one inch out of my course to gain fame . . .

"My books have sold largely in England, have been translated into many languages, and passed through several editions in foreign countries. I have heard it said that the success of a work abroad is the best test of its enduring value. I doubt whether this is at all trustworthy; but judged by this standard my name ought to last for a few years . . .

"But I was also ambitious to take a fair place among scientific men, —whether more ambitious or less so than most of my fellow-workers, I can form no opinion."–Charles Darwin

"Since the real world in the absolute sense is independent of individual personalities, indeed independent of all human intelligence, every discovery made by an individual acquires a very general significance. This gives the scientist, who struggles with his problem in quiet isolation, the certainty that every result which he finds, will be appreciated by all specialists throughout the world, and this feeling of the significance of his work is his joy, it gives him full compensation for many a sacrifice in his daily life."–Max Planck

I have met few scientists, if any, who are uninterested in the approval of their colleagues and do not care whether or not they get credit for their discoveries. Few of them pick up a book or a reprint on their own subject without immediately consulting the author index to see whether they are quoted. Why are most of them so desperately ashamed of this?

We have established a visiting professorship at our Institute which has brought us into contact with some of the most eminent medical scientists of our time. It has become our tradition to invite these distinguished guests for an informal dinner followed by a leisurely chat. This gives us a chance to learn more about the intimate characteristics, drives and satisfactions of these men. One question which is always asked, concerns the motives for research. The most common answer is, "Curiosity." When pressed for additional motives, a scientist may also mention his wish to be useful, or even admit that he got into his career by sheer accident because there was an opening in a research laboratory and he needed the money. But a desire for credit is always violently denied. Why?

I shall never forget the time when my youngest graduate student innocently asked our distinguished guest on such an occasion: "Well, sir, in that case, would you mind if I published the experiment you showed us this afternoon? I have been assisting you with it and I did quite similar work —though, I admit, not very successfully—before. It would be a useful addition to my thesis, sir . . . That is if you don't mind, sir." It did not prove to be a practical request, but it was a good question.

Scientific curiosity can be satisfied much more easily by reading the publications of others than by working in the lab. It may take years to prove by experimentation what we can learn in the few minutes needed to read the published end result. So let us not fool ourselves; the driving force is hardly sheer curiosity. Could it merely be the wish to do good? Few scientists would get much pleasure from doing good by political or charitable activities, or by providing livelihoods through business.

The fact is that we are vain, very vain. We adore the feeling of having found some important law of Nature through our own ingenuity. Why should we be so ashamed of it? "Vanity as an impulse has without doubt been of far more benefit to civilization than modesty has ever been" [William E. Woodward].

Vanity becomes objectionable only when the legitimate pride in a recognized accomplishment turns into an indiscriminate craving after fame for its own sake. No scientist worthy of the name measures his success by the number of people who acclaim him. No scientist wants credit for a discovery erroneously attributed to him, nor would he trade places with the most famous politicians, millionaires or generals. No scientist that I ever knew could possibly have felt envy for the enormous fame of a ventriloquist admired on the television screens by millions throughout the nation. Scientists are vain, they like recognition, they are not immune to the pleasures of fame; but they are very choosy about whom they want to be recognized by and what they want to be famous for.

Actually, scientists are extremely discriminating in this respect. The greater they are, the smaller the number of people whose recognition means something to them. But it is a heart-warming experience for one who has assiduously labored in the solitude of his laboratory on a highly intricate mechanism of Nature to know that, somewhere in the world, there are some people—even though perhaps only half a dozen—who truly understand the importance of his work and appreciate the difficulties he had to surmount. These colleagues he accepts as his peers and he is deeply gratified that, through his work, he has acquired their spiritual kinship. He has earned a place in their select, intellectual aristocracy. He can communicate with them across the enormous geographic distances, the language and social barriers, and all the petty hatreds and competitions that separate other men. In this age of cold and shooting wars, of bitter racial, political, and religious intolerance, or of simply trite platitude of purpose, I do not think that the basic scientist need be ashamed of his vanity.

## THE GLORY OF SUCCESS; HERO-WORSHIP AND A DESIRE TO IMITATE OUR HEROES

"Men of genius do not excel in any profession because they labour in it, but they labour in it, because they excel."–William Hazlitt

"Which one of us·has not gained fortitude and faith from the incarnation of ideas in men, from the wisdom of Socrates, from the wondrous creativity of Shakespeare, from the strength of Washington, from the compassion of Lincoln, and above all, perhaps, from the life and death of Jesus?"–Arthur Schlesinger, Jr.

I am a passionate hero-worshipper myself; my great ideals are Claude Bernard, Louis Pasteur, Robert Koch, Paul Ehrlich and Walter Cannon. But I profited mainly from Dr. Cannon, whom I knew personally as a pure man and a pure scientist. He had the greatest influence on me, and throughout my life I always felt very close to him. My work on stress has been largely inspired by his discovery of the sympathetic "emergency reactions" and even these Notes bear the imprint of his spirit. I seem to be tied to Dr. Cannon by bonds I cannot sever. I hope that he would not mind if he were still alive. After all, he himself said.

"I am a son of Bowditch, who led me into physiological investigation. Dr. Bowditch in turn was the son of Karl Ludwig, to whose laboratory in Leipzig in the last century he resorted together with other young men from many lands. Through my grandfather Ludwig, I am related to others of his descendants, among them the Italian physiologist Mosso, the English pharmacologist Brinton, and the Russian physiologist Pavlov. In my own place in this sequence of familial relationship I have scattered sons —and some grandsons."–Walter Cannon

I have embraced so many of Cannon's ideas! I can only be grateful, but I cannot help it. For sons cannot help resembling their fathers; it would be irreverent if the offspring tried to be different just to avoid being accused of imitation. Besides, transmitted characteristics manifest themselves differently in successive generations. No scientist arises spontaneously without predecessors, but, unlike the son by blood, the son by mind can at least choose his parent.

The development of real excellence and genius has been greatly impeded by a misunderstanding of what Lincoln meant when, on the battlefield of Gettysburg, he dedicated his nation to "the proposition that all men are created equal." Taken literally, this proposition is obviously untrue: Some men are small, others big; some are fat, others thin; some are intelligent, others stupid. What Lincoln meant was that all men should have the same birthright to develop whatever qualifications they possess.

In practice, even this is impossible, so we are told to do the next best thing and treat everybody in the manner that suits most people. We cannot adjust our teaching to every pupil in the class—so the "democratic" thing is to adjust it to the mean. This turns Lincoln's proposition into a motto of mediocrity, especially if even in daily life, every measure—from taxes to prejudice—is leveled against those who rise above the mean. There must always be an aristocracy of some kind (in royalist, democratic, and communist societies alike), or else the gifted receive neither the chance nor the inducement to develop their excellence and the nation must remain middle-class. It is most unfortunate that:

> "Our contemporary American society . . . has little use for the individualist. Individualism implies dissent from the group; dissent implies conflict; and conflict suddenly seems divisive, un-American and generally unbearable. Our greatest new industry is evidently the production of techniques to eliminate conflict, from positive thoughts through public relations to psychoanalysis, applied everywhere from the couch to the pulpit. Our national aspiration has become peace of mind, peace of soul. The symptomatic drug of our age is the tranquilizer. 'Togetherness' is the banner under which we march into the brave new world."–Arthur Schlesinger, Jr.

Under present circumstances, it may not be practical to decide general community problems otherwise than by a majority vote but in scientific, artistic and other cultural matters it is certainly true that: "Any man more right than his neighbors, constitutes a majority of one" [Henry David Thoreau].

## THE FEAR OF BOREDOM

Much has been written about all these motives that unceasingly push the creative mind on to the path of glory; but I have heard little about boredom —one of the mightiest motives of all which acts by ruthlessly blocking all other avenues of escape.

All living things have to do or die. The mouse can restlessly dart hither and thither, but it cannot keep still for long; the bird must fly, the fish must swim, even the plant must grow.

The minimum requirement for activity varies from species to species, from individual to individual, from time to time. It drops quite low when life is slow during sleep or hibernation, during senility or severe disease; it rises high when body and mind are blooming and bursting with the vigor of youth.

The need for physical exercise tends to decrease more rapidly with age than the craving for mental activity. Usually, the body ages sooner than the mind. But if we find no outlet for our energies, they viciously begin to bore inward, destroying themselves and their casing by morbid self-dissection. Enforced inactivity—be it due to laziness or compulsory retirement—breeds insecurity, depression, and hypochondriac preoccupation with body and mind. Busy people have no time to worry even about major setbacks; the inactive fret themselves to while the time away.

Creative people have a tremendous appetite for spiritual outlets; since they have acquired a taste for the great adventures of the mind, nothing else seems to them worthwhile by comparison. Few scientists are amused by anything but science, and I believe that their terrifying fear of boredom drives them away from more worldly occupations just as strongly as their enthusiasm for science attracts them toward research.

# 17

## Politics and Science

F. BURLATSKII

To say that science is called upon to play a great role is to repeat the commonplace. You can hardly find a literate person who has any doubt about it. In our time, when science advances in Seven League Boots, when any contemporary person can see its achievements literally at each step, there is no need to prove that science is a necessary element for social progress.

In this article, I wish to express several ideas not about science alone, but about its role in those areas of the social sciences that are most closely linked with practice, with politics.

We frequently encounter the ideas of the scientific leadership of society. It resounds in the speeches of governmental leaders, the statements of managers, and in the articles written by publicists, journalists, and scholars. The characteristic feature of our times, the real demands of life, are—rationally and comprehensively considered decisions about problems based upon a precise understanding of the facts, the study of social processes, the evaluation of different points of view and of alternative proposals—in a word, managerial ability.

Scientific leadership is a necessary feature of socialism. Of course, the very idea of socialism carries within itself the vision of the scientifically organized society, of a society that profoundly studies and contemplates its own development, so that it can achieve better conditions for rapid and steady progress. There is also another side of this question: contempt for the laws of science and practical experience, mistakes in the leadership of social tasks that cruelly exact their own revenge, bringing waste of vast material resources and influencing the daily life of the people.

F. Burlatskii, "Politika i Nauka," *Pravda,* January 10, 1965, p. 4. (Trans. by Glenn D. Paige).

It is no accident that the last works of V. I. Lenin, which were dedicated to the concrete tasks of economic and state construction, spoke with such insistence and penetrating understanding of the role of science: "Only socialism," wrote Lenin, "makes it possible to distribute widely and actually to subordinate social production and the distribution of products according to scientific considerations related to making the lives of all workers easier, and of securing for them the possibility of prosperity. Only socialism can accomplish this. And we know that it must accomplish this; to understand this truth is to know all the difficulty of Marxism and all its power."

Its power stems from the fact that only Marxism makes it possible for a society truly to understand itself, to take its fate into its own hands; its difficulty lies in the fact that truly scientific methods of leadership by no means emerge overnight. There must be truly unceasing efforts, great practical work, and critical evaluation and assessment of what has been done, in order to discover the truly scientific forms and methods of leadership in the various social enterprises, and to perfect these methods in correspondence with changes taking place within the country and in the world arena, all of these related to the concrete tasks of building Communism.

The Party recently has cautioned with special insistence against haste and subjectivism, and has stressed the necessity for careful analysis of facts and for taking penetrating decisions based upon comprehensive consideration of related elements. The lessons of the reorganization which has been undertaken in recent years show the necessity of a scientific approach to managerial problems. To be sure many of these projects were in substance of a doubly apical character. Fundamental problems of management connected with the task of stimulating the activities of millions of productive workers often were set aside. It is possible in accordance with some rational scheme to construct a managerial apparatus from above, but if the lower levels, where material wealth is produced—enterprises, construction sites, collective farms, state farms—are not in circumstances such that it is profitable for the collective to increase production, the quality of production, the productivity of labor, the profitability and earnings of production, then any reorganization will bring little results.

Is it not obvious that if the reorganization of the managerial apparatus had been based upon scientific analysis then it would have been possible to escape many negative consequences? This experience teaches again and again the deep wisdom of the Leninist idea that under socialism each political decision on any problem—big or small—should be based upon scientific research. This is the only way to make it truly comprehensive, effective, and acceptable to the masses.

It is understandable, therefore, that in the socialist countries the closest union between practitioners and scholars is not only a desirable condition but a genuine social requirement. However, it must be admitted that over the course of a long time the cooperation between practical workers and workers in the social sciences has been inadequate. There are many reasons for this, and they cover many areas. Regrettably the phenomena warned against earlier by Lenin became widespread; for example, "an increase in commandism" and an unwillingness "to take into account that which already has been established by science." But on the other hand, it is impossible to deny the fact that practitioners by no means found in the works of scholars—economists, philosophers, jurists—concrete answers to the problems with which life confronted them.

Recently many interesting and profound works have been published in the social sciences. Nevertheless it must be admitted that the commentary still remains permeated by sickness. Commentaries in philosophy limit themselves to the explication of a well-known text; in economics, to the explanation of an economic plan; in the juridical sciences, to the explication of laws and other legal norms. In the best of circumstances propositions are systematized and illustrated. But surely genuinely profound research proposes to raise a question, the answer to which previously was not known. In this is everything. If there is no answer to an unsolved problem, then there is also no recommendation needed by practice.

At the present time, very favorable conditions are opening up for the development of science as a whole, particularly in those of its administration, which will serve practice. The significance being acquired by economic science is evident to all. In the last one to two years, a lively discussion of economic problems has arisen in the pages of our newspapers and journals. This discussion has great significance for solving basic problems of the economy.

Significantly, it evoked great interest among economic managers, and economists in our country, but also in many socialist countries. Those who were present in these countries can easily testify to this. Recently there also has emerged abroad a wide ranging discussion of problems related to the management of the economy. Just as with us, they seek more effective forms and methods of leadership. The basic directions of the changes which have been adopted are along the same lines that many participants in our own economic discussions have proposed: the establishment of trusts and firms; the enlargement of authority at the level of the individual enterprise; the calculation of profits as an important factor in assessing its activity; change in planning practices; creation of a more flexible price system, etc. I think that ideas which are expressed along these lines in socialist countries, experience which is accumulating there, in turn, should attract the interest of our economic managers and economists.

There is also great interest in other areas of social science which are closely linked with practice. In our newspapers there are often writings on the role of empirical sociological investigations. We want to draw attention to the necessity of working on problems of *political science.*

The concept "political science" recently is coming more and more to acquire the rights of citizenship within our society. And this is not by accident. We speak about that branch of knowledge, the development of which is necessary at the present time in connection with important and complex problems facing the country. The object of this science is to provide answers to basic questions related to the perfection of forms and methods of leadership by society, the precise delineation of functions, the rights and obligations among all levels of the administrative apparatus, and the problem of selection and training of cadres.

This science emerges in the interface of many other sciences; for example, scientific communism, theory of state and law, sociology, and also economics. By way of comparison, recall that natural scientists—physicists, chemists, biologists—have written much recently about the special significance of those areas of knowledge that emerge at the point of abutment of other sciences. We observe something analogous in the relationship of political science to the general development of Marxist-Leninist knowledge about society.

The process of further differentiation in Marxist-Leninist social sciences is a phenomenon that is completely natural and explicable. In essence, this is a process of the deepening of theory, of the greater penetration of scientific analysis into all corners of social life as an expression of its multifaceted nature. In the not too distant past it was deemed necessary to introduce scientific communism as an independent subject. Experience proves the correctness and timeliness of that decision. Now, in our opinion, it is the turn of political science.

We do not define our task to be an exhaustive discussion of questions related to political science. It is suggested that the main object of investigation of this science should be political (class) relations in both socialist and capitalist society, and relations between states in the international arena. More concretely we can suggest that this science must concern itself with the study of problems related to the structure and activity of the state, political parties, social organizations, mass movements, international relations and organizations, forms and methods of diplomatic activity, the study of public opinion, methods of propaganda, etc. This is not to say that these problems are completely overlooked at present, but it remains a fact that they are studied predominently in a historical framework or in a legal framework, and many problems in general fall outside the scholarly focus of attention.

The development of political science as an independent area of social research, will permit study of the problems mentioned in a thorough manner —but more importantly, in close relation to the needs of practical politics.

Of course, political science cannot take upon itself the study of everything related to state policy. This is the task of the social sciences as a whole. The point of view of political science is the study of leadership by society by dynamic [processes]; that is, the study of how it functions and of what is required for its improvement and development. Lenin wrote that the most essential thing in politics was "the construction of state power." There is no doubt that this is also the most essential problem in political science.

What is involved, of course, is not only the question of recognizing political science as a separate branch of the social sciences. The main thing is to study deeply those problems which form the subject matter of political science. Can it be considered normal that questions of administration at present are not studied by a single branch of the social sciences? And might it not be that deficiencies involved in efforts to solve problems related to the improvement of the structure and methods of the state apparatus were linked in some degree with this omission?

It is interesting to recall that in the 1920's much attention was devoted to this question. For many years, for example, the journal *Economy and Administration* . . . was published. Now when you peruse the pages of this journal you are struck with the seriousness and business-like manner in which in those years they studied questions concerning the improvement of the apparatus for managing the economy and indeed the whole state apparatus.

Another fact must be given attention: for many years the history of political knowledge has been a separate field of inquiry which pursues the study of political science in a historical framework. A question: Why must there not also be a special science which would study contemporary political institutions, contemporary political trends, and theories?

It is significant that political science recently is receiving its greatest recognition in many socialist countries where corresponding scientific research institutes and faculties are being created in universities.

How can the successful and rapid development of these branches of science that are most closely related to politics be achieved? Naturally a decisive role can be played if problems of political science can be included more widely in the program of the existing scientific institutes. But this alone will hardly solve the problem. The experience of past years shows that without the creation of special scientific institutions devoted to political science, it is difficult to expect any substantial achievements. Such institutions, in addition to working on theoretical problems, would carry out directly tasks for party and state organs, and also would prepare a cadre of specialists of whom there are still very, very few.

It is obvious that scientific institutions engaged in political science can develop successfully only under conditions where they are closely linked to party and state organs, where they have the necessary information at their disposal, and where they rely on a broad base of practical workers.

The attainment of the objectives of political science presupposes a special method in formulating and studying its problems, especially wide usage of the empirical sociological approach. Attracting practical workers, journalists, teachers, and other representatives of the intelligentsia to work on the concrete problems of the social and cultural development of each district, province, city, and republic, the scientific institutions will have many opportunities to bring forth practical recommendations and proposals.

Certainly the development of political science is by no means the sole condition for achieving scientific leadership by society. The task of strengthening the ties between science and politics involves in the final analysis all branches of the social sciences. Undoubtedly an exchange of opinions on the present proposal will help to move forward a decision on this important problem.

# 18

The Fighting Task Confronting Workers in Philosophy
and the Social Sciences

CHOU YANG

Forming a powerful contingent of Marxist-Leninist theorists capable of weathering any storm is a task having both urgency and long-term strategic significance. It is an arduous task to develop Marxist-Leninist philosophy and social science through the criticism of modern revisionism, the summing up of the lessons of contemporary revolutionary struggles, and the sorting out of our historical legacy. For a few people to continue at their present level will not be sufficient for this task; we must strive to train more theorists and constantly raise their level.

Workers in philosophy and social science are spokesmen of the ideology of a class; they are an important force in creating intellectual values and influencing the minds of the people. Proletarian workers in philosophy and social science serve the interests of the proletariat, and bourgeois workers in these fields serve those of the bourgeoisie. Their different class stands make them play opposite roles. Hence, the great importance of the question of how to educate the ranks of our philosophers and social scientists.

What should be the orientation and method of training for our theorists? There are two fundamentally different lines on this question. One is to train them in the proletarian orientation, that is, train them to serve the people whole-heartedly and to strive to be both "red and expert" so that they will take an active part in practical struggle and manual labor and become proletarian fighters closely linked with the working people. This is the correct proletarian line. This application will make it possible to produce good Marxist-Leninist theorists. The other line is to train them in a bourgeois orientation, that is, train them to seek personal fame and

Chou Yang, *The Fighting Task Confronting Workers in Philosophy and the Social Sciences* (Peking: Foreign Languages Press, 1963), pp. 61–68.

fortune and to become experts devoid of socialist consciousness, so that they will divorce themselves from reality and the working people and lord it over the people as intellectual aristocrats. This is a wrong line, the bourgeois line. Its application can only result in producing revisionists and new reactionary bourgeois experts, or the degeneration of revolutionary specialists into revisionists and bourgeois Philistines. The lessons of certain socialist countries in this respect are a warning to us all. In his article "On the Correct Handling of Contradictions Among the People," Comrade Mao Tse-tung calls on Chinese intellectuals to "gradually acquire a communist world outlook, get a better grasp of Marxism-Leninism, and identify themselves with the workers and peasants." In other words, it is necessary for intellectuals to effect a fundamental change in their world outlook, the key to which lies in linking themselves closely with the workers and peasants.

Twenty-one years have passed since the Yenan forum on literature and art where Comrade Mao Tse-tung advanced the view that literary and artistic workers must go among and identify themselves with the workers, peasants, and soldiers. And now a goodly number of comrades have accepted this view and put it into practice. It is a fundamental matter of principle for the orientation of workers in philosophy and social science, too. Although social science and literature and art are different ideological forms, both are unquestionably reflections in people's minds of social life and are instruments for understanding and remolding society. Writers and artists epitomize the lessons of the people's struggle in artistic form, whereas social scientists sum them up in theoretical form. Therefore, like workers in literature and art, those in philosophy and social science must go into the midst of the workers and peasants, participate in their labor and struggle, do practical work in organizations at the lower level, learn and study the lessons of the workers' and peasants' struggles, and study the complex phenomena of social life so as to discover its laws and its new problems and provide theoretical explanations for them. To do so is our bounden duty and the only way we can insure ourselves against separation from the masses and reality and against atrophy in our thinking; hence, it is the only way to avoid revisionism and dogmatism. No one can contribute to the revolutionary cause in the field of science if he does not link himself with the workers and peasants but belittles the lessons of their revolutionary struggles and immerses himself in books behind closed doors. No one aspiring to be a Marxist-Leninist will ever become one so long as he feels out of his element among the workers and peasants.

While engaged in the practice of class struggle and production, the masses of workers, peasants, and cadres raise all kinds of theoretical questions for solution, and they advance many original views. But they lack the requisite book knowledge and theoretical equipment while many of the professional workers in philosophy and social science lack the steeling and experience acquired in practical struggles. In 1942 in his speech, "Rectify the Party's Style of Work," Comrade Mao Tse-tung asked the people with book-learning to combine with those experienced in work: "Those with book-learning must develop in the direction of practice; only so will they not rest content with books, only so will they not commit dogmatist errors. Those experienced in work must take up the study of theory and must read seriously; only then will they be able to systematize and synthesize their experience and raise knowledge and the level of theory, only then will they not mistake their partial experience for universal truth and not commit empiricist errors."

The combination of these two kinds of people, so, that they can make up for each other's deficiences and raise each others level, will prove very helpful not only to theoretical work but to the revolutionary cause as a whole. Man's correct ideas come only from social practice. Man's social being determines his consciousness. Once grasped by the masses, the correct ideas which a progressive class represents become a material force capable of changing society and the world. The movement from the material to the mental and then back from the mental to the material, i.e., the movement from practice to knowledge and from knowledge back to practice, has to be repeated many times before correct knowledge takes shape. The dialectical process of the transformation of the material into the mental and the mental into the material in the course of social struggle will be more consciously grasped and will give rise to still greater achievements in the revolutionary cause as a result of the combination of professional theoretical workers with those engaged in practical work. Promising theorists will emerge from among the practical workers. A powerful contingent of theorists, with the professional theorists as its center but comprising large numbers of practical workers too, will grow relatively rapidly.

In stressing the need for workers in philosophy and social science to link themselves with the workers and peasants and to keep in contact with and understand reality, we do not in the least minimize the importance of book knowledge. Workers in philosophy and science must be proficient in their own fields as well as being well versed in the Marxist-Leninist classics; they must acquire knowledge of a wide range of subjects and become truly learned.

Marx's theories are revolutionary and critical because he had the courage not only to make a thorough criticism of the old world but also to assimilate critically the whole range of human knowledge, past and present, thus enriching and fortifying his theories. Speaking of Marx, Lenin said: "He critically reshaped everything that had been created by human society, not ignoring a single point. Everything that had been created by human thought he reshaped, criticized, tested on the working-class movement, and drew conclusions which people restricted by bourgeois limits or bound by bourgeois prejudices could not draw." [1]

The same is true of Lenin himself, of Engels and of Stalin. It is also true of Comrade Mao Tse-tung. When discussing party spirit in philosophy in *Materialism and Empirio-Criticism,* Lenin pointed out: "The task of Marxists in both cases (i.e., in economics and philosophy) is to be able to master and refashion the achievements of these salesmen (for instance, you will not make the slightest progress in the investigation of new economic phenomena without making use of the works of these salesmen) and to be able to lop off their reactionary tendency, to pursue your own line, and to combat the whole line of the forces and classes hostile to us." His statement tells us how to study modern bourgeois academic theories.

There are communists as well as noncommunist among our workers in philosophy and social science; some are Marxists, and some have not yet become Marxists. Party and non-Party Marxist-Leninists should form the strong backbone and nucleus of our ranks in philosophy and social science. Marxist workers in philosophy and social science should unite with all non-Marxists scholars who can be united with, help them to come over to Marxism gradually and consciously and, at the same time, modestly learn from them. In study it is harmful to show even the slightest self-complacency or conceit.

Just as the great socialist era has produced a host of people's heroes, it should also produce a galaxy of brilliant scholars. Both bourgeois and feudal societies had their flourishing periods in the intellectual field, periods which gave birth to many outstanding thinkers and writers. In Germany before Marx, there were Kant and Hegel in philosophy and Lessing and Goethe in literature. In Russia before Lenin there were such outstanding revolutionary thinkers and men of letters as Pushkin, Herzen, Belinsky, Chernyshevsky, and Tolstoy. In the past hundred years and more, China produced such figures as Kung Ting-an, Kang Yu-wei, Tan Sze-tung, Tsou Jung, Chang Tai-yen, and Li Ta-chao, the great revolutionary Sun Yat-sen, and the great writer Lu Hsun. Historical figures have generally emerged in the course of radical social changes and acute class struggles. In the period of the Spring and Autumn Annals and of the Warring States, in the classical age of ancient Greece and in the period of the European Renaissance, radical social changes and fierce class struggles pushed many outstanding thinkers, writers, and artists to the foreground on the historical stage. Their splendid activities and magnificent achievements still command our admiration. Engels said in praise of the Renaissance: "It was the greatest progressive revolution that mankind had so far experienced, a time which called for giants and pro-

---

[1] "The Tasks of the Youth Leagues," *Selected Works,* Vol. 2, Part 2 (Moscow: Foreign Languages Publishing House), p. 478.

duced giants—giants in powers of thought, passion, and character, in universality and learning." [2]

We are now in the midst of a new, great socialist era which calls for new giants, not by scores but by the thousands. With their heroic labor and struggle and their boundless strength, the great liberated Chinese people have created the necessary conditions for our work, stimulated our intellectual capacities, and inspired us to advance. We have also before us the great example of Comrade Mao Tse-tung's creative development of Marxism-Leninism. Should we not achieve results in the academic field far surpassing those of our predecessors? In the early days of liberation, Comrade Mao Tse-tung said: "The great, victorious Chinese People's War of Liberation and the great people's revolution have rejuvenated and are rejuvenating the great culture of the Chinese people." [3] A new great renaissance, a socialist renaissance, is approaching. We should live up to the challenge of our era and greet it with new efforts, new achievements, and new creations. Let us work and march forward together!

---

[2] *Dialectics of Nature* (Moscow: Foreign Languages Publishing House, 1954), p. 30.

[3] "The Bankruptcy of the Idealist Conception of History," *Selected Works,* Vol. 4 (Peking: Foreign Languages Press, 1961), p. 458.

# 19

## Professors and Citizen Activism

PAUL L. ADAMS

I

Being a professor entails a complicated life of multifaceted and interacting roles. The professor has the following four tracks along which he runs:

*1. Scholar.* As a scholar he is playing a role with both conservative and innovative meanings. As a scholar who teaches he has the basic residual role of a guardian, conserver, condenser and transmitter of knowledge. As an investigator, however, he finds himself often in league with—or operating in the same mode as—the rebel, the iconoclast, the disillusioner. Now some teachers do not teach only what is accepted but stir up their students with questions that require answering. Similarly, some investigators are busily carrying out research that is so intimately entrenched in the approved channels of their special fields that anyone would be hard-put to call it either imaginative or innovative; it is only industrious at best. There is, then, an exceptional researcher who manages to remain aloof from the fires of rebellion; and there are teachers who question as much as they transmit knowledge. But a professor lives out his dual functions as a conserver and as a critic when he acts as a scholar.

*2. Specialized technician.* Every professor has some special tools and some special know-how connected with his field of professional work. The physician with his technology for diagnosis and healing, the philosopher with his brightly shining verbal and cognitive skills, and the experimental psychologist with his laboratory-managerial skills: we are all technicians with practical arts and gadgets that societies such as ours value to some degree. We struggle very hard at times to keep our knowledge esoteric and

Paul L. Adams, "Professors and Citizen Activism," *Philosophical Psychologist,* Vol. 4 (1970), 25–30. Copyright 1969 by Paul L. Adams. Reprinted by permission of the author.

sequestered from the masses (Hughes, 1963). Occasionally, it is by moon-lighting or consulting that professors are made aware of their technical worth, for having marketable skills.

3. *Employed professional.* Even when his official professional ide-ology, by cultural lag, proclaims the model of the private practitioner there is no escaping the observation that professional persons are more and more the hirelings of agencies and corporations. Professors increasingly live from pay checks, not from their students' private fees; and from teaching required courses, not electives. All of this contributes to job security but diminishes the free play of idiosyncrasy to be seen in an ideal entrepreneur. We are not private entrepreneurs. We are employees of large and enlarging organizations. Our employers and administrators are not our "fellow offi-cers" of the universities, they have many more of the characteristics of in-dustry bosses as time passes. The rhetoric of the American Association of University Professors cannot undo that reality. Our administrators, and we professors ourselves, have ever widening connections with agents such as professional associations and guilds outside the particular campus on which we are stationed: we are a part of an apparatus that reaches at least across this continent. I am not alluding merely to the Pentagon's shadow on the ivy which is indeed a deepening shadow; but also to the complex tie-in of church-college-industry-military-executive branch of federal government-foundation-professional association. Interlocking nationwide bureaucracies impinge upon the professor nowadays. Still, he remains in one aspect of his operations a hired or employed professional in the local workshop.

4. *Citizen.* The professor is a participant in the power relations that characterize his society. That is to say, he is a political man. He is a mem-ber of his nation and is involved in civic life. He cannot escape the fact that his citizenship in the United States gives him a role as a person, and often-times as a professor, in the nation—a nation characterized by features such as the reign of greed or profit and economic inequality; a vaunting of war-fare and derogation of welfare; racism; alienation; and then on the other hand a rarely surpassed edifice of civil liberty; a recurrently forceful ide-ology of democracy, etc. He is a partisan, even if he is a liberal, in a mas-sive multi-group pluralistic nation dominated by a relatively small complex of military, industrial and governing men. He can always be put down by Socrates' judges.


II

It is to the professor as a citizen, or more definitely as a politico-social activist, that I would like to pay most attention. However, the pro-fessor's role as a citizen is always shaped and colored by certain values that enshroud his other roles as scholar, technician, and employee.

Professors I have known, both as colleagues and as patients or as parents of young patients, are a fascinating lot—so verbal, so intellectual, so sick, so well, so callous and competitive, so precious and so selfless. What a crowd, so deserving of fuller study by psychologists and philosophers! Professors collectively are a complicated mixed bag; and the same can be stated with respect to the individual professor: a complicated mixed bag.

As a citizen the professor is no simple cipher either. He goes in and out of active participation in political affairs, and in or out on the oddest and most sophistic of philosophic grounds. My goal is to proceed as a taxonomist would, however crudely and incompletely the labor is wrought, and to offer a tentative empirical classification of the positions taken or the arguments advanced by professors in the two camps, activist and passivist. These terms are inadequate certainly but they are meant to suggest a natural division between professors who demonstrate, vote, teach in, speak out, and join up as opposed to those who keep aloof from such activities. Terms such as "highly participant" and "minimally participant" might carry less disparaging connotations than the terms "active or passive," and, if they are more denotative, the member of the audience must substitute them for the feebler terminology that I employ.

### Ideology and Behavior of the Effectively Uninvolved Professor

*1. Nihilist, dropout, retreatist, delinquent.* There are professors who are devoid of either conventional or unconventional values, who in the terminology of Ignazio Silone (1955), are nihilists who determinedly set out to deflate and to unmask all values. They are retreatist, in Robert K. Merton's sense of the term, and they are delinquent in the Latin sense of delinquere as drop out. They are not joiners, and they are not fighters. They are nonbelievers who approximate being non-doers as far as their role as citizens is concerned. Some of them have told me that they used to be fighters but that they have despaired of achieving anything by fighting, and they prefer to withdraw from citizenship into their libraries and laboratories. They have concluded that values are not of worth as guides to our destiny but are only presentable masks for entirely selfish interests. They may say it in exalted, "professorial" language, but their message content is like that of the hippie adolescent who is dropping out of active citizenship and valuing only the doing of one's own thing.

*2. Eclectic, pluralist, dually committed.* Some professors hold to the liberal ideal so profoundly that in matters intellectual and civic they see both sides so clearly that they are incapacitated in moving toward a partisan position. There are many more true cowards than true liberals and there are many more avowed liberals than there are true liberals. Professors have a penchant for portraying themselves as in the tradition of Erasmus. The position of the authentic eclectic is subjected to abuse by many professors. Yet there is a rare Morris R. Cohen, to name a liberal philosopher whom I admire, and a Gardner Murphy, to mention a psychologist whose genuine eclecticism I admire. Both of these men knew so much and with such depth that their students respected their eclecticism, saw them as "telling it like it is" even when they told it as liberal, dual and mixed. There is indeed an elegance about the humanist Erasmus perched above the grubbier battles of everyday life, and there is an inescapable attractiveness about the peace-maker who loves the warriors on both sides. It is such people who end our wars and who remind us of our common humanity. I would not attempt to derogate the man who actively advances both sides because he feels both sides are right. Such a man is Milovan Djilas (1966) who, often imprisoned by the Yugoslavian Establishment, can state a position, devoid of rancor, that all will be well if we in the west strive for a socialist economy whilst advancing individual liberties and if we in the east strive for political democracy with civil liberties whilst vigilantly maintaining a socialist economy. Czechoslovakia notably is still trying the latter course against great obstacles from the USSR. The liberal ideal is fated always to be fighting uphill, it seems.

    *3. Diphasic, obsessive, with limited commitment.* Here is the professor who is effectively uninvolved because his conflicting involvements are weak. He is involved on two sides, but weakly on both. He cancels out a commitment to citizenship as soon as the commitment starts. He prides himself on his maintenance of his "critical faculties," meaning that he never makes even a false start without an abundance of self-doubt. Such a professor will contribute to the teachers' union behind the scenes but will not join because of his loyalties to a vice-president on the other side. He will repent his lukewarm conservatism as soon as he has avowed it, and will proffer a lukewarm and fleeting liberalism or libertarianism in its stead. He truly vacillates with only a limited investment in either of his phases. His motto could well be that anything worth doing is worth doing in moderation. Often the person with limited commitment to any values will denounce partisanship, praise his passage from bland phase to bland phase, and extol obsessive doubting. For some this lukewarmness is what it is to be "professorial."

    *4. The laissez-faire conservative.* Here is a species of minimally "involved" who is comfortably committed to the Establishment, to the status quo. By doing nothing apparently he in reality supports what is: the control of the university not by professors and students but by administrators —who are trained typically not in education but in political, industrial and military bureaucracies, and who when at a university have only *formal* authority, not *functional authority* (Peabody, 1962); the warfare state, military conscription, the trammeling of the university by the Pentagon and the

Department of Defense, the advancement of patriotic imperialism; the enthronement of greed not welfare as the dominant economic motive; the perpetuation of racism; the subjugation of females; the development of violence and repression in the form of rioting police; and the rest of the ugliness in Amercia as it is.

At the local university level it is this conservative professor who, not militant but laissez-faire, stands for such forms of law and order as arming cops against students, urging administrators to be strong, voting for resolutions that blur real differences between the administrator and the faculty hireling, and in general proclaiming that activism only leads to "polarization" of issues and groups. The implications are that polarization separates people who belong together (such as state senators and university presidents) and that polarization is the end of civilized discourse (as if sharply drawn issues necessarily will make murderers out of the opponents). These cautions against confrontation and polarization are, underneath, only conservative counsels to let what is good enough remain as it is, and to reduce activity in order to let the powerful enjoy uncontested power over the powerless.

5. *Paralyzed by fear.* Some professors whom I have known initially come on as indifferent and inactive, only to show later on in some safe self-disclosure that they do have values which condone active citizenship and active participation in town and gown activities. Several of these professors move off to northern universities and there become declared activists; hence it is only in the South that they are afraid to get involved. Others move north for hibernation after being involved in activism in the Southeast. The fear of being lynched is not a thing of the past in the USA. Albert Camus (1946) knew our condition when he wrote that the foremost reality of our time is *fear,* the fear of being either a victim of murder or an executioner, the fear of living in a society where murder is legitimate. Professors know this fear and they know the softer preludes to murder: denial of tenure, denial of academic freedom, cutting off funds for positions (you have a guaranteed job but it carries no salary), ostracism, foot-dragging, letters and conversations aimed to intimidate the professor, the professor's wife and even his children. Threats of bombings, and actual bombings are not beyond occurring in most university towns where professors are radically activist. Hence, some professors lie low, seeming to be uninvolved, but in reality they are waiting opportunistically for a *milieu* more favorable to their vigorous activities as citizens. They are not uncommitted really; they are scared radicals.

6. *Believer that activism is uncouth, unscholarly or unprofessional.* The sixth variety, or species, of minimally participant professor is one who invokes values pertaining to his being teacher, investigator, professional, and specialist. In the name of these values he dons the professional man's muzzle (B. Spock, 1965), and renounces all but conformist citizenship

activities. He says, with the establishment organizations among professors, that strikes are unprofessional; unions are unprofessional; professors contract to do as they are told when they accept appointments at a university; the only truly "professional" organization for teachers is an organization such as the National Education Association which includes bosses as well as employees in its ranks, or an organization such as AAUP which confines its work to "nice" projects—especially, as Harry Elmer Barnes (1965) put it, to the writing of eloquent obituaries when professors have already been denied irretrievably their academic freedom and tenure. The esthetic sensibility of a snobbish professor who encounters something "not nice" is a formidable foe. When outraged by the impropriety of a colleague's defiant stand such a professor who vaunts non-action climbs to dazzling heights of scorn and disdain. From his perch he utters the kind of thing that is actually not very "nice" for it can cut a tender soul to shreds. One such scornful colleague told me that he thought it would be the death of our teacher's union at the University of Florida if we installed a certain "gauche and indelicate" professor as president, adding, "He shows the city slums in everything he says."

Six of these types are enough to characterize the minimally participant professors who, with Prince Sihanouk of Cambodia, would "rather switch than fight"; and those who are conservatives, liberals, fearful radicals, and nihilists but who muster up a host of arguments that support their participating feebly as citizen activists.


III

Let us turn next to the classes of activist professors. There are activists of many species also; but among professors activists are a minority, and detailed taxonomy may not be warranted. However, among professors there is more activism than among students. My experience would drive me to concur with the observation of Richard E. Peterson (1968) that no more than two per cent of students are "left-activist" whereas it is closer to 10 per cent of every faculty group that I have known. (And who says the youth initiate change?)

A. Reactionists. Not all activists are leftists and not all right-wingers are easy-going conformists. There is a "radical right" among professors. They are often in arts and sciences, or in medicine; but mostly they are in engineering, agriculture, and business schools. There are, to be blunt about it, trade school professors who are right-wing militants when it comes to citizenship. They are vocal—for war, for greed, for flag and patriotism, and for a capitalistic system that was. These are the reactionaries who counter-picket me and my friends, and to be honest they are as small a minority as are we. But they often seem to have better connections.

*B. Issue protesters.* Some leftist professors are anti-ideological but can be counted on to hit out hard on some isolated issues. To have a general program or rationale is regarded by such people as boringly Old Left. They go for spontaneity and unpredictability to such a degree that they sometimes seem to be against thinking itself. They'd prefer spilling guts to spilling brains. Nevertheless, there they are, ready to dissent when the issue arises.

*C. Revolutionists.* These are the professors who want to change the world. They differ amongst themselves principally in their attitudes toward violence. The two varieties, I feel, in the final analysis are what in Anglo-Saxon speech we can call the haters and the lovers. These are imprecise terms, a recurrent problem that one, but my general intent of meaning can be conveyed. The "hater" is a person who is illiberal, totalitarian, resentful and vengeful (Roodkowsky, 1969). He often feels that short of achieving violent cataclysm there is nothing of consequence, nothing worthy of doing, so he writes and plans violent Revolution with little daily involvement in practical affairs and issues. The "lover" on the other hand does not lust to take anyone's blood; he will allow coexistence to his enemy; he knows forgiveness and leniency. Perhaps he is not totally "politicized." He is more likely to be vigorously involved in the here-and-now of revolutionary living. He emphasizes the relations of men and women and children as much as he concentrates on the market place. He is more worldly, more pragmatic, more inclined to live in give-and-take, than is the violent revolutionist, he who hates. Albert Camus has dissected out the "yes" and the "no" of rebellion. The subscriber to revolutionary violence (perhaps a self-contradictory term in our era) knows only the "no" of rebellion, and shuns the loving, affirming, empathetic "yes" of human solidarity. It is just the practical but global issue of acceptance of the pacifist ethic that provides a convenient line for dividing the revolutionary professors into these two radically different groups. Indeed pacifism may be the most telling single criterion of humane citizenship, today and tomorrow. Where we stand on violence is what counts.

## IV

To conclude, this essay has not pretended to be "cool" and unfeeling. Nor has it gone over to "soul" entirely, inasmuch as that entails at times the losing of one's head, one's mind. Its author obviously wants to change the world, and in concrete particular to change the structure of the university.

The college professor has been viewed as a highly verbal, subtle being with an endless repertoire of subterfuge and casuistry available to him. He often cops out on citizenship, often claiming that as a scholar-technician-professional the cop-out is the only tenable course. In some cases, though, he is with it—as a liberal, conservative, reactionist and revolutionist—and playing one of these roles he participates in direct social action. He knows that he is a citizen and as an ethical being he accepts certain obligations of citizenship.

In my own mind the ethic of pacifism can invigorate citizenship. The pacifist ethic has the highest revolutionary potential. Pacifism gives an energetic force that can remake the world, that can remake revolution itself, and that can certainly remake the university professor as a citizen and as a total Being.

## REFERENCES

Barnes, Harry Elmer, *An Intellectual and Cultural History of the Western World.* Third Rev. Ed. (New York: Dover Publications, 1965), p. 1230.

Camus, Albert, "Neither Victims nor Executioners." *Politics* 4 (1947): 141–147.

Djilas, Milovan, "An Open Letter to President Tito." *Encounter* XXVII (1966): 88–89.

Hughes, Everett C., "Professions." *Daedalus* (1963): 655–668.

Peabody, Robert L., "Perceptions of Organizational Authority: A Comparative Analysis." *Administrative Science Quarterly* VI (1962): 643–682.

Peterson, Richard E., "The Student Left in American Higher Education." *Daedalus* 97 (1968): 293–317.

Roodkowsky, Nikita D., "The Lesson of Russian Nihilism." *America* (Jan. 4, 1969): 13–18.

Silone, Ignazio, "The Choice of Comrades." *Dissent* 2 (1955): 7–19.

Spock, Benjamin, "The Professional Man's Muzzle," *American Journal of Orthopsychiatry* 35 (1965): 38–40.

T UNION          DATE DUE